Exploring Newspaper Language

Studies in Corpus Linguistics (SCL)

SCL focuses on the use of corpora throughout language study, the development of a quantitative approach to linguistics, the design and use of new tools for processing language texts, and the theoretical implications of a data-rich discipline.

For an overview of all books published in this series, please see *http/benjamins.com/catalog/scl*

Volume 49

Exploring Newspaper Language. Using the web to create and investigate a large corpus of modern Norwegian
Edited by Gisle Andersen

Exploring Newspaper Language

Using the web to create and investigate a large corpus of modern Norwegian

Edited by

Gisle Andersen
Norwegian School of Economics, Bergen

John Benjamins Publishing Company
Amsterdam / Philadelphia

The paper used in this publication meets the minimum requirements of the American National Standard for Information Sciences – Permanence of Paper for Printed Library Materials, ANSI Z39.48-1984.

Cover design: Françoise Berserik
Cover illustration from original painting *Random Order*
by Lorenzo Pezzatini, Florence, 1996.

Library of Congress Cataloging-in-Publication Data

Exploring newspaper language : using the web to create and investigate a large corpus of modern Norwegian / edited by Gisle Andersen.
p. cm. (Studies in Corpus Linguistics, ISSN 1388-0373 ; v. 49)
Includes bibliographical references and index.
1. Norwegian language (Nynorsk)--Usage. 2. Norwegian language (Nynorsk)--Syntax. 3. Newspapers--Norway. 4. Mass media--Norway. 5. Information technology--Norway. I. Andersen, Gisle.
PD2914E97 2012
439.8'20188--dc23 2011045662
ISBN 978 90 272 0354 0 (Hb ; alk. paper)
ISBN 978 90 272 7499 1 (Eb)

John Benjamins Publishing Co. · P.O. Box 36224 · 1020 ME Amsterdam · The Netherlands
John Benjamins North America · P.O. Box 27519 · Philadelphia PA 19118-0519 · USA

Table of contents

Building a large corpus based on newspapers from the web*

Gisle Andersen & Knut Hofland
NHH Norwegian School of Economics / Uni Computing

The Norwegian Newspaper Corpus (NNC) is an initiative to create a large monitor corpus representing contemporary Norwegian language in both its written varieties, Bokmål and Nynorsk. The corpus is compiled through daily harvesting and processing of published texts from the web edition of Norwegian newspapers. This introductory chapter gives a survey of work on corpus building, tool development and research in connection with the NNC project. It provides an overview of the corpus and its system architecture, describing the work flow, tools and methods used in the data processing. The chapter also gives a presentation of the individual research contributions to this volume.

1. Introduction

The Norwegian Newspaper Corpus (NNC) is an undertaking which started in 1998 with the set-up of an automatic system for extracting Norwegian newspaper text from the web (Wangensteen 2002; Hofland 2000; Andersen 2005, 2010). There were originally 10 newspapers in the corpus, but from that point this effort has been extended in various ways, in terms of the number of newspapers retrieved (now 24), the technologies applied, the range of topics researched, the number of users, etc. This book serves the twofold purpose of describing the procedures, methods and tools developed in the NNC project, as well as presenting new research based on the corpus. This introductory chapter first provides an overview of the corpus and its system architecture (Section 2) and then gives a brief presentation of the individual contributions to this volume (Section 3).

* We are grateful to a number of institutions for their contributions to the Norwegian Newspaper Corpus project, especially the Research Council of Norway (the AVIT programme), the University of Bergen (Faculty of Humanities), NHH Norwegian School of Economics and Uni Research.

In corpus linguistics there has been a tremendous development of new language resources, technologies and methods over the past few decades. We consider the emergence of dynamic corpora and web-based corpora to be among the most significant events in recent corpus development (Fairon et al. 2007; Hundt, Nesselhauf & Biewer 2007; Renouf 2007). Equally crucial is the exploitation of large corpora in lexicography and terminology (Grefenstette 2002; Atkins & Rundell 2008; Pulcini 2008). The Norwegian Newspaper Corpus project is both inspired and directly influenced by these developments and represents the first initative to create a large monitor corpus of contemporary Norwegian language in both its written varieties, Bokmål and Nynorsk. The NNC is compiled through daily harvesting and processing of published texts from the web edition of Norwegian newspapers. It is a 'modern diachronic corpus', in the sense described by Renouf (2007), enabling the study of language change, neologistic usage and lexical productivity and creativity as it unfolds in written language. This open-ended monitor corpus can be used to study language as an evolving phenomenon at the diachronic micro-level, by comparing time frames calibrated on a daily, weekly, monthly or yearly basis within the time-span the corpus represents – from 1998 to the present. This makes it particularly well suited for studying ongoing innovation in contemporary language, such as lexical, morphological, syntactic and pragmatic innovation (Hundt, Nesselhauf & Biewer 2007: 3). Naturally, it can also be used as a comparison with other synchronic or diachronic Norwegian corpora or as a basis for cross-linguistic comparison with similar corpora representing other languages.

As the contributions to this book will reveal, the corpus has been used as the basis for a variety of case studies. However, we should emphasise that the corpus is particularly tailored for lexicographical work (Hofland 2000; Wangensteen 2002; Andersen 2005, 2010). An important source of inspiration has been the Collins COBUILD project and subsequent corpus development projects using a similar methodology. Initiated by Atkins and Sinclair in the 1970s, this was the first lexicography initiative which systematically used a corpus as its main source of knowledge about words and their use in the language (Sinclair 1987). This effort has been described as a revolution which "changed the principles and methods of dictionary making" (Pulcini 2008: 189) and which enabled lexicographers to "view the evidence of how a word was used without the arbitrary filter of who thought what was an interesting example of a word" (Kilgarriff & Tugwell 2002: 125). An important driving force behind our efforts has therefore been to enable systematic corpus resources for the study of lexical neography in Norwegian (Fjeld & Nygaard this volume). Indeed the project team has consisted of lexicographers who utilise the corpus for this purpose and several of the language processing tools to be described in Section 2 are meant to make life easier for the lexicographer and, more generally, to stimulate research in lexicology, terminology, morphology and related fields. Until the compilation of our corpus, Norwegian lexicography had been largely based on manual extraction of new words, but now it is possible to use the method of corpus lexicography "for measuring hard evidence of the lexical behaviour of words since this will (arguably) result in a more representative, coherent and consistent output than a lexicon produced from conventional means" (Ooi 1998: 37).

We also draw on methods used in the AVIATOR project, which developed "the first 'dynamic' corpus of unbroken chronological text" (Renouf 2007: 36). This was established in 1990 using the *Times* newspaper as its source. The efforts of the Birmingham-based RDUES group were followed by other efforts to monitor and classify new words in the APRIL and ACRONYM projects (Renouf 1996, 2007). Since the turn of the millennium, it has also become increasingly common to develop and explore web-based corpora, aka. 'cyber-corpora' (Renouf 2007), resulting in a growing body of corpus-based studies using the web as their prime source of data (Kilgarriff & Grefenstette 2003; Fletcher 2007; Hundt, Nesselhauf & Biewer 2007). Corpus-building efforts such as WebCorp (Renouf, Kehoe & Banerjee 2005), the Corpus of Contemporary American English (Davies 2009) and the WaCky initiative (Baroni et al. 2009) use web crawler technology to make the web serve as a linguistic corpus. In line with this approach, we regard the World Wide Web as "a mine of language data of unprecedented richness and ease of access" (Lüdeling, Evert & Baroni 2007: 7) and our overall aim has been to exploit the web as a language resource for the compilation of a large corpus.

Further, we consider newspapers to be a relevant source on which to base a large corpus of Norwegian. Web newspapers lend themselves to use in a corpus for a number of reasons, such as their ease of access, their large and regular text production, their wide range of topics, their systematicity and coherence in text categorisation, their coverage of local, regional, national and global events, etc. (van Dijk 1988; Cotter 2010). Unlike many other sections of the World Wide Web, newspapers contain journalistic text which is professionally written and edited. This entails a certain level of quality and standardisation in terms of spelling, language use, genre conventions and other features. The initiation of a project of compiling a web-based corpus might nevertheless raise the question "Why not just use Google?" In response to this we would argue, like Kilgarriff and Grefenstette (2003: 12) that for most scientific purposes a systematically compiled and annotated corpus is preferable to relying on Google searches for a number of reasons. First, a corpus such as the NNC enables the extraction of all instances of a token within a set period of time and within a certain genre, in our case web newspapers. Second, it allows for the presentation of more context than Google gives, and for the restriction of the search to predefined categories such as newspaper type, date of publication, type of article, author's gender, etc. Third, a structured corpus allows the researcher to sort and select tokens according to transparent linguistic criteria, such as word form, lemma, word class, collocational features and the like. Fourth, it serves as a basis for extracting reliable usage and distribution statistics according to linguistic and non-linguistic criteria such as the ones mentioned.[1]

Note that the NNC is a *web-based* newspaper corpus. We have restricted the inclusion of newspapers to the web edition of newspapers that also have a *printed counterpart*. This means that fully web-based media, such as the web newspaper *Nettavisen* or the web news service of NRK, the Norwegian national broadcasting corporation, are not included. Given this restriction, we have aimed at a maximally broad selection of regionally and distributionally different newspapers, and the collection includes local, regional, national and special interest (niche) newspapers. Table 1 gives a survey of the newspapers included in the corpus and their sizes (measured in total number of words in the corpus) as of April 2011.

Table 1. Survey of newspapers in the Norwegian Newspaper Corpus

Newspaper	Code	Distribution	Category	Written standard	Million words	%
1. Adresseavisen*	AA	Regional – middle	General	BM	100.32	9.3%
2. Aftenposten*	AP	National	General	BM	136.62	12.7%
3. Bergens Tidende*	BT	Regional – west	General	BM/NN	58.35	5.4%
4. Dagsavisen*	DA	National	General	BM	46.23	4.3%
5. Dagbladet*	DB	National	General	BM	128.71	12.0%
6. Dagens Næringsliv*	DN	National	Financial	BM	59.404	5.5%
7. Dag og tid	DT	National	Niche	NN	4.389	0.4%
8. Firda	FI	Local – west	General	BM/NN	16.29	1.5%
9. Fædrelandsvennen*	FV	Regional – south	General	BM	101.78	9.5%
10. Gudbrandsdølen Dagningen	GD	Local – east	General	BM/NN	11	1.0%
11. Hallingdølen	HD	Local – east	General	BM/NN	8.79	0.8%
12. Hordaland	HO	Local – west	General	NN	0.88	0.1%

(Continued)

1. Most of these objections can also be raised against using a commercial text archive such as Atekst, which, although large and useful, is not tailored for corpus linguistic research (like the WWW itself).

Table 1. (Continued)

Newspaper	Code	Distribution	Category	Written standard	Million words	%
13. Klassekampen	KK	National	Niche	BM/NN	8.18	0.8%
14. Morgenbladet	MB	National	Niche	BM/NN	25.6	2.4%
15. Nationen	NA	National	Niche	BM/NN	20.06	1.9%
16. Nordlys*	NL	Regional – north	General	BM	55.86	5.2%
17. Stavanger Aftenblad*	SA	Regional – southwest	General	BM/NN	101.31	9.4%
18. Sunnhordland	SH	Local – southwest	General	BM/NN	3.99	0.4%
19. Sogn avis	SO	Local – west	General	NN	11.8	1.1%
20. Sunnmørsposten	SP	Local – northwest	General	BM/NN	30.95	2.9%
21. Vikebladet	VB	Local – northwest	General	NN	2.43	0.2%
22. Verdens Gang*	VG	National	General	BM	130.35	12.1%
23. Vårt land	VL	National	Niche	BM	6.8	0.6%
24. Vest-Telemark blad	VT	Local – east	General	NN	2.9	0.3%

The asterisk indicates that the newspaper is among the original ten newspapers that were included from the start of the harvesting in 1998, while the other newspapers are later additions; hence their text material does not necessarily cover the whole period (cf. Section 2). Note that some national newspapers such as *Aftenposten* also serve regional functions in their respective areas (Oslo/Central Eastern Norway in this case). The categorisation in Table 1 follows the official classification used by the Norwegian Ministry of Culture in their calculation of the annual public funding for Norwegian newspapers, which distinguishes between *lokalaviser* 'local newspapers', *regionaviser* 'regional newspapers', *riksaviser* 'national newspapers' and *nisjeaviser* 'niche newspapers'. The niche newspapers are also known as *riksspredde meningsbærende aviser* 'nationally distributed opinion-making newspapers'. The ones included in the corpus are: *Klassekampen,* the newspaper of the political left; *Dag og Tid,* a weekly Nynorsk newspaper for a academic readership; *Morgenbladet,* a weekly newspaper primarily for an academic readership; *Nationen,* a newspaper representing agro-pastoral/agricultural communities and readers; and *Vårt Land,* a newspaper for a Christian readership. Our policy in compiling the corpus has been to be *maximally inclusive* and to achieve a balance between different types of newspapers. And, indeed, the corpus comprises all the national newspapers; all major regional newspapers from Norway's largest cities (Oslo, Bergen, Trondheim, Stavanger, Tromsø, Kristiansand); the five most important opinion-making/niche newspapers, each with its own relatively well-defined readership; as well as a number of regional newspapers representing most parts of the country, though not all due to time restrictions of the NNC project. The full political spectrum is also represented, ranging from the business newspaper *Dagens Næringsliv* to *Klassekampen* representing the political left. Of course, any newspaper corpus based on printed newspapers may end up having a different composition than the NNC in terms of content, text types, distribution, etc. Nevertheless, we are convinced that the NNC is a rich resource that covers a very broad range of topics and vocabulary, with a number of different stylistic levels, from information-dense technical terminology to highly informal slang (G. Andersen this volume).

Before the compilation of the NNC, no large corpus of Norwegian was available. Given the experience of previous national corpus-building projects in other countries, we knew that shipments of texts at regular intervals from newspapers or publishers is costly and involves manual work at both ends. The overall aim of our venture has thus been to compile the largest possible corpus of the best possible quality, while minimising the need for manual work. As of April 2011, the NNC is a little short of 1 billion words, which makes it the largest searchable corpus of Norwegian. Our motivation for collecting a large corpus can be viewed against the experience of the British National Corpus (BNC). In this 100 million word corpus "the bulk of the lexical stock occurs less than 50 times in it, which is not enough to draw statistically stable conclusions about the word. For rarer words, and combinations of words, we frequently find no evidence at all" (Kilgarriff & Grefenstette 2003: 336). Concerning representativity, we concur with Kilgarriff and Grefenstette, who state that "the web is not representative of anything other than itself" (Kilgarriff & Grefenstette 2003: 333). We do not conceptualise the NNC as a representative sample of a larger population, but have rather aimed at including the whole population of Norwegian web-based newspapers in the corpus, in agreement with Manninng & Schütze who state that "one should simply use all the text that is available" (Manning & Schütze 1999: 120).

2. An overview of the Norwegian Newspaper Corpus and its system architecture

The text collection for the Norwegian Newspaper Corpus began in 1998. The growth of this dynamic corpus is on average approximately 230,000 words per day. The corpus currently consists of the full web version of 24 Norwegian newspapers. This includes large, national newspapers like *Aftenposten, Dagbladet* and *VG*, major regional newspapers like *Bergens Tidende* and *Stavanger Aftenblad* and local newspapers like *Sogn Avis*. Most of the newspapers are of general interest, but important niche publications are also included. The selection of newspapers has resulted in a large corpus with broad topical coverage containing relatively homogeneous data, despite the fact that it is harvested from the web. Although maximal efforts have been made to ensure a balance between the two language varieties, the Bokmål variety is massively larger than Nynorsk (cf. Section 2.3). This discrepancy reflects the degree to which Bokmål and Nynorsk are used in newspapers on the web, but it is not necessarily representative of the use of the two varieties in other contexts.

The system involves several stages of processing, most of which run automatically due to a self-executing cron job. Its architecture is visualised as a data flow diagram in Figure 1 and involves the following main steps:

1. *harvesting*: a web-crawler programme (*w3mir* or *wget*) downloads the full internet versions of Norwegian newspapers
2. *boilerplate and duplicate removal*: a set of specifically designed programs automatically selects the core text, including the body text, headline, lead paragraph and picture caption, but discarding advertisements, navigation menus, etc.
3. *language classification*: the texts are classified as either Bokmål or Nynorsk, while English and other foreign texts are discarded
4. *text annotation*: metadata concerning date, author and source are extracted from the source texts, and the texts are machine-classified according to topic and morphosyntactically tagged by the Oslo-Bergen tagger
5. *user interface*: the annotated texts are made available for search via Corpus Workbench and Corpuscle, a new in-house search system
6. *neology extraction*: the inventory of word forms of newly harvested texts is compared with an accumulated list of word forms, and a list of forms not previously recorded is extracted and added to the accumulated word list
7. *neology classification*: new word forms are classified according to orthographic criteria, and anglicism candidates are identified
8. *frequency profiling and lexical database entry*: statistical filters are used to identify neologisms that are most relevant for lexicography and registered in the Norwegian Word Bank and subsequently used by the Oslo-Bergen tagger
9. *extraction of multiword expressions*: sequences of words with a strong tendency to co-occur are extracted from the corpus and added to the lexical database

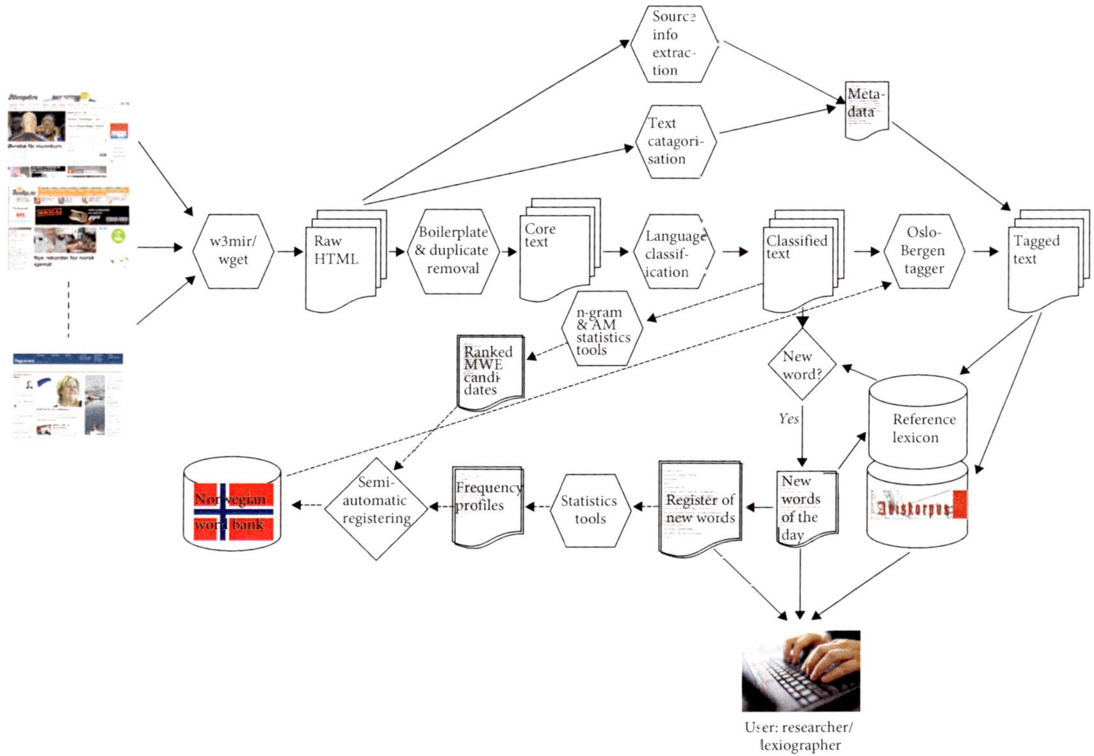

Figure 1. System architecture for the Norwegian Newspaper Corpus

Parts of this system have been running fully automatically since 1998, but some of the modules are of a more recent date. The system runs on a Sun Unix system and uses a number of custom-made programs and shell scripts. Steps 1–7 are performed automatically on a daily basis, while steps 8–9 require manual intervention and are performed in less regular batches (hence the dotted arrows in Figure 1). In the following, we describe each of these steps in more detail. Each of the subsections below corresponds to the numbering of procedural steps in the list above.

2.1 Text harvesting

The NNC uses a web crawler in combination with a variety of different specifically developed scripts (cron, grep, UNIX shells, perl, etc.) in a system which is fully automatic from web text harvesting to corpus text indexing and neology extraction. When the project was started in the late 1990s, a web mirroring and batch download program, w3mir, was chosen.[2] This was one of the few web crawler programs available at the time. W3mir is a set of Perl scripts which can be run from the command line, and it is thus easy to call from other scripts. It has an advantageous option to return a list of all the web-references in a document in addition to the document itself. For technical reasons the web crawler was later replaced by wget, which is a more well-known Linux software package.[3] Originally, the system downloaded all referenced pages recursively, but we soon realised that recursive web crawling led to unduly large downloaded files and a lot of duplication, so the system was adjusted so as to download selected files non-recursively. When a newspaper site is visited by the web crawler program, a list of all URLs referred to on this page is compiled. This list is sorted by means of a series of grep patterns and compared with an accumulated list of previously retrieved URLs from the newspaper, to ensure that only unique and corpus-relevant references are selected. A shell script is used to retrieve these individual pages and to update the accumulated list of retreived URLs. All the articles retreived from an individual newspaper on a particular day are collected in one file. A cron job is set to run automatically every day at 10 PM, and this activates a series of shell scripts which collect the articles and process them further. Since URLs may refer to older newspaper articles, the corpus contains some text that is written before the text collection started.

As part of the administrative project work, each of the newspaper editors was contacted in writing for permission to use the material. In our correspondence, we emphasised that the project represented a non-profit, coordinated, national effort

2. http://www.langfeldt.net/w3mir/

3. http://www.gnu.org/software/wget/

(a text collection *dugnad* 'voluntary effort') which was meant for non-commercial research purposes only. Further, we explained that only registered users would have access to the corpus and its derived data, that they would only be given limited access to the data via concordance views, and that no transfer of the material to any third party would take place. Most importantly, we stressed that the inclusion of their texts in the corpus required no effort on their part, except for an e-mail granting us the right to use their material under the conditions stated in the letter. We received only positive responses from the editors.

2.2 Boilerplate and duplicate removal

The development of tools for the removal of boilerplates and duplicates turned out to be a particularly time-consuming and complicated task. Boilerplate is the name given to repetitive, marginal text which is not part of the core text of the newspaper article (Fairon et al. 2007). Anyone who has visited a web newspaper has seen the large amount of such marginal text. Consider Figure 2:

OBAMA BER GBAGBO GÅ: Obama med klar tale Foto Ap/Charles Dharapak/SCANPIX

- Gbagbo må gå

Obama ber Elfenbenskystens president slippe makten.

Obama gjentok oppfordringen han kom med under en telefonsamtale med Gabons president Ali Bongo om krisen i Elfenbenskysten.

Laurent Gbagbo fortsetter å klamre seg til makten, selv om hans rival Alassane Ouattara vant presidentvalget i fjor høst.

Etter at alle forsøk på å forhandle fram en løsning mislyktes, innledet Ouattara en militær offensiv mot Gbagbos styrker. Han har fått kontrollen over mesteparten av landet og planlegger nå et angrep på landets største by Abidjan.

Mandag kveld skjøt helikoptre fra Frankrike og FN mot presidentpalasset i Abidjan, der Gbagbo trolig oppholder seg, og noen av basene til Gbagbos styrker i byen. (NTB)

Del på Facebook 20 TIPS

annonse

De bortgjemte krigsfrimerkene:
- fra partiet funnet på slottet av Milorg mai 1945!

SAMLERHUSET
KLIKK NÅ!

Nyheter
mest lest siste 24 timer

Drept av støt i dusjen på ferie i Thailand
Et svensk turistpar døde i dusjen da den ble strømførende på drømmeferien i Thailand.

- Pasienten var veldig glad for at han fikk bli med
Flykaptein Inge Sollerud sier pasienten gikk foran alt og alle da han ble med på kongeflyet.

Har funnet lik i

Figure 2. Sample web newspaper article (*Dagbladet* 5 April 2011)

Boilerplate removal involves separating the wheat from the chaff in pages like this one. What we are interested is only the editorial and non-repetitive text parts. The corpus is therefore meant to include only the body text of the article (framed with a dotted line in Figure 2), its headline, the lead paragraph and the picture caption. In addition, we exploit the information in the byline and dateline as metadata about author and publication date in the categorisation of the corpus data (cf. Section 2.5), but this is not meant to be part of the retrievable text in the corpus. All other material is uninteresting and is removed as part of the text cleaning process. A typical web newspaper article also contains a main image (not seen in Figure 2) and a lot of additional text material, and most of this is repetitive and shared across many other articles on a particular day. This includes advertisements, links to other articles, links for sharing the article via social media, links to specific sections of the newspaper, etc. Moreover, it has become customary to let readers comment interactively on the topic of newspaper articles. We do not include these comments in the corpus, but by storing the originally retrieved HTML files we have retained the possibility of compiling a separate subcorpus from these comments or integrating them in the newspaper corpus in the future.

Web newspapers come in many different formats, but there is a general tendency to use XML coding converted to HTML via style sheets. Every day about 85–100 MB of HTML files is retrieved, a little less at the weekends (c. 50 MB). One MB of HTML-coded newspaper text roughly approximates 15,000 running words in the corpus. Usually it is possible to retrieve the core text by selecting text between certain HTML codes or hidden comments in the document. Generally speaking, each newspaper has its own system, so the text selection procedure has to be given unique selection codes for each newspaper. However, some newspapers appear to be using the same web publishing tools, so some synergies can be drawn from reusing the code for picking out the core text across some of the newspapers in a semi-generic system. Further complicating these matters is the fact that the structure of the HTML code used by the newspapers may well change over time; hence there is a need for constant monitoring of the text cleaning procedure. Most of the HTML codes are stripped off and the entity names for national or foreign characters are transferred to their ISO 8-bit character equivalents. This process brings the size of the documents down to one seventh of the original size.

Some newspaper articles are based on or are direct copies of a national news wire service, and these articles may appear in several newspapers on a given day. In fact, this is the case with the article shown in Figure 2, which is from the newswire service NTB (*Norsk telegrambyrå*); hence no specific author is mentioned. Moreover, duplicates may be the result of parallel publishing of the same article in several newspapers that belong to the same corporation; this concerns especially Media Norge ASA, which owns the newspapers *Aftenposten*, *Bergens Tidende*, *Stavanger Aftenblad* and *Fædrelandsvennen*. For this reason, users of the corpus may come across duplicates and near-duplicates which have been intentionally included, in cases where several newspapers publish more or less the same text on the same day. However, if the same text occurs more than once in the same newspaper, we consider this to be an illegitimate duplicate, which should be removed. It may happen as part of the automatic text harvesting procedure that the same article is downloaded more than once. We have made efforts to eliminate this problem using different tools for the automatic detection of illegitimate duplicates. However, in such a large and automatically compiled corpus it is virtually impossible to eliminate all unwanted duplicates, and the improvement of the algorithms for duplicate removal is a continuous process.

2.3 Language classification

As mentioned, Norwegian has two written standards, Bokmål and Nynorsk, and it is crucial for many uses of the corpus to separate the two. It has been our aim throughout the project to build a corpus which covers both varieties, but which also incorporates separate subcorpora that allow the user to focus on a specific variety. As seen from Table 1 above, some newspapers are exclusively written in one variety while others contain both varieties. The downloaded HTML files do not contain any explicit indicators about which variety is used. Therefore, we needed to develop a tool for automatic classification of the two varieties. This language classification tool simultaneously performs a necessary related function, namely identifying articles written in a foreign language, of which English is by far the most common, although other languages also occur (e.g. German). The language classification tool uses a small list of unique and frequent words from Bokmål, Nynorsk and English (cf. Table 2) and matches the inventory of each file against these lists. Texts that contain more than 80 per cent of the Bokmål or Nynorsk key words are included in the corpus, and the variety-specific articles are grouped into different files, one for each language on a given day.

Table 2. Language/variety classification key words

Bokmål	*en, de, ikke, et, fra, jeg, ble, sier, da, hun, være, mer, vært*
Nynorsk	*ein, dei, ikkje, eit, frå, eg, ei, seier, ho, me, då, meir, vart*
English	*the, and, in, that, is, was, it, he, as, with*

We knew from the start that the majority variety Bokmål would be overrepresented in web newspapers, simply because most web newspapers use this variety. Since our aim is to be maximally inclusive of Norwegian web newspapers, we consider it unrealistic to have an even distribution of corpus text in the two varieties. However, in order to even out at least a part of the expected bias, we attempted to maximise the number of newspapers that publish in Nynorsk. Although as many as 14 of 23 newspapers include Nynorsk, the Bokmål component massively outnumbers Nynorsk in the corpus. As of April 2011, the corpus consists of a mere 5.2 per cent Nynorsk text, amounting to 56 million words.

2.4 Text annotation

Once converted from HTML to a text file, each article is provided with a header in an in-house corpus format which contains various metadata. A sample document header is shown in Figure 3. The metadata include file name, URL of the source text, name of the newspaper, date of publication, information about author's name and gender, text category and language variety.

```
<header>
<attribute name="file" value="AP/nob/2009/09/30/20090930-3296557.xml"/>
<attribute name="url"
value="http://www.aftenposten.no/kul_und/anmeldelser/article3296557.ece"/>
<attribute name="source" value="AP"/>
<attribute name="date" value="2009-09-30 16:17"/>
<attribute name="author" value="Cecilie Asker"/>
<attribute name="gender" value="K"/>
<attribute name="class1" value="kul_und/anmeldelser"/>
<attribute name="class2" value="kultur,musikk"/>
<attribute name="language" value="nob"/>
</header>
```

Figure 3. Sample corpus text file header

The data categories and their possible values are described in subsections 2.4.1–4 below.

2.4.1 *Annotation of source, date and author information*

By source we simply mean the newspaper the text was retrieved from. This information is conveniently drawn from the URL of the text and is annotated in the header as a two-letter code, according to the scheme shown in the second column of Table 1 above.

The date is extracted from one of three sources, depending on availability and the structure of the HTML pages of the newspapers. It can often be extracted directly from the file name of the URL. In other cases it has to be extracted from the text file itself, and conventionally, the newspapers print it immediately above the core text, as seen in Figure 2 above. If the date is not explicitly available, we must rely on the date when the text was retrieved. At any rate, the annotation of date is among the more trivial parts of the text annotation. The date is stored in the format 2009-09-30, as seen in Figure 3.

The annotation of author, i.e. the name of the journalist, is a less trivial task and has, due to time restrictions, only been implemented in a subset of the corpus. So far, this information has only been exploited in one specific study, namely Dyvik (this volume), and the sections of the corpus where this is annotated are the four newspapers studied in his paper, namely parts of *Aftenposten*, *Bergens Tidende, Dagbladet, Klassekampen, Dag og Tid, Hallingdølen, Nationen* and *Sogn Avis*. We extract this information from the HTML files, which will typically contain a specific code identifying the author, as seen from this XML code:

```
<div class="articleByline withByWho">
<span class="byWho pad-5 f-fff">AV</span>
<a href="mailto:kjersti.nipen@aftenposten.no">
KJERSTI NIPEN</a></div>
```

However, this is not done consistently across the newspapers, and each newspaper requires specific rules in order to capture the author's name. For those newspapers where author information can be provided, we also include author's gender. This information is retrieved automatically on the basis of (regularly updated) gender-specific name lists, each containing about 1,000 first names.

2.4.2 *Topic classification*

Far from trivial is the task of classifying the corpus texts according to their topic, such as sports, politics, local news, international news, etc. This part of the project is described in detail by Hagen (this volume). The main topic of a text can sometimes be extracted from its file name or from HTML tags in the text. We have experimented with machine learning techniques for automatic topic classification with some success. Metadata from the code can be used as a basis for topic classification, but the categories applied by the newspapers are unreliable and inconsistently used within and across newspapers. Moreover, news topics are notoriously overlapping; for example, is an article about Norwegian Prime Minister Jens Stoltenberg giving a speech on carbon capture and storage in Moscow to be considered 'politics', 'foreign', 'environment' or 'technology'? Manual annotators, and people in general of course, make different judgments about this, as seen from Hagen's (this volume) work on creating a manually annotated gold standard against which the automatic classification is compared. As Hagen explains, we started out with an unrealistically complex set of topics, but ended up with nine news categories: 'Culture', 'Entertainment', 'Foreign', 'Domestic', 'Economy', 'Politics', 'Consumer', 'Science and Technology' and 'Sports'. Due to the complexity of this task, the project did not allow for a manual classification of the corpus. Consequently, users should be warned that the topic classification is not fully reliable and is to be tentatively applied in research. We nevertheless think that the classification can be useful in order to compare general tendencies of linguistic phenomena across the various sections of the corpus, or to describe the language of one particular section, for instance sports, which turned out to be among the most easily identifiable topics.

2.4.3 *Part-of-speech tagging*

The NNC uses the Oslo-Bergen Tagger (OBT) for word class tagging of the corpus. The OBT is a rule-based Constraint Grammar (CG) tagger that provides each word with a morphosyntactic tag containing information about word class, inflectional paradigm, morphosyntactic category (definiteness, gender, number, tense), etc. The tagger covers both language varieties Bokmål and Nynorsk (Johannessen, Hagen & Nøklestad 2000) and it uses a large tagset with 358 morphological tags. It was originally developed in 1996–1998 by the Tagger Project at the University of Oslo and is currently used for a large variety of language resources in addition to the NNC. As part of the NNC project, the tagger has been developed further in order to meet specific requirements of this large corpus. This work principally involved adding a statistical module to the tagger as well as reimplementing the rules from the CG1 rule formalism to the newer CG3 format. The linguistic CG rules are developed by the Text Laboratory at the University of Oslo, while Paul Meurer at Uni Computing has created a stand-alone multitagger module, and the CG3 rule interpreter now replaces the earlier one implemented by Meurer. These efforts and their results and current status are described in detail by Johannessen et al. (this volume). The OBT utilises an electronic lexicon called *Norsk Ordbank* 'Norwegian Word Bank'. This lexicon is regularly expanded with new words from the register of new words in the NNC, as seen from Figure 1 above, and it is quality assured by lexicographers from the University of Oslo (Fjeld & Nygaard this volume).

We acknowledge, however, that morphosyntactic tagging has its limitations. For instance, it is not possible, or at best it is highly complicated, to search for passive constructions or relative clauses using only a word class tagged corpus. These and many other types of searches require annotation of syntactic structure in terms of hierarchical phrase structure, functional relations and the like. A corpus with this kind of annotation is commonly referred to as a treebank, and there are plans to develop a Norwegian Treebank based on the NNC as a source of data. However, this is a major effort that lies outside the current project, and is being carried out within the INESS project (Norwegian Infrastructure for the Exploration of Syntax and Semantics). These plans are described in detail by Rosén (this volume).

2.5 Search system and user interface

After downloading and subsequent processing of text, the corpus texts become available for search via the search interface the next morning. This means that users never have access to today's newspapers via the corpus, but the most recent files contain yesterday's news. From the start of the project, we have used Corpus WorkBench (CWB) from IMS at the University of Stuttgart,[4] and most of the research presented in this book is based on this system. However, Paul Meurer at Uni Computing has recently developed a new search system and user interface. Currently the two systems co-exist but we may in the future opt for using the in-house system only.

2.5.1 *Corpus WorkBench*

Corpus WorkBench is a well-known system for administering, indexing and querying large text corpora and can be used for corpora of several hundred million running words. The texts can have structural attributes such as source or date and positional attributes such as word class. CWB comes with a command line query user interface (CQP) and in the project we have made a web-based user interface to this command line query program. The user can get a traditional concordance output either as a KWIC concordance or a sentence concordance. In our case the CWB interface has been integrated into the Plone-based project web page, which contains news, statistics, background information, administrative information, etc. Figure 4 shows the CWB interface to the NNC.

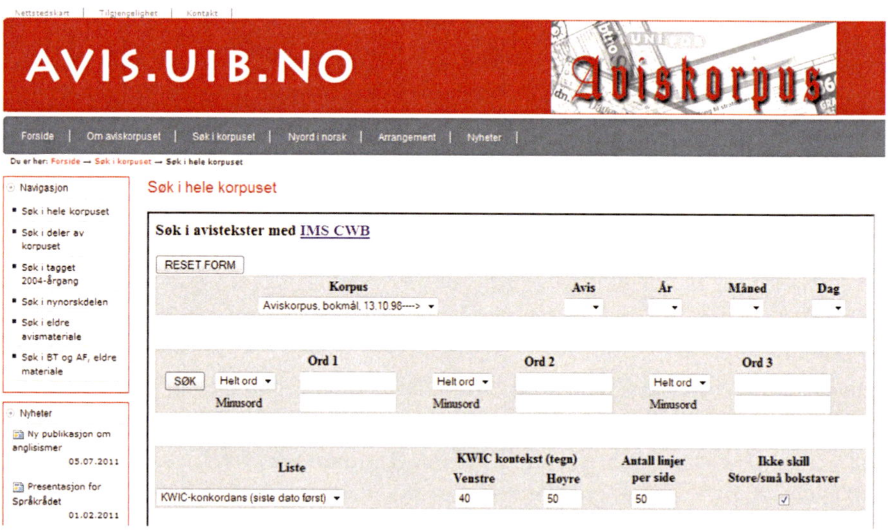

Figure 4. The Corpus WorkBench interface to the Norwegian Newspaper Corpus

4. http://www.ims.uni-stuttgart.de/projekte/CorpusWorkbench/

The user can view concordances and lists of collocates and sort these according to different criteria. The search can be restricted according to various structural attributes, in this particular case limited to *Avis* 'newspaper' *DN* (*Dagens Næringsliv)* from 16 June 2010. Users may also access distribution statistics for the result of a query across the different structural attributes, and the search pattern may be truncated to the left, right or both ways.

2.5.2 *Corpuscle*

Corpuscle is a new corpus query engine and web-based corpus management system that has been developed at Uni Computing for the benefit of NNC and other corpus-building projects. Its technical details and functionality are described by Meurer (this volume), while G. Andersen (this volume) illustrates the value of this interface for a specific research task, namely the study of anglicisms in Norwegian. The main design goals of Corpuscle have been the ability to handle very large corpora, support for structured XML data and seamless integration of manual corpus annotation and editing. New algorithms have been developed which allow for the implementation of multi-valued and set-valued attributes. Queries can be input in a graphical, menu-driven way, freeing the user from dealing with the complexities of the query language. The Corpuscle user interface is shown in Figure 5.

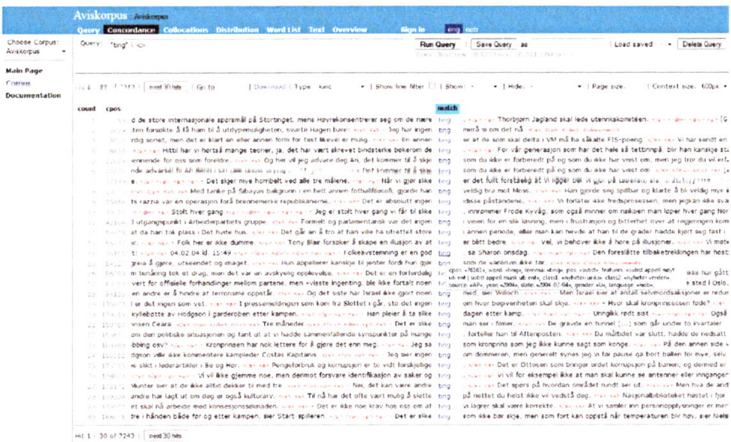

Figure 5. The Corpuscle interface to the Norwegian Newspaper Corpus

As can be seen, the web interface offers rich functionality for concordancing, collocations, distribution statistics, and more. While the figure shows the Concordance view, basic or advanced searches can be typed in the leftmost Query tab. The Collocations view allows users to view ranked collocation patterns and to select among different association measures (token frequency, relative frequency, mutual information, log likelihood, etc.). The Distribution tab gives distributional statistics for the search pattern for the various sections of the corpus, compared by absolute or relative frequencies. The Word List view gives a clickable alphabetical/frequency-sorted list of all forms which match the search pattern; this is highly useful for instance when studying inflections of compounding (e.g. G. Andersen this volume). The Text tab is automatically activated when clicking a concordance for more context, while the Overview tab provides statistical data about the whole corpus, its size, number of unique word forms, distribution of text across attributes, etc. Note also that all key words and XML elements (tags) have a mouseover functionality which shows all the attributes of the elements. This is seen in the middle of Figure 5 in the text box, which gives information about corpus position, word, lemma, part-of-speech, morphosyntactic features (alternative interpretations of the ambiguous form *ting* 'thing' are separated by the hash ("|") symbol), news category, source, year, date, author's gender and name, and finally language (*nob* 'Norwegian Bokmål'). All concordances, statistics and word lists can be downloaded as a text file by clicking the Download button, and the file can then be further explored using other software, such as Excel.

2.6 Extraction of new words

As mentioned in Section 1, the NNC project is especially tailored for lexicography and the study of new words in the language, and one of the most important features of the NNC architecture is a system for monitoring the development of lexical neologisms. Each day the lexical inventory of all the harvested text is checked against a comprehensive, accumulated word list which as of April 2011 consists of some 5.292 million word forms. This reference list comprises all the previously recorded words in the NNC combined with the inventory of all other Norwegian language resources collected at Uni Computing[5] over the last 20 years, including a full-form lexicon derived from the comprehensive dictionary *Bokmålsordboka*. Of the c. 230,000 running words that are daily added to the text database, on average 1,300 are previously unrecorded word forms. It should be pointed out that we are using technical definitions here; a 'word' is any sequence of graphemes (letters, digits, punctuation or other symbols) found between two spaces in a running text. A 'new word' is any word that is not included in the accumulated reference list mentioned. The daily lists of neologisms can be viewed at the *Nyord i norsk* 'Norwegian Neologisms' section of the NNC's web page.

5. And its organisational predecessors the HIT Centre, Unifob AKSIS and Uni Digital.

2.7 Classification of new words

Naturally, only a subset of the new forms retrieved on a given day are relevant for lexicographical purposes. Since it is not feasible to check manually all word forms on a daily basis, we apply pattern-matching and statistical techniques for selecting what appear to be the most relevant word forms from a lexicographical point of view. As an initial classification, new words are automatically distinguished according to some of their orthographical features. Table 3 shows this classification and the distribution of word forms among the new words in the corpus.

Table 3. New word categories in the Norwegian Newspaper Corpus

Category	Examples	Frequency	%
General neologisms/spelling errors	*glera, bursdagsrevyer, inkosekvente*	895,336	46.0
Anglicism candidates	*cinefilt, eurodancegjengen*	104,217	5.4
Abbreviations	*omg.*	2,838	0.1
Name candidates	*Awarta, Navarrrggsete, McCluskeys, al-Fetori, PARTIC*	477,828	24.6
Hyphenated name candidates	*May-Tordis, United-Dæhli*	104,960	5.4
Hyphenated compounds	*med-tunga-rett-i-munnen, mafia-søppel*	212,413	10.9
Compounds with other marking	*brukeren/kjøperen, kg/person*	62,510	3.2
Digits and abbreviations	*47LE850N*	16,802	0.9
Pure digits	*49,00–48,67*	358	0.0
URLs and e-mail addresses	*sportsjournalists.co.uk*	22,968	1.2
Garbage	*mÃ¸, belkolleksjon, BerlinA*	44,790	2.3
TOTAL		1,945,020	100.0

In the first category of Table 3, we find words that are orthographically unmarked, that is they contain no capital letter, hyphen or the like but consist of lower-case letters only, accounting for almost half of the new words. Real neologisms, that is, new linguistically motivated and authentic lexical items are typically found in this category, represented here by forms such as *glera*, a kind of wine grape, and *bursdagsrevyer* 'birthday reviews', a new compound. But the first category also includes lower-case spelling errors not previously recognised, such as *inkosekvente* (*inkonsekvente* 'inconsistent'). These are irrelevant from a lexicographer's point of view, but could be relevant to the developer of spell checking systems or to the psycholinguist focusing on error studies or the like. Some new words, about 5 per cent, are classified as anglicism candidates, including *cinefilt* and *eurodancegjengen*. The procedure for classification is described briefly in Section 2.7.1 below, and further by Losnegaard and Lyse (this volume). Some new words have special orthographic features which make them less relevant for inclusion in dictionaries. About 10 per cent of the new words are productive, hyphenated compounds. Newspaper language refers widely to names of people, places, companies and products, and, unsurprisingly, a substantial proportion of new words, about 30 per cent, are orthographically distinguishable as name candidates (including hyphenated/compound names). Besides, the new words include abbreviations, digits, URLs and e-mail addresses, and a relatively small proportion of garbage (2.3 per cent), that is, letter/symbol combinations that do not conform with any recognisable pattern but which are the likely result of an error in character conversion or the like, an example being *mÃ¸belkolleksjon* (*møbelkolleksjon* 'furniture selection').

2.7.1 *Anglicism detection*

For lexicography and language policy purposes, we find it relevant to single out words which appear to be of English origin from the rest of the new words. We have developed an in-house language processing tool which identifies words with English orthography. The module, described in (Andersen 2005, 2011, Fortcoming), uses a hybrid method combining n-gram statistics, dictionary look-up and regular expressions. English and Norwegian have rather different orthographies, and this can be exploited in anglicism detection. By considering grapheme typicality for English or Norwegian, the tool extracts words like *crew*, *quiz* and *comeback* as anglicisms, as they all contain character n-grams (chargrams) that do not occur in words of Norwegian origin. For each neologism, the program considers the orthographic inventory and looks for letter combinations that are typically English and atypically Norwegian. However, due to the typological closeness of English and Norwegian, many anglicisms cannot be identified using this method, since their orthography is not specifically English-looking. This applies to a work such as *nerd*, whose chargrams are not atypical for domestic Norwegian words. For this reason, the anglicism identifier also uses lookup in a specifically tailored dictionary based on the BNC lexicon to identify words of English origin. In the project we have also experimented with methods using supervised machine learning techniques based on TiMBLE in combination with the Java-based data mining software Weka (Losnegaard & Lyse this volume). The current precision of the module is about 75 per cent, based on a gold standard of 10,000 manually identified anglicisms. The module identifies 128,588 anglicism candidates from 1,469,925 unique word forms in the corpus, amounting to 8.7 per cent.

2.8 Frequency profiling and lexical database entry

Given the vast number of new words that occur in the corpus, it is particularly important to consider frequency, as this information holds the key to whether or not a particular form or meaning should be included in the dictionary, and if so, in which orthographic form it should be entered (Stubbs 2007:90). Overall frequency and frequency development over time has a direct bearing on the relevance for lexicographic inclusion of individual word forms and neologistic phrases. Generally, new words with a high frequency are more relevant than lower-frequency words, and words with a steady or gradually increasing frequency in the period represented in the data are more relevant than those with a fluctuating or decreasing frequency. The work on lexicography based on the NNC is described in detail by Fjeld and Nygaard (this volume). Lexicographers and other users of the NNC can retrieve usage statistics of individual words as images created on-the-fly (Andersen 2011). For more systematic considerations of frequency developments, the NNC project team have developed frequency filters which systematically extract frequency profiles for new words and select the words that look the most interesting from the point of view of frequency development over time. The filters are based on linear regression statistics calibrated with the least square method (Fjeld & Nygaard this volume). The first filter picks out non-frequent words (n<10), and these are discarded and not included among the neologism candidates for manual inspection. The second filter picks out words with a high and stable frequency. These are manually checked by a lexicographer, and the most relevant words are included in the Norwegian Word Bank. The third filter identifies words with a high overall frequency and gradually increasing frequency, most of which are included in the Norwegian Word Bank. Examples of some of the words that have been picked out by the various filters are given in Table 4.

Table 4. Result of frequency-based filtering of new words

Not included in the Norwegian Word Bank	*alpindamene, bøllefri, dettestår, vikig, viestad*
Included but not new	*akilles, bakfull, lukeparkere*
Included and new	*dyssosial, fistet, flatskjermen, foodprosessor, hacker, hajj, lagbygging, omrokeringer, zappe*

In the category of words not relevant for inclusion we find spelling errors (*dettestår, viestad, vikig*) and non-lexicalised compounds (*alpindamene, bøllefri*). Among forms which proceed further to manual lexicographical edition, we find both real neologisms like *hajj* and *foodprosessors*, but also, interestingly, lexicographical lacunae, that is, words which are not new, but which nevertheless are missing from existing dictionaries, like *akilles, bakfull* ('hung over') and the verb *lukeparkere* ('parallel park'). This shows that the inductive and corpus-driven method (Tognini-Bonelli 2001) for neologism extraction has an advantage over manual methods, in that it may lead to better coverage of existing words in the language.

2.9 Identification of multiword expressions

Finally, in the NNC project we have also considered it important to explore tools and methods for segmenting and identifying multiword expressions (MWEs), that is, pairs or longer combinations of words which co-occur more often than would be predicted by chance (Renouf & Sinclair 1991). As mentioned in Section 2.5, users of the NNC can search for and retrieve MWEs in the CWB and Corpuscle interfaces, but we have also given priority to a more systematic, large-scale effort to identify all candidate MWEs that occur using corpus-driven methods. This effort is described in detail by Lyse and Andersen (this volume; see also Andersen 2011). It is not part of the day-to-day processing which runs automatically, but is performed in less regular batches according to the needs of lexicographers and other users of the corpus (and is thus marked with a dotted line in Figure 1 above). The category of MWEs incorporates an array of structurally and conceptually different items, and the correct identification and segmentation of MWEs is necessary for a variety of purposes in natural language processing, terminology, lexicography and related fields. For instance, technical terminology is very often realised as phrasal units. Examples that occur in the NNC are *acute respiratory distress syndrome*, *predatory pricing*, *tabula gratulatoria* and *spinal muskelatrofi*, some of which also illustrate terms realised as anglicisms or other foreign items. For more general lexicographical purposes, a systematic data-driven approach can be used to identify various types of phrasal idioms such as *sakens kjerne* 'the core of the matter' and idiomatic formulae such as *abra kadabra* etc. Moreover, the performance of language processing tools such as word class taggers and grammatical parsers (treebanks) can be enhanced with knowledge of which forms constitute different types of grammatical MWEs, for instance phrasal prepositions such as *på grunn av* 'because of', adverbs such as *i tide* 'on time', etc. These should be segmented as phrasal units and not processed further by the tagger. Thus, the main concern of this part of the project is to find ways of distinguishing between, on the one hand, "frequent collocations … which are of no real interest to lexicography" (Atkins & Rundell 2008: 166) and on the other hand "phrases which have some degree of idiomatic meaning or behaviour" (Atkins & Rundell 2008: 166). To this end, Lyse and Andersen (this volume) have produced n-gram statistics for the entire corpus and calculated rank scores using a variety of different association measures.

3. The content of the research contributions to this book

In the sections above, we have already partly described those contributions to this book which have a specific methodological focus and concern the development of the corpus itself, its search system and user interface, so these will only be dealt with briefly here. Three papers are concerned with various aspects of annotating the corpus. **Paul Meurer** describes Corpuscle, the new corpus query engine and web-based corpus management system, and shows that the system is flexible enough to handle very large corpora like the NNC in an efficient way. He evaluates its performance compared to Corpus WorkBench and shows its usefulness for the diversity of corpus projects that Uni Computing is involved in (see Section 2.5.2 above for a fuller description). The contribution by **Janne Bondi Johannessen, Kristin Hagen, André Lynum and Anders Nøklestad** gives a survey of the work on development of the Oslo-Bergen tagger, specifically how they met the challenges of tagging the large NNC by reimplementing the constraint grammar rules to the CG3 system and by adding a data-driven statistical disambiguation module for word class, morphological tags and lemmas (cf. 2.4.3). **Victoria Rosén** explores the usefulness of the NNC as a resource for creating a Norwegian treebank. Data from the NNC are used as a basis for the ongoing INESS project (Norwegian Infrastructure for the Exploration of Syntax and Semantics), and the Norwegian treebank will provide detailed annotation of hierarchical phrase structure, functional relations and the like. This in turn will enable much more powerful searches than are currently possible in the corpus, for instance searching for passive constructions, relative clauses and the like.

Further, the contribution by **Gunn Inger Lyse and Gisle Andersen** provides a step-by-step account of the data-driven effort to detect MWEs in the NNC. The authors evaluate a range of different association measures by inspecting ranked lists of bi- and trigrams. The most striking observation they make concerns the considerable differences between the various rankings, and consequently the differences in suitability of the methods to the task of identifying lexicalised phrases such as multiword terms, idiomatic phrasal expressions, multiword prepositions, etc. (cf. Section 2.9). **Thomas M. Hagen** describes how machine learning methods, combined with a limited amount of manual classification, have been used in a fairly successful attempt to automatically classify newspaper articles from the NNC according to their topic, using a programming language called CRM114 (cf. Section 2.4.2). **Gyri S. Losnegaard and Gunn Inger Lyse** describe how anglicisms are automatically detected among new words in the corpus through a series of experiments with data-driven methods to identify anglicisms in Norwegian text. They show that memory-based learning using chargrams provides a valuable complement to the existing hybrid tool used for anglicism detection (Andersen Fortcoming; cf. also Section 2.7.1).

The remaining chapters of the book all explore the research potential of the corpus from different perspectives. Four contributions are concerned with various aspects of the lexicon, including anglicisms (G. Andersen), neologisms

(Fjeld & Nygaard, and De Smedt) and terminology (Kristiansen). Two chapters focus on morphological aspects, including variation in stem forms and inflections (Dyvik) and the development of deverbal nouns (Ø. Andersen), while two contributions explore the NNC in investigations of metonymy (Halverson) and metaphor (Breivik & Swan).

The paper by **Gisle Andersen** is an investigation of English influence on Norwegian lexis. Specifically he looks into the orthographic adaptation of import words, such as the change from *blog* to *blogg*, or *squash* to *skvåsj*. This adaptation can be viewed from a top-down perspective, by considering the effect of standardisation decisions made by the Norwegian Language Council, or from a bottom-up perspective, by considering unsolicited adaptation initiated by language users. Through a quantitative and qualitative inspection of a large set of data, he gives a survey of a set of linguistic and contextual factors that appear to have important bearings on the degree to which different words undergo spelling adaptation. The paper also illustrates the usefulness of several of the facilities of the Corpuscle search engine and interface.

Helge Dyvik describes an innovative method of applying correspondence analysis and implication analysis to investigate interdependencies between morphosyntactic variants in Norwegian. Each of the two written standards, Bokmål and Nynorsk, allows an unusual amount of variation among alternative stem forms such as *skole/skule* 'school' and inflectional endings such as *boken/boka* 'the book'. Dyvik's study is a corpus-driven account that aims to chart significant patterns of variation, construed as so-called 'norm clusters', i.e. subnorms that emerge from the data. It is evident from the investigation of actual newspaper texts that there are intricate interdependencies among the alternative morhosyntactic options. For instance, there is an implicational relationship between the choice of feminine gender for nouns denoting abstract concepts and the choice of feminine gender for concrete and everyday words, where the former choice implies the latter, but not vice versa. The study shows the strength of corpus-driven methodology, in that we now are able to explore such intricate patterns of dependency among morphosyntactic variants without having to rely on our intuitive assumptions. Further it shows that the resources and tools that have been developed in connection with the NNC project provide a good basis for investigating such interdependencies empirically on a larger scale.

Further, **Ruth Vatvedt Fjeld and Lars Nygaard** present a short history of Norwegian neography and some of the problems in the field of lexical development. They argue that the methodology and coverage of previous efforts to chart the development of neologisms have been insufficient. Further, they present a classification of neologisms and give a detailed account of the new method of semi-automatic identification of neologisms from the NNC (cf. Section 2.8).

Their study demonstrates the usefulness of the corpus-driven approach to lexicography through results which show that the overwhelming number of new words in Norwegian are inherited words, mostly compounds, and that genuinely new words are fairly rare.

Koenraad de Smedt looks into a very specific aspect of neologisms, namely 'ash compounds' – compounds such as *askefast* 'ash stranded', created in association with the explosive volcanic eruption at Eyjafjallajökull in Iceland in April 2010. His research displays the dynamics of word formation and linguistic creativity in newspaper accounts of this specific event, demonstrating the usefulness of the NNC for the purpose of obtaining data on this theme. De Smedt's method is to use truncated corpus searches combined with post-processing and varying the time frame of the searches. He shows how the news coverage occurred in rough waves of about five to ten days and how this correlates with the formation of new ash compounds, which shows a clear increase during the initial period with peaks in relevant news coverage, followed by a flattening of the word formation curve.

The contribution by **Marita Kristiansen** illustrates that the NNC can also be a useful resource for the study of terminology. She looks into the financial jargon associated with the financial crisis starting in 2008, such as *credit crunch, subprime* and *hedge fund*, and shows that the NNC provides a solid representation of relevant financial jargon used in Norwegian in the period of the financial crisis and can be used as a basis for term development in accordance with official language policy. Through a primarily concept-based analysis, Kristiansen outlines the morphosyntactic variation of terms, their degree of Englishness, inflectional variation, conceptual relations, etc, concluding that data from the NNC make it possible to outline relations that hold among several of the most topical concepts and to discover new concepts belonging to the concept field of the financial crisis.

Sandra Halverson gives an account of metonymy and vagueness associated with the place names *Schengen* and *Kyoto*. The metonymic uses of place names often involve reference to events located at specific places or to the participants or the results of such events. For instance, the place name *Schengen* may be used metonymically to refer to the Schengen Agreement, to the membership or group of Schengen treaty signatories or to the geographical territory defined by the agreement, i.e. its area of jurisdiction. Halverson's data show that there are several fluid cases where more than one interpretation of an utterance is possible. Her contribution illustrates the value of using a monitor corpus such as the NNC to study the emerging uses of existent linguistic forms, as the new senses developed are observable as cases of short-span diachrony. Moreover, her findings show that the two place names are at different stages of development in terms of the metonymic senses that emerge.

Leiv Egil Breivik and Toril Swan investigate a set of spatial metaphors from a cognitive perspective. The authors explore certain patterns of conceptual association, specifically conceptual metaphors such as UP IS MORE and UP IS POSITIVE EVALUATION as well as their linguistic realisations based on data from the NNC. Their investigation shows that the large majority of the UP/DOWN words studied are used metaphorically, while the assumed prototypical use – i.e. the concrete literal use – is very infrequent. Further, the number of positive (UP) words by far exceeds the number of negative (DOWN) words in their data. The corpus-based findings show the ubiquity and pervasiveness of metaphor even in newspaper language which is primarily associated with informative functions rather than with poetic functions and linguistic creativity.

In the final chapter of the book, **Øivin Andersen** takes a diachronic perspective and explores the development of six zero suffix deverbal nouns in Norwegian in the course of the twentieth century using data from the NNC. Deverbal nouns are nominalisations such as *skudd* 'shot' derived from the verb *skyte* 'shoot'. He hypothesises that these nouns tend to develop into prototypical nouns the older they get, and that they follow a diachronic path leading from imperfect noun to perfect noun. His investigation draws not only on the NNC but also some supplementary data consisting of older newspaper texts used for comparative reference. Andersen devotes special attention to the occurrence of prepositional dependents in the form of an argument coded with the preposition *av* versus the presence of a participant coded by the preposition *på*, and brings to bear the challenges associated with studying diachronic developments on the basis of contemporary newspaper data.

4. Concluding remarks

The Norwegian Newspaper Corpus is a fully automatic dynamic corpus of considerable size and coverage, and the collection of papers in this volume is meant to show that it is a valuable resource for a variety of research purposes, illustrating the advantages of using a large monitor corpus as a basis for linguistic research. First, the corpus captures new micro-level developments involving new word forms and new uses of old word forms. Second, it allows for large-scale quantitative studies. Third, it provides a continuously updated repository of evidence for language usage. Fourth, it involves continuous monitoring of language development by statistical comparison between different time sections of the corpus, thus enabling the study of short-term change in diachrony. Thanks to recent advances in corpus building and technology, Norwegian word formation, neology and other language features can now be studied in quantitative detail. The monitor corpus allows us to become less dependent on our intuitions and instead rely on statistical facts. We have argued that the corpus-based approach is a valuable supplement to traditional lexicography and terminography, and hopefully it will lead to a significant reduction of the manual work and a radical simplification of the task of looking for the needle in the linguistic hay-stack. However, we should stress that there are many aspects of Norwegian language that are yet to be explored using state-of-the-art corpus-based/corpus-driven methods. Thus, we hope that this book merely represents the beginning of such explorations.

References

Andersen, Gisle. 2005. Assessing algorithms for automatic extraction of anglicisms in Norwegian texts. *Proceedings from Corpus Linguistics 2005.* ⟨http://www.corpus.bham.ac.uk/pclc/Birmingham_paper.doc⟩.

Andersen, Gisle. 2010. Halvautomatisk ekserpering av anglisismer i norsk. *Nordiska studier i leixcografi* 10: 72–85.

Andersen, Gisle. 2011. Corpora as lexicographical basis: The case of anglicisms in Norwegian. *VARIENG – Studies in Variation, Contacts and Change in English* 6. ⟨http://www.helsinki.fi/varieng/journal/index.html⟩.

Andersen, Gisle. Fortcoming. Semi-automatic approaches to Anglicism detection based on corpus data. In *The Anglicization of European lexis,* Virginia Pulcini & Christiano Furiassi (eds). Amsterdam: John Benjamins.

Atkins, B.T. Sue & Rundell, Michael. 2008. *The Oxford Guide to Practical Lexicography.* Oxford: OUP.

Baroni, Marco, Bernardini, Silvia, Ferraresi, Adriano & Zanchetta, Eros. 2009. The WaCky Wide Web: A collection of very large linguistically processed web-crawled corpora. *Language Resources and Evaluation* 43(3). 209–226.

Cotter, Colleen. 2010. *News Talk: Investigating the Language of Journalism.* Cambridge: CUP.

Davies, Mark. 2009. The 385+ million word Corpus of Contemporary American English (1990–2008+): Design, architecture, and linguistic insights. *International Journal of Corpus Linguistics* 14(2): 159–190.

Fairon, Cédrick, Naets, Hubert, Kilgarriff, Adam & de Schryver, Gilles-Maurice (eds). 2007. *Building and Exploring Web Corpora.* Louvain-la-Neuve: UCL Presses Universitaires de Louvain.

Fletcher, William H. 2007. Concordancing the web: promise and problems, tools and techniques. In *Corpus Linguistics and the Web,* Marianne Hundt, Nadia Nesselhauf & Carolin Biewer (eds), 25–46. Amsterdam: Rodopi.

Grefenstette, Gregory. 2002. The WWW as a resource for lexicography. In *Lexicography and Natural Language Processing,* Marie-Hélène Corréard (ed), 199–215. Gothenburg: Euralex.

Hofland, Knut. 2000. A self-expanding corpus based on newspapers on the Web. Paper read at The Second International Language Resources and Evaluation Conference (LREC), at Paris.

Hundt, Marianne, Nadja Nesselhauf, & Carolin Biewer. 2007. *Corpus linguistics and the web, Language and computers.* Amsterdam: Rodopi.

Johannessen, Janne Bondi, Hagen, Kristin & Nøklestad, Anders. 2000. A constraint-based tagger for Norwegian. In *17th Scandinavian Conference of Linguistics*, Carl-Erik Lindberg & Steffen Nordahl Lund. Odense: University of Southern Denmark.

Kilgarriff, Adam & Grefenstette, Gregory. 2003. Introduction to the Special Issue on Web as Corpus. *Computational Linguistics* 29(3): 1–15.

Kilgarriff, Adam & Tugwell, David. 2002. Sketching words. In *Lexicography and Natural Language Processing*, Marie-Hélène Corréard, 125–137. Gothenburg: Euralex.

Lüdeling, Anke, Evert, Stefan & Baroni, Marco. 2007. Using web data for linguistic purposes. In *Corpus Linguistics and the Web*, Marianne Hundt, Nadia Nesselhauf & Carolin Biewer (eds), 7–24. Amsterdam: Rodopi.

Manning, Christopher & Schütze, Hinrich. 1999. *Foundations of Statistical Natural Language Processing*. Cambridge MA: The MIT Press.

Ooi, Vincent B.Y. 1998. *Computer Corpus Lexicography*. Edinburgh: Edinburgh University Press.

Pulcini, Virginia. 2008. Corpora and lexicography: The case of a dictionary of Anglicisms. In *Investigating English with Corpora: Studies in Honour of Maria Teresa Prat*, Maria Teresa Martelli & Virginia Pulcini (eds), 189–203. Monza: Polimetrica.

Renouf, Antoinette. 1996. The ACRONYM Project: Discovering the textual thesaurus. In *Synchronic Corpus Linguistics*, Carol E. Percy, Charles F. Meyer & Ian Lancashire (eds), 171–187. Amsterdam: Rodopi.

Renouf, Antoinette. 2007. Corpus development 25 years on: From super-corpus to cyber-corpus. In *Corpus Linguistics 25 Years on*, Roberta Facchinetti (ed), 27–50. Amsterdam: Rodopi.

Renouf, Antoinette, Kehoe, Andrew & Banerjee, Jay. 2005. The WebCorp search engine: A holistic approach to web text search. Paper read at Corpus Linguistics 2005, at Birmingham.

Renouf, Antoinette & Sinclair, John McHardy. 1991. Collocational frameworks in English. In *English Corpus Linguistics – Studies in Honour of Jan Svartvik*, Karin Aijmer & Bengt Altenberg (eds), 128–143. London: Longman.

Sinclair, John McHardy (ed). 1987. *Looking up*. London: Collins ELT.

Stubbs, Michael. 2007. An example of frequent English phraseology: Distributions, structures and functions. In *Corpus Linguistics 25 Years on*, Roberta Facchinetti (ed), 89–106. Amsterdam: Rodopi.

Tognini-Bonelli, Elena. 2001. *Corpus Linguistics at Work* [Studies in Corpus Linguistics 6]. Amsterdam: John Benjamins.

van Dijk, Teun A. 1988. *News as Discourse*. Hillsdale NJ: Lawrence Erlbaum Associates.

Wangensteen, Boye. 2002. Nettbasert nyordsinnsamling. *Språknytt* (2): 17–19.

PART I

Exploiting the web as a corpus – Methods and tools

Corpuscle – a new corpus management platform for annotated corpora

Paul Meurer
Uni Computing, University of Bergen

Corpuscle is a new corpus query engine and Web-based corpus management system. The main design goals were the ability to handle very large corpora, support for structured data (XML), and seamless integration of manual corpus annotation and editing. New algorithms have been developed, among them a technique for running finite state automata from edges with lowest corpus counts, and an implementation of regular expressions on suffix arrays for fast reverse index lookup. These algorithms allow for a clean and elegant implementation of multi-valued and set-valued attributes. The web interface offers rich functionality for concordancing, collocations, distribution statistics, and more. Queries can be input in a graphical, menu-driven way, freeing the user from dealing with the complexities of the query language.

1. Introduction

In this chapter, I describe Corpuscle, a new corpus query engine and corpus management system that is under active development and already in use for a variety of corpora of different types at Uni Computing and the University of Bergen.

The corpus engines that are most widely used today (e.g. Open Corpus Workbench (CWB), Manatee/SketchEngine) were developed in the 1990s, when corpora still were well below 100 million tokens in size, and harddisk and memory capacity were limiting factors. Consequently, much effort was put into achieving high data compression, whereas search algorithms were not overly sophisticated. Some of those systems also suffer (or have suffered until recently) from missing Unicode support, missing support for structured data, a complex programming interface, and restrictive licensing. In contrast, today's largest corpora are approaching a billion tokens or are already significantly larger, and disk space and memory are cheap commodities. Support for Unicode and structured data (XML) are important concerns.

With these changed circumstances in mind, I started designing and implementing Corpuscle in late 2009.[1] My goal was to create a state-of-the-art corpus system that would be flexible enough to handle very large corpora like the Norwegian Newspaper Corpus (around 900 million tokens) in an efficient way and at the same time be useful for the diversity of corpus projects Uni Computing is involved in. Considerable effort has been put into the design of fast search algorithms, whereas data compression has had no priority. Several novel algorithms[2] were developed, among them a technique for running finite state automata from edges with lowest corpus counts,[3] and an implementation of regular expression matching on suffix arrays for fast lexicon lookup.[4]

An evaluation of our system against Corpus Workbench using the Norwegian Newspaper Corpus and other large corpora (see Section 6) shows that our system is comparable in speed or significantly faster on most types of queries.

In the design of the new corpus system, the main requirements were the following:

- Full Unicode support[5]
- Support for hierarchically structured data (e.g. XML)
- Clean implementation of multi-valued attributes (used to encode ambiguity) and set-valued attributes (used to encode sets of features)
- Support for very large corpora (order of magnitude 2 billion tokens and more)

---

1. The development of Corpuscle was financed through a grant from the Meltzer Foundation.

2. These algorithms will be described in detail in a forthcoming paper.

3. See Evert (2007) for a discussion of the shortcomings of invariably running the automata from the start edge.

4. See Section 2.

5. Corpuscle supports presently only the Basic Multilingual Plane (BMP) subset of the Unicode code range. The BMP consists of the first $2^{16} = 65536$ Unicode characters and contains characters for almost all modern languages, whereas some ancient languages (e.g. Gothic) are not fully covered. If there is a need, Corpuscle can easily be extended to support all of Unicode. Using the BMP alone has however significant advantages, as every character can be uniformly stored as a two-byte integer (in the UCS-2 format) and does not have to be decoded when read in again. This is in contrast to the popular format UTF-8, which is capable of encoding any Unicode character, but costly decoding is necessary when reading from a file.

- Query execution speed comparable to or better than Corpus Workbench, in particular on queries with high-frequent initial position and on queries involving certain types of regular expressions
- Powerful query syntax, comparable to and modeled along CQL ("Corpus Query Langugage", the querying language of Corpus Workbench), with better support for structured data
- Seamless integration of manual corpus annotation and editing, with live querying, at least for smaller corpora
- Rich functionality for concordancing, collocations, distribution statistics etc.
- Well-defined API[6] (Application Programming Interface)
- Integrated Web interface

2. Design principles

The overall design of the query engine of Corpuscle is quite similar to that of Corpus Workbench.

In a technical sense, a corpus can be described as a sequence of corpus positions that are annotated with values for one or several attributes (also called positional attributes). The words of the underlying texts comprise the mandatory attribute *word*, that is, a minimally annotated corpus consists of a sequence of words. Other possible attributes may encode grammatical features (part of speech, morphosyntax etc.), other linguistic annotations and metadata. Attribute values can be atomic or structured. Corpuscle has built-in support for structured attributes, both for multi-valued and set-valued attributes and combinations thereof.

In addition to corpus positions that encode word tokens together with their annotations, Corpuscle also uses corpus positions to encode structural data.[7] Here, Corpuscle differs from CWB, where structural attributes are tied to the corpus position of the following word token. The advantage of giving structural data their own dedicated corpus positions is twofold: First, the original order of consecutive XML tags can always be unambiguously reconstructed from the encoded corpus. And second, structural data can also have positional attributes. This can be an

6. An API is a formal specification of how other software programs can be built on top of the core functionality of a system (here, Corpuscle).

7. Since structural data is represented in the vertical file as XML start, end and empty tags, possibly containing arbitrary XML-style attribute-value-pairs, I will use the terms XML tag and structural attribute (value) synonymously.

advantage when attributes that scope over more than a single corpus position are coded as positional attributes.[8]

A collection of annotated documents has to be formatted as a *vertical file* before it can be imported into Corpuscle. The vertical file has a format similar to CWB's vertical file. Each line in the vertical file corresponds to a corpus position, and the values of the positional attributes that are defined for the given corpus are separated by tab characters. Structural positions are represented by XML-style tags that may include attribute-value pairs (e.g. ⟨text id = "314" lang = "kat"⟩). They, too, can have positional attribute values.

A vertical file can be automatically derived from XML-encoded documents; the resulting corpus will then only contain structural positions (corresponding to XML tags) and the *word* attribute, corresponding to the sequence of word tokens in the document. When the corpus documents are linguistically annotated, it is however desirable to encode the linguistic annotation as separate attributes, which necessitates preprocessing of the data in a more sophisticated way.

A corpus cannot be searched efficiently without an *index*. An index is (much like a book index) a set of data structures that encode for every word in the corpus the positions of all its occurrences in the corpus. Thanks to the index, it is not necessary to scan the whole corpus position for position to find the occurences of a given search word. Such an index exists for every corpus attribute; it is called an *inverted index*.

For efficiency reasons, the annotated corpus text itself is encoded as a set of sequences of numerical value *ids* (numbers), one sequence per attribute. For each corpus position, the value of a given attribute is represented by a unique id, equal values having equal ids.

The data structure that implements the mapping between attribute values and value ids and vice versa is called the *attribute lexicon*. In Corpuscle, I have chosen *suffix arrays* (Manber & Myers 1991) as the data structure to implement the lexica. A suffix array is an index data structure that indexes every substring of a given (potentially very long) string, which means that the occurrences of any substring can be looked up very efficiently. In our case, this long string is the attribute lexicon.

Suffix arrays are also well suited for the implementation of fast regular expression matching in the lexicon. In CWB and elsewhere (e.g. in the Unix utility *grep*), a regular expression is evaluated by linearly scanning the lexicon

8. As a consequence, the query language of Corpuscle has a semantics that differs slightly from that of CQL. See also Section 3, where an extension of the query language is described that makes it possible to easily ignore structural positions in queries.

for matching strings. Although linear search can be quite fast in many cases when techniques like Boyer-Moore search are used, it is slow when the regular expression contains few consecutive characters. An example is the expression ".*ja.*zz.*", which matches a string containing the substrings 'ja' and 'zz', in that order. Since the lexicon suffix array indexes every substring of all lexicon strings, the strings containing 'ja' and 'zz' are found efficiently without the need to scan the lexicon.[9]

In Figure 1, the vertical file, encoded corpus, inverted indexes and attribute lexica are given for a small corpus with attributes *word* and *pos* (part of speech).

vertical file		*word* corpus		*word* lexicon/inv.i.			*pos* corpus		*pos* lexicon/inv.i.		
word	**pos**	**cpos**	**id**	**id**	**value**	**inv .i.**	**cpos**	**id**	**id**	**value**	**inv.i.**
⟨NP⟩		0	4	0	girl	2	0	0	0		0, 4, 7, 8
the	Det	1	2	1	telescope	6	1	1	1	Det	1, 5
girl	N	2	0	2	the	1, 6	2	2	2	N	2, 6
with	PP	3	3	3	with	3	3	3	3	PP	3
⟨NP⟩		4	4	4	⟨NP⟩	0, 4	4	0			
the	Det	5	2	5	⟨/NP⟩	7, 8	5	1			
telescope	N	6	1				6	2			
⟨/NP⟩		7	5				7	0			
⟨/NP⟩		8	5				8	0			

Figure 1. A small corpus with vertical file, encoded corpora, lexica and inverted indexes

An additional data structure, the *structure tree*, encodes the hierarchical structure of the corpus. The structure tree contains for every corpus position a pair $(pl(c), pr(c))$ of pointers that point to the structural element that immediately contains the position. More exactly, if c is a start tag position, $pl(c)$ points to the start tag of the enclosing element and $pr(c)$ points to the corresponding end tag; if c is an end tag position, $pl(c)$ points to the corresponding start tag and $pr(c)$ points to the end tag of the enclosing element; otherwise, $pl(c)$ and $pr(c)$ point to the start and end tags of the enclosing element. In Figure 2, the structure tree of the corpus in Figure 1 is displayed.

Using the structure tree, it is straightforward to navigate in the XML tree of the underlying texts and to calculate sentence and other contexts for a given corpus position. The structure tree is also consulted when it has to be checked whether matches of balanced tags (start and end tags with equal name) in a query correspond to matching tags in the corpus.

9. For this query, Corpuscle is almost 5 times faster than CWB.

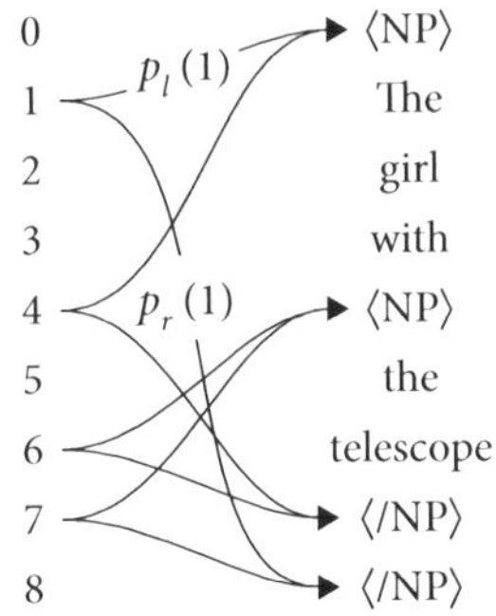

Figure 2. The corresponding structure tree. Not all pointers are drawn

As CWB and Manatee do, Corpuscle uses a static, file-based representation of the encoded corpus, the inverted indexes and the attribute lexica.

3. Querying the corpus

The query language Corpuscle has a query language in which complex queries can be succinctly formulated. It is based on regular expressions over strings, corpus attributes and corpus positions. The query language is similar to CQL, the query language of Corpus Workbench, and tries to be compatible with it as far as possible. On the other hand, since Corpuscle implements features that are missing in Corpus Workbench, and vice versa, there are necessarily differences in the query languages.

Overview of the query language[10] The basic building blocks of a query are *positional constraints*. A positional constraint matches a corpus position if all attribute values in that corpus position satisfy the conditions of the positional constraint. Normally, a positional constraint is written as '[…]'. In the simplest case, the brackets are empty ('[ ]'), they contain no condition, which means that the constraint matches any corpus position. *Attribute constraints* are of the form '*attribute* = "*value*" '. A constraint containing an attribute constraint would be '[word = "fish"]', which would match every corpus position where the *word* attribute had the value "fish". This constraint can be written abbreviated as '["fish"]' or even "fish". In a positional constraint, attribute constraints can be combined using the boolean operator *and* (' & '), e.g.: '["fish" & pos = "V"]'. This query matches all occurrences of "fish" that are marked with part of speech "V".

10. An exhaustive description of the query language can be found in the on-line documentation of Corpuscle at ⟨http://iness.uib.no/corpuscle⟩.

In addition to a literal string, the value expression in an attribute constraint can be a regular expression, e.g. '[lemma = "book.*"]', which would match all corpus words starting with "book". To give characters that have a special meaning in regular expressions their literal meaning, they have to be escaped, e.g. "\." matches a dot, whereas " . " would match any character.

Positional constraints can be combined into a regular expression using the sequence operator (juxtaposition of positional constraints) and the following operators that apply to the preceding expression (which can be a positional constraint or a complex expression in parentheses):

*	Kleene star: arbitrary many repetitions, including zero
+	Kleene plus: at least one repetition
{*n*,*m*}	bounded repetition: between *n* and *m* repetitions
?	optionality
|	disjunction

A query expression that illustrates the use of some of those operators would be

(1) "I" [pos = "V"] + [] {1,2} "to" [pos = "V"]

This query searches for occurences of "I", followed by some verbs, followed by one or two arbitrary positions, followed by "to", and finally followed by a verb again. Thus, it would match the phrase "I would want these things to happen", but not "I have to go".

Structural positions (XML tags) can also be queried for. They are simply written in standard XML notation (e.g. '⟨s⟩' or '⟨/s⟩'). When a start and an end tag with the same element name appear in a query expression, it is assumed that matching tags should correspond to each other; they should be start and end tag of the same XML element. This means for example that a query like

(2) ⟨s⟩ []* "jeg" []* "deg" []* ⟨/s⟩

always should find "jeg" and "deg" in the same sentence. It also means that in a situation where XML elements can be embedded in elements of the same type, the retrieved start and end tags always correspond. A query like

(3) ⟨NP⟩ []* "girl" []* ⟨/NP⟩

would match the phrase

(4) ⟨NP⟩ the girl with ⟨NP⟩ the telescope ⟨/NP⟩⟨/NP⟩

and not the shorter sequence

(5) ⟨NP⟩ the girl with ⟨NP⟩ the telescope ⟨/NP⟩,

since here, the ⟨/NP⟩ is not the corresponding end tag of the leftmost ⟨NP⟩.

Attributes of XML tags can also be queried. The syntax is equal to the XML tag syntax, with the difference that values of attributes can be regular expressions. A valid query would be:

(6) ⟨s type = "main" lang = "nob|nno"⟩

When writing a query, one has to be aware that structural positions are corpus positions in their own right, in contrast to CWB. A query like

(7) "with" "the" "telescope"

will not, as perhaps intended, match the subsequence "with ⟨NP⟩ the telescope" of (5), because of the intervening ⟨NP⟩. A query that would match that subsequence can be written like this:

(8) "with" ⟨⟩* "the" ⟨⟩* "telescope"

to allow for XML tags between the words, where '⟨⟩' denotes an arbitrary start or end tag. The same query can be formulated in a more succinct and elegant way using the *ignore tag* operator (written as backslash, '\'), followed by the tags that should be ignored:

(9) "with" "the" "telescope" \ ⟨⟩

In some situations, for example when non-textual material is interspersed with text, it is desirable to ignore not only XML tags, but entire XML elements. This can be achieved using the *ignore element* operator (written as double backslash, '\\'). In query evaluation, all elements with start tags listed after the *ignore element* operator will be disregarded.

A typical corpus where the *ignore element* operator is essential is an electronic critical edition of a literary œuvre, like for example Ludvig Holberg's[11] writings. The XML format of the edited texts is rather complex. In the main text, which basically follows the first edition, notes and deviating readings from later editions are inserted as XML elements. In the example fragment (10), the main text is in boldface; it consists of the top-level text and those parts that are enclosed in ⟨lem⟩ elements inside ⟨app⟩ (apparatus) elements.

(10) **… thi jeg fik aldrig saa mange Hug i** ⟨app type = "tc"⟩⟨lem wit = "A A-2 a2 B C"⟩ **ti** ⟨/lem⟩⟨rdg resp = "Liebenberg"⟩ de ti ⟨note type = "last"⟩ (fulgt af Martensen) ⟨/note⟩⟨/rdg⟩⟨/app⟩ **Aar …**

11. Ludvig Holberg was a central figure in the Danish-Norwegian literature of the 18th century. A critical edition of Ludvig Holberg's writings has been imported into Corpuscle for testing purposes.

Thus, in a corpus fulltext search, one would like to search exactly in that part (11) of the encoded document, and exclude text in ⟨rdg⟩ (denoting deviating readings) and ⟨note⟩ elements.

(11) ... thi jeg fik aldrig saa mange Hug i ti Aar ...

A search for “Hug i ti Aar” could then be achieved with query (12), which ignores all XML tags and all ⟨rdg⟩ and ⟨note⟩ elements:

(12) “Hug” “i” “ti” “Aar” \ ⟨⟩ \\ ⟨rdg⟩ | ⟨note⟩

Attribute values can be *atomic* or *structured*. The ‘*word*’ attribute is atomic, but attributes that encode grammatical features (part of speech, morphosyntax etc.) and other linguistic annotations can be structured in two different ways; attributes can be multi-valued, and they can be set-valued, or even a combination of both.

A typical multi-valued attribute is the ‘*lemma*’ attribute in a lemmatized corpus where the readings are not totally disambiguated. When using a statistical tagger for morphosyntactic parsing, all readings are normally fully disambiguated, but rule-driven parsers like for example Constraint Grammar parsers output ambiguous readings (cf. Johannessen et al. this volume).

The morphosyntactic tags that a Constraint Grammar parser attaches to a reading are a good example of a set-valued attribute (‘*morph*’). Since readings can be ambiguous, this attribute is multi-valued at the same time.

Corpuscle has built-in support for structured attributes, both for multi-valued and set-valued attributes and combinations thereof. This support is also reflected in the query language. Plain multi-valued attributes do not need special syntax; a corpus position matches a constraint on such an attribute if at least one of the values matches the constraint.

Consider for example the Norwegian word “fisker”, which can mean “fishes” (*pl*) or “fisherman” (*sg*). Thus, a non-fully disambiguated reading could have

(13) word = *fisker*, lemma = *fisk* | *fisker*

Both a search for ‘[lemma = “fisk”]’ and for ‘[lemma = “fisker”]’ will match that position, as one would expect. It is however also possible to search for unambiguous readings only, by using the *unambiguously equal-* or *strict equal-*operator (‘ == ’):

(14) [lemma == “fisk”]

Query (14) would not match the corpus position in (13).

Similarly, there is, besides the *not-equal*-operator (‘!=’), a *strict-not-equal-*operator (‘!!=’) which can be used to demand that none of the readings should match the value in the query:

(15) [lemma !!= “fisk”]

Again, query (15) would not match the corpus position in (13), whereas the query

(16) [lemma != "fisk"]

would match (13).

The values of set-valued attributes are stored as strings with separator characters (*space*, '|' or similar) enclosing the set members. Thus, the '*morph*' value set '(*N m pl*)' (i.e. *Noun masculine plural*) would be encoded as the string "␣N␣m␣pl␣", and in principle, a regular expression could be used to search for subset containment. Corpuscle has however a much more efficient implementation of subset search which is based on suffix arrays, and a syntax extension that makes it easy to formulate queries on set-valued attributes. The values that are searched for can be given in the query expression as a set themselves. Consider the morphosyntactic annotation of the previous example:

(17) word = *fisker*, lemma = *fisk* | *fisker*, morph = (*N m pl*) | (*N m sg*)

A query for plural nouns can be formulated as (18), which would match the corpus position (17).

(18) [morph = ("N" "pl")]

The *morph* attribute is in fact an example of an attribute that is both multi-valued and set-valued.

4. API and Web interface

Corpuscle is both a corpus query engine and a corpus management system. As such, it has both a well-defined Application Programming Interface (API) and a flexible and elaborate Web interface.

Since many users are reluctant to learn the syntax of the query language, Corpuscle has a graphical query interface (see Figure 3) which allows the user to compose most queries in a menu-driven, graphical way. Almost all constructions of the query language are accessible in the query interface; in addition, the user gets all necessary help in chosing admissible attributes and values.

4.1 The API

The Corpuscle tool is written entirely in Common Lisp. It includes a Web server that makes most of the functionality of the system accessible via a simple HTTP-based protocol. Requests to the query engine and other parts of the tool can be sent to the server as *post-* or *get-*requests with documented parameters. Replies are sent in the form of XML and JSON pages. When the server is contacted for the first time

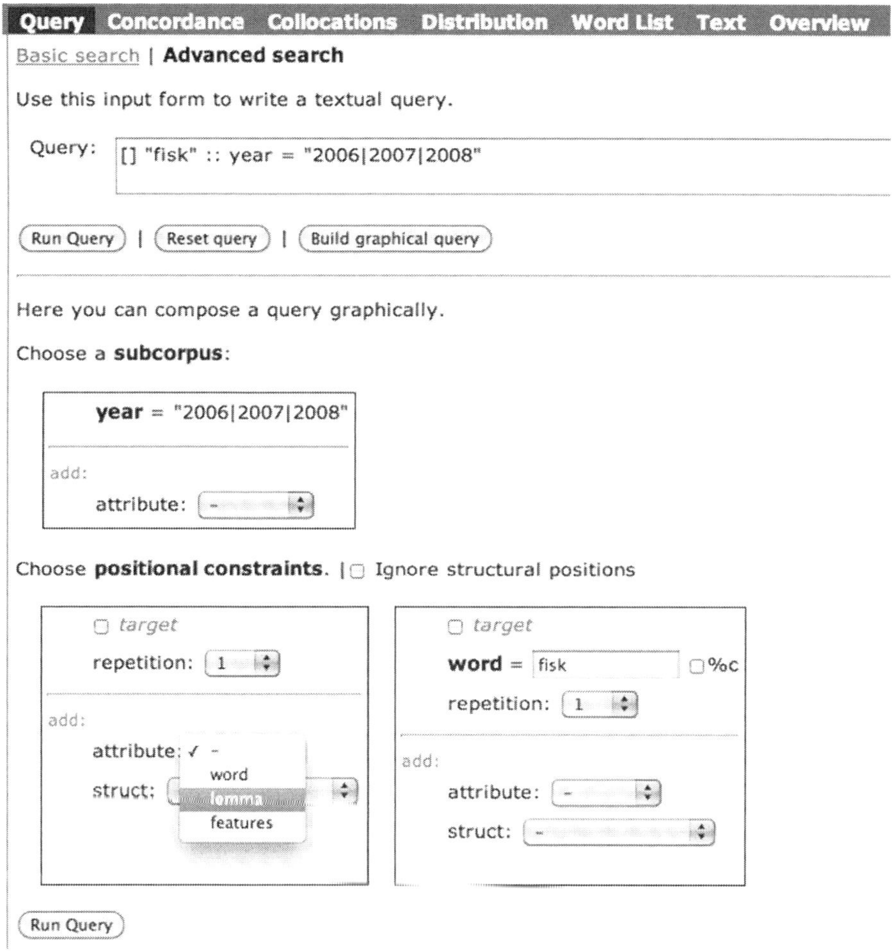

Figure 3. The graphical query interface

and authentication has taken place, a session object is established in the server that preserves state information of the connection, and a session identifier is sent back. On every following request, the session identifier has to be sent along.

This HTTP/XML/JSON-based interface is presently the only external API that is implemented. It is naturally well suited for building Web applications around the Corpuscle core functionality. When the Corpuscle system is run in default mode, the XML pages are processed by internal XSLT stylesheets that generate the HTML pages and Javascript code for the built-in Web interface. Alternatively, external style sheets can be run; in this way, programmers can adapt the Corpuscle system to their needs without having to touch the Common Lisp code.

4.2 The Web interface

Corpuscle's built-in Web interface offers typical corpus tool functionality: concordances, word lists, collocations, distribution statistics, exporting tools and more.[12]

Queries can be input either in textual form in Corpuscle's query syntax, or via a flexible menu-driven interface.

When a query is started, the matching corpus positions are displayed as concordance lines in the order they are calculated, already before the query evaluation is finished. The user can choose which attributes to display in the concordance and how to sort the results. Concordances can be displayed either as KWIC-concordances (see Figure 4) or as matches in a context defined by a structural attribute (e.g. sentence or paragraph). In the concordance view, additional functionality can be available. Figure 5 for instance shows a concordance from an annotated Georgian corpus; clicking on a context word makes the dictionary entry of the associated lemma pop up. As can be seen from this example, when a structural attribute is queried, token and word counts for the attribute are displayed: the numbers are the number of tokens resp. words between start and corresponding end tag. Those counts are also available when statistics are calculated.

When the corpus can be edited, an edit mode is available in the concordance view. From a concordance line, it is possible to jump to more context, typically the whole document.

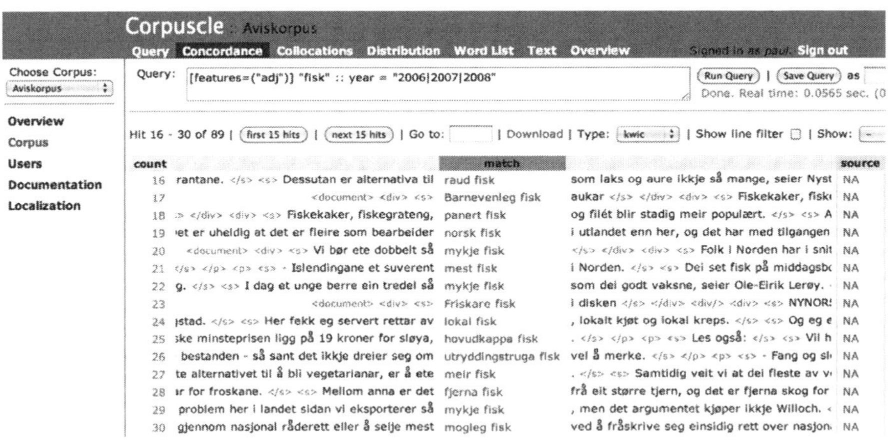

Figure 4. The KWIC concordance page of the Corpuscle Web interface

12. See G. Andersen (this volume) for a specific study using Corpuscle with the Norwegian Newspaper Corpus, demonstrating the value of some of these features.

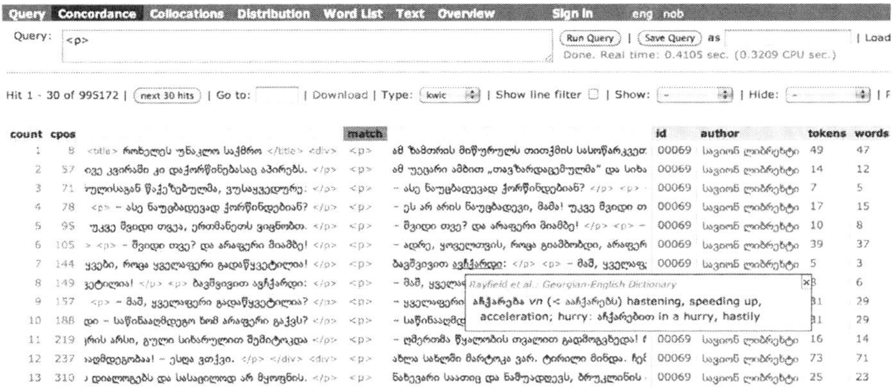

Figure 5. Query for the structural attribute ⟨p⟩; clicking on a context word makes the dictionary entry of the associated lemma pop up

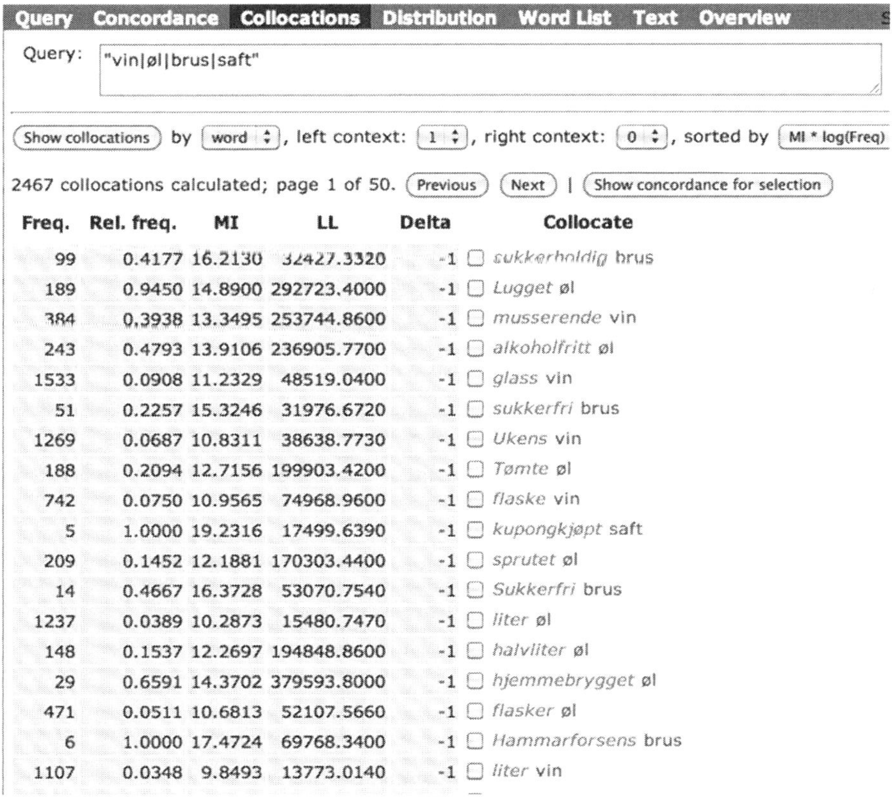

Figure 6. A collocation for the words *vin* 'wine', *øl* 'beer', *brus* 'lemonade', *saft* 'juice', sorted by *MI* log (*Freq*)

On the Word list page, all different query matches are listed together with their counts in the result. Here, it is possible to list the matches for other attributes than *word* only. When an attribute is set-valued, both the matches for the sets as a whole and for the occurring set members can be displayed. Each match word or phrase is linked to a concordance of all contexts the match occurs in.

More advanced frequency and distribution statistics are available on the Distribution page. Here, match counts can be categorized and grouped along up to four attribute axes, and absolute and relative frequencies are calculated. For each attribute, a regular expression filter can be defined that groups attribute values together. Values that do not match the filter are collected into a rest group. Values can also be manually grouped together via drag-and-drop. In addition, some useful filters that cannot be easily expressed as regular expressions (e.g. numeric ranges) are hard-coded.

All concordances, collocations and distributions can be downloaded in a format suitable for further processing in a spreadsheet or statistical application.

Corpuscle has built-in user management with fine-grained access control; corpora can be open for querying to anybody, or access is restricted to groups of users. Similarly, access to entire texts can be restricted, as well as the possibility to edit and to annotate.

There is extensive on-line documentation. The documentation is written using an integrated Wiki-system that is similar to Redmine's Wiki system or the Wikipedia.

The main language of the user interface is English, but the interface has also been localized to Norwegian. Due to an integrated localization interface, localization to other languages is easy and does not involve editing source code or text files.

5. Editing and manual annotation

In many applications, it is essential to be able to edit or annotate a corpus. It can be necessary to edit a corpus in order to correct errors of different types, like OCR or transcription errors, or to manually disambiguate or correct automatic morphosyntactic annotation. Editing can mean to correct the values of attributes in certain corpus positions or even to delete or to add corpus positions. When structural positions are added or deleted, it is important to make sure that the structure of the corpus remains valid; e.g. when start tags are added or deleted, corresponding end tags should also be added or deleted.

Interactive manual annotation gives the corpus user the possibility to add interpretive information to a concordance or query result. This can be very valuable when query results have to be cleaned up or further annotated with a specific research question in mind. The manual annotation can be private or accessible to all users of the corpus. Smith et al. (2008: 175) argue convincingly for the importance of manual corpus annotation. They review existing corpus tools, discuss their functionality and shortcomings with respect to manual annotation and set up a list of "requirements for future tools". They demand greater flexibility in entering and manipulating manual annotations, and they stress the importance of data exchange between the corpus tool and other (spreadsheet and statistical) applications in both directions.

In Corpuscle, a relational database (PostgreSQL) is used to implement editing and manual annotation. The database is fully integrated into the tool; patched (edited) attribute values and manual annotations are stored in the database, and patches and annotations are searchable in the same way as attributes and values that are stored in the regular index. When a query is run, both the static index and the database are considered; the index does not have to be recompiled to make patches or annotations visible in the query result.

Manual annotations are treated in most respects like ordinary corpus attributes. There can be different types of manual annotations as there can be different types of attributes, depending on the structure of the corpus and the user's needs. Annotations can be free text, which is useful for adding all sorts of comments to concordance lines. Annotations can also be enforcibly restricted to a finite set of values and then be used to classify matches according to a finite set of classes. If more than one classifying criterium is used, annotations are set valued, each set member being an attribute-value pair on its own. In addition, annotations can be private and only visible to the user that created them, and they can be public and thus be used to enrich the corpus with specialized information that is not available through automatic linguistic annotation.

Figure 7 shows the use of annotations in the Norwegian dialect corpus project "Talebanken". The corpus consists of transcribed dialect recordings that are annotated grammatically and with sociolinguistic metadata. The text is linked to the sound files, and any text segment can be listened to via a keyboard shortcut in the concordance page. In Talebanken, annotations are used to classify the pronunciation of dialect words according to a set of phonetic features or variables (in the figure: F21, L02 and L12) that can have a finite set of possible values. The features and their admissible values can be edited in a separate page of Corpuscle.

After having searched for words to annotate, the annotator can put a concordance line into focus and listen to the match word in its utterance context. Then he can pick a value for a selected feature simply by using a keyboard shortcut, and the feature-value pair is added to the annotation of that word, or the annotation is changed accordingly if the feature had been present before. More than one concordance line can be put into focus simultaneously (the grayed lines in the screenshot) and a feature value can be assigned for all focussed words at once.

Figure 7. The annotation interface of the "Talebanken" project

Implementation issues Since lookup in a relational database is intrinsically slower than lookup in a static index, extensive annotation and patching can lead to decreased query performance. This is especially true for large corpora. One way to deal with this problem is to merge the patches with the main index when the patch database has grown too large, and in the same way to maintain and update a static index for annotations.[13] A disadvantage of this approach is that the index cannot any longer be recompiled from the original texts when patches are incorporated into the index.

The structure of the tables containing the patches and the annotations has to be designed carefully. We have seen that the corpus positions are coded as consecutive integers. Since this is a problem when new positions are to be inserted, corpus positions are stored arithmetically shifted by a fixed positive integer Δ.[14] New (integer-valued) corpus positions are then inserted in the middle between existing or added (shifted) corpus positions. This allows for the insertion of many new corpus positions; even if all new positions are inserted consecutively behind an existing position, up to Δ new positions can be inserted before there is no

13. This is however not yet implemented in Corpuscle.

14. This integer can be chosen on a per-corpus basis; in Corpuscle, $\Delta = 28$ is chosen for technical reasons. An arithmetic shift by Δ is equivalent to a multiplication with 2^{Δ}.

gap available to insert the next position. Many more positions can be accommodated if new positions are inserted in a balanced way, and if inserted positions are rebalanced if necessary. There is room for up to 2^{Δ} new corpus positions between two consecutive positions that are coded in the index. It is obvious that all algorithms that deal with corpus positions have to be adapted to this extended coding scheme.

Another difficulty arises when documents are added to or deleted from an existing annotated or patched corpus. When the corpus is reindexed, all documents that follow the added or deleted document will have changed corpus positions. Since annotations and patches are tied to corpus positions, the corpus positions of the annotations and patches will have to be recomputed. This can be done by storing, in addition to the corpus positions, a combination of document name, a document-internal unique identifier of a structural (XML) element containing the corpus position and the offset of the corpus position relative to that element's start tag. If the documents have no structural coding, the offset can be taken relative to document start.

This technique allows one to recode the corpus positions of the annotations and patches by searching for the position of the document and the unique identifier using the new index, provided that both document name and unique identifier are indexed.

6. Evaluation and concluding remarks

In this section, I give an informal evaluation of the query execution speed of Corpuscle measured against Corpus Workbench.

It is difficult to benchmark two corpus engines against each other in a systematic and fair way. The best strategy to compare their performance would be to measure query execution times on the basis of a typical usage pattern collected from the queries of several users over a longer time period. Since I do not have such data, I benchmarked some arbitrary queries that exemplify the strengths and weaknesses of both query engines. The test corpus is the English Wikipedia corpus, containing 1,200,904,250 corpus positions. The runtimes in Table 1 are in seconds, measured on a 2 × 3 GHz Quad-Core Intel Xeon Macintosh Pro with 26 GB of memory. Queries are ordered by relative performance; those performing best in Corpuscle being on top. The Corpuscle system was compiled with Steelbank Common Lisp (SBCL). The benchmark times include both query compilation and execution and matchlist construction, and they are taken on a second run of the queries, when the needed index data were fully loaded into main memory. Ratios higher than 1 are in favor of Corpuscle.

Table 1. Running times of selected queries in Corpuscle and CWB

<table>
<tr><th>CWB</th><th>Corpuscle</th><th>Ratio</th><th>Query</th></tr>
<tr><td>7.106</td><td>0.020</td><td>355.3</td><td>“and” “fish”</td></tr>
<tr><td>10.227</td><td>0.450</td><td>22.7</td><td>“I|you” “found|read” “this”</td></tr>
<tr><td>0.228</td><td>0.038</td><td>6.0</td><td>“.*fish.*”</td></tr>
<tr><td>0.550</td><td>0.093</td><td>5.9</td><td>“not” “even”</td></tr>
<tr><td>0.409</td><td>0.086</td><td>4.8</td><td>“.*ja.*zz.*”</td></tr>
<tr><td>0.028</td><td>0.014</td><td>2.0</td><td>“heavy” “weather”</td></tr>
<tr><td>0.285</td><td>0.183</td><td>1.6</td><td>(“I” | “you”) (“found” | “read”) “this”</td></tr>
<tr><td>0.266</td><td>0.217</td><td>1.2</td><td>“had”</td></tr>
<tr><td>336.694</td><td>290.300</td><td>1.2</td><td>#a:[] #b:[]:: #a.word = #b.word</td></tr>
<tr><td>0.018</td><td>0.018</td><td>1.0</td><td>“fish” “and”</td></tr>
<tr><td>0.212</td><td>0.218</td><td>1.0</td><td>“confus.*” []{0,8} “by”</td></tr>
<tr><td>0.713</td><td>1.688</td><td>0.4</td><td>“look|bring” [word != “i.*”]{0,10} “up|down”</td></tr>
<tr><td>0.010</td><td>0.030</td><td>0.3</td><td>[word = “fish” & path = (“title”)]</td></tr>
</table>

Some remarks to the benchmark numbers are called for. As expected, Corpuscle significantly outperforms CWB on queries that have a high-frequent token in initial position; for the query “and” “fish”, Corpuscle is 355 times faster than CWB. Whereas CWB has to check which of the 29 million occurrences of “and” are followed by “fish”, Corpuscle tests which of the 61.000 occurrences of “fish” are preceded by “and”. If we reverse the order of the query tokens (“fish” “and”), both systems use the same index lookup and perform equally well. In general, all queries involving only sequences of regular expressions on words are in Corpuscle as least as fast as in CWB.

The long running time of the query searching for two equal words in a row is explained by the fact that the whole corpus has to be scanned to find the matches; here, no indexes can be used to speed up the search.

The Corpuscle system has now been in use for over a year in several projects at the University of Bergen and has proven to be a versatile, robust and fast corpus management system. It is used to host diverse corpora of small to large size, among which are:

- The Norwegian Newspaper corpus (940 million tokens)
- The ASK Corpus, a Norwegian Learners’ corpus (1.1 million tokens)
- Talebanken, a Norwegian dialect corpus (1.3 million tokens)
- A Georgian corpus of fiction and non-fiction texts (125 million tokens)
- The English Wikipedia corpus (1.2 billion tokens)

The development of the Corpuscle software is not completed. Among the plans for the future development of the system are:

- implementation of more advanced statistics capabilities through the integration of the R statistics package
- graphical visualization of statistics
- extensions for handling of parallel corpora
- integration of multimedia capabilities that go beyond the linking of text to sound

In addition, the Corpuscle platform is becoming an integral part of INESS, the Norwegian Infrastructure for the Exploration of Syntax and Semantics.[15] Although the main focus of INESS is on treebanks, databases of syntactically annotated sentences, the INESS infrastructure will also host traditional corpora. Finally, it is planned to make Corpuscle open source in the near future, such that interested parties will have the possibility to try and use the Corpuscle system with their own corpora.

References

Evert, Stefan. 2007. Inside the IMS Corpus Workbench. ⟨http://www.iula.upf.edu/materials/080925evert_ hdout.pdf⟩.

Manber, Udi & Myers, Eugene. 1991. Suffix arrays: A new method for on-line string searches. *SIAM Journal on Computing* 22(5): 935–948.

Smith, Nicholas, Hoffmann, S., Rayson, P. 2008. Corpus tools and methods, today and tomorrow: Incorporating linguists' manual annotations. *Literary and Linguistic Computing* 23(2): 163–180.

15. See Rosén, this volume.

OBT+stat

A combined rule-based and statistical tagger

Janne Bondi Johannessen, Kristin Hagen, André Lynum & Anders Nøklestad
The Text Laboratory, University of Oslo

The paper describes the improvement of the rule-based Constraint Grammar (CG) Oslo-Bergen Tagger (OBT) by the addition of a statistical module. It is in the nature of CG taggers to leave some words ambiguous between different readings, due to a lack of coverage by the linguistics-based rules. Such ambiguities are often a problem for applications that use the tagger, among them the Norwegian Newspaper Corpus. Our statistical module not only removes part of speech (PoS) and morphological ambiguities, but also disambiguates lemmas. We show how this new system, referred to as OBT+stat, in a straightforward manner combines the strengths of the linguistic knowledge-based CG approach with data-driven methods. The result is a high-performing, fully disambiguating PoS/morphological tagger and lemmatizer with very satisfactory evaluation results.

1. Introduction[1]

The purpose of this paper is to describe how we have improved the existing rule-based Constraint Grammar (CG) Oslo-Bergen Tagger (OBT) (Johannessen, Hagen & Nøklestad 2000: 31–48) by adding a statistical module. Due to lack of full coverage in the linguistic rules, CG taggers will generally leave some ambiguity behind in their output as we will show later in this paper. This is a problem for many applications in which the tagger is used – among them the Norwegian Newspaper Corpus.[2] Within this project we found the opportunity to improve this aspect of the OBT tagger.

---

1. We would like to thank the two anonymous reviewers for very helpful comments that we think have definitely improved the paper.

2. Some other corpora that have been tagged by the OBT (though not with the new OBT+Stat) are The Oslo Corpus of Tagged, Norwegian Texts (Bokmål & Nynorsk), the Norwegian parts of the Oslo Multilingual Corpus, the RUN Russian Norwegian Parallel

Statistical taggers are often preferred in applications because they are faster to build and use, and leave no ambiguity behind. Rule-based taggers, however, are generally very reliable with high precision, i.e. their output tends to contain a large portion the correct tags, which is why we explore the possibility of combining the two types. For this purpose we trained a statistical Hidden Markov Model tagger (HMM, see Brants 2000) on an existing development corpus. We describe how we have applied the new statistical module on the ambiguous output of the OBT, resulting in a new system, OBT+stat, which disambiguates all previous ambiguities in PoS category, morphology and lemmata, leaving a single preferred morphological tag and lemma pair. The performance of the new system is very good, with an accuracy of about 96 percent. Since this result is close to the 95.4 percent precision of the original OBT (Hagen & Johannessen 2003: 90), it is fair to say that the OBT+stat in one sense outperforms the original OBT, as we show in Section 8.2, since the system retains the ratio of correct tags produced while users are no longer exposed to the risk of considering incorrect tags left alongside correct ones.

The paper is organized as follows. First we give a short description of the history of the OBT tagger and state of the art for Norwegian PoS taggers. This chapter is followed by a description of OBT's main architecture. Then we discuss our reasons for improving the OBT, followed by a discussion about ambiguities that occur, and ways of resolving them. Finally, we describe statistical disambiguation, the integration of the statistical module and an evaluation of the performance of the new system.

2. Background

2.1 The history of the Oslo-Bergen Tagger

The Oslo-Bergen Tagger is a rule-based Constraint Grammar tagger for Norwegian originally developed in 1996–1998 by the Tagger Project at the University of Oslo. As part of this effort the project developed an electronic lexicon – later known as *Norsk Ordbank* ('Norwegian Word Bank', see reference list). The linguistic CG rules were developed by the Text Laboratory (University of Oslo), and used the CG1 rule formalism (Karlsson et al. 1995) along with an interpreter from the

Corpus, and The Lexicographical Bokmål Corpus. (For more information on these corpora, please see the Text Laboratory home page.)

Finnish company Lingsoft AB – the only such technology available at the time. The tagger covers both official written language varieties, Bokmål and Nynorsk, but the work in the present paper has focused primarily on Bokmål (both varieties are described in Johannessen, Hagen & Nøklestad 2000: 31–48). From the start, the development of OBT was focused on giving linguistically precise descriptions. This resulted in a rather large tagset with 358 morphological tags (with further 2,000 or so for full morphosyntactic analysis).

The original tagger achieved high performance when tested on an unseen evaluation corpus of 30,000 words based on a wide variety of material such as literary fiction, magazines and newspapers. Precision and recall were 95.4 and 99.0 percent respectively, with a combined F-measure of 97.2 percent (Hagen & Johannessen 2003: 90). In 2000 the Lingsoft rule interpreter was replaced by a reimplementation made by Paul Meurer at Aksis (now Uni Computing) based in Bergen, and the tagger was named the Oslo-Bergen Tagger. The new rule interpreter was implemented in Allegro Lisp and included a user-friendly web-based rule-writing system. The tagger was also made available online. While the old version is no longer available, the new OBT+stat that we discuss in this paper is available online from the OBT homepage.

2.2 State-of-the-art for Norwegian PoS taggers

There are two main types of part of speech taggers. Some use manually made linguistic rules, while some use statistics computed from a tagged training corpus. The landscape of Norwegian part of speech tagger efforts is regrettably a sparse one, with the rule-based Oslo-Bergen tagger as the only publicly available tagger with a performance competitive with taggers for other languages. To our knowledge there is only one other part of speech tagger with published results, the statistics-based Xerox tagger for Norwegian developed by Anders Nøklestad (1998: 181–197). This tagger achieved 96 percent accuracy for Bokmål and Nynorsk on a tagset of 95 tags using a combination of a lexicon and a HMM model, but is not publicly available. An unpublished effort by Emiliano Guevara during the compilation of a new, Norwegian web corpus (NoWaC, Norwegian Web as Corpus, see reference list) achieved 94.4 percent accuracy with a Support Vector Machine (SVM) tagger (Ratnaparkhi 1996 and Giménez & Màrquez 2004) on a tagset of 165 tags, with a HMM-based tagger based on TnT (Brants 2000) achieving close to the same result with 94.0 percent accuracy. The tagsets covered by those efforts are considerably smaller than the one covered by OBT, and our own investigations indicates that training a HMM tagger in a straightforward manner on the OBT training corpus and tagset achieves an accuracy of around 88 percent.

3. The architecture of the Oslo-Bergen Constraint Grammar tagger

The Oslo-Bergen Tagger consists of four different modules which run in sequence with the output of each module being the input for the next one. The four modules can be briefly described as follows:

a. A combined morphological analyzer/tokenizer that segments text into sentences, tokenizes their content and assigns each token possible tags and lemmas from the lexicon, including productively formed compounds and unknown words. We refer to this module as the multitagger.
b. A morphological disambiguator based on CG rules that select or remove tags attached to the input tokens. We refer to this module as the CG or rule-based disambiguator.
c. A syntactic multitagger and disambiguator that uses CG rules to assign a syntactic label to each token.
d. A named entity recognizer (see Johannessen et al. 2005).

In this paper we will focus on the first two modules, which together form a part of speech tagger, including a sophisticated tokenizer, a morphological analyzer and a compound word analyser (guesser) for Norwegian Nynorsk and Bokmål. To illustrate the internal operation of the CG tagger, example (1) shows an example multitagger output, where one or more tags from the lexicon are assigned to each token in the sentence. Note that the multitagger can only use the morphological information already given in the lexicon.

(1)
```
"⟨Dette⟩"
        "dette" verb inf
        'verb infinitive'.
        "dette" pron nøyt ent pers 3
        'pronoun neuter singular 3. person'.
        "dette" det dem nøyt ent
        'determiner demonstrative neuter singular'
"⟨er⟩"
        "være" verb pres
        'verb present'
"⟨et⟩"
        "en" det nøyt ent kvant
        'determiner neuter singular quantifier'
        "ete" verb imp
        'verb imperative'
"⟨eksempel⟩"
        "eksempel" subst appell nøyt ub ent
        'noun common neuter indefinite singular'
        "eksempel" subst appell nøyt ub fl
        'noun common neuter indefinite plural'
```

```
"⟨.⟩"
        "$." clb <<< ⟨punkt⟩ 'punctuation'
```

'This is an example'

In example (2) we show the corresponding output after the rule-based disambiguator. In this case the tagger has fully disambiguated all PoS tags and lemmas in the sentence.

(2)

```
"⟨Dette⟩"
        "dette" pron nøyt ent pers 3
        'pronoun neuter singular 3. person'
"⟨er⟩"
        "være" verb pres a5 pr1 pr2 ⟨aux1/perf_part⟩
        'verb present'
"⟨et⟩"
        "en" det nøyt ent kvant
        'determiner neuter singular quantifier'
"⟨eksempel⟩"
        "eksempel" subst appell nøyt ub ent
        'noun common neuter indefinite singular'
"⟨.⟩"
        "$." clb <<< ⟨punkt⟩
```

However, as we shall see in Section 5, the original OBT tagger does not always resolve ambiguities. This is the task covered by the new statistical disambiguation module described in Section 6 onwards.

4. Methodology of improvements to the Oslo-Bergen Tagger

Although the Oslo-Bergen Tagger is considered to be robust and produces output with high precision, there are some aspects that we wanted to improve upon in the context of the Norwegian Newspaper Corpus project. The first was the speed of the tagging process. Over the last ten years, the size of Norwegian corpora has increased considerably. The Norwegian Newspaper Corpus has more than 900 million words, while the NoWaC corpus (Norwegian Web as Corpus, Guevara 2010) at the Text Laboratory has more than 700 million words. The relatively slow performance of the Oslo-Bergen Tagger made it difficult to annotate such large amounts of text. Another opportunity for improvement was the Constraint Grammar rules themselves, since more efficient and expressive Constraint Grammar versions have become available since the project started in 1996, most notably CG3 (see reference list) developed by the VISL project at the University of Southern Denmark, Odense. A third concern has been the output of the Oslo-Bergen Tagger. Not every sentence analyzed by the tagger leaves us with an unambiguous sequence of PoS tags and lemmas as in example (2). The tagger might leave some words ambiguous due to a conscious choice by the rule writers or unintended lack of coverage in the CG rules. Furthermore, the tagger does not attempt to disambiguate lemmas. For many purposes – both in applications and research – it is desirable to have a totally unambiguous output with only a single annotation for each token. This may be motivated by technical considerations such as easier implementation of corpus search and storage, but corpus users may also often be better served by fully disambiguated annotations.

To meet these concerns we have improved the Oslo-Bergen Tagger in two steps. First, the rules were reimplemented from CG1 to the newer CG3 format. Paul Meurer at Uni Computing created a stand-alone multitagger module for this purpose, and the CG3 rule-interpreter replaced the earlier one implemented by Meurer. As these steps are reasonably straightforward we will not discuss them further in this paper, although we can report that they have improved the tagger both in terms of tagging speed and evaluation performance. The recall remains at 99.0 percent while precision has increased to 96.0 percent, resulting in an F-score of 97.5 percent (see OBT homepage). In light of this progress we consider the reimplementation a sound and worthwhile effort. We have also added a complete disambiguation module for PoS/morphological tags and lemmas to the tagger, and it is this latter step that is the focus of the present paper.

There were in principle three options for developing the Oslo-Bergen tagger into a fully disambiguating tagger. The least desirable one was to manually write more CG rules. This would have been very costly and time-consuming, as rules would have to be developed to account for increasingly marginal linguistic phenomena. It would also have been a task that would be hard to ever consider completed given the productivity of human language. Furthermore, some words are genuinely ambiguous in a given context, and are hard to disambiguate in a linguistically meaningful manner, a phenomenon that has been measured with regard to inter-annotator agreement as in Babarcy, Carrol and Sampson (2006). A second option would have been to manually write heuristic rules that would generalize the ambiguous linguistic phenomena. In our experience such rules are often too broad and often end up as arbitrary when applied to specific cases. A third option, and the one we have chosen for the Oslo-Bergen Tagger, is to build a data-driven statistical disambiguation module that works on the output of the rule-based tagger. This disambiguation module does not change the disambiguated output, but selects a preferred annotation among the readings left by the CG disambiguation process – effectively ranking the remaining output of the CG tagger.

5. Dealing with left-over ambiguities in the Oslo-Bergen Tagger

5.1 Morphological ambiguities

The lemmas and PoS/morphological tags considered by the rule-based disambiguator are produced by the multitagger, which is based on the lexicon *Norsk Ordbank*. The PoS classifications, including morphological information, are used in accordance with The Norwegian reference grammar (Faarlund et al. 1997). The CG rules are motivated by Norwegian morphology, syntax and to some extent semantics. They operate by eliminating incorrect annotations (as in Examples 1 and 2), leaving one or more annotations. As noted, PoS and morphological ambiguities left by the Oslo-Bergen Tagger have two different origins. The first consists of unintended ambiguities that are the result of inadequate coverage by the CG rules, a consequence that is in practice unavoidable. The second, which we consider deliberate ambiguities, are those where the CG system developers and linguists cannot reach a preference between two or more annotations, in essence considering several annotations to be correct. This happens, for instance, with nouns that can be classified as either masculine or feminine, which, in fact, is the case for all feminine nouns in Bokmål (cf. Dyvik this volume). One such example is the word *bok* 'book', which yields the annotations in example (3).

(3)
```
"⟨bok⟩"
        "bok" subst fem appell ent ub
        'noun feminine common singular indefinite'
        "bok" subst mask appell ent ub
        'noun feminine common singular indefinite'
```

In a context like *Per kjøper ei bok* 'Per buys a book' it is easy to disambiguate "book" to the feminine *"fem"* reading since it agrees syntactically with the feminine determiner *ei*. But if there is no determiner, like in the grammatical sentence *Neste prosess er å skrive bok.* (lit. 'The next process is to write (a) book'), there is not enough context to discriminate between the two gender readings.[3] A related kind of ambiguity occurs between singular and plural readings of neuter nouns. In the grammatical and acceptable Norwegian sentence *Han kjøpte hus* 'He bought (a) house/houses', one cannot ascertain whether there is one or more houses involved

3. Linguistically speaking, it is possible to analyze the object of the verb not as a proper verb argument, but rather as part of a complex verb *skrive bok* 'engage in book writing'. We cannot choose this option here, since the tagger is tied to the grammatical tags given in the lexicon. Here the noun *bok* 'book' has two entries, and one of them has to be selected.

and the Oslo-Bergen Tagger leaves both *"ent"* (singular) and *"fl"* (plural) annotations in the final output as in example (4).

(4)

```
"⟨hus⟩"
        "hus" subst nøyt appell ent ub
        'noun common neutre indefinite singular'
        "hus" subst nøyt appell fl ub
        'noun common neutre indefinite plural'
```

5.2 Lemma ambiguities

In most circumstances the Oslo-Bergen Tagger only disambiguates between different PoS tags or other morphological information and ignores different lemmas. Since there is no semantic information incorporated in the tagger, it is unable to differentiate between them. One example is the pair *regel* 'rule' and *regle* 'verse', which have several identical, inflected forms, despite their different stems. Given a specific context, a human annotator can easily select the correct form in a sentence like *Det er få formelle regler for oppførsel* 'There are few formal rules for behaviour', but the tagger cannot. As a consequence both of the annotations shown in example (5) are left in the output.

(5)

```
"⟨regler⟩"
        "regel" subst mask appell fl ub ⟨Correct!⟩
        'noun masculine common plural indefinite'
        "regle" subst fem appell fl ub ⟨Correct!⟩
        'nounfeminine common plural indefinite'
        "regle" subst mask appell fl ub <Correct!
        'noun masculine common plural indefinite'
'rules,verses'
```

In some cases a word can have several alternative forms according to the lexicon, even when the meaning is exactly the same. Also in such cases the human annotator has to make a decision, although it may be an arbitrary one. This is illustrated by example (6).

(6)

```
"⟨vinger⟩"
        "ving" subst mask appell fl ub
        'noun masculine common plural indefinite'
        "vinge" subst mask appell fl ub
        'noun masculine common plural indefinite'
'wings'
```

Our statistical disambiguation module, described in the next section, extends the Oslo-Bergen Tagger and enables it to deal with these and other PoS/morphological and lemma ambiguities.

6. Statistical disambiguation

In order to provide fully disambiguated output with the least amount of effort, a statistical post-processing module was built using the existing development corpus for the Oslo-Bergen Tagger. A data-driven module is especially advantageous since it can use information from a training corpus where annotations have been manually disambiguated in the context of the full text. In addition, training a statistical module is relatively cheap in terms of resources and implementation, even when the manual annotation of the training corpus is taken into account. The OBT development corpus we used for training originally consists of 120,000 words from different sources, such as literary fiction, magazines and newspapers with correct analyses marked accordingly. As more than one analysis could be marked as correct in that corpus, we had to first fully disambiguate the corpus to make it suitable for training the disambiguation module. We chose to keep the original tagset instead of introducing new collapsed tags for unsolved cases like the 'masc/fem' and 'neutre single/plural' ambiguity described above to avoid expanding an already large tagset. Instead, we determined some general disambiguation guidelines – for example, in case of masculine/feminine gender ambiguity we decided to choose the feminine reading – while some ambiguities were left to the judgement of the annotator based on context and common semantic knowledge.[4,5]

One might ask whether disambiguating these kinds of grammatical ambiguities is actually worthwhile, and indeed if this can be done correctly. It is our opinion that it is, since a correct analysis is important for many tasks, for example when tagged texts are used in an anaphora resolution system. If a system tries to identify the reference of a singular pronoun, it would be highly problematic if the noun referred to were not tagged as singular, since most systems use identity in grammatical features as an important guideline for reference resolution.

The statistical module takes output sentences from the tagger and selects a single tag where the disambiguation module earlier in the pipeline left several tags. It has the current sentence tokens and their annotations available for consideration. Given this, two approaches were considered for modelling a suitable

4. Arne Martinus Lindstad annotated both the traditional and the new fully disambiguated development and evaluation corpus.

5. One anonymous reviewer asks how much context is used. For the manual lemma disambiguation, the whole corpus can be used. The statistical lemma disambiguation model uses no such context.

statistical disambiguator. The first method is alignment, which is simple and uses readily available tools. It runs a statistical tagger on the original input sentence and then the output of this tagger is aligned with the Oslo-Bergen tagger output. Whenever an ambiguity is encountered, the analysis of the statistical tagger is used to select the appropriate tag. This approach has been found successful in earlier work on disambiguating CG taggers (Tapanainen & Voutilainen 1994) and is the one we have used here. The second method uses a statistical tagging model to select the highest ranked PoS tag sequence among those enumerated by the Oslo-Bergen Tagger. This is similar to discriminative ranking approaches in NLP, and is briefly described in the context of CG tagging in Hajič et al. (2001) and Lynum, Evensberget and Skjærholt (2011).

For both approaches a separate model handles ambiguity among lemmas, but we perform lemma disambiguation only if such ambiguities remain after PoS/morphological tag disambiguation. It is natural to give the tag selection preference during disambiguation, given that earlier experience with the rule-based tagger has shown that nearly all lemma ambiguities are of a semantic nature originating from the lexicon.

The first approach of using an aligned tagger might be considered somewhat *ad hoc* and the second approach may appear as more principled as it explicitly models the disambiguation task, selecting among the available annotations directly. One would expect the alignment process to fail for some amount of ambiguous tokens where the statistical tagger output and the OBT output do not overlap. Still, we consider this approach the most practical one, since it is simple and builds existing tools that are good and robust. In our experience more sophisticated methods may not be as robust considering the small amount of training data.

While much data-driven work on CG taggers is concerned with automatic or semi-automatic derivation of suitable rules or the use of frequency-based annotations in CG rule writing, there has been some exploration of statistical disambiguation as a completely separate module. A recent example is the Czech tagger of Hajič et al. (2001) and Spoustová et al. (2007), which is the most thorough work on incorporating a statistical module separate from the CG rules themselves. Although the work of the present article is closely related to Hajič's work, the basis and motivation for our work differs. In contrast to the Czech tagger, the Oslo-Bergen Tagger already boasts a fairly high precision and has also proven itself as a highly accurate and useful technology. It is the need for full disambiguation and the assumption that the remaining ambiguities cannot be clearly formulated in linguistic terms that motivates our effort. As such, the earlier efforts of Tapanainen and Voutilainen (1994) – which might be construed as a less sophisticated approach than the one we describe in this paper – can be viewed as more closely related.

As shown in the work cited above, and perhaps to the dismay of the CG research community, adding statistical modules to CG taggers often yields positive results and helps highlight deficiencies in the CG rule sets. In this light we view statistical disambiguation both as a complementary module to any fully developed CG tagger, and as a useful tool during rule development.

7. Modelling challenges and engineering concerns

The disambiguation module is left with the unenviable task of performing the most difficult analyses left by the rule-based tagger. The ambiguities involved can be quite subtle and for some there may not be a single analysis that is broadly agreed upon. Even worse, the tagset used by the Oslo-Bergen Tagger is also quite large, with about 350 different tags representing a combination of morphological features.

The statistical tagger used for the aligning approach is HunPos (Halácsy, Kornai & Oravecz 2007), an open source reimplementation of TnT, the well known HMM tagger developed by Brants (2000). The HMM model is one of the simpler ones used for tagging, conditioning its probabilities on the immediate context only. But in our experience HunPos provides robust performance when trained on modest amounts of training data such as ours.

For the purpose of lemma disambiguation the training data available is quite sparse (summarized in Table 1) and therefore a simple frequency-based disambiguation was preferred. The lemma with the highest frequency given the word form is selected based on the same training data that was used for the statistical tagger. As the results show, this primitive model is able to disambiguate most of the lemmas. In addition, a backoff disambiguator was used for word forms not found in this training data, based on the notion that most of the lemmas will occur as words at some point in natural text. Recognizing this, a backoff model selects the lemma that corresponds to the most frequent word form from the NoWaC corpus (Norwegian Web as Corpus), a corpus compiled by Guevara (2010) with 700 millions words collected from the .no domain on the web.

Table 1. Characteristics of the training corpus

Tokens	Sentences	Ambiguous tokens	Mean ambiguity
122,523	8,178	6,317	2.2

The lemma and PoS/morphological tag disambiguator and Oslo-Bergen Tagger have been packaged into a combined system named OBT+stat, which provides fully disambiguated PoS tags and lemmas.

8. Evaluation of the statistical module

8.1 How to evaluate

Since the disambiguation module selects a single reading as output for each token, its performance is not directly comparable to the published precision and recall measures for the Oslo-Bergen Tagger (Hagen & Johannessen 2003: 90). PoS tagging results are usually not reported in terms of precision and recall but by a single accuracy measure, which is the frequency of correctly annotated tokens in the output. One might suggest that the accuracy should be comparable to the F-score or precision of a CG tagger with near 100 percent recall, but the task of creating fully disambiguated output is arguably more difficult than leaving several alternatives while retaining a high recall. This makes it difficult to compare the accuracy reported here and the earlier evaluation, but we consider the precision of the rule-based OBT tagger as the yardstick against which we will compare the accuracy of the fully disambiguating OBT+stat tagger.

Before looking at the evaluation results, we would like to emphasize the fact that the OBT evaluation corpus contains very diverse texts with a minimum of cleanup. It contains raw text from a variety of magazines, newspapers and fiction among other genres. This makes the evaluation material more difficult to analyze than single domain corpora such as the WSJ Penn Treebank. Our evaluation corpus represents a more natural utilization scenario containing diverse running text where one cannot expect to match the performance reported using simpler corpora. Giesbrecht (2009) shows that such state-of-the-art results do not necessarily hold when given more diverse input documents.

8.2 Evaluation results

The final model was evaluated on the fully disambiguated OBT evaluation corpus. The characteristics of the evaluation corpus are summarized in Table 2.

Table 2. Oslo-Bergen Tagger evaluation corpus statistics

Tokens	Sentences	Ambiguous tokens	Mean ambiguity
32,677	2,213	2,869	2.2

We evaluated OBT+stat in two contexts. First the pure disambiguation task is evaluated in Table 3.

Table 3. Evaluation of pure disambiguation tasks

PoS and morphological disambiguation accuracy	79.8%
Lemma disambiguation accuracy	95.1%

Here the accuracy of the PoS/morphological tagging is reported for tokens where OBT provides more than one annotation, i.e. the ambiguous ones. The lemma model accuracy is reported in the same manner, i.e. over all ambiguous lemmas in the evaluation data including lemmas disambiguated through the tag disambiguation. The coverage of the alignment between the OBT output and statistical tagger, i.e. the ratio of ambiguous tokens left by OBT where the statistical tagger has predicted one of the ambiguous tags, is 82.8 percent, while accuracy of the HMM tagger for aligned disambiguities is 84.9 percent.

The end-to-end performance of the entire Oslo-Bergen Tagger was also measured, and accuracy is reported for PoS/morphological tagging, lemmatization and the combined analysis in Table 4.

Table 4. Final evaluation results – PoS tagging, lemmatization and combined analysis accuracy

OBT+stat	Accuracy
PoS and morphological tagging	96.0%
Lemmatization	98.3%
Combined	95.7%

Compared to the earlier precision and recall scores of 96.0 percent and 99.0 percent for OBT, OBT+stat retains this high precision while producing fully disambiguated results. We interpret this as an improvement in performance in light of the below 100 percent recall of the OBT output. This is a surprisingly good result given the resources available, and validates the choice of robust statistical tools and simple integration with the CG tagger.

9. Conclusion

In this paper we have described how we have improved the Constraint Grammar based Oslo Bergen Tagger (OBT) (Johannessen, Hagen & Nøklestad 2000)

by adding a statistical module. Rule-based taggers tend to produce competitive results, but will generally leave some ambiguity behind in their output. In contrast, statistical taggers excel at ranking subtle linguistic phenomena based on annotated data. We therefore found it a good idea to combine the two approaches. We trained a statistical HMM tagger and applied the new statistical module on the ambiguous output from the OBT resulting in a new system, OBT+stat, which disambiguates all previous PoS and morphological ambiguities and ambiguities in the lemmatization. The performance of the new system is very good, with an accuracy around 96 percent, which compares favourably to the precision of the original OBT, even if the tasks are not directly comparable.

In OBT+stat we have gained the best of both worlds: The rich linguistic knowledge embodied in the CG rules and the data-driven disambiguation of more marginal linguistic phenomena by the statistical tagger. The strengths of the two approaches are combined to create an even better Oslo-Bergen Tagger with a wider area of application in the Norwegian Newspaper Corpus and beyond. The OBT+stat is now available on GPL conditions and can be downloaded from the OBT homepage.[6]

References

Babarcy, Anna, Carrol, John & Sampson, Geoffrey 2006. Definitional, personal, and mechanical constraints on part of speech annotation performance. *Natural Language Engineering* 12(1): 77–90.

Brants, Thorsten. 2000. TnT: A statistical part-of-speech tagger. 2000. In *Proceedings of the Sixth Conference on Applied Natural Language Processing* 224–231. Stroudsburg, PA: ACL.

CG3. ⟨http://beta.visl.sdu.dk/constraint_grammar.html⟩.

CLARIN. ⟨http://www.clarin.eu/⟩.

Faarlund, Jan Terje, Lie, Svein & Vannebo, Kjell Ivar. 1997. *Norsk referansegrammatikk*. Oslo: Universitetsforlaget.

Giesbrecht, Eugenie & Evert, Stefan. 2009. Is part-of-speech tagging a solved task? An evaluation of POS taggers for the German web as corpus. In *Proceedings of the Fifth Web as Corpus Workshop (WAC5)*, 27–35 San Sebastian, Spain.

Giménez, Jesús & Màrquez, Lluís. 2004. Svmtool: A general PoS tagger generator based on support vector machines. In *Proceedings of the 4th International Conference on Language Resources and Evaluation*, 43–46.

Guevara, Emiliano. 2010. NoWaC: A large web-based corpus for Norwegian. In *Proceedings of the NAACL HLT 2010, Sixth Web as Corpus Workshop* 1–7. Stroudsburg, PA: ACL.

6. We also expect to make it available within a prospective NO-CLARIN portal (see CLARIN homepage).

Hajič, Jan, Krbec, Pavel, Květoň, Pavel, Oliva, Karel & Petkevič, Vladimir. 2001. Serial combination of rules and statistics: A case study in Czech tagging. In *Proceedings of the 39th Annual Meeting on Association For Computational Linguistics*, 268–275. Stroudsburg, PA: ACL.

Halácsy, Péter, Kornai, András & Oravecz, Csaba. 2007. HunPos – an open source trigram tagger. In *Proceedings of the 45th Annual Meeting of the Association for Computational Linguistics Companion Volume Proceedings of the Demo and Poster Sessions*, 209–212. Stroudsburg, PA: ACL.

Hagen, Kristin & Johannessen, Janne Bondi. 2003. Parsing Nordic Languages (PaNoLa) – norsk versjon. In *Nordisk Sprogteknologi 2002*. 89–97. Copenhagen: Museum Tusculanums Forlag.

Johannessen, Janne Bondi, Hagen, Kristin & Nøklestad, Anders. 2000. A constraint-based tagger for Norwegian. In *17th Scandinavian Conference of Linguistics* [Odense Working Papers in Language and Communication 19], Carl-Erik Lindberg & Steffen Nordahl Lund (eds), 31–48. Odense: University of Southern Denmark.

Johannessen, Janne Bondi, Hagen, Kristin, Haaland, Åsne, Nøklestad, Anders, Jónsdottir, Andra Björk, Kokkinakis, Dimitris, Meurer, Paul, Bick, Eckhard & Haltrup, Dorte. 2005. Named Entity Recognition for the Mainland Scandinavian Languages. *Literary & Linguistic Computing* 20(1): 91–102.

Karlsson, Fred, Voutilainen, Atro, Heikkilä, Juha & Anttila, Arto. 1995. *Constraint grammar: A language-independent system for parsing unrestricted text*. Natural Language Processing 4 Berlin and New York: Mouton de Gruyter.

Lynum, André, Evensberget, Johan Benum & Skjærholt, Arne. 2011. PoS tagging with sparce resources. In proceedings of the India-Norway. Workshop on Web Concepts and Technologies, Trondheim, Norway, October 2010, Tapir Academic Press, Trondheim.

Norwegian Newspaper Corpus. ⟨http://avis.uib.no/⟩.

NoWaC. ⟨http://www.hf.uio.no/iln/om/organisasjon/tekstlab/prosjekter/nowac/index.html⟩.

Norsk Ordbank 'Norwegian Word Bank'. ⟨http://www.hf.uio.no/iln/om/organisasjon/edd/forsking/norsk-ordbank/⟩.

Nøklestad, Anders. 1998. Statistisk disambiguerende tagging av norsk. In *MONS 7. Utvalde artiklar frå det 7. Møtet Om Norsk Språk i Trondheim 1997*, Jan Terje Faarlund, Britt Mæhlum & Torbjorn Nordgård, T (eds), 181–197). Oslo: Novus forlag.

Oslo-Bergen Tagger homepage. ⟨ http://tekstlab.uio.no/obt-ny/⟩.

Ratnaparkhi, Adwait. 1996. A maximum entropy model for part-of-speech tagging. In *Proceedings of the Conference on Empirical Methods in Natural Language Processing EMNLP-96 of* 133–142. Philadelphia PA: University of Pennsylvania.

Spoustová, Drajomira, Hajič, Jan, Votrubec, Jan, Krbec, Pavel & Květoň, Pavel. 2007. The best of two worlds: Cooperation of statistical and rule-based taggers for Czech. In *Proceedings of the Workshop on Balto-Slavonic Natural Language Processing: Information Extraction and Enabling Technologies*, 67–74. Stroudsburg: ACL.

Tapanainen, P. & Voutilainen, A. 1994. Tagging accurately: don't guess if you know. In *Proceedings of the Fourth Conference on Applied Natural Language Processing*, 47–52. Stroudsburg: ACL.

Text Laboratory, University of Oslo. ⟨http://www.hf.uio.no/iln/om/organisasjon/tekstlab/⟩

Exploring corpora through syntactic annotation

Victoria Rosén
University of Bergen

Syntactic analysis is a valuable addition to corpus annotation, since it enables the retrieval of structural information which is otherwise difficult to access. The Norwegian Infrastructure for the Exploration of Syntax and Semantics is adding syntactic information to the Norwegian Newspaper Corpus and is effectively producing a treebank as a parsed corpus.

1. Introduction

Annotation of corpora facilitates their analysis for research purposes. While some research on the Norwegian Newspaper Corpus presupposes only plain text with minimal metadata (cf. elsewhere in this volume), other research questions may benefit from lemmatization and morphosyntactic tagging. However, even common morphosyntactic tagging has serious limitations. How could one for instance search for relative clauses or cleft constructions, or investigate the placement of adverbial constituents, using only a morphosyntactically tagged corpus? These examples illustrate that morphosyntactic tagging may be insufficient, as such studies are difficult to carry out without annotation in terms of hierarchical phrase structure, functional relations and the like. A corpus with this kind of syntactic annotation is commonly referred to as a treebank.

The Norwegian Newspaper Corpus project included preliminary methodological steps towards treebanking. These treebanking efforts will be continued and extended in the INESS project, which aims at constructing a large treebank for Norwegian. In the following section a brief overview of treebanking methodologies will be provided. Then the INESS project will be presented. In the final section, illustrations will be given of the kinds of searches that presuppose a treebank.

2. Treebanking

A treebank is a corpus that is annotated with linguistic information beyond the part of speech level. Treebanks are so called because the first type of syntactic annotation used in treebanks was in the form of phrase structure trees. The term treebank is however also used for parsed corpora that have representations of syntactic and sometimes also semantic structures in other formats (Abeillé 2003).

Many different methods are used for building treebanks. The earliest treebanks relied on mostly manual methods, so that linguists annotated the phrase structure bracketing by hand. There are two main drawbacks to manual annotation. Firstly it requires a huge effort and is consequently expensive. Secondly it requires a lot of work in specifying how the annotation should be done.[1] But even with extensive guidelines, there is a problem achieving interannotator agreement. It is namely a considerable problem that different people annotate in different ways. In fact, it can be difficult to get the same annotator to annotate similar phenomena in the same way over time.

More common today is a semiautomatic approach where some analysis is done automatically, for example automatic parsing. If the corpus is analyzed automatically, it is essential that there is manual checking and correction to ensure high quality. One reason for this is that natural languages have so much lexical and syntactic ambiguity that automatic parsing will often result in many analyses. Until reliable automatic disambiguation can be applied, a human disambiguator is indispensable for determining which analysis is the intended one so that it can be stored in the treebank.[2] The greatest advantage with automatic parsing is that all analyses produced are consistent with the computational grammar that is used in parsing. It is therefore much easier to ensure that similar constructions receive similar annotation with automatic parsing than with manual annotation. Another advantage is that complicated syntactic structures can be more efficiently built automatically than by an annotator. Automatic parsing must however always rely on a previous manual analysis, either in the form of manual analysis of a corpus, or a handwritten computational grammar which provides input to a parser. There is, in other words, no way around the fact that constructing a treebank is a large investment in terms of both time and money, but with great potential benefits, as will be exemplified below.

The type of annotation used varies between treebanks. Syntactic annotation usually encodes constituent structure or functional structure, or a combination of

1. Geoffrey Sampson has noted that the book which defines the annotation scheme for the SUSANNE treebank contains a larger number of words than the treebank itself (Sampson 2003:35).

2. In rare cases there may be a genuine ambiguity that cannot be resolved by considering the context, sometimes even an intended ambiguity. In such cases more than one analysis may be stored in the treebank.

the two. Perhaps the most influential treebank has been the Penn Treebank, created at the University of Pennsylvania between 1989 and 1996 (Taylor et al. 2003). This treebank includes texts from different genres, including computer manuals, nursing notes, and Wall Street Journal articles. During the first phase of the Penn Treebank project, the syntactic annotation was "a skeletal context-free bracketing with limited empty categories and no indication of non-contiguous structures and dependencies" (Taylor et al. 2003: 7). After the release of the first version, feedback from users indicated that the treebank could be more useful if the annotation were richer. In the second phase of the project a new style of annotation was developed that included information about syntactic functions and semantic predicate-argument structure. In Figure 1 an example is given of the annotation used in the second version of the Penn Treebank for the sentence *The ball was thrown by Chris* (Taylor et al. 2003: 12).

```
(S  (NP-SBJ-1 The ball)
    (VP was
        (VP thrown
            (NP *-1)
            (PP by
                (NP-LGS Chris)))))

Predicate Argument Structure:
throw(Chris, ball)
```

Figure 1. Example of Penn Treebank II annotation for the sentence *The ball was thrown by Chris*

In addition to phrase structure categories such as S, NP, VP and PP, we see here annotation of syntactic functions such as subject (SBJ), semantic arguments such as "logical subjects in passives" (LGS), and a predicate-argument structure. The annotation also introduces a null element to account for the 'movement' of the object of the verb *throw* to the subject position in the passive, the null element being encoded by an asterisk that is coindexed with the subject NP.

Early treebanks were often quite theory neutral, encoding only the least controversial types of structure. More recently theory-specific treebanks have been built. There are two main types of theory-specific treebanks: those that use dependency theory and those that use a unification-based generative theory, such as Head-Driven Phrase Structure Grammar (HPSG) (Sag et al. 2003) or Lexical-Functional Grammar (LFG) (Bresnan 2001). The Prague Dependency Treebank is one of the oldest and most important dependency treebanks (Böhmová et al. 2003). The LinGO Redwoods project has been developing a dynamic HPSG treebank for English for the past ten years (Oepen et al. 2004b). The INESS project will develop an LFG treebank for Norwegian in the INESS project, which will be the subject of the following section.

3. INESS – the Norwegian treebanking infrastructure

INESS, the Norwegian Infrastructure for the Exploration of Syntax and Semantics, is a project cofunded by the University of Bergen and the Norwegian Research Council as part of its initiative for research infrastructure (http://iness.uib.no/). The project will provide a virtual eScience laboratory for linguistic research. The infrastructure will make treebanks directly accessible from a modern browser via the Internet. This will be made possible through a state of the art high performance computing cluster at the University of Bergen, eliminating the need for users to acquire special software and install it themselves, something that has often been prohibitively complex in practice. The INESS infrastructure will thus make treebanks much easier to exploit by end users. Treebanks for several different languages will be made available through the infrastructure, initally including Norwegian, German, English and Sami.

Since there is currently no extensive treebank for Norwegian, the most important content in the infrastructure will be a new, large coverage treebank for Norwegian Bokmål and Norwegian Nynorsk. The corpus will consist of texts from various genres, and the Norwegian Newspaper Corpus will provide newspaper texts for the treebank.

The Norwegian treebank in INESS will build on the competency acquired in the NorGram, LOGON and TREPIL projects. The NorGram (Norwegian Computational Grammar) project began development of a computational LFG grammar for Norwegian Bokmål more than a decade ago (Dyvik 1999, 2000) as part of the Parallel Grammar Project (Butt et al. 2002). The Xerox Linguistic Environment (XLE) developed at the Palo Alto Research Center is used as a parsing platform (Maxwell & Kaplan 1993). This grammar was subsequently used in the LOGON machine translation project (Oepen et al. 2004a), which also supported the initial development of treebanking tools and techniques further developed in the TREPIL pilot project (Rosén et al. 2006). The main result of TREPIL was the LFG PARSEBANKER, a toolkit and platform for constructing LFG parsebanks (Rosén et al. 2009). Although originally conceived as a means of constructing a treebank for Norwegian, the LFG PARSEBANKER is language and grammar independent, so that it may be used to construct a treebank for any language that has an LFG grammar implemented in XLE.

The use of LFG as a theoretical framework for dynamic treebank analysis has been thoroughly explored and motivated in the TREPIL project. LFG representations are aimed at 'deep' parsing using a grammar that projects different aspects of grammatical structure into different structural representations. The c(onstituent)-structure provides surface phrase structure trees. The f(unctional)-structure is an attribute-value matrix providing information about grammatical features and functions. This theory thus gives prominence to traditional grammatical concepts such as subject and object. In addition, the Norwegian grammar has a semantic component in the form of MRS-structures (minimal recursion semantics; cf. Copestake et al. 2005). Together, these levels of analysis provide a very detailed picture of the syntactic and semantic structure of a language and can form a solid basis for any derived representations, such as dependency trees, depending on the end user and application area.

The grammar and lexical resources necessary for this treebank have so far been developed and tested for Norwegian Bokmål, but will also be extended to Norwegian Nynorsk in INESS. The NorGram computational grammar will need only minor adjustments to be able to accommodate Nynorsk, while a lexical resource for Nynorsk has already been obtained from the lexical database Norsk Ordbank (http://www.edd.uio.no/prosjekt/ordbanken/).

As mentioned above, automatic parsing often produces multiple analyses requiring efficient human disambiguation. A simple example of an ambiguous sentence from the Norwegian Newspaper Corpus is (1).[3]

(1) *Sannheten kompliserer den politiske historien.*
truth:DEF.SG complicates the political history:DEF.SG
'The truth complicates political history.' or
'The truth, political history complicates.'

Norwegian is a verb second language, the finite verb occurring in second position in main clauses regardless of whether the subject or some other constituent occurs in first position. In example (1) it is therefore not possible to determine what the subject and object of the sentence are based on word order; the first constituent *sannheten* 'the truth' can either be interpreted as the subject or the topicalized object. In (2), there is also a nominal phrase both before and after the verb, but in this example, the nominative case of the pronoun *jeg* 'I' makes it clear that the object has been topicalized.

(2) *Denne bilen liker jeg.*
this car:DEF.SG like I
'This car, I like.'

In the LFG Parsebanker, a human annotator may specify that the intended reading of (1) is that the initial nominal is the subject, thereby choosing the c-structure

3. The Norwegian examples in this chapter, except for (2) and (7), are taken from the Norwegian Newspaper Corpus.

and f-structure in Figure 2. Efficient disambiguation techniques based on discriminants for LFG grammars were developed in the TREPIL project (Rosén et al. 2007). A discriminant is an elementary property of an analysis, such as that an NP functions as subject.

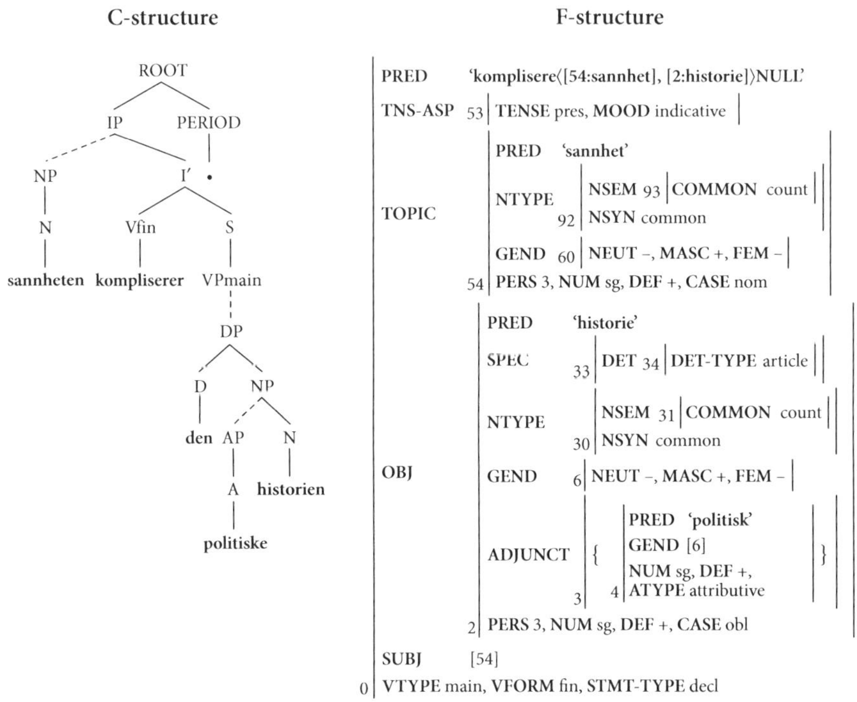

Figure 2. C- and f-structure for the sentence *Sannheten kompliserer den politiske historien*

As this example shows, the LFG structures provide a wealth of grammatical information about the sentence. The c-structure is a phrase structure tree which follows the principles of X-bar theory as proposed by Bresnan (2001), with necessary adjustments for Norwegian (Dyvik 2000). The attributes and values in the f-structure come either from the lexical entries for the words in the sentence or from the grammatical rules that are used in the analysis. The f-structure includes grammatical features such as person, number, definiteness and case. There are also features for grammatical functions such as subject (SUBJ), object (OBJ), topic and adjunct. The NP *sannheten* functions simultaneously as the topic and the subject, which share the same value; this is shown in the f-structure through coindexation.[4]

4. See http://prosjekt.aksis.uib.no/projects/inesspublic/wiki/NorGram_documentation for detailed documentation of the LFG grammar for Norwegian used in INESS.

A treebank is built up in the LFG Parsebanker by first parsing a corpus. This is followed by discriminant disambiguation by human annotators. Whenever the intended analysis is among the analyses produced by the parser, this analysis is stored in the treebank. When the intended analysis is not present, the disambiguation process will often help to diagnose the problem, for instance that an item is missing from the lexicon, or that a grammatical construction is not yet covered by the grammar. Therefore disambiguation will be followed up by improvements to the grammar and lexicon. This process can be repeated in cylces, thus gradually improving coverage of the corpus and resulting in a dynamic treebank. Annotators' choices of discriminants are saved and may be reapplied automatically in most cases, thereby reducing the need for human intervention in subsequent cycles.

4. Searching for complex syntactic constructions in a treebank

The wealth of grammatical information in our treebank annotation makes it possible to exploit powerful search strategies involving any grammatical properties in the annotation. This section illustrates how passive constructions may be found by using f-structure properties in the search expression and how relative clauses may be found using c-structure properties. Both c-structure and f-structure properties may also be included in the search expression when necessary.

4.1 Passive constructions

Passive constructions have been a popular theme for linguistic research for decades. There are many aspects of the passive that could be interesting to investigate in a large corpus, for instance, pragmatic aspects tied to its use for agent demotion. But it is not trivial to find passive constructions automatically even in a morphosyntactically tagged corpus. The reason is that, at least in some languages, the passive cannot be unambiguously identified through a single passive marker. In English the passive voice is expressed by an auxiliary, usually *be* or *get*, together with the past participle of the main verb. Since the past participle has numerous other uses, and the passive auxiliaries also can be used as main verbs, passive constructions cannot be found simply by searching for one word; a combination of auxiliary and past participle must be used in the search expression. Although this can be rather complicated, since one must allow for different auxiliaries and for words possibly intervening between the auxiliary and the past participle, it can be done. The search results will however be noisy, with many active sentences among the results.

The Norwegian passive is similar to the English one, but in addition to the periphrastic passive with an auxiliary and a past participle, there is also a morphological passive, the so-called *s*-form. This form of the verb also has other uses than the passive, however. The Norwegian reference grammar *Norsk referansegrammatikk* (Faarlund et al. 1997: 511) distinguishes between several different meanings that these verbs can have, including reflexive and reciprocal, illustrated by examples (3) and (4) respectively (with the *s*-forms marked in boldface).

(3) *Vi* ***skjemmes*** *over vår innsats.*
we are.ashamed over our effort
'We are ashamed of our efforts.'

(4) *Lederne* ***møttes*** *i Jerusalem.*
leader:DEF.PL met in Jerusalem.
'The leaders met (each other) in Jerusalem.'

Thus, in Norwegian as in English, it is complicated to search for passives through morphosyntactic tags alone.

Agentive phrases are expressed in English through preposisitonal phrases headed by the preposition *by* and in Norwegian through prepositional phrases headed by the preposition *av* 'by'. If one were interested in investigating how often passive constructions include agentive phrases, it would not be sufficient to identify all of the passive constructions with PPs headed by these prepositions, since in both languages, these prepositions have many other uses. Examples of passives from the Norwegian Newspaper Corpus are given in (5) and (6).

(5) *Da funnet ble oppdaget, ble det foretatt*
when find:DEF.SG became discovered became it undertaken
DNA-undersøkelser av bakterien.
DNA-test:INDEF.PL of bacteria:DEF.SG
'When the discovery was made, DNA-tests of the bacteria were undertaken.'
'When the discovery was made, DNA-tests were undertaken by the bacteria.'

(6) *De positive prøvene ble tatt av et parti sauekjøtt [...]*
the positive sample:DEF.PL became taken of a batch mutton
'The positive samples were taken of a batch of mutton [...]'
'The positive samples were taken by a batch of mutton [...]'

Both of these examples are ambiguous, as indicated by the two idiomatic translations for each of them. The PPs headed by *av* could be agentive phrases, but in these sentences the agentive reading is not the intended one.

In order to reliably identify passives with and without agentive phrases, it seems that detailed syntactic analysis is therefore necessary. The f-structure for the sentence in (7) is given in Figure 3.

(7) *Prøvene tas av kontrolløren.*
sample:DEF.PL are.taken of inspector:DEF.SG
'The samples are taken by the inspector.'

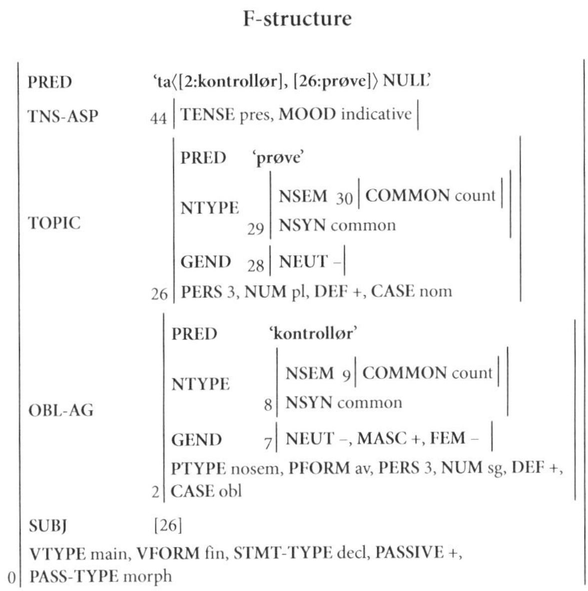

Figure 3. F-structure for the sentence *Prøvene tas av kontrolløren*

If a construction has been analyzed as a passive, the attribute-value pair 'PASSIVE +' will occur in the f-structure. If an *av*-phrase has been analyzed as an agentive, the feature 'OBL-AG' will appear on the same level of the f-structure (in this case the outer level, indexed with 0). One can therefore easily search for passives with agentive phrases by specifying that both of these features must occur on the same level of the f-structure. Since the search mechanism in the LFG PARSEBANKER includes a negation operator, it is also easy to search for f-structures with the attribute-value pair 'PASSIVE +' that do not have an 'OBL-AG' feature, thus enabling one to find agentless passives.

4.2 Relative clauses

Like passive constructions, relative clauses are difficult to search for in a corpus without syntactic annotation. In English, many relative clauses begin with the complementizer *that* or one of the relative pronouns (*who*, *which*, etc.). In a morphosyntactically tagged corpus one could search for nouns followed by these functions words, thereby potentially locating the beginning of a relative clause. But since these grammatical words all have other functions in addition to introducing relative clauses, the results of such a search would still require a large amount of manual work to locate the actual relative clauses. Norwegian is similar to English in that the complementizer *som* (modern Norwegian has few relative pronouns) also has many other functions, thus rendering this type of search of little value.

The situation is further complicated by the fact that many relative clauses, in both English and Norwegian, lack an initial function word. One might want to explore under what conditions relative clauses occur with and without complementizers or relative pronouns, or the relative frequency of the two types of relative clauses. Without syntactic annotation, identifying these constructions reliably in a corpus seems impossible. With syntactic annotation, it is simple. Example (8) contains a relative clause without a complementizer; the position where *som* 'that' could occur is marked with this word in brackets, and the relative clause is underlined.

(8) *Amerikansk politi ble torsdag kveld sendt hjem*
American police became Thursday evening sent home
til popstjernen Britney Spears i forbindelse med konflikten
to pop.star:DEF.SG Britney Spears in connection with conflict:DEF.SG
[som] hun og eksmannen har når det gjelder omsorg
[that] she and ex-husband:DEF.SG have when it concerns care
for deres to felles barn.
for their two common children.
'American police were Thursday evening sent to pop star Britney Spears' home in connection with the conflict she and her ex-husband have concerning the care of their two children.'

In Figure 4 an abbreviated form of the NP containing the relative clause in (8) is shown with and without the complementizer *som*.

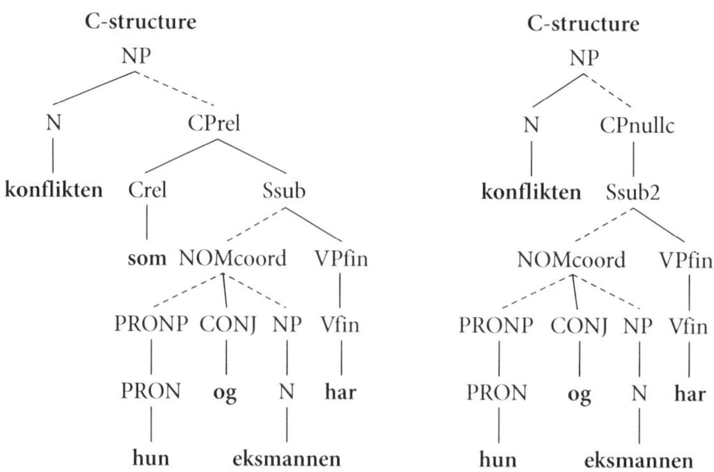

Figure 4. C-structures for the NPs *konflikten som hun og eksmannen har* and *konflikten hun og eksmannen har*

Relative clauses of both types can be easily found through a search for the relevant phrase structure category, either CPrel or CPnullc.

5. Conclusion

Syntactic annotation fundamentally changes the type of research that can be done with corpora. The examples in Section 4 illustrated what a powerful tool such annotation can be for linguistic research. Treebanks are also of great importance in the area of language and speech technology. They are used for inducing various kinds of resources, such as lexica and grammars, and they are also essential for training and testing different kinds of tools for automatic natural language processing, such as taggers and parsers. The texts from the Norwegian Newspaper Corpus which are included in the INESS treebank for Norwegian will be an important source of information about contemporary Norwegian language use.

References

Abeillé, Anne. 2003. Introduction. In *Treebanks: Building and Using Parsed Corpora* [Text, Speech and Language Technology 20], Anne Abeillé (ed), xiii–xxvi. Dordrecht: Kluwer.

Böhmová, Alena, Hajič, Jan, Hajičová, Eva & Hladká, Barbora. 2003. The PDT: A 3-level annotation scenario. In *Treebanks: Building and Using Parsed Corpora* [Text, Speech and Language Technology 20], Anne Abeillé (ed), 103–127. Dordrecht: Kluwer.

Bresnan, Joan. 2001. *Lexical-Functional Syntax*. Malden MA: Blackwell.

Butt, Miriam, Dyvik, Helge, King, Tracy Holloway, Masuichi, Hiroshi & Rohrer, Christian. 2002. The Parallel Grammar Project. In *Proceedings of COLING-2002 Workshop on Grammar Engineering and Evaluation*, Taipei, Taiwan.

Copestake, Ann, Flickinger, Dan, Sag, Ivan A. & Pollard, Carl. 2005. Minimal recursion semantics: An introduction. *Journal of Research on Language and Computation* 3(4): 281–332.

Dyvik, Helge. 2000. Nødvendige noder i norsk. Grunntrekk i en leksikalsk-funksjonell beskrivelse av norsk syntaks. In *Menneske, språk og felleskap*, Øivin Andersen, Kjersti Fløttum & Torodd Kinn (eds), 25–45. Oslo: Novus forlag.

Dyvik, Helge. 1999. The universality of f-structure. Discovery or stipulation? The case of modals. In Proceedings of the LFG99 Conference, Tracy Holloway King & Miriam Butt (eds). Stanford CA: CSLI.

Faarlund, Jan Terje, Lie, Svein & Vannebo, Kjell Ivar. 1997. *Norsk referansegrammatikk*. Oslo: Universitetsforlaget.

Maxwell, John T. & Kaplan, Ronald M. 1993. The interface between phrasal and functional constraints. *Computational Linguistics* 19(4): 571–589.

Oepen, Stephan, Dyvik, Helge, Lønning, Jan Tore, Velldal, Erik, Beermann, Dorothee, Carroll, John, Flickinger, Dan, Hellan, Lars, Johannessen, Janne Bondi, Meurer, Paul, Nordgård, Torbjørn & Rosén, Victoria. 2004a. Som å kapp-ete med trollet? Towards MRS-based Norwegian–English Machine Translation. In *Proceedings of the 10th International Conference on Theoretical and Methodological Issues in Machine Translation*, Baltimore MD.

Oepen, Stephan, Flickinger, Dan, Toutanova, Kristina & Manning, Christopher D. 2004b. LinGO Redwoods, a rich and dynamic treebank for HPSG. *Research on Language & Computation* 2(4): 575–596.

Rosén, Victoria, De Smedt, Koenraad & Meurer, Paul. 2006. Towards a toolkit linking treebanking to grammar development. In *TLT 2006: Proceedings of the Fifth Workshop on Treebanks and Linguistic Theories*, Jan Hajič & Joakim Nivre (eds), 55–66. Prague: Institute of formal and applied linguistics.

Rosén, Victoria, Meurer, Paul & De Smedt, Koenraad. 2007. Designing and implementing discriminants for LFG grammars. In *Proceedings of LFG07*, Tracy Holloway King & Miriam Butt (eds), 397–417. Stanford CA: CSLI.

Rosén, Victoria, Meurer, Paul & De Smedt, Koenraad. 2009. LFG parsebanker: A toolkit for building and searching a treebank as a parsed corpus. In *Proceedings of the Seventh International Workshop on Treebanks and Linguistic Theories*, Frank Van Eynde, Anette Frank, Koenraad De Smedt & Gertjan Van Noord (eds), 127–133. Utrecht: LOT.

Sag, Ivan A., Wasow, Thomas & Bender, Emily M. 2003. *Syntactic Theory: A Formal Introduction*. Stanford CA: CSLI Publications.

Sampson, Geoffrey. 2003. Thoughts on two decades of drawing trees. In *Treebanks: Building and Using Parsed Corpora* [Text, Speech and Language Technology 20], Anne Abeillé, (ed), 23–41. Dordrecht: Kluwer.

Taylor, Ann, Marcus, Mitchell & Santorini, Beatrice. 2003. The Penn Treebank: An overview. In *Treebanks: Building and Using Parsed Corpora* [Text, Speech and Language Technology 20], Anne Abeillé, (ed), 5–22. Dordrecht: Kluwer.

Collocations and statistical analysis of n-grams

Multiword expressions in newspaper text

Gunn Inger Lyse & Gisle Andersen
University of Bergen / NHH Norwegian School of Economics

Multiword expressions (MWEs) are words that co-occur so often that they are perceived as a linguistic unit. Since MWEs pervade natural language, their identification is pertinent for a range of tasks within lexicography, terminology and language technology. We apply various statistical association measures (AMs) to word sequences from the Norwegian Newspaper Corpus (NNC) in order to rank two-and three-word sequences (bigrams and trigrams) in terms of their tendency to co-occur. The results show that some statistical measures favour relatively frequent MWEs (e.g. *i motsetning til* 'as opposed to'), whereas other measures favour relatively low-frequent units, which typically comprise loan words (*de facto*), technical terms (*notaries publicus*) and phrasal anglicisms (*practical jokes*; cf. G. Andersen this volume). On this basis we evaluate the relevance of each of these measures for lexicography, terminology and language technology purposes.

1. Introduction

Multiword expressions (MWEs) may be defined as words that co-occur so often that they are perceived as a linguistic unit (for instance *pit stop* and *by and large*). Linguistically, MWEs comprise several phenomena, ranging from idioms, semi-fixed expressions, foreign expressions (such as anglicisms in Norwegian) and technical terminology. MWEs are surprisingly ubiquitous in natural language, being estimated to be as frequent as one-word expressions Jackendoff (1997). The identification of MWEs is therefore pertinent for a range of tasks within lexicography, terminology and language technology, including for instance the correct segmentation of phraseological units and the extraction of terminology (*ulcerøs kolitt, notarius publicus*).

In the field of Natural Language Processing, MWEs are sometimes referred to as "a pain in the neck" (Sag et al. 2002), because their meanings usually cannot be determined compositionally from the meanings of the individual words. In the context of machine translation, for instance, this means that the system needs to know if a sequence of words can be translated word by word or if it has a special meaning, requiring a particular translation, in virtue of being an MWE. Moreover, since many MWEs have a marked syntax, they may seriously impede syntactic parsers (cf. the expression *by and large*, which is a juxtaposition of a preposition and an adjective). Norwegian, like German but unlike English, follows the convention of representing compounds as one word; hence MWEs are not as relevant for the identification of (domestic) compounds as is the case for English. Nevertheless, for the Norwegian newspaper project it is desirable to explore the vast amount of data by identifying MWEs that are lexicographically or terminologically relevant.

The identification of MWEs is valuable for several purposes. First, multiword expressions are needed in lexical databases used for general lexicographical purposes as well as for NLP purposes. Recurring MWEs should be systematically identified and correctly segmented in a corpus-driven approach, and added to the national lexical database, the Norwegian Word Bank (cf. Fjeld & Nygaard this volume). Second, we know that the syntactic tagger used by the Norwegian Newspaper Corpus (NNC; Andersen & Hofland this volume), the Oslo-Bergen tagger (Johannessen et al. this volume) makes errors related to MWEs, especially pertaining to phrasal prepositions such as *på grunn av* 'because of, due to' and adverbs such as *i tide* 'on time'. These should be segmented as phrasal units and not processed further by the tagger. Therefore the overall performance of the tagger may be improved through added knowledge about multiword expressions in Norwegian text. Third, technical terminology is very often realised as MWEs, and the identification of recurrent collocational patterns is relevant for term extraction, even in non-technical texts such as newspaper language.

In line with the "re-emergence of empirical linguistics" Abney (2000), statistical methods have been introduced as a way to quantify an intuition about words that "belong together" (e.g. Church et al. 1991, Baldwin & Bond 2002, Banerjee & Pedersen 2003, McInnes 2004; Evert 2004). So-called association measures (AMs) analyse the relation between how often words in a sequence occur together and the frequency of each of the words individually.

However, the interplay between statistical measures, corpus material and the identification of MWEs is still not very well explored, among other things because the choice of statistical measure depends on which type of MWEs one is attempting to extract. The norm seems to be to provide a variety of statistical measures with minimal guidelines as to which will probably suit the needs of the user best (Banerjee & Pedersen 2003; Evert 2004; Baldwin 2004, Baldwin & Kim 2010). In other words, there seems to be a knowledge gap in terms of how to use (and how to choose) association measures to extract MWEs. To explore this relation further, we have applied nine common statistical measures to two-word sequences (bigrams) in the NNC and four statistical measures to three-word units (trigram).

Our main objective is to evaluate the usefulness of the alternative association measures, when applied to a large set of Norwegian data, in terms of their ability to pick out relevant MWEs representing the different lexical and terminological categories sketched above. This is based on the *a priori* assumption that certain AMs will pick out items with a relatively low frequency and thereby be better at finding rarely used technical terms (*trojansk hest* 'trojan horse' in computing), anglicisms (*corned beef, practical jokes*), other foreign expressions (*per capita* 'per head', *gefundenes fressen* 'delicacy, tidbit'), and possibly also different domestic MWEs (e.g. the dessert *tilslørte bondepiker*). Other AMs may be better suited for picking out high-frequency multiword units such as phrasal prepositions and adverbs (*stort sett* 'mostly', *blant annet* 'among other things'). Yet other AMs may well be better suited for the automatic detection of multi-word proper nouns (*Gro Harlem Brundtland*), which are of less lexicographical value but important for NLP purposes such as named entity recognition.

The paper is structured as follows. Section 2 provides an overview of general concepts relevant for the study of phraseology and MWEs. Section 3 describes the material used and the methods applied in order to extract collocational statistics and test the association measures. In Section 4 we present the results and discuss the relevance of the different association measures from the point of view of lexicography and terminology, while Section 5 contains concluding remarks and proposals for future work.

2. Background

2.1 Multiword Expressions (MWEs)

The concept of MWE is an attempt to capture the intuition that meaningful units in our language are often larger than individual words. Intersecting with a wide range of linguistic phenomena, Baldwin and Bond conclude that "there is much descriptive and analytic work on MWEs that has yet to be done" (Baldwin & Bond 2002: 3). In so-called compositional semantics, open-class words (nouns, verbs, adjectives and adverbs) are commonly assumed to have a lexical meaning which contributes to the meaning of an utterance, i.e. the meaning of the utterance is composed of the meanings of the parts. Linguistic analyses of meaning often rest solely on words as a basic lexical unit, which is also reflected in the way we tend to organise our vocabulary in terms of lexicons or dictionaries that are usually based on looking up individual words.

This approach poses problems when we encounter sequences of words where the meaning is *not* unambiguously composed of the meaning of the parts. There is an emerging awareness that MWEs are not just sporadic exceptions in our vocabulary (Sinclair 1991; Stubbs 1996; Sinclair 1996, Tognini-Bonelli 2001; Biber 2009). Jackendoff (1997) estimates that MWEs are as common as simplex words in our vocabulary; similarly Sag et al. (2002) assert that 41 per cent of the entries in WordNet (Fellbaum 1998) are multiword units.

We adopt the definition by Baldwin and Kim (2010:3), who define MWEs as units that (i) can be decomposed into more than one (space-separated) lexical unit; and (ii) display lexical, syntactic, semantic, pragmatic and/or statistical idiomaticity. This is a useful definition because it states that some form of idiomaticity is a necessary feature of MWEs, as opposed to applying loose criteria (as an example, the 'single-word phrasability' criterion states that if an MWE can be paraphrased by a single word, then it usually counts as an MWE).

'Idiomaticity' is taken to mean that the expression is somehow 'marked' or deviates from the linguistic properties of the component words, and may apply at the lexical, syntactic, semantic, pragmatic, and/or statistical levels (Baldwin & Kim 2010:4), as described below. From this definition it also follows that MWEs are somehow lexicalised, in virtue of having some additional property which cannot be deduced directly from its component words.

Following Baldwin and Kim (2010), *lexical idiomaticity* is defined as an expression being "lexically marked" in that one or more lexical components of the expression are not part of the conventional lexicon of the language in question (consider the Latin phrase *de facto*, or a phrasal anglicism such as *bottom line* in Norwegian). Since such phrases are not part of the domestic vocabulary, lexical idiomaticity usually entails semantic idiomaticity, since the meaning of the expression is then usually not deduced from the meanings of the parts (unless the listener has adequate knowledge of the language from which an expression is taken and the meaning of the phrase can be deduced from its parts in that language). For the same reason, lexical idiomaticity usually also entails syntactic idiomaticity.

Syntactic idiomaticity, as defined by Baldwin and Kim (2010), occurs when the syntax of the MWE deviates from the constructions that one would expect in the given language – although in that case, it is perhaps more accurate to call it *morphosyntactic* idiomaticity. Consider the Norwegian adverb *i tide* 'on time', whose archaic word form *tide* does not belong to the ordinary inflectional paradigm of the lexeme *tid* 'time', making *i tide* syntactically idiomatic. The noun cannot be derived by the rules of the grammar, but its use in this idiomatic context has to be learnt.

Semantic idiomacity is the property that the meaning of an MWE is not fully predictable from its component parts. The Norwegian expression *på kant med* 'in disagreement with' is semantically marked in that its meaning is not derivable from the components *på* 'in/on', *kant* 'edge', *med* 'with'. The expression is, incidentally, also syntactically marked in that one cannot inflect the noun or insert a modifier before the noun (**på kanten med* lit. 'on the edge with'), illustrating why such idiomatic expressions often cause problems for foreign learners.

Baldwin and Kim (2010: 5) observe that there are a range of borderline examples of semantic idiomacity, where the meaning is partially predictable, for instance due to metonymic extensions (Halverson this volume) or the use of metaphor (*around the clock*, meaning '24 hours', refers to counting the hours on a clock as a metaphor.)

Pragmatic idiomaticity pertains to MWEs that are associated with particular communicative situations or discourse contexts, for instance expressions like *good morning, how do you do* or *welcome back*, performing specific pragmatic functions, for instance at the speech act level (e.g. Sag et al. 2002).

Finally, *statistical idiomacity* is the phenomenon of particular combinations of words occurring with markedly higher frequency in comparison to alternative phrasings of the same concept. Statistical idiomaticity thus appears to correspond to what Sag et al. (2002: 7) refer to as 'institutional phrases'. For instance, there is no principled linguistic reason for not saying *computer translation* when meaning *machine translation*, or *pepper and salt* instead of *salt and pepper*, but statistically we find that particular lexicalisations are simply more frequent. Statistical idiomacity encompasses notions such as 'naturalness' and 'conventionalisation' of word sequences; for instance one may say *strong tea* and *powerful car*, but their so-called anti-collocations *?powerful tea* and *?strong car* are markedly less common.

A problem in delimiting MWEs is that there are many sequences of words which intuitively have a strong association but which may or may not be characterised as MWEs – consider for instance so-called formulaic sequences such as *I don't want to, the fact that*. Biber et al. (1999: 999) introduce the term 'lexical bundles' to denote "sequences of word forms that commonly go together in natural discourse" and that are characterised by a high frequency. Lexical bundles are compositional expressions that are not lexicalised, although they may become so in the course of time, and which may allow for a certain variability (e.g. Biber 2009).

There are several phenomena that intersect with the MWE category, although not all examples of these phenomena are multiword units. Therefore, when we attempt to identify MWEs automatically, we expect to discover that the identified MWE candidates belong to different linguistic categories. One category is technical terminology, defined by Baldwin (2004) as "a lexical unit consisting of one or more words which represents a concept inside a domain". Although terms are not necessarily multiword units, Sag et al. (2002: 2) observe that "specialized domain vocabulary, such as terminology, overwhelmingly consists of MWEs". According to Baldwin and Kim (2010: 11), the field of terminology is "broader in scope than MWEs in the sense that simple lexemes can equally be technical terms, and narrower in the sense than non-technical MWEs are not of interest to the field". Anglicisms are often lexicalised phrases (G. Andersen this volume) such as *due diligence, easy listening, straight edge*, etc. Further, even though compounds are written without whitespace in Norwegian, it is not inconceivable that the systematic retrieval of MWEs may identify certain compounds that are commonly spelt as separate words in disagreement with the spelling norms (the phenomenon known as *særskriving*). Finally, there are named entities (names of persons, places, events, organisations, titles, expressions of time and quantity, numerical expressions, etc. (*New York, Melodi Grand Prix, cand. scient., tomorrow morning, one million*).

Among these phenomena, there are certain kinds of multiword sequences that we are particularly interested in identifying in the context of the Norwegian Newspaper project, due to their potential relevance for general lexicography and terminology. This applies to multi-word terms from various professional domains, such as *amyotrofisk lateralsklerose* (medicine), *pater familias* (law) or *vennligsinnet oppkjøp* 'friendly acquisition' (business), as well as recurrent MWEs in general language, i.e. idioms such as *gemene hop* 'common folk', conventionalised metaphors such as *hellige kuer* 'holy cows' and multiword anglicisms such as *make or break* or imported interjections and discouse markers like the irony marker *yeah right*.

As we will see, different association measures vary in terms of their ability to retrieve elements in these groups.

2.2 Collocations

Sag et al. (2002) define a 'collocation' as an arbitrary statistically significant association between co-occurring items; that is, collocations subsume MWEs.

Association measures (AMs) are statistical measures that calculate the association strength between tokens in an n-gram. An n-gram is a sequence of *n* units, in our case a unit is a string of characters separated by white space. A bigram contains two units, a trigram contains three units, etc. There are many statistical AMs available; some are relatively simple to calculate whereas other are more complex. Two freely available statistics software packages illustrate the range of AMs that have been suggested in the literature: The UCS Toolkit[1]

1. URL: http://www.collocations.de. Last verified July 8, 2010.

provides a repository for almost 30 AMs for bigrams (Evert 2004). The n-gram Statistics Package (NSP)[2] provides 13 AMs for bigrams and four measures for trigrams (Banerjee & Pedersen 2003).

The relation between statistical measures of collocation and linguistic concepts such as MWEs has not been fully explored in the literature. Baldwin and Kim (2010: 23) observe that although AMs have been applied to a wide range of extraction tasks over a number of languages, the general finding is that it is often unpredictable which association measure will work best for a given task in a given language. Thus, it seems to be the norm to present a group of "common statistical measures" with minimal statements relating to the applicability of each statistical test.

The approach taken in this paper is that, although the numerical values for ranking n-grams according to collocational strength are not comparable across statistical measures, we may evaluate the different measures applied on the same data by comparing whether one n-gram is ranked higher or lower than another. Our intension is therefore to scrutinise the kinds of MWE candidates that are captured by each statistical measure, in an attempt to improve our understanding of the relation between statistical AMs and linguistic phenomena of MWEs, as observable in a large Norwegian dataset. To this end, we adopt a subset of the common statistical measures that are given in the UCS toolkit and in the NSP package. Although we follow the definitions given from these two sources, all calculations have been performed in Common LISP by the authors.

3. Methodology

3.1 Data and n-gram extraction

In order to apply statistical AMs, all word sequences in the NNC first had to be organised into lists of n-grams. In the description below, n-grams are represented in square brackets in which the first element is the frequency of the n-gram, and the rest is the sequence of words. For instance, the bigram [38759 *på forhånd*] tells us that the bigram *på forhånd* 'in advance, beforehand' occurred 38,759 times in the corpus.

In order to maximise the amount of text from which n-grams were extracted, we merged the texts from the NNC with Norwegian newspaper texts collected by the company Nordisk Språkteknologi. This additional dataset contains electronic

2. URL: http://www.d.umn.edu/tpederse/nsp.html. Last verified July 8, 2010.

text from the newspapers *Bergens Tidende, Aftenposten* and *VG* from the 1980s and 1990s. The two sources were combined in order to broaden the time span of the newspaper articles, and the resulting corpus material thus covers three decades and contains both Bokmål and Nynorsk, the two written standards of Norwegian.

The extraction of n-gram lists from the corpus of newspaper texts was done by Knut Hofland at Uni Computing. He first filtered out boilerplates and other elements that do not belong to the core text (Andersen & Hofland this volume). For the subsequent multiword extraction, only bigrams and trigrams have been considered so far, motivated by considerations of re-usability, allowing a user to modify the original list according to the specific needs of a given task. The n-grams were compiled according to the principle of keeping the data as unmodified as possible, in order to allow subsequent users of the data to modify the original n-gram lists according to the specific needs of a given task. Specifically, case-sensitivity was retained, i.e. n-grams that occur both with lower and upper case are counted separately, allowing for subsequent users to count them separately or collapse them into joint n-grams.

For the same reason, the n-grams also record all punctuation marks as separate tokens in a sequence. Finally, in this strictly corpus-driven approach, the extraction of n-grams or the subsequent analysis does not rely on any linguistic or other annnotation of the data, such as parts of speech, lemma information or the like.

3.2 Post-processing of n-gram lists

The initial analysis of the raw n-gram lists and preliminary experiments for MWE extraction revealed that it would be beneficial to filter the data by removing certain n-grams prior to the application of statistical AMs. First, more than half of the n-grams only occurred once in this large dataset, and we have no reason for claiming that they represent "recurrent" phenomena. Moreover the hapax legomena occupy much computer memory, and therefore only bigrams that occur more than once were extracted. Based on initial MWE experiments we decided to weed out all n-grams that occur less than 5 times. Only the results of applying AMs on this subset of n-grams are reported here.

Second, statistical AMs generally capture sequences of words that co-occur more often than would be expected by chance. Among the categories that are ranked high are multiword proper nouns and titles, which, for our current purposes are not seen as relevant. For instance, the upper-case version of the adjective form *Røde* 'Red' predominantly occurs in the sequence *Røde Kors* 'Red Cross'. We therefore needed to perform processing operations to remove or collapse n-grams according to their relevance.

Third, the preliminary experiments revealed another category of unwanted high-ranked items, namely string sequences that are not words but the result of formatting errors and boilerplates that should have been removed in the initial text processing. For example we found [*reC sultat*] as an erroneous division of the noun *resultat* 'result'. Although this erroneous collocation was not frequent overall, the AMs that favour low-frequent associations ranked such examples high. Thus, the n-gram lists to be used as input for the AMs were filtered according a set of rules, as described in points 1–5, in which each string separated by a space in an n-gram is referred to as a *token*):

1. *Only alphanumeric characters*: remove n-grams with non-alphanumeric characters ([*i 1998*] 'in 1998', [, *og*] ', and').
2. *Remove proper nouns*: Proper nouns are identified simply on the basis of case sensitivity and are discarded from the main file. An n-gram is assumed to be a proper noun if each token is capitalised (*Røde Kors*) or all letters are written in upper-case (*RØDE KORS, SAS Norge*), although we define some exceptions from this general rule (see main text below).
3. *Merging the frequencies of pairs of n-grams*: We merge the frequencies of n-grams pairs that are only distinguished by whether the first token is capitalised or not (*[Det er]* 'It is'–*[det er]* 'it is'), and we also merge the frequencies of n-gram pairs where an assumed non-proper noun has a capitalised/upper-case variant (see main text below).
4. *Remove erroneous word segmentations, when possible*: erroneous word segmentations such as *reC sultat* 'result' are removed by discarding all n-grams where the initial character is lower-case and one or more succeeding characters are upper-case.
5. *Frequency*: Of the remaining n-grams after filtering, remove n-grams that occur less than 5 times (a heuristic threshold).

It may be added that some n-grams were recorded both in upper-case (all-caps or capitalised) and lower-case. For instance, the proper noun *Røde Kors* had an appellative lower-case variant *røde kors*, whereas the adverbial *stort sett* 'generally' and the anglicism *easy listening* had upper-case variants (*STORT SETT* and *Easy Listening*, respectively).

In such cases, the most frequently used variant was taken to be the most probable one. If the lower-case variant is the most probable, we tentatively merged the frequencies of the case variants and then discarded the upper-case. In the opposite case (cf. *røde kors*–*Røde Kors*), both variants were filtered from our data file, since they were assumed to represent a proper noun. We also discarded n-grams where the latter token(s), but not the first one, are capitalised (*i Europa* 'in Europe').

Possible abbreviations – characterised by a period after each token (*dr. med.*) – were moved from the data file and moved to a separate list of proper noun candidates, for the benefit of future users of such a resource.

The size of the n-gram lists before and after filtering is shown in Table 1. The figures show the number of unique bigrams and trigrams, respectively, but do not show how many times each n-gram occurred in the corpus. The top row shows the total number of unique n-grams in the unfiltered list of n-grams occurring more than once. Rows two and three show the number of proper nouns and other items that were filtered out. The fourth row shows the number of remaining words after the filtering. It is this dataset that will be used for the statistical ranking of MWE candidates in this study.

As can be seen, the number of token combinations is much higher for trigrams than for bigrams. The high number of discarded proper nouns illustrates their preponderance in newspaper language.

Table 1. The number of n-grams (type level) before and after filtering proper nouns and other unwanted items

	Bigrams	**Trigrams**
n-grams (where $n > 1$) before filtering	24,512,294	62,040,589
discarded proper nouns	1,102,927	347,260
other discarded n-grams	8,476,622	29,063,290
n-grams after filtering (**where** $n \geq 5$)	4,945,930	8,542,891

It is worth pointing out that when weeding out elements *a priori*, as we have done here, this has consequences for the statistical basis for our study. We nevertheless believe that such a filtering of names and other unwanted material is necessary in order to enhance the extraction of relevant candidates for MWEs. The NSP package offers two alternatives: either include unwanted items while counting frequencies, but ignore them in the final ranked lists of MWE candidates, or alternatively – as we do – discard unwanted n-grams prior to frequency counts.

3.3 Contingency tables

Having filtered the list of n-grams, each remaining n-gram was associated with a set of observed frequencies and estimated frequencies. These frequency counts were conveniently plotted into a *contingency table* (henceforth CT). We will first consider the bigram CT and then the trigram CT.

3.3.1 *Bigram contingency tables*

Each observed frequency in a bigram CT is represented as a numeric value, o_{ij}, where *i* and *j* represent the presence (value=1) or absence (value=2) of each token in the n-gram. For instance, the value o_{11} tells how many times the bigram sequence [a b] occurred in the corpus, and o_{12} indicates how many times *a* occurred in n-grams without being followed by *b*. The marginal frequencies are the sums of each line: o_{1p} is the sum of $o_{11} + o_{12}$, and so on. Marginal frequencies are sometimes referred to as R1, R2, C1 and C2, respectively (cf. Table 2). O_{pp} is the sum of the marginal frequencies (sometimes the notation N is used), and thus sums up the total number of n-grams.

Table 2. Contingency table (CT) for a bigram [a b]: observed frequencies

	b	not b	
a	o_{11}	o_{12}	o_{1p} (R1)
not a	o_{21}	o_{22}	o_{2p} (R2)
	o_{p1} (C1)	o_{2p} (C2)	o_{pp} (N)

Each CT of observed frequencies has a parallel table of *estimated frequencies*, which provides the *expected* frequencies, given the null hypothesis that there is no association between the words in the given n-gram. If there is no association between *a* and *b* we would expect that the chance of seeing them together is proportional to the frequency of each of the tokens individually. Thus, if one or both tokens are highly frequent, then we may expect a high frequency for their estimated e_{11}, too.

Table 3. Contingency table for a bigram [a b]: estimated frequencies

	b	not b
a	$e_{11} = \frac{R1C1}{N}$	$e_{12} = \frac{R1C2}{N}$
not a	$e_{21} = \frac{R2C1}{N}$	$e_{22} = \frac{R2C2}{N}$

Table 4 contains a number of illustrative examples of bigrams and trigrams that we consider relevant for the purposes of lexicography or technical terminology, because they represent genuine MWEs, as well as some n-grams that are not relevant but nevertheless included in the table for comparison (bottom section of the table). Each n-gram is listed with the observed value of the full n-gram, and the number of times each word of the n-gram occurred in contexts other than the n-gram (bigrams: o_{11}, o_{12}, o_{21}; trigrams: o_{111}, o_{122}, o_{212} and o_{221}). Each expression in the table is given an English gloss in parenthesis. Due to their foreign origin, we consider multiword anglicisms as a separate category, which may subsume English-based technical terms (*due dilligence*) or other lexicalised items.

Table 4. Examples of bigram and trigram multiword expressions (MWEs). Observed frequencies (o_{11}) and the number of times each token occurs in this position

n-gram	o_{11}/o_{111}	o_{12}/o_{122}	o_{21}/o_{212}	o_{221}
Anglicisms:				
banana split (a dessert)	15	0	16	
due diligence (examination of company)	35	805	0	
practical jokes (a prank)	67	33	0	
corned beef (brine-cured beef)	78	0	16	
easy listening (music style)	85	129	13	
get a life (multiword discourse marker)	29	258	6298	403
Other foreign expressions:				
gefundenes fressen (Ger. 'delicacy, tidbit')	47	0	0	
in vitro (Lat. 'in a test tube')	66	14859	0	
quod erat demonstrandum (Lat. 'that which was to be demonstrated')	12	0	0	0
Terms:				
anaerob terskel 'anaerobic threshold' (medicine)	6	9	1429	
perfektum partisipp 'perfect participle' (linguistics)	8	0	4	
ulcerøs colitt 'inflammation' (medicine)	24	18	0	
notarius publicus 'public secretary' (law)	69	4	0	
per capita 'per head' (statistics)	96	43651	3	
trojansk hest 'virus, Trojan horse' (computing)	140	4	9546	
acute respiratory infection	5	0	5	0
Idioms:				
tilslørte bondepiker (a dessert)	50	68	4	
tenners gnissel 'despair'	106	23	5	

(Continued)

Table 4. (Continued)

n-gram	o_{11}/o_{111}	o_{12}/o_{122}	o_{21}/o_{212}	o_{221}
navns nevnelse 'by name'	156	16	2	
hellig ku 'holy cow'	277	5362	1593	
på fersken 'in the act'	1133	9051906	266	
i tide 'on time'	9527	16400611	18348	
på tide 'about time'	18199	9034840	9676	
rusk og rask 'bric-a-brac'	190	329	6650950	15421
katta i sekken 'buy a pig in a poke'	255	123	11940228	916
på kant med 'in opposition to'	1741	5985152	1299	5694890
rett og slett 'simply'	48827	161950	6598278	18904
Complex grammatical expressions (syntactically idiomatic):				
på forhånd 'in advance'	38769	9014270	22	
stort sett 'generally'	52403	159845	216228	
blant annet 'among other things'	257627	338086	208987	
på en måte 'in a way'	16600	5612405	7619609	94091
i motsetning til 'as opposed to'	26154	11463279	1304	7848663
i forhold til 'compared to, in relation to'	134768	11462650	55016	7811917
på grunn av 'because of, due to'	178525	5655710	146367	7170521
Multiword formulaic sequences that *are not* multiword expressions:				
på bananen 'on the banana'	5	9053034	74	
millioner kroner 'million NOK'	411623	245778	250644	
det er 'it is'	1170464	9424660	7343062	
jeg vil ikke 'I don't want to'	4738	1974296	1428425	3640209
grunn til å 'reason to'	85136	203451	5087841	7028596

Intuitively bigrams such as the phrasal anglicism *banana split* (a dessert), the linguistic term *perfektum partisipp* 'perfect participle' and the phrasal idiom *på fersken* 'red-handed, in the act' are more strongly associated than highly frequent formulaic multiword sequences such as *det er* 'it is' or less frequent syntactic phrases such as *på bananen* 'on the banana'. In other words, for our purposes a 'good' AM measure is one that ranks highly the members of the first-mentioned categories (seen in the upper five sections of Table 4), since they represent true MWEs.

For instance, the phrase [*på fersken*] may happen to instantiate a non-lexicalised regular prepositional phrase in a situated context (*tenke på fersken* 'think of a peach'), but the bigram is usually instantiations of an idiomatic expression that means 'red-handed, in the act'. In this meaning, one cannot insert anything between the two elements, nor can the noun be inflected and still convey the meaning of the idiom. By contrast, the bigram [*på bananen*] is intuitively just a regular prepositional phrase (cf. *tenke på bananen* 'think of the banana'). This is clear because the noun can be inflected and still retain the same lexical meaning, and a modifier may be inserted between the two bigram words (*på en uhyre liten banan* 'on an incredibly small banana').

As Table 4 shows, the bigram frequencies appear to reflect this intuition. Considering the anglicism and the linguistic term, the bigrams are not particularly frequent, but both tokens in both bigrams nonetheless occur more often in this particular collocation than in any other collocations. Comparing the observed frequencies of [*på fersken*] (idiom) and [*på bananen*] (prepositional phrase), we note that the idiomatic *på fersken* is by far more frequent than the non-lexicalised phrase (1,133 against 5, respectively).

3.3.2 *Trigram contingency tables*

Trigram contingency tables are more complicated since they are three-dimensional. To generate the trigram contingency tables, we re-implemented the NSP package in Common LISP. Given a trigram [a b c], where 1 denotes the presence of a token and 2 the absence of a token, the observed frequencies are shown in Table 5. The marginal and estimated frequencies are listed in Tables 6 and 7, respectively. As with bigrams, *p* means that the count is not conditioned by what appears in the position *p*.

Table 5. Contingency table for a trigram [a b c]: observed frequencies

		c	not c
a	b	o_{111}	o_{112}
a	not b	o_{121}	o_{122}
not a	b	o_{211}	o_{212}
not a	not b	o_{221}	o_{222}

Table 6. Marginal frequencies: trigrams (three-dimensional)

o_{1pp}, o_{p1p}, o_{pp1}	= the number of trigrams where the first token is *a*, *b* and *c*, respectively.
o_{2pp}, o_{p2p}, o_{pp2}	= the number of trigrams where the first token is **not** *a*, *b* and *c*, respectively.
o_{11p}, o_{1p1}, o_{p11}	= the number of trigrams where the first and second token; first and third token and second and third token are (respectively) *a–b*; *a–c* and *b–c*.
(the marginal frequencies o_{22p}, o_{2p2}, o_{p22} are not needed for any of the AMs)	
O_{ppp}	= the total number of occurrences of all trigrams.

3.4 Bigram association measures

For bigrams, our experiments mainly follow the definitions found in the UCS Toolkit[3]. Some of the statistical tests have several variants (for instance with and without statistical correction measures). In the following we provide all formulae, as implemented in Common LISP by the authors, and motivate the various choices that have been made. For each formula, an abbreviation is given in parenthesis. For a more thorough, theoretical discussion of the different measures, we refer to Evert (2004) and Banerjee and Pedersen (2003).

Table 7. Estimated frequencies: trigrams (three-dimensional). The o_{ppp} corresponds to the *N* value in the bigram contingency table, i.e. the total number of trigram occurrences

$e_{111} = \frac{o_{1pp} * o_{p1p} * o_{pp1}}{(o_{ppp})^2}$	$e_{222} = \frac{o_{2pp} * o_{p2p} * o_{pp2}}{(o_{ppp})^2}$	
$e_{112} = \frac{o_{1pp} * o_{p1p} * o_{pp2}}{(o_{ppp})^2}$	$e_{121} = \frac{o_{1pp} * o_{p2p} * o_{pp1}}{(o_{ppp})^2}$	$e_{211} = \frac{o_{2pp} * o_{p1p} * o_{pp1}}{(o_{ppp})^2}$
$e_{122} = \frac{o_{1pp} * o_{p2p} * o_{pp2}}{(o_{ppp})^2}$	$e_{212} = \frac{o_{2pp} * o_{p1p} * o_{pp2}}{(o_{ppp})^2}$	$e_{221} = \frac{o_{2pp} * o_{p2p} * o_{pp1}}{(o_{ppp})^2}$

Pearson's chi-squared homogeneity corrected $\left(X^2_{h,c}\right)$ Pearson's chi squared test (X^2) measures the difference between the observed values and the estimated values, i.e. those values one would expect if the tokens in the bigram were independent. The higher the score, the more strongly they are associated. It was chosen to implement a special version of the X^2 formula, namely the *chi-squared homogeneity corrected*, as this version, according to Evert (2004), is often used in applications.

$$X^2_{h,c} = \frac{N\left(\left|o_{11}o_{22} - o_{12}o_{21}\right| - \frac{N}{2}\right)^2}{R1R2C1C2} \tag{1}$$

Log-likelihood ratio (LL) The Log-likelihood ratio measures the difference between the observed values and the expected values. It is the sum of the ratio of the observed and expected values. According to Evert (2004), the Log-likelihood ratio is expected to perform better than the Pearson's chi-squared for lexical word

3. URL: http://www.collocations.de. Last verified July 8, 2010.

collocations, since lexical (as opposed to grammatical) words tend to have a low o_{11} in comparison to a generally high N value. The standard formula is:

$$\text{Log-likehood ratio} = 2 * \sum_{ij} o_{ij} \log(\frac{o_{ij}}{e_{ij}}) \tag{2}$$

Logarithmic Odds Rato$_{disc}$ (OR) The Logarithmic odds ratio returns the proportion between how many times the tokens in an n-gram co-occur and how many times each of the tokens occur individually. Since the logarithm is undefined if any of the numbers in the denominator (o_{21} or o_{22}) are zero, Evert (2004) proposes a 'discounting' technique by which 0.5 is added to every observed value (written in the formula below as $_{disc}$). As an alternative solution, Banerjee and Pedersen (2003) propose a "smooth-by-one" technique by which only zero values are replaced by 1. We chose to apply this latter discounting technique because Evert (2004) claims that since it produces slightly higher figures, it might be beneficial for low-frequency bigrams.

$$\text{Odds ratio}_{disc} = log \frac{(o_{11} + 0.5)(o_{22} + 0.5)}{(o_{12} + 0.5)(o_{21} + 0.5)} \tag{3}$$

Z-score (regular and corrected) (Z-s, Z-s$_{corr}$) The z-score is a relatively simple measure which computes a probability score for the observed frequency in comparison to the expected value. According to Evert (2004) it can be used to find "significant word pairs".

$$\text{z-score} = \frac{o_{11} - e_{11}}{\sqrt{e_{11}}} \tag{4}$$

A problem of the z-score measure is its use of the continuous normal distribution to approximate a discrete (binomial) distribution. According to Evert (2004), *Yates' continuity correction* improves this approximation by adjusting the observed frequencies according to the following rules, which we also implemented:

$$\text{z-score}_{corrected} = \frac{o_{11} - e_{11}}{\sqrt{e_{11}}} \begin{cases} o_{ij} - 0.5 & \text{if } o_{ij} > e_{ij}, \\ o_{ij} + 0.5 & \text{if } o_{ij} < e_{ij}. \end{cases} \tag{5}$$

Yates' continuity correction can be applied to all cells of the contingency table, although only o_{11} is relevant for the z-score measure.

T-score (T-s) Church et al. (1991) use the co-called Student's *t*-test as an alternative to the *z*-test. The t-score determines whether the association between two words is non-random, by computing the quotient of the observed and estimated value divided by the square root of the observed frequency value. As opposed to the z-test, the variance (the denominator) is estimated directly from data, and not through the estimated frequency. According to Evert (2004), the t-test is theoretically dubious for collocations and produces extremely conservative values.

$$\text{z-score} = \frac{o_{11} - e_{11}}{\sqrt{o_{11}}} \tag{6}$$

Pointwise Mutual Information (PMI) In general, Mutual Information ranks n-grams according to the principle of comparing the frequency of the MWE candidate to the frequency of the components of the MWE. This is expressed in the formula below in that the o_{11} value tells how often the sequence occurs, whereas the estimated value of the sequence is based on how often each of the two words in the sequence occur independently. This measure is biased towards low-frequency n-grams, i.e. n-grams where o_{11} is low (Evert 2004, Manning & Schütze 1999). The pointwise MI is calculated as follows:

$$\text{Pointwise MI} = \log(\frac{o_{11}}{e_{11}}) \tag{7}$$

Dice coefficient, Jaccard coefficient (D, J) The two measures Dice coefficient and Jaccard coefficient are often used in information retrieval technology and are easily calculated. The dice coefficient considers the frequency of a and b occurring together and their individual frequencies.

$$\text{Dice} = \frac{2o_{11}}{R1 + C1} \tag{8}$$

$$\text{Jaccard} = \frac{o_{11}}{o_{11} + o_{12} + o_{21}} \tag{9}$$

3.5 Trigram association measures

The calculations are not straightforward when treating sequences that are longer than bigrams. Banerjee and Pedersen (2003) list the following tests as suitable for trigrams: Log-likelihood ratio, Mutual Information, Pointwise Mutual Information and Poisson Stirling. The trigram measures below are based on the perl code of the NSP package.

Log-likelihood (LL) As with bigrams, the Log-likelihood method measures the tendency for words to co-occur by considering the deviation between observed and expected values for each observed value in (Table 5):

$$\text{Log-likelihood} = 2\sum_{ijk} o_{ijk} log \frac{o_{ijk}}{e_{ijk}} \tag{10}$$

Poisson-Stirling (PS) The Poisson-Stirling measure is computed as:

$$\text{Poisson-Stirling} = o_{111}(log(o_{111}) - \log(e_{111} - 1) \quad (11)$$

Pointwise Mutual Information (PMI) As with bigrams, Pointwise Mutual Information measures the association strength by considering the frequency of the MWE candidate in comparison to the frequency of the components of the expression.

$$\text{Pointwise Mutual Information} = \log_2(\frac{o_{111}}{e_{111}}) \quad (12)$$

True Mutual Information (TMI) True Mutual Information measures the extent to which the observed frequencies differ from the expected frequencies, by computing the weighted average of the pointwise mutual informations for all the observed and expected value pairs.

$$\text{True Mutual Information} = \sum_{ijk}(\frac{o_{ijk}}{N})(log_2\frac{o_{ijk}}{e_{ijk}}) \quad (13)$$

4. Results

4.1 Bigrams

In what follows, we will propose a grouping of the nine tested AMs for bigrams, according to their ability to rank bigrams that we perceive to be of high lexicographical or terminological relevance. First we compare how the different AMs rank the example bigrams in Table 4 using *Spearman's rank correlation coefficient*. Then we present an evaluation based on a manual inspection of the 500 most highly ranked items for each AM.

Given a set of n-grams which has been ranked by two different AMs, Banerjee and Pedersen (2003) suggest to compare the rankings using *Spearman's rank correlation coefficient*. The formula is given in Equation (14), in which r is the rank, n is the total number of n-grams considered and D_i is the difference between the rank assigned to an n-gram i by two different AMs (if an n-gram i was ranked second by the first AM and fourth by the second AM, then $D_i = 4-2 = 2$). An r value close to 1 indicates that the two measures rank n-grams in the same order,

-1 that the two rankings are exactly opposite to each other, and the value 0 indicates that they are not related.

$$r = 1 - \frac{6\sum_{i}^{n} D_i^2}{n(n^2 - 1)} \tag{14}$$

It was beyond the scope of the present experiments to run comparisons on the entire material (almost 5 million bigrams); instead a pairwise comparison of the AMs was run based on the list of example bigrams in Table 4. As will be shown below, the results from this sample-based comparison seem to concord with the general findings when considering the top-ranked bigrams for each AM. With nine bigram measures and 36 combinations, we only present the main conclusions from the Spearman's comparison.

Ranking all 36 *r* scores from 1 to -1, a clear "upper ten" of AM comparisons is singled out with values in the range of 0.99–0.77. For instance, the highest *r* value was found when comparing the Z-score and Z-score$_{corrected}$ (r=0.9993162), which indicates that they are very similar in how they rank the set of example bigrams. The next (11th) *r* score is as low as 0.36. Among the top ten most similar AMs, some of them have direct or indirect links (cf. the way the *r* score close to 1 linked Z-score and Z-score$_{corrected}$) whereas others are never linked to each other. Thus, three clusters of AMs with a similar behaviour are suggested through Spearman's, as itemised below. Based on the small example set of bigrams, the Chi-squared$_{corr}$ measure is "the odd one out" and is not found to be similar to any other measure. Its highest score is 0.36 (which was in comparison to Dice), but being closer to 0 this value rather indicates unrelatedness.

- Z-score, Z-score$_{corr}$, PMI and Odds Ratio
- Log-Likelihood and T-score
- Jaccard and Dice
- Chi-squared$_{corr}$

In order to analyse the behaviour of each association measure in more detail, all the 500 top-ranked MWEs for each AM were classified manually according to the following set of categories: *anglicism MWE*, *foreign MWE*, *grammatical MWE*, *idiomatic phrase*, *concept structure appositional phrase*, *term candidate* (examples of each category are given below). Thus we may analyse the kinds of MWEs singled out by each AM. The findings for the bigram AMs are summed up in Figure 2 (which excludes n-grams that were not classified as belonging to any of the mentioned catgories).

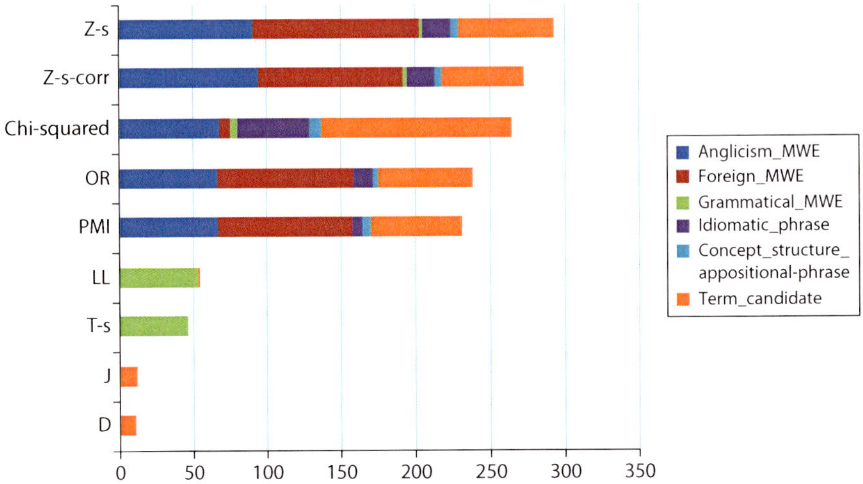

Figure 1. A manual classification of the 500 top ranked MWEs for each bigram Association Measure (AM)

The manual analysis indicates that there are major differences between the different measures in their ability to retrieve bigrams that are considered terminologically of lexicographically relevant. Starting at the bottom of the figure, two AMs, Dice and Jaccard, are only able to retrieve a very limited number of lexicographically or terminologically relevant items, amounting to a mere 2 per cent of the manually inspected ranked n-grams, including *langvarig konjunkturoppgang* 'sustained cyclical expansion' and *maritime industri* 'maritime manufacturing'. Two measures, T-score and Log Likelihood, are particularly suited for detecting grammatical MWEs and not any other MWE types. The retrieved items include multiword adverbials and prepositions such as *for eksempel* 'for example', *i tillegg* 'in addition', *etter hvert* 'gradually' and *blant annet* 'among others' as well as one phrasal verb, *regne(r) med* 'take into account'. Their respective 10.8 and 9.2 per cent must be considered a high proportion of grammatical MWEs, given that this is a semi-closed category, which generally can be expected to have fewer members than open categories such as nouns, which is where most terms would be included.

The remaining five AMs are all relatively successful in retrieving lexically and terminologically relevant items, ranging from 46.2 (PMI) to 58.6 per cent (Z-score regular). One of these measures, Pearson's chi square, is particularly able to pick out term candidates, including *alternative energikilder* 'alternative energy sources' and *blokkerende mindretall* 'blocking minority' as well as appositional noun phrases of the type *tungmetallet cadmium* 'the heavy metal cadmium', which we also consider to be relevant for term extraction purposes since it gives not only a term but also its superordinate concept. The other four measures are to a lesser degree able to identify domestically based term candidates but are better than Pearson's at extracting MWEs (including terms) of foreign or English origin, such as *consumer confidence, joint ventures, annus horribilis* and *garam masala*.

The similarities and differences between the AMs might be better understood by considering the frequency patterns that tend to be ranked high with the different AMs. Table 8 shows the top ten ranked bigrams of four AMs that seem well-suited for the identification of extracting MWEs (including terms) of foreign or English origin, namely Pointwise Mutual Information, Odds Ratio$_{discr}$, Z-score and Z-score$_{corr}$. Recall that we set a lower threshold of 5 tokens; hence no bigrams occurring fewer times are included in the tables. These four measures favour bigrams where the o_{11} is low, and where the individual words of the bigrams only occur in the context of this particular bigram, as can be seen from the contingency figures of almost all n-grams in Table 8.

(It may be noted that if several bigrams have the same statistical score in the leftmost column, they are simply ranked alphabetically, for instance this applies to the PMI and the Z-score measure).

We note that the n-grams typically consist of words that only occur in this particular expression, which we would expect to be the case for xenomorphic MWEs. Several of the English-based n-grams that are highly ranked with these measures indeed represent technical terminology from different professional domains. This includes anglicisms such as *rollon rolloff* 'ships designed to carry wheeled cargo', *unit linked* 'a type of (insurance) fund' and *whistle blower* 'person who alerts about a wrongdoing', which are linked to shipping and the economic-administrative domains.

By contrast, multiword anglicisms that are part of the general vocabulary do not achieve a particularly high rank according to these four measures, due to the higher overall frequency of the n-grams and their components, of which *body lotion* (9 – 78 – 12), *dark horse* (153 – 28 – 22), *sudden death* (1158 – 5 – 261) and *all right* (738 – 147517 – 370)) are notable examples.

Furthermore, Latin expressions tend to dominate in these lists, and the most highly ranked items are drawn from technical terminology rather than general language. In the top ten lists we find for instance the biological term *tussilago farfara*, which is the Latin name of the flower coltsfoot, and the medical term *Retinitis pigmentosa* 'an eye disease'. There are also terms of Norwegian origin among these highly ranked n-grams, such as the biological *rødøret terrapin* 'red-eared terrapin' (a turtle) and the medical *radiær keratotomy* 'eye surgery'. Incidentally, these lists also highlight the importance of detecting and investigating longer n-grams before shorter ones. For instance, *twam asi* is part of the Sanskrit sentence *tat tvam asi* 'that thou art', while the bigram *jaska beana* is part of the Sami sentence (which is also the title of a song) *oro jaska beana* 'be quiet, dog'.

Pearson's chi-square could have been grouped with those in Table 8, but we list it alone (Table 9) since it is particularly well-suited to single out domestically based term candidates. The vast majority of highly ranked n-grams with this are straightforward phrases with rather low overall frequencies, such as *knus hvitløken* 'crush the garlic' and *buddhistiske munker* 'Buddhist monks'. However, we do find the odd n-gram of terminological relevance, namely the medical term *obstructive lungesykdommer* 'obstructive lung diseases' and the biology term *tissue engineering*.

Table 8. Top ten ranked bigrams: 4 AMs favouring low-frequent associations

Pointwise Mutual Information (PMI)				
18.409534	vilkårsett skattefritaking	5	0	0
18.409534	varannan damernas	5	0	0
18.409534	unio mystica	5	0	0
18.409534	twam asi	5	0	0
18.409534	tussilago farfara	5	0	0
18.409534	suvas bohciidit	5	0	0
18.409534	skrimmi nimmi	5	0	0
18.409534	rollon rolloff	5	0	0
18.409534	rødøret terrapin	5	0	0
18.409534	radiær keratotomi	5	0	0
Odds Ratio$_{discr}$ (OR)				
25.34685	chop suey	51	0	0
25.265997	gefundenes fressen	47	0	0
24.916813	nobis pacem	33	0	0
24.855255	jaska beana	31	0	0
24.789658	lorem lipsum	29	0	0
24.75517	lipsum lorem	28	0	0
24.75517	hæ hæ	28	0	0
24.603941	retinitis pigmentosa	24	0	0
24.518784	eines fahrenden	22	0	0
24.425692	haemophilus influenzae	20	0	0

(Continued)

Table 8. (Continued)

Z-score (Z-s)				
22236.418	byssan lull	15	0	0
22236.416	yada yada	6	0	0
22236.416	whistle blowers	7	0	0
22236.416	visibility corp	6	0	0
22236.416	vilkårsett skattefritaking	5	0	0
22236.416	varannan damernas	5	0	0
22236.416	utsletti respateksbord	8	0	0
22236.416	unio mystica	5	0	0
22236.416	uisge beatha	11	0	0
22236.416	twam asi	5	0	0
Z-score$_{corr}$ (Z-s$_{corr}$)				
22018.41	chop suey	51	0	0
21999.857	gefundenes fressen	47	0	0
21899.498	nobis pacem	33	0	0
21877.762	jaska beana	31	0	0
21862.246	hokus pokus	263	6	2
21853.03	lorem lipsum	29	0	0
21839.336	lipsum lorem	28	0	0
21839.336	hæ hæ	28	0	0
21773.154	retinitis pigmentosa	24	0	0
21744.455	unit linked	111	2	2

Table 9. Top ten ranked bigrams for Pearson's Chi-square

Chi-squared$_{h,corr}$ ($X^2_{h,c}$)				
9996430.0	ss tomatpure	220	5361	207
9996173.0	knus hvitløken	22	63	247
9983254.0	våpentekniske korps	88	62	2440
9983179.0	obstruktive lungesykdommer	10	0	437
9980703.0	all sannsynlighet	5164	143091	3739
9980339.0	red anm	87	1864	103
9980115.0	buddhistiske munker	112	400	1091
9967788.0	ferjefritt veisamband	9	55	47
9966970.0	nordatlantiske fiskeriorganisasjonen	22	446	27
9962959.0	tissue engineering	5	0	196

The next category of AM measures, in Table 10, includes AMs that seem to favour grammatical MWEs, namely the Log-likelihood ratio and the T-score. These lists predominantly consist of highly frequent formulaic sequences of lexical and function words with a low relevance to lexicograpical or terminological purposes. Virtually all of them consist of at least one function word, e.g. prepositions (*på* 'on, at', *til* 'to, for'), the infinitive marker (*å* 'to'), subjunctions (*at* 'that', *som* 'which'), etc.

According to Evert (2004), the Log-likelihood ratio works better when bigrams containing grammatical words are ignored. However, given our strict corpus-driven method, we did not exclude any items on the basis of syntactic category. If we isolate only the Log-likelihood bigrams where both components are lexical words, i.e. verbs, nouns, adjectives or adverbs, or combinations thereof, the top-ranked items seem to have a varying degree of lexicalised status. Some, like *millioner kroner* 'million NOK', are clearly not lexicalised MWEs, while others, like *administrerende direktør* 'managing director', can be seen to have terminological value in the economic-administrative domains. In other words, we cannot rule out the relevance of these three AMs for the identification of multiword lexemes and terminology.

However, and importantly, these AMs do appear to be capable of identifying highly frequent MWEs that are grammatically significant, namely multiword prepositions. An example of this is *blant annet* 'among other things', which is ranked among the top ten in two of the AMs in Table 10. In passing, we ought to mention that it may be fruitful in a future study to test all AMs on lists of n-grams that solely contain lexical words, and lists of n-grams where at least one of the words is a lexical word.

Table 10. Top ten ranked bigrams: 2 AMs favouring grammatical MWEs

Log-likelihood				
6512751.0	til å	1965359	6805145	8333315
6221586.0	for å	1904212	6759186	8394462
4913251.0	millioner kroner	411623	245778	250644
3253937.2	å få	642768	9800294	634097
3172030.5	at det	1233788	6813598	8599093
2953856.0	blant annet	257627	338086	208987
2943812.0	har vært	544440	7822106	575711
2596295.2	det er	1170464	9424660	7343062
2009919.6	at han	619027	7428359	2766184
1954526.4	løpet av	264615	21286	9123515

(Continued)

Table 10. (Continued)

T-score				
1271.6094	til å	1965359	6805145	8333315
1249.1697	for å	1904212	6759186	8394462
966.686	at det	1233788	6813598	8599093
913.2606	det er	1170464	9424660	7343062
850.10693	er det	1205511	12478853	8627370
768.0912	å få	642768	9800294	634097
716.75714	at han	619027	7428359	2766184
712.1745	har vært	544440	7822106	575711
709.274	at de	671512	7375874	4876299
686.3624	som er	803092	10116108	7710434

Table 11 shows the top ten bigrams for the final two AMs, Dice and Jaccard, which only seem to identify very few terminologically relevant items. By and large they seem to extract a bit of a 'word salad' not particularly fitted for any of our needs. Characteristic for them is that the high-ranked bigrams are mainly composed of lexical, as opposed to grammatical words.

Table 11. Top ten ranked bigrams: 2 final AMs, not well-suited for MWEs

Dice (D)				
0.001	engasjerende valgkamp	7	1225	12761
0.001	folk sa	251	368926	132572
0.001	froskemenn lette	11	437	21541
0.001	innkalle statsråden	9	2764	15218
0.001	konsernet realiserte	6	11549	439
0.001	manglende gjennomslag	28	41751	14193
0.001	militæret opplyser	18	2744	33220
0.001	overveie konsekvensene	11	1667	20311
0.001	strengere sikkerhetsforskrifter	7	13857	129
0.001	undersøkt påstander	15	11606	18364
Jaccard (J)				
0.001	arrangerte seminar	14	5815	8171
0.001	begår voldelige	11	3945	7044
0.001	fekk raudt	8	7906	86

(Continued)

Table 11. Top ten ranked bigrams: 2 final AMs, not well-suited for MWEs (Continued)

Jaccard (J)				
0.001	flott representant	49	26459	22492
0.001	hjemlige filmmiljø	6	5790	204
0.001	høyerestående planter	7	203	6790
0.001	human kapital	19	1115	17866
0.001	kapitalistisk ånd	5	545	4450
0.001	konfliktene oppstår	21	3928	17051
0.001	lidende dyret	5	868	4127

4.2 Trigrams

As with bigrams, we compared how the different AMs rank the example trigrams in Table 4 using *Spearman's rank correlation coefficient*; then the 500 most highly ranked items for each AM were manually inspected. The Spearman's comparison did not shed much light on the relation between the four AMs being compared, maybe due to the low number of trigram examples in the comparison. Based on the manual evaluation, on the other hand, there seem to be striking differences between the four different trigam AMs in their ability to pick out word sequences that are of terminological or lexicographical relevance (Table 2).

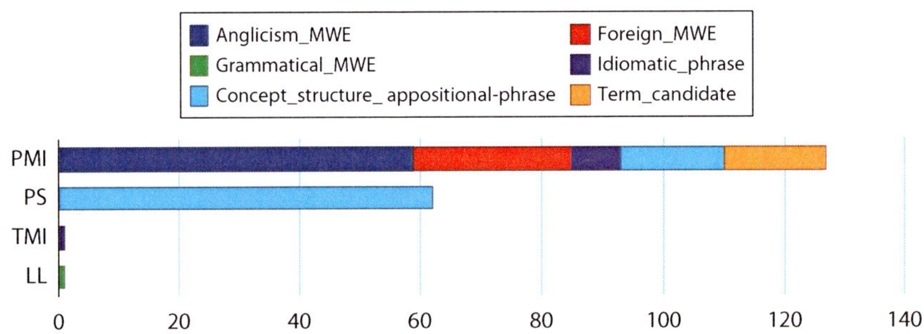

Figure 2. A manual classification of the 500 top ranked MWEs for each trigram Association Measure

Based on the analysis of the 500 top-ranked items, two of the AMs, Log-likelihood (LL) and True Mutual Information (TMI), were unable to rank highly any relevant items, with the exception of one token each, the idiomatic phrase *grøss og gru* 'shiver and horror' (TMI) and the phrasal verb *kommer til å* 'is going to' which counts as a grammatical MWE (LL). To give an indication of the kinds of items ranked highly with these measures, the top ten trigrams with these two measures are listed in Tables 12 (LL) and 13 (TMI).

Table 12. Top ten ranked trigrams: Log-likelihood

Log-likelihood					
	AM-score	o_{111}	o_{1pp}	o_{p1p}	o_{pp1}
til å få	9680734.0	47806	6391902	9844607	1099442
for å få	9259922.0	204938	6485314	9844607	1099442
til å ha	8226067.0	26364	6391902	9844607	1058478
til å ta	7820512.0	71232	6391902	9844607	505870
for å ha	7761713.0	100968	6485314	9844607	1058478
til å bli	7748718.0	85448	6391902	9844607	922553
til å være	7624434.0	61043	6391902	9844607	1164046
til å gjøre	7609440.0	39591	6391902	9844607	393839
til å i	7546252.0	76	6391902	9844607	15570426
for å ta	7411975.5	35027	6485314	9844607	505870

As we also saw with bigrams, the Log-likelihood tends to assign a high rank to high-frequency items which include grammatical words and which are formulaic sequences rather than lexicalised phrases (*for å få* 'in order to get', *til å ha* 'to have/having'). According to McInnes (2004), Log-likelihood generally encounters problems with large sample sizes. Since the marginal values will then be very large, the expected values are increased, yielding extremely low observed values compared to the expected values. Paradoxically, this means that very independent and strongly dependent n-grams may end up with the same values. She notices similar characteristics with true mutual information; if this is true this may mean that these AMs are not well-suited for our material. The top-ranked trigrams with TMI are rather reminiscent of the 'word salad' that we saw for Dice and Jaccard with bigrams. To illustrate, the three top trigrams in Table 13 are translated as 'us the necessary confidence', 'researchers that a', 'end the boycott of', respectively.

As seen in Figure 2, based on the manual inspection of the 500 top-ranked items using Poisson-Stirling, this measure is highly capable of picking out one specific type, namely grammatical MWEs, as 12.4 per cent of the inspected trigrams were of this category, and no other categories were represented. Its top ten

Table 13. Top ten ranked trigrams: True Mutual Information

True Mutal Information	AM-score	o_{111}	o_{1pp}	o_{p1p}	o_{pp1}
oss nødvendig selvtillit	9.999997e – 7	5	329746	83870	7994
forskere at et	9.999991e – 8	7	14296	6738145	3119515
avslutte boikotten av	9.999989e – 6	10	6383	1826	7602876
det store endringer	9.9999845e – 5	69	10219653	478697	31431
politiske strid i	9.9999794e – 5	11	99326	39182	15570426
om hvorvidt amerikanerne	9.999977e – 5	11	3391818	12656	12779
er kjent ugyldig	9.999971e – 5	52	11305572	152137	1956
an å bygge	9.999971e – 4	156	51684	9844607	91208
vei et lavt	9.99997e – 6	5	99877	3552803	15550
han kræsjet med	9.999967e – 6	8	3596157	154	5800181

trigrams are given in Table 14 to give an idea of the kinds of frequencies that yield a high rank with this measure. Grammatical MWEs are exemplified by complex prepositions like *i løpet av* 'in the course of' and *i forbindelse med* 'in connection with', and adverbs like *først og fremst* 'first and foremost', etc.

Finally, Pointwise Mutual Information is a more versatile measure that is capable of picking out a variety of MWEs, totalling 25.4 per cent of its 500 most highly ranked items. Note that no types representing grammatical MWEs were picked out by this AM. This shows very clearly the need for selecting

Table 14. Top ten ranked trigrams: Poisson-Stirling

Poisson-Stirling	AM-score	o_{111}	o_{1pp}	o_{p1p}	o_{pp1}
i løpet av	1607657.0	263659	11929615	278965	7602876
på grunn av	1110109.4	178525	6090499	327900	7602876
for å få	988856.9	204938	6485314	9844607	1099442
at det er	897022.25	259845	7064920	9035186	5503500
når det gjelder	848167.8	102058	783030	9035186	151384
i forbindelse med	845152.0	133840	11929615	149389	5800181
først og fremst	828941.2	81313	236761	6652225	82358
i forhold til	746500.1	134768	11929615	227855	8315633
etter å ha	620644.8	105565	1209267	9844607	1058478
ferd med å	589744.1	85702	88570	4773377	8883188

the right AM depending on the specific objectives of the term extraction or lexical acquisition. However, all the other types were identified. The multiword anglicisms include multiword terms from various domains such as *hypertext markup language*, *deficit hyperactivity disorder*, *joint stock companies*, *checks and balances*, *frequently asked questions*, *catch and release* and *stream of consciousness*, as well as other salient multiword anglicisms of a more general nature, such as *worst case scenario* and *trick or treat*. The foreign multiword trigrams are especially culinary terms, such as *gambas al ajillo*, *spaghetti alla carbonara*, *chili con carne*, *biff chop suey*, *cafe au lait* and *pain au chocolat*, but also include terms from other domains such as *homo sapiens sapiens* and *tae kwon doe*, and also more general foreign multiwords such as *quod erat demonstrandum*, *cage aux folles* and *persona non grata*. Further, this AM picks out idiomatic phrases like the formulaic *snipp snapp snute* (used at the conclusion of fairy tales) and *bitte litte granne* 'teeny weeny bit'. The term candidates are mostly from medicine and include *viral hemoragisk septikemi*, *amyotrofisk lateral sklerose* and *hemolytisk uremisk syndrom*.

The top ten ranked trigrams using Pointwise Mutual Information can be inspected in Table 15, showing that it seems to be capable of extracting relevant term candidates. The top-ranked item is a proper noun written in lower-case that failed to be weeded out during filtering. The second item illustrates the importance of looking for longer sequences before approaching trigrams and bigrams. *nil nisi bene* is part of the Latin proverb *de mortuis nil nisi bene* (approximately: '(speak) of the dead only good'), whereas *ludens nomadic machines* is part of the sequence *Homo Ludens Nomadic Machines*. The third item is a term referring to a

Table 15. Top ten ranked trigrams: Pointwise Mutal Information

Pointwise Mutal Information	AM-score	o_{111}	o_{1pp}	o_{p1p}	o_{pp1}
lars myhren holand	51.51715	6	6	6	6
nil nisi bene	51.195225	5	5	5	9
viral hemoragisk septikemi	51.102116	6	8	6	6
remote operated vehicle	51.102116	6	6	8	6
geht besser nun	51.102116	6	8	6	6
acute respiratory infection	51.043217	5	5	10	5
ludens nomadic machines	50.932186	6	6	6	9
zero visibility corp	50.905716	5	11	5	5
sub specie aeternitatis	50.709797	7	9	7	7
hypertext markup language	50.401676	6	6	6	13

fish disease, other terms are *acute respiratory infection* (medicine) and – below the top ten – *file transfer protocol* (computers).

5. Conclusion and future work

This paper has approached multiword expressions by applying statistical association measures to two- and three word sequences (bigrams and trigrams) from the Norwegian Newspaper Corpus. To this end, lists of bigrams and trigrams were compiled, and they were pre-filtered for proper nouns and other named entities. This was necessary since statistical measures of collocation strength capture a wide range of phenomena, among these named entities. Another way of looking at it is to say that proper nouns are easily detected, by virtue of getting high ranks, by the same measures that work well for n-grams where the observed frequency of the components outside of the n-gram is low.

Based on our observations when testing nine different AMs on bigrams and four different ones on trigrams, the following conclusions seem justifiable. First, there are great differences with respect to the different AMs' abilities to extract n-grams that are relevant for lexicographical and terminological purposes, and a grouping of AMs according to these abilities has been proposed. Second, a necessary methodological strategy for future work is to begin with the longest sequences using a methodology for weeding out longer-sequence n-grams before moving to shorter-sequence n-grams. Third, future work should also aim at testing the AMs on a morphologically analysed version of the corpus, to test the different AMs on lists of n-grams that contain at least one lexical word or exclusively lexical words, to see if this may improve the performance of some of the AMs.

References

Abney, Steven. 2000. *Statistical methods*. London: Macmillian.

Baldwin, Timothy. 2004. Multiword Expressions. Advanced course at the Australasian Language Technology Summer School (ALTSS 2004), Sydney, Australia.

Baldwin, Timothy and Bond, Francis. 2002. Multiword Expressions: Some Problems for Japanese NLP. In *The Eigth Annual Meeting of the Association of Natural Language Processing*, 379–382. Keihanna.

Baldwin, Timothy and Su Nam Kim. 2010. Multiword Expressions. In N. Indurkhya and F.J. Damerau, eds., *Handbook of Natural Language Processing, Second Edition*, 267–292. Boca Raton, FL: CRC Press, Taylor and Francis Group.

Banerjee, Satanjeev and Pedersen, Ted. 2003. The design, implementation, and use of the n-gram statistic package. In *Proceedings of the Fourth International Conference on Intelligent Text Processing and Computational Linguistics*, 370–381. Mexico City.

Biber, Douglas. 2009. A corpus-driven approach to formulaic language in English: Multi-word patterns in speech and writing. *International Journal of Corpus Linguistics* 14(3): 275–311.

Biber, Douglas, Johansson, Stig, Leech, Geoffrey, Conrad, Susan, Finegan, Edward, and Hirst, Graeme. 1999. Longman Grammar of Spoken and Written English. London: Longman.

Church, Kenneth, Gale, William, Hanks, Patrick, and Hindle, Donald. 1991. Using statistics in lexical analysis. In *Lexical Acquisition: Exploiting On-Line Resources to Build a Lexicon*, 115–164. Erlbaum.

Evert, Stefan. 2004. *The Statistics of Word Co-occurrences: Word Pairs and Collocations*. Ph.D. thesis, IMS, University of Stuttgart.

Fellbaum, Christiane, ed. 1998. *WordNet. An Electronical Lexical Database*. MIT Press.

Jackendoff, Ray. 1997. *The Architecture of the Language Faculty*. Cambridge, MA: The MIT Press.

Manning, Christopher and Schütze, Hinrich. 1999. *Foundations of Statistical Natural Language Processing*. Cambridge: Massachusetts: MIT Press.

McInnes, Bridget T. 2004. *Extending the Log Likelihood Measure to Improve Collocation Identification*. Master's thesis, University of Minnesota.

Sag, Ivan, Baldwin, Timothy, Bond, Francis, Copestake, Ann, and Flickinger, Dan. 2002. Multiword expressions: A pain in the neck for NLP. In *Proceedings of the Third International Conference on Intelligent Text Processing and Computational Linguistics*. Mexico City, Mexico.

Sinclair, John M. 1991. *Corpus, Concordance, Collocation*. Oxford: Oxford University Press.

Sinclair, John M. 1996. The search for units of meaning. *Textus* 9:75–106.

Stubbs, Michael. 1996. *Text and corpus analysis*. London: Blackwell.

Tognini-Bonelli, Elena. 2001. *Corpus Linguistics at Work*. Amsterdam: John Benjamins.

Automatic topic classification of a large newspaper corpus

Thomas M. Hagen
Uni Computing

This paper describes how machine learning methods, along with a limited amount of manual classification, were used in a fairly successful attempt to automatically classify, by topic, newspaper articles from The Norwegian Newspaper Corpus.

The Norwegian Newspaper Corpus is a challenge to automatically classify, since not all of it has been boilerplate cleaned. Our automatic topic classifier achieved 54% accuracy, while our human annotators achieved only slightly more; 59% accuracy.

We used several machine learning methods built into the programming language CRM114. We used used six annotators, who manually classified 1,400 articles from the corpus. The machine learner trained only on errors it made when attempting to classify these articles.

1. Introduction

The Norwegian Newspaper Corpus consists of articles from 10 Norwegian newspapers harvested from the web since the late nineties. The harvesting is ongoing (Andersen & Hofland this volume), and more newspapers are being added to the collection. The corpus contained about 850 million words at the time of these experiments.

To facilitate relevant research, the corpus is annotated with morphosyntactic and other metadata (Andersen & Hofland this volume). One of the attributes is the topic of the newspaper articles. Topic classification is a demanding routine task. Hence the need for an automatic topic classifier.

The material contained in the corpus is quite varied, both in content and format, which makes automatic topic classification quite difficult. Even deciding which texts to include in the corpus, and which to exclude, was fodder for discussion during the work.

This paper is organized as follows: Section 2 describes the background and related work and Section 3 contains a description of the material used. Section 4 discusses the overview of our approach, while Section 5 discusses our approach in more detail, and contains an introduction to the CRM114 programming language used in the project (Yerazunis 2006). Section 6 discusses the datasets and experimental evaluation, Section 7 describes achieved results, and finally, Section 8 concludes and gives suggestions for future work.

2. Background and related work

A general observation that has been made in the field of topic classification is that classification is relatively easy when features are well defined and static. However, when the features are dynamic, and interpretation of them is left to the classifier itself, things become more difficult (Masud et al. 2009). Historically, support vector machines and k-nearest neighbour have been the most successful approaches to automatic topic classification (Folch et al. 2000; Yang & Liu 1999). Naive Bayesian, or Markovian classifiers, have been used for similar tasks, most notably for spam detection, which is a two-category genre classification problem (Graham 2002, 2003; Zdziarski 2005). Currently, Deep Boltzmann Machines appear to be a very good machine learning method for pattern recognition, but they have, as yet, not been applied directly to topic classification. They have, however, been used for document retrieval, resulting in a 2-dimensional plot of mostly discrete category variables (Salakhutdinov & Hinton 2009).

There are two basic approaches to automatic classification; rule-based and pattern matching, described below.

2.1 The rule-based approach

The rule-based approach is *ad hoc* and brittle. Rule-based systems cannot adapt to changes in style, unless explicit exceptions are introduced. Each such exception will, of course, introduce further vulnerability to change. Rule-based systems are also limited to formal knowledge, as they cannot generate their own.

If we were to use rule-based systems, there would be a large initial burden on the developer, since we would have to rely on insufficient *a priori* assumptions as to which features distinguish various categories from each other in each domain.

When using rule-based systems, a large part of the work is defining what features to use. This would be a difficult, time-consuming and error-prone phase.

Furthermore, creating a rule-based system forces the developer to wear two hats; he must be an expert in the formal knowledge of the field, as well as being adept at coding this knowledge into a program.

If two people were to collaborate, i.e. one expert and one implementer, such a setup would impose considerable communication constraints.

An advantage of rule-based systems is that they place little burden on the computer. However, now that computers are becoming powerful enough to do robust pattern matching, there is no need for this tradeoff. Thus, rule-based automatic classification was ruled out in this project.

2.2 The pattern-matching approach

Pattern matching methods make their own internal model of the input, and could be constructed so the model adapts as the input changes (Scholz & Klinkenberg 2005; Wang et al. 2008).

Four different pattern matching or machine learning approaches are typically used for topic classification; k-nearest neighbor, neural networks, support vector machines, and Bayesian filtering. Common to all four is that there are two phases; training and classification.

Also, all four methods use the same basic approach; when classifying, they consider the features (words, html tags, formatting, etc.) in each text, and try to determine which pre-defined category most resembles that text. The underlying insight is that the words and names that appear, and the way they appear together, in a sports article will differ from the composition of words and names in an article about culture.

Bayesian filtering evaluates the probability that each word will occur in a certain category. It then adds the probabilities for all or some of the words together, according to Bayes' theorem, in order to find the total probability that the article belongs to a certain category. It does this for all categories, and the one with the highest probability is selected.

As an example of Bayesian filtering common in spam filtering techniques, the word 'Viagra' would have a score of, say, 0.999, indicating it was spam. An *a priori* threshold could be set for instance at 0.9, and every text above that would be considered spam. If, now, the word 'scam', which might have a score of 0.07, also appeared in the text, things would change. In that case, the two probabilities would be combined, and the result would be that, based on those two words alone, the text in question is probably non-spam, because the overall probability score would be below the 0.9 threshold.

Markovian filtering is a variant of Bayesian filtering that also takes into account the order of the words appearing in the article (Puterman 2005). A window of, say, five words is moved along the text, and each five-word sequence is examined to find the probability that it belongs in a certain category. A variant of this is to use sparse matrices, which do not store the whole five word window, but only the unique two-word pairs in each window.

K-nearest neighbor (Daelemans & van den Bosch 2005) and support vector machines (Vapnik & Kotz 2006; Joachims 2002; Shawe-Taylor & Christianini

2000) are variants of the same method. They both place each article in an n-dimensional space, and try to determine the distance to other articles based on the aggregate of features in the article. Thus, they store much more information for each article learned in the training phase, and the training material must therefore be smaller than for Markovian.

Neural networks are useful, but demand a lot of tuning in order to be effective. They have the ability to store enormous amounts of information, since they store models of the real world as simple relations of differing numerical value between a (relatively) non-increasing number of artificial neurons. The programming language used in our experiments, CRM114, allows for implementation of all these methods.

2.3 Promising results

Hillard et al. (Hillard 2008) and Purpura et al. (Purpura 2006) report accuracies of 78 per cent with a very large training material. Hillard and Purpura used roughly 400,000 US Congress bill titles classified by highly trained annotators with years of experience, while we used roughly 1,400 Norwegian newspaper articles classified by untrained annotators.

Purpura and Hillard achieved the above accuracy on 21 main categories, and about 71 per cent on 226 subcategories, of US Congress bills (Purpura 2006). They then refined their accuracies to 87 per cent with limited aid from highly trained annotators (Hillard 2008). They first used a Support Vector Machine, and later an ensemble of three automatic classifiers; SVM, MaxEnt and Boostexter.

3. Material

The Norwegian Newspaper Corpus consists of about 2.7 million articles, so the training material could have been vast if we had chosen unsupervised training. Since we used supervised training, we had to create a training set from scratch.

Since The Norwegian Newspaper Corpus has not been completely boilerplate-cleaned, the vast majority of articles contain boilerplate, html tags and Javascript in addition to the text itself. For our first approach, we decided to use these as they were, and feed everything into the learner.

Boilerplate is a catch-all term for anything that is not really a relevant part of a text, and should be removed. For a newspaper article, this includes things like ads, links to similar articles, disclaimers and instructions. On the other hand, things like captions and bylines are relevant, and should be kept. Boilerplate removal is a non-trivial problem which is far from solved.

For our second approach, we chose to use articles stripped of boilerplate, html and Javascript. This greatly reduced the size of data the learner had to store, which turned out to be a considerable advantage, since the size of the learner's statistics files (see Section 5.3) is limited.

We also tried training on texts that had been annotated with metadata (but not with topic category).

We changed the number and nature of the categories between the first and second approach, so some work had to be done remapping the gold standard (see Section 3.4) manually. Fortunately, some of it could be done automatically. E.g. 'Local' always became 'Domestic'.

3.1 Manual annotation

The annotators worked with a rather simple interface, where only the last part of an article was visible to them (they could scroll up to view more). They then had to type the correct three-letter code for the category they felt the article belonged in. In the first phase, articles were often surrounded by large amounts of boilerplate or whitespace, which made it difficult for the annotators to quickly see the article itself, but this was reduced in the second round of experiments.

```
Ifølge 30-åringens hjemmeside har han de siste årene investert penger
i aksjer og eiendommer i Norge og utlandet. I fjor kjøpte han en Mercedes-Benz
SLK kabriolet, og nylig kjøpte han også en ny leilighet  på Askøy utenfor
Bergen.¶
På ulike diskusjonsforum forteller 30-åringen om hyppige feriereiser.
Blant annet til Thailand, Sør-Amerika, USA, og Sør-Europa.¶
Selve forretningsvirksomheten hevder Andersen at han har styrt fra
flere europeiske byer, deriblant London og Minsk. Fra den hviterussiske
hovedstaden skrev han følgende innlegg i 2005, under et alias:¶
(VG 15.09.2008 kl. 08:38, Sist oppdatert 15.09.2008 kl. 09:04)¶

======================================================================

Topics:
con (consumer),        for (foreign),
cul (culture),         pol (politics),
dom (domestic),        sct (science & technology),
eco (economy),         spo (sports),
ent (entertainment).

Special categories:
unc (uncertain),        out (stuff that doesn't belong in the corpus).

Please type the correct three-letter topic: █
```

Figure 1. The annotator interface

For our first approach, the annotators classified 3,000 articles. However, we only used about 1,200 of those as training material. This reduction was largely due to deliberate cropping of the largest categories, since we realized that all the categories should contain the same amount of material. One annotator contributed more than the others in this phase; he classified about 1,000 articles.

For the second attempt, we could not use the 3,000 articles already classified, because we had changed both the number of categories and the definitions of some categories. Furthermore, there did not exist boilerplate-cleaned copies of all the articles used in the first run. We wanted to use only boilerplate-cleaned text in the second run.

In order to secure inter-annotator agreement, the annotators were given the following set of guidelines before the manual classification. In addition, there was continual informal discussion between annotators during the work.

There are nine categories. They are as follows:

Culture: film, theatre, literature, opera, comics, obituaries. Example: "Michael Jackson makes a new record", "'Watchmen' to become movie".

Entertainment: actors, celebrities, TV, computer games. Examples: "Michael Jackson dies", "Gerrard Arrested for Bar Brawl".

Foreign: things that happen outside Norway, and are not already classified as some other category. Examples: "Michael Jackson's Physician Suspected of Murder". "Norwegians Sentenced to Death in Congo".

Domestic: same as above, if it happens in Norway. Example: "Swedish Murderer Caught in Oslo".

Economy: commerce, financial crisis, mortgages, loans and interest, the stock market.

Politics: polemics, policy. Examples: "Putin visits Oslo", "Jens Stoltenberg [the Norwegian premier minister], Speaks Highly of the Beach Zone". Many letters from readers belong here.

Consumer: product reviews, wine, housing, travel, health food. Examples: "New Ear Phones for the iPhone", "New Gaming Console from Sony".

Science and Technology: research, space travel, astronomy. Examples: "Cheap Hearing Aid for Developing Countries", "New G3 Net in the EU".

Sports: football, competitive chess, rally, long distance swimming in ice water.

Out: articles in other languages, empty articles, tables.

Since the program can only place the article in a single category, choose the one that makes the most sense topically – think of what an alien, or an AI, would do.

Other than that, choose the narrowest category; "Iranian Ambassador Called on the Carpet" belongs to 'Politics' rather than 'Domestic', because 'Politics' is more specific.

Figure 2. Annotator guidelines

3.2 Feature extraction

The features collected from the articles by the learner were simply whitespace-separated 'words' of one or more letters. These were not stemmed or lemmatized, nor sorted by grammatical class.

Choosing the best feature representation is a non-trivial task, and a research area in its own right. Stemming or lemmatizing, although seemingly obvious choices, are only two of a great many methods that can be applied, with very varying results, depending on the task.

3.3 Cleaning the text

During the first phase, we applied the classification on raw text, i.e. the version prior to boilerplate removal. This consisted of the entire raw text from the newspapers' websites, including html tags, boilerplate and Javascript. This was done because Bayesian filtering tends to pick up features humans have not thought about, including features from, say, html tags. A relevant example is the html tag for bright red, which is a good indicator of spam in Bayesian spam filtering.

Due to the lack of boilerplate removal, 80–90 per cent of the bulk of each article would be non-prose. This, of course, led to the articles being very large, which again meant that the program had to store a large number of features.

It turned out that training on articles which included all the boilerplate was impractical. The statistics files quickly became too large for the CRM114 system to handle properly. Also, the statistics files, although large, did not contain enough relevant learning. This was probably due to the relatively low ratio of relevant newspaper prose to boilerplate in the raw texts.

3.4 The gold standard

The term 'gold standard' is most often used to mean the best method or approach for measuring. In this case, we define it to mean 'the standard measured against'.

Six people were involved in classifying a set of 106 articles. This set contained examples from every category. This became the gold standard, or test material, against which the accuracy of the classifier was measured. The learner did not train on any of articles in the gold standard.

There were never fewer than three people agreeing on a category for any article. We took that agreement to be the definition of 'correct category' for that article. In two instances, three people agreed on one category, while the three others agreed on a different category. In one of those cases, one person arbitrarily decided on 'Consumer' over 'Economy'. In the other, 'Entertainment' was chosen over 'Culture'.

When all six annotators agreed, we took that to be a correct human classification. This meant that human accuracy was 59 per cent. When that requirement was relaxed to 5 out of 6 agreeing, human accuracy was 81 per cent.

The low human accuracy shows very clearly how desirable it is to be able to allow for more than one topic tag for each article, rather than pigeonholing each article in a single category.

4. Overview of our final approach

In the initial stage, human annotators manually classified roughly 1,400 short newspaper articles in order to create a training material for the statistical machine learner to learn from. We then trained the machine learner on the result; roughly 200 articles from each of nine categories.

The machine learner trained only on errors, and used a method built into CRM114 called Hyperspace, which is a variant of k-nearest neighbour, in that it places texts in an n-dimensional (hyper)space.

This method collects features in the same way as the sparse-matrix variant of Markovian filtering. The only features used were whitespace-separated words.

Finally, human annotators classified a set of 106 articles with examples from each category, on the basis of which we measured inter-annotator agreement and the final accuracy of the automatic classifier.

5. Our approach in detail

5.1 Hypothesis

We hypothesized that a relatively simple program written in CRM114 would be able to classify multiple topics quite well, and better than a support vector machine, although not as accurately as CRM114's reported accuracies on two-genre classification (spam vs. non-spam).

We later refined our hypothesis: it is probably easier for the classifier to do things stepwise, i.e. a binary classification, where the material is first organized into two groups, starting with sport vs. non-sport, then each of those are organized into two, and so on.

A further refinement of this hypothesis would be that annotating each article with several topic tags would result in better accuracy and relevance than pigeonholing the article into a single category. This has not been tested within the confines of the current project.

5.2 Defining categories

We started out by defining 29 categories of newspaper articles, roughly similar to the ones in the Topic Codebook (Policyagenda.org, 2010). This selection of categories was created by the Policy Agendas Project at the University of Austin, Texas, in order to standardize topic classification of government documents in the US. However, we soon reduced the number of categories to 19. These were even more similar to those described in the codebook. Soon after, we reduced the number to nine. The reason for this was that the machine learning did not seem to be able to converge at all with 29 or 19 categories. Nine seemed a more promising level of granularity, and we proceeded with that number.

5.3 Tools

CRM114 (Yerazunis 2006) was developed for a subtype of automatic classification, namely spam-filtering, which is essentially a two-way genre classifier.

The CRM114 programming language is a regular expression manipulator with several built-in methods of classification. By changing a few keywords and using different statistics files, the method can be set to Bayesian, Markovian, Markovian with sparse matrices (aka OSBF), k-nearest neighbor, Hyperspace, or neural networks.

Reported accuracies achieved by CRM114 in spam filtering are well above 99%. However, classifying more than two categories, although comparable, was assumed to be much more difficult. Also, CRM114's strength is genre classification, while we wanted to use it for topic classification.

All CRM114's methods are supervised. That is, they need feedback from users to gain accuracy, so an amount of manually classified material was required in order to train the program.

During training, CRM114 gathers features from each article in statistics files; one file for each topic. The size of these files increases as the program learns by incorporating more 'feature-collections' (articles) into the statistics files. The size of these files vary depending on which method is used.

A technique called 'boosting' can be used to reduce the size of the statistics files. In short, this means using the old files as correction input while training new files from scratch on the errors made. This will often also increase accuracy by weeding out early learning of lower quality.

A drawback with CRM114 is that it does not store features in human-readable form. The features are stored as a hash. Thus, retrieving them, while not impossible, is a cryptographic exercise. This means that the exact composition of the features collected is not known. Consequently, no manual intervention was done to remove 'non-features' from the material, or manipulate the features in any way.

Another drawback is that, although CRM114 can output several candidate topics after a classification attempt, it can only use a single one of these for actual learning. This makes consistently tagging an article with more than one tag difficult.

5.4 Programming and experimenting

At first, about 3,000 articles from The Norwegian Newspaper Corpus were manually classified. We then wrote a program – the learner – which tried to automatically classify these articles without looking at the topic tags. The tags were then used as correction input to the program.

The program learned from the errors it made. That is, it did not learn anything from getting things right, but stored the features from the article into the correct statistics file only whenever it had made a mistake.

The first version of the learner used the built-in OSBF-method from CRM114. This method is a Markovian sparse-matrix approach (see Section 2.2). It has achieved very good results in spam filtering, and is the default method of Spamreaver, a spam filter created with CRM114. However, with OSBF, there is always a chance that it may not converge on stable learning. This problem increases with more categories, and the initial results were disappointing, even with only nine categories.

Boosting (see Section 5.3) was attempted, with only modest accuracy improvement as a result.

In this phase, we operated with relatively large a number of categories, several of which overlapped:

Business Climate Consumer Domestic Economy Education
Energy Entertainment Environment Foreign Health Local
Politics Science Sports Technology Travel Work

It proved impossible for the learner to separate all these categories from each other due to the large degree of topical overlap, so several of them had to be combined, and others removed entirely.

For example, 'Business' and 'Economy' were merged to 'Economy'; 'Travel' and 'Consumer' were merged to 'Consumer'. 'Climate', 'Energy' and 'Environment' were at first merged to 'Environment', and then dropped altogether. 'Local' was subsumed by 'Domestic'.

In addition to manual training, we also experimented with using the article's URL to derive the topic. During this phase, if the URL yielded an unequivocal result, that was trained as the correct topic for the article. An example of an informative URL is

http://www.dn.no/privatokonomi/article1616562.ece

which indicates that the article belongs to the topic 'Economy' (it could even be refined to 'Personal Economy' if we had used a more fine-grained classification).

If, however, the URL did not give unequivocal topical information, the article was ignored. This method turned out to be not very successful. The URLs of articles were found to be sometimes inaccurate, and therefore not reliable. Furthermore, the machine learner "trained on everything", i.e. it did not only train on newspaper articles it had erroneously classified, but trained every newspaper article into its statistics files.

The original idea behind URL-based training was that training on a large part of the corpus would give the learner a good base from which we could start training on errors. It turned out, however, to be better to start from scratch, and let the learner make huge mistakes at first while training exclusively on errors.

It was decided that the OSBF-based solution was not going to work. The second version of the programs used the built-in Hyperspace method, which is a variant of k-nearest-neighbor. The Hyperspace training was done on cleaned text.

Before this second round of manual classification, we changed the specification of the 'Foreign' category from being 'everything that happens abroad' to 'anything that happens abroad that has not already been classified as something else'. Thus, the 'Foreign' category became very similar to the 'Domestic' category, since they both tend to contain descriptions of disasters, accidents and crime.

One annotator went through some of the manually classified material to weed out obvious errors. This revealed that several kinds of errors were quite common. For example, a lot of material was classified as 'Out' because the interface had not shown the article properly to the annotator. Also, some of the articles in the material were far from representative of their category.

In addition to training on error, correctly classified articles that the classifier was not confident about were also trained. This technique is known as 'single-sided thin threshold training' (Yerazunis 2006). This increased accuracy noticeably.

The size of the training material from each category turned out to be important. This is also suggested by Breeman (Breeman 2009), who shows that the accuracy increases by an average of 1.75% for each 500 entries that are added to the training material (see Table 1). The highest accuracies were reached when all the categories were trained on the same amount of material. This ensured that the larger categories did not dominate. For us, this meant we could only use roughly as much material as there was in the smallest category. This was 'Science and Technology', of which we only had 73 manually classified articles.

Several attempts at improving the accuracy were made at this stage. First, it was thought that tagging the material with lemma-and grammatical information would help, but it only seemed to make things much worse. This experiment was undertaken quite close to the deadline for the project, and only a token effort was made. The result might have differed if the approach had been investigated more thoroughly.

Table 1. Size of training material, from Breeman (Breeman 2009)

Articles	Accuracy
1,500	48.0%
2,000	50.2%
2,500	51.0%
3,000	53.0%
3,500	55.4%
4,000	56.6%

Second, we tested using word-pairs as features rather than single words. This definitely turned out not to be a good idea, since the Hyperspace method already makes sparse bi-grams out of single word features. These single word features are defined by the TRE-compatible regular expression '[[:graph:]]+' which is the default feature detector in CRM114 (Yerazunis 2006). It defines printed characters (letters or punctuation) surrounded by whitespace. Using two-word features only served to reduce the information density in the sparse bi-grams.

Third, we decided to try a binary classification process in order further boost accuracy. Here each category was separated from the remaining material, one after the other, starting with 'Sports' vs. all the non-sport categories. The result was a binary, right-branching tree of classification, as seen in Figure 3.

Fourth, we felt that separating the categories one by one, thus ending up with a right-branching tree, was perhaps not an optimal way of proceeding. Thus, we tried to separate the material into two categories of equal size (each containing several topic categories) in each step. This however, proved difficult, and with dismal initial results the attempt was abandoned. The various categories were, after all, designed to be different from each other from the outset.

Separating one category from others, however, proved to be relatively easy, since each category was sufficiently different from the aggregate of the remaining ones to make it recognizable with a certain level of accuracy. The possible exceptions were 'Politics' and 'Entertainment', which both had quite a few false positives.

Using this procedure, we started by separating 'Sports' from everything else, which seemed the obvious choice, since it seemed the most easily classifiable category. We trained on about 200 'Sports' articles and a collection of about 300 articles picked from all the other categories.

After a bit of experimenting, and looking at what accuracies we got when separating each topic from all the others, we chose 'Domestic' to be the next one out. We removed all the sports articles from the training material, and trained on about 200 'Domestic' articles and about 250 non-domestic articles.

We repeated this procedure in the following order: 'Economy', 'Science and Technology', 'Politics', 'Consumer', 'Foreign', 'Culture', and finally 'Entertainment', which was not explicitly trained, since all the remaining articles would belong to this category by default.

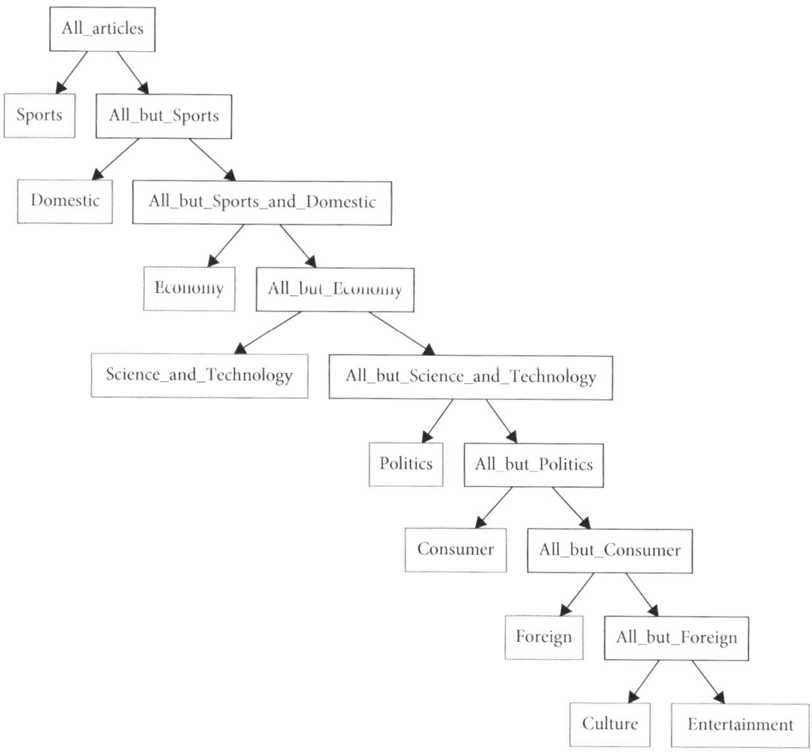

Figure 3. Order of binary classification

Fifth, we experimented further with separating each article from all the other categories each time, rather than diminishing the material in each step. This was not successful. The advantage of binary classification seems, as expected, to be that the material becomes simpler at each step, and therefore easier to split into two categories.

We noticed a considerable difference between letting the training run until convergence and stopping it earlier. The recall was much better when learning had converged, but at the cost of precision. The number of false positives became impractically high long before the classifier managed to find all the articles on a given topic. We therefore had to decide on an acceptable number of both false positives and false negatives at each step.

At the same time, we had to keep an eye on the size of the generated statistics files. Each topic category had a statistics file, where all the training on that topic was contained (as a hash, see Section 5.3). We saw that when one statistics file was much larger than the others, that topic would get many more false positives than any other topic. Thus, we had to stop the training run before the statistics file for the topic at hand became so large it would dominate the other topics. We kept the sizes of the statistics files within 50% or so of each other.

Due to time constraints, the 'boosting' technique (see Section 5.3) was not undertaken during this phase.

The automatic classification was computationally not intensive. A corpus of 850 million words could be worked through in a few hours, given access to an ordinary 8-core server. This applies to the classification, after training has happened. The training phase only took a few minutes of processor time, since the training material was quite small.

6. Data and experimental evaluation

6.1 Measuring inter-annotator agreement

Cohen's *Kappa* value is the standard measure of inter-annotator agreement while controlling for chance agreement (Cohen 1968). It is defined as:

$$\kappa = \frac{p(A)p(E)}{1p(E)}$$

where, $p(A)$ is the probability of the observed agreement between two decisions:

$$p(A) = \frac{1}{N}\sum_{n=1}^{n} I(Human_n == Computer_n)$$

Here, N is the number of examples. *I()* equals 1 when the two annotations (e.g., human and computer) agree on a particular example. *P*(*E*) is the probability of the agreement expected by chance:

$$p(E) = \frac{1}{N^2} \sum_{c=1}^{C} (HumanTotal_c \times ComputerTotal_c)$$

The argument of the sum is a multiplication of the marginal totals for each category. For example, for 'Sports', the argument would be the total number of articles a human annotator marked as 'Sports', times the total number of articles the computer system marked as 'Sports'. This multiplication is computed for each category, summed, and then normalized by N^2.

We used Kappa to measure inter-annotator agreement. We also used it to measure agreement between the annotators and the gold standard, as well as agreement between the machine classifier and the gold standard.

6.2 Possible sources of error

The biggest source of error is probably the small amount of training done. We only trained each category on very roughly 200 (often fewer) representative articles from each category, and about 300 or fewer articles from other topics in each step.

CRM114 is designed to be continuously corrected by users when used as a spam filter, and it is that continuous training input – the long tail – which yields its high accuracy rates (often above 99.95%). Thus, over time, each user will train a large number of emails into both the spam and non-spam categories.

Possibly, not enough was done to ensure that training examples were as representative as possible of their respective topics. One person went through some of the material to correct obvious mistakes, but a methodical selection of representative articles was not done.

The accuracy of boilerplate removal remains an unsolved problem, so the purity of the texts used in the Hyperspace-phase was not optimal. For instance, many of the articles in the training material had erroneous – and differing – character encodings for Norwegian letters, as well as visible formatting marks and obvious advertisement links. No attempt was made to clean all the articles of these blemishes to increase accuracy.

The system in place for harvesting text from the web is also not optimal. Specifically, some articles in the corpus contain no text at all. Fortunately, this is not a significant problem to the users of the corpus. There is a considerable tolerance for 'junk data'.

Articles that would have been classified as 'Out' – mostly foreign articles – were not included in the training material, nor in the gold standard. In hindsight, some should have been included, since the raw text of the corpus does contain some rogue English and Spanish articles. The automatic classifier would probably have been able to help weed them out if the 'Out' category had been included in the final version.

The selection of the 106 articles in the gold standard (see Section 3.4) was done by one person without any clear instruction on how to pick articles. Many of the articles were therefore picked for their 'interestingly ambiguous' nature, which made it difficult for both humans and machine to classify them confidently.

The program displaying the articles to be manually classified was not optimal. It relied on primitive *ad hoc* techniques for removing boilerplate text. As a result, it often displayed confusing text to the human annotator. A relatively small number of errors has been discovered in the gold standard, perhaps because of this. Other errors are probably due to disagreement between annotators.

Only a partial correction of the gold standard was subsequently done, and so, the extent of errors in the gold standard – although probably low – is unknown.

7. Results

A survey of the results of the testing described above is given in Table 2.

Table 2. Results

Method	Accuracy
OSBF	18%
Hyperspace, URL-based	28%
Hyperspace	45%
Binary hyperspace	54%

As seen from the table, the best method yielded an accuracy of 54 per cent. We consider this to be satisfactory as an initial machine-based classification of the corpus, as a basis for subsequent manual improvement.

It is worth noting that we achieved this while training on a very small training material, thereby achieving better results than those predicted by Breeman (Breeman 2009). According to his exploration of training material size (see Table 1), we should have ended up with an accuracy below 48%.

For classification tasks similar to ours, Kappa (see Section 6.1) is the standard measure of inter-annotator agreement. A Kappa of 0.70 or higher is considered a very good agreement between annotators (Carletta 1996).

In our own round of in-house classification, Kappa between pairs of annotators varied from 0.72 to 0.86. Average Kappa between annotators was 0.79.

As for the machine learning methods, the OSBF method used in our first attempt only yielded about 18 per cent accuracy measured against the gold standard.

With the Hyperspace method, accuracy went up to above 28 per cent when 'Domestic' and 'Foreign' was taken as two separate topics. These two topics are, however, almost identical in nature. When they are treated as one topic, the accuracy went up to more than 43 per cent.

After URL-based pre-training was removed, accuracy increased to 45 per cent.

Finally, after a stepwise binary classification, the overall accuracy was 54 per cent (see Table 2), i.e., a Kappa of 0.48.

Kappa between the human annotators and the correct category was on average only slightly better; 0.49, or 59 per cent accurate.

Thus, we see that although the automatic classifier's accuracy is far from exact, it does not lag far behind human accuracy, with the method used.

Still, our accuracy is considerably lower than reported accuracies when Support Vector Machines are used to classify large training sets (Hillard 2008).

8. Conclusions and future work

It seems difficult to make a very accurate automatic classifier based on a corpus with so many similar and overlapping categories when the classifier is restricted to a single output category rather than several tags to indicate topic. A point to note is that the articles in this corpus, although their topics are discernable by humans, are all of the same genre, in contrast to spam versus non-spam. The accuracy achieved is, however, far above randomness, which means automatic classification can at the very least be used as an initial measure to assist subsequent manual classification.

In that regard, CRM114 is helpful in that it allows the programmer to define a threshold for confidence, below which the program will ask a user for the correct category. The user's feedback will then be trained on, in order to improve future accuracy.

The number of categories, and the specific type of machine learner, clearly has a major impact on the accuracy. With too many categories, no convergence could be seen towards learning with the OSBF method. The Hyperspace method, with fewer categories, worked better.

The nature of the categories also plays an important role. In our project, having two separate topics called 'Domestic' and 'Foreign' was problematic, since these categories tend to contain the same type of subject matter; namely descriptions of accidents, crimes, trials, and natural disasters.

In our work, more effort could have been put into extracting more appropriate features. As it was, we used CRM114's default way of extracting features, namely words defined by taking any combination of printed characters separated by whitespace (see Section 5.4). In the future, this approach can probably be refined.

A lot of manual training is required to boost the accuracy. This is time-consuming, and would be better solved by using pre-classified articles as training. A large, manually classified corpus of Norwegian newspaper articles would be beneficial for training an automatic classifier like this one. If an appropriate corpus could be found, much higher accuracy could probably be achieved.

An API for harvesting newspaper articles from the web would be highly desirable, in order to avoid, or at least reduce, the boilerplate problem. This API should, of course, contain a requirement for journalists to classify their articles themselves, which would further aid the searchability of the articles and their usefulness as learning material in automatic topic classification.

Our results show that we managed to separate single topic categories from the rest with accuracies around 90 per cent (varying from 61% to 93%). However, when done in succession, the errors accumulated, so that the final accuracy fell to 54 per cent.

One possible solution to the lack of training material in our project could be to create a web-interface to the interactive training, so that researchers – and anyone else – could contribute to the classification and correction on a voluntary basis. User-generated and -corrected content has proved valuable in projects like Wikipedia, for example.

As mentioned, the CRM114 programming language can only assign each article a single category. It would be preferable to be able to give each article several topic tags. Many of the articles were almost impossible to put into a single category, even after discussion among the annotators, and a system that used topic tags instead of discrete categories would be advantageous.

It could also prove worthwhile to base the classification on texts tagged with grammatical information. It is likely this would improve accuracy, even though our attempt yielded disappointing results.

It would probably have been helpful to put the material through a simple, good, lemmatizer or stemmer before feeding it into the automatic classifier, as was suggested by Breeman (2009). Note that this technique is different from tagging the tokens with grammatical information.

Moreover, it would be interesting to experiment with the order in which each category was separated out from the rest during the binary classification, to see if the number of false positives would decrease. For instance, 'Politics' and 'Domestic' had a lot of false positives. If these two had been tackled near the end of the process, the number of errors might have been reduced.

An important dimension in topic classification is topic drift. Topic drift is the introduction of new topics, and the disappearance of obsolete topics over time. Topic drift is often the result of technological obsolescence or invention, but could also be due to shifts in, for example, ideological, geographical or religious climate. This challenge has been addressed in fields such as website intrusion detection and data mining by using en ensemble of a handful of automatic classifiers, where new ones are trained and outdated ones are removed continuously (Scholz & Klinkenberg 2005; Wang et al. 2008). A similar approach could easily be implemented in a robust topic classification system.

References

Breeman, Gerard et al. 2009. Strategies for improving semi-automated topic classiffication of media and parliamentary documents. *Midwest Political Science Association 67th Annual National Conference 2009.*

Carletta, Jean. 1996. Assessing agreement on classification tasks: The kappa statistic. *Computational Linguistics* 22(2): 249–254.

Cohen, Jacob. 1968. Weighted kappa: Nominal scale agreement provision for scaled disagreement or partial credit. *Psychological Bulletin* 70: 213–220.

Daelemans, Walter & van den Bosch, Antal. 2005. *Memory based Language Processing*. Cambridge: CUP.

Folch, Helka, Heiden, Serge, Habert, Benoit, Fleury, Serge, Illouza, Gabriel, Lafon, Pierre, Nioche, Julien & Provost, Sophie. 2000. Typtex: Inductive typological text classification by multivariate statistical analysis for NLP systems tuning/evaluation. In *Proceedings of the Second Language Resources and Evaluation Conference,* 141–148.

Graham, Paul. 2002. A plan for spam. Paul Graham's website. <http://paulgraham.com/spam.html>.

Graham, Paul. 2003. Better bayesian filtering. Paul Graham's website. <http://paulgraham.com/better.html>.

Hillard, Dustin. 2008. Computer assisted topic classification for mixed methods. *Journal of Information Technology and Politics* 31: 46.

Joachims, Thorsten. 2002. *Learning to Classify Text using Support Vector Machines: Methods, Theory, and Algorithms*. Berlin: Springer.

Masud, Mohammad. M., Jing Gao, Khan, Latifur, Jiawei Han & Thuraisingham, Bhavani. 2009. Integrating novel class detection with classification for concept-drifting data streams. In *Proceedings of 2009. European Conference on Machine Learning and Principles and Practice of Knowledge Discovery in Databases*, 79–94. Berlin: Springer.

Policyagenda.org. Topics Codebook. policyagendas.org website. 2010.

Purpura, Stephen. 2006. Automated classification of congressional legislation. In *Proceedings of the Seventh International Conference on Digital Government Research*, San Diego CA.

Puterman, Martin L. 2005. *Markov Decision Processes: Discrete Stochastic Dynamic Programming* Wiley Series in Probability and Statistics. New York: John Wiley and Sons.

Salakhutdinov, Ruslan & Hinton, Geoffrey E. 2009. Deep boltzmann machines. *Artificial Intelligence & Statistics* 5:448–455 .

Scholz, Martin & Klinkenberg, Ralf. 2005. An ensemble classifier for drifting concepts. In *Proceedings of the Second International Workshop on Knowledge Discovery in Data Streams*, Porto, Portugal, 53–64.

Shawe-Taylor, John & Christianini, Nello. 2000. *Support Vector Machines and other Kernel-based Learning Methods*. Cambridge: CUP.

Vapnik, Vladimir & Kotz, Samuel. 2006. *The Nature of Statistical Learning Theory*. Berlin: Springer.

Wang, Haixun, Fan, Wei, Yu, Philip S. & Jiawei Han. 2008. Mining concept-drifting data streams using ensemble classifiers. In *Proceedings of the Ninth ACM SIGKDD International Conference on Knowledge Discovery and Data Mining*.

Yang, Yiming & Liu, Xin. 1999. A re-examination of text categorization methods. In *Proceedings of ACM SIGIR Conference on Research and Development in Information Retrieval*, 42–49.

Yerazunis, Bill. 2006. CRM114 Revealed. Sourceforge website <http://crm114.sourceforge.net/docs/CRM114_Revealed_20061010.pdf>.

Zdziarski, Jonathan. 2005. *Ending Spam: Bayesian Content Filtering and the Art of Statistical Language Classifcation*. San Francisco: No Starch Press.

A data-driven approach to anglicism identification in Norwegian

Gyri Smørdal Losnegaard & Gunn Inger Lyse
University of Bergen

Anglicisms are words of English origin that have entered into Norwegian, either denoting conceptual innovations such as *interface* or denoting existing concepts in parallel with their Norwegian counterparts (*boots*). In this chapter we investigate whether machine-learning methods could improve the anglicism component of the classification tool that is currently used to categorize new words appearing in the Norwegian Newspaper Corpus. We derive classification features by extracting three-character sequences (trigrams) from long lists of uniquely English and Norwegian words. Next, we test two frequency-based and a statistics-based approach to selecting features from this initial pool of trigrams. Finally, using the TiMBL memory-based learning system, we train a classifier with our selections of trigrams, identifying the sets of trigrams that are most predictive for identifying anglicisms. The results show that the data-driven frequency approach, although not sufficient as a stand-alone method for automatic anglicism identification, provides a valuable supplement to the existing knowledge-based classification tool.

1. Introduction

In the Norwegian Newspaper Corpus (NNC) project, G. Andersen (2011, this volume) has built a hybrid tool that combines statistical, lexicon-based and rule-based methods to categorise new words (neologisms) appearing in the corpus. The current level of precision is about 75 per cent, calculated on the basis of a gold standard of 10,000 words.

Of the strategies employed in the hybrid system, the most promising is to consider sequences of characters (chargrams) below word level. For instance, an unadapted anglicism never contains the sequence ⟨*kjø*⟩ (but a Norwegian word might), whereas the sentence-initial sequence ⟨*co*⟩ is indicative of an anglicism. Andersen employs a set of intuition-based, handcrafted chargrams as well as a set of English chargrams from a list of English phrases. He observes that many significant chargram patterns seem to be missing, which gives a lower recall for the anglicism classification tool, i.e. it will not identify all anglicisms in a dataset. In the following we describe experiments with automatic, data-driven methods to identify anglicisms in Norwegian text. We investigate whether such methods could complement or improve the existing classification tool.

With the increasing availability of large collections of language data, machine-learning methods have become powerful tools for exploring language regularities. In machine learning the system attempts to 'learn' from a sample illustrating the phenomenon at hand (Hagen this volume). We hypothesise that anglicisms (or at least certain types of anglicisms) may be detected by learning orthographical characteristics from a sample of general English words. Thus, we generate training data from a compiled list of uniquely English word forms, i.e. word forms that do not occur in a Norwegian reference lexicon, and similarly, a list of unique Norwegian word forms. All words are broken down to three-character sequences (trigrams), and we run a series of experiments to identify the set of trigrams that have the best predictive power to identify previously unseen anglicisms. As a gold standard we use Andersen's (2005, 2011) manually classified list of words from the NNC's neology database (Andersen and Hofland this volume).

We explore two frequency-based criteria for selecting trigrams; *simple frequency*, testing whether the *n* most frequent trigrams are more predictive, and *productivity*, where we assume that a predictive trigram should be found in a minimum of *n* words, and vary *n* to find the optimal threshold. We also try automatic feature selection to see whether a statistically based selection of features gives better results.

The motivating questions of the present machine learning experiments are thus as follows: to what extent may anglicisms be detected automatically based on the characteristics of general English words; and how does the machine learning methodology compete with the hybrid strategy described in Andersen (2005, 2011)?

2. Background

2.1 Anglicisms

Anglicisms are often treated as a subgroup of *neologisms*, that is, new words in our vocabulary (Andersen 2006). In general, we may distinguish between two main types of English words in Norwegian (Graedler 1998; Görlach 2001; Andersen 2006 this volume): some anglicisms denote things and phenomena where a Norwegian term has not yet been established (typically new inventions, e.g. *server, podcasting*), while in the other group, we find words that do have Norwegian counterparts but where a language user nonetheless prefers the English word in certain contexts (e.g. *anyway* 'uansett', *boots* 'støvler', *project manager* 'prosjektleder'). The use of English terms in this latter group is typically motivated by sociolinguistic factors, for instance signalling a particular style (Graedler 1998; Johansson & Graedler 2002) or belonging to a particular group, c.f. the use of English expressions among adolescent Norwegians, such as *chille* 'to relax'.

Linguistically, there are many subtypes of anglicisms that need an adequate description and analysis. The systematic identification of anglicisms is also "potentially relevant for linguistic, language-political and language-technological purposes" (Andersen 2005: 3). Anglicisms in Norwegian have often been studied as a sociolinguistic phenomenon where the main question is whether Norwegian, being a relatively small language, is encroached upon by English, and whether there is a risk of domain loss for Norwegian in particular domains (G. Andersen this volume; Johansson & Graedler 2002; Stortingsmelding nr. 35 (2007–2008)). Given their language-political consequences, such concerns beg the question of the extent to which anglicisms do, in fact, replace Norwegian words in our vocabulary, both in professional language and in everyday language. To this end, it is vital to be able to identify anglicisms on a large scale across different texts and genres, which is hardly feasible by manual labour alone.

In language technology, anglicisms pose a different kind of problem: since their markedness as "non-Norwegian" words often surfaces through morphological or orthographical properties that deviate from what the computer expects to find in Norwegian text, they cause problems for computational language analysis. This especially holds true for speech technology, which relies on a consistent mapping between spelling and pronunciation (Andersen 2005). In other words, it is desirable to be able to identify previously unseen anglicisms on the basis of their spelling.

2.2 Modelling anglicisms computationally

The task of automatic identification of anglicisms illustrates a general challenge when modelling linguistic phenomena computationally: how to formulate principles which are sufficiently practical to be 'translated' into observable clues for a computational system, and which simultaneously are sufficiently close to our ideal criteria for calling something an anglicism. Following Pedersen (1999), a good predictive model should be sufficiently complex in the sense that it must encapsulate the important dependencies that exist in our dataset; but on the other hand, the predictive power of a model hinges on model simplicity: if the knowledge demanded by the model is too complex, we cannot hope to acquire it consistently and reliably; and in that case we cannot make reliable predictions about new instances either. Hence, it seems well motivated to begin by some broad criteria, which may then be evaluated and modified as needed.

According to G. Andersen (this volume), anglicisms typically retain their original orthography in Norwegian text (*crew, big deal, reality*). However, they are also found with alternative orthography: for instance, the anglicism *dull* is attested in the NNC both as *dull* and with a spelling that reflects its Norwegian pronunciation; *døll* (G. Andersen this volume). While some anglicisms remain completely unaffected by Norwegian morphology (these may be referred to as *non-adapted*, following Furiassi (2008)), others are subject to a variety of morphological, syntactic and semantic processes in the new language. Plural nouns, for instance, can be realised by the English plural form (*shots*), by adding a Norwegian plural suffix to the stem (*shotene*), or by adding a suffix to the English plural form. For instance, in the corpus-attested anglicism *shotsene* 'the shots', the original plural form is combined with the regular Norwegian plural affix +*ene* (Andersen 2005). Anglicisms are often introduced into Norwegian as parts of compounds, which in Norwegian are written as one word without a space (*verdenscup* 'world cup'). A Norwegian compound containing an anglicism will thus yield some chargrams that reflect Norwegian characteristics, and some that reflect English. Variations in morphhological adaptation, varying degrees of 'norwegification' and anglicisms with features typical for both languages all present challenges in the computational modelling and identification of anglicisms.

Making a trade-off between ideal definitions and what is possible to implement computationally, Andersen (2011) suggests four criteria for discriminating anglicisms and non-anglicisms for the specific task of automatic identification: A word is an anglicism if (i) the word is an existing English word (e.g. *condominiums* 'a kind of housing tenure'), or (ii) the word contains at least one compound part of English origin (*slengbuksefunky* 'flared denims-funky'; literal translation). We do *not* call it an anglicism if (iii) it is a well-established anglicism *sport*, *starte* 'start'), or (iv) if the word is of a non-English, foreign origin (cf. *sudoku*, *celle* 'cell', *pizza* or the compound *nettjournal* 'web journal', where *journal* has a French origin). Several strategies can be used to meet the mentioned challenges, but anglicisms with unmarked orthography with respect to Norwegian are especially difficult to recognise computationally; *date* for instance, is an anglicism due to criterion (i), but it is also a valid Norwegian sequence of characters. We thus add to these criteria a fifth (Andersen 2005): we do not consider anglicisms whose orthography is normalised with regard to Norwegian pronunciation (cf. *døll* 'dull').

There are mainly two conceivable ways of implementing the first criterion, where an English word is taken to use in Norwegian in its original orthographic form: either by lexicon lookup or by exploiting orthographic differences between Norwegian and English. Andersen (2005) presents two main experiments based on lexicon lookup and two experiments based on orthography below word level. Classification was measured in terms of anglicism precision and overall accuracy (cf. the equations in Section 3.2). In the first lexicon experiment, anglicism candidates were looked up in a large lexicon based on the British National Corpus (BNC) (Andersen 2005: 6), and in the second experiment a lexicon of uniquely English word forms was compiled with the English word forms that did not appear in the Norwegian reference lexicon SCARRIE (De Smedt & Rosén 2000: 7). The two lexicon experiments resulted in an anglicism precision of 45.78 and 58.73 per cent, respectively (overall accuracy: 94.30 and 94.48 per cent). A main problem concerns anglicisms that are used in hybrid compounds, i.e. compounds with an English and a Norwegian component.

While a lexicon lookup method is confined to the level of word forms, orthographic characteristics may be captured below word level. In *chargram matching*, the character sequences of an anglicism candidate are matched against sequences of characters that are assumed to indicate the "englishness" of a word (Andersen 2005: 8; Furiassi & Hofland 2007; Furiassi 2008). Significantly, this methodology enables the discovery of anglicisms that are parts of Norwegian compounds, meeting our second criterion.

The chargram list in Andersen (2005) was retrieved from a list of English phrases and contained 1,074 character sequences of length 4–6 that were *uniquely English*, i.e. not found in the Norwegian reference lexicon, and that were *productive* in virtue of occurring in at least 100 unique word forms. The results were promising, yielding an anglicism precision of 74.73 per cent and an overall accuracy of 95.72 per cent. As will be seen, the present experiments suggest that an *a priori* threshold of 100 is not necessarily optimal, as classification seems to improve when lowering the threshold, at least for our data. The gold standard test in Andersen (2005: 8) revealed that certain anglicisms were not detected because the necessary chargrams were absent from his list, and he concludes that a more comprehensive and refined list of typically English chargrams might yield further improvements. Andersen does not state, however, whether all the chargrams in his list contributed to the classification, or if only a subset of them did. Hence, we cannot say for sure if the problem was his particular selection of chargrams, or if this list was highly relevant but incomplete.

In a rule-based experiment, Andersen (2005) developed a set of manually defined regular expressions, defining for instance typically English character clusters that occur specifically in the beginning (*co-*), in the middle (*-atio-*) and at the end of words (*-ly*). A list of stop words (exceptions) was included to prevent overgeneration. This approach resulted in an anglicism precision of 60.60 per cent (overall accuracy: 95.15 per cent). The anglicisms that were not identified by the classifier roughly corresponded to those missed by the chargram method.

In a final experiment, Andersen (2005) combined the two most promising methods, viz. the chargram-based and the knowledge-based (rule-based) method, by first applying the rules (and stop word list) and then matching against chargrams. Intuitively, this is a reasonable approach because the combination of different views on the data ought to provide a more robust system. This experiment improved both the anglicism precision (77.46 per cent) and the overall accuracy (96.32 per cent); a result which is supported by other linguistic classification tasks, in that a combinatorial system "helps to improve results in almost all learning scenarios and it constitutes a very helpful and powerful tool for system engineering" (Màrquez et al. 2006: 204). However, the fact that Andersen's (2005) methods reportedly retrieve roughly the same anglicisms (and overlook the same anglicisms) may mean that their combined benefit is only marginal in practice. An evaluation study in the classification task of Word Sense Disambiguation (identifying the relevant sense of an ambiguous word in context), indicates that if several systems are largely in agreement, then there is little benefit in combining them since they will simply reinforce each other; but a combination of approaches with *combinatorial* benefits may improve performance significantly (Pedersen 2002).

2.3 A machine learning approach to anglicisms

During the past two decades, data-based methods have demonstrated measurable success in fields such as speech recognition, text categorisation, syntactic parsing and part-of-speech tagging (cf. for instance Abney 2000; Daelemans & Van den Bosch 2005, Manning & Schütze 1999). As a subtype of data-based methods, corpus linguistics represents an appealing alternative to introspection and enables us to quantify the representativeness of linguistic phenomena (Sæbø 2004). *Machine learning methods* attempt to discern regularities associated with a particular phenomenon (such as orthographic characteristics) by analysing statistically examples from a training set. In a supervised approach, the training examples are labelled in advance and the system subsequently uses its acquired knowledge to classify previously unseen examples, hence the term "classifier".

In the following we propose a machine learning approach to explore chargram characteristics of anglicisms from lexicon and corpus data. We build on the observation in Andersen (2005) that anglicisms can be recognised, at least in part, on the basis of their orthography. Our hypothesis is that anglicisms may be detected by learning the general orthographical characteristics of English. Since the list of chargrams used in Andersen's experiments was incomplete in the sense that chargrams that could have contributed to the successful classification of certain words were missing, we believe that by using a larger set of chargrams derived from all words in the training material, a classifier will be able to identify a broader set of anglicisms than would be the case with a handcrafted set of chargrams.

3. Methodology

3.1 Machine learning algorithm: TiMBL

We use the TiMBL software package for our experiments (Daelemans & Van den Bosch 2005; Daelemans et al. 2007). TiMBL stores all training instances explicitly in memory, hence the term Memory-Based. The system has been found useful for a wide range of areas in natural language processing, and the software is optimised for fast and accurate classification with large numbers of examples. It is also easy to set up TiMBL experiments in a way that resembles the chargram pattern matching in the chargram experiments in Andersen (2005), because TiMBL builds on a kind of pattern matching. New instances are classified by selecting the class of the most similar stored instances. If the new instance does not resemble any of the stored examples, TiMBL chooses the most frequent class in the training material by default (simple majority voting). Importantly, as our main concern is the "well-informed" classifications, i.e. those that are based on successful chargram pattern matching, our experimental setup is devised to ignore words where TiMBL resorts to the default classification by the most frequent class.

TiMBL requires all training and test instances to be represented as a feature vector with a fixed, user-defined length. The vector consists of *n* features, which in our case are trigrams derived from the words in the training set. Each trigram has a fixed position in the vector, and each training or test instance is represented as an instance of this feature vector, where binary values denote the absence (0) or presence (1) of each vector feature. The word *beetle*, for instance, would yield the trigrams ⟨bee⟩ ⟨eet⟩ ⟨etl⟩ ⟨tle⟩.[1] If all these trigrams were included as features in the vector, the word *beetle* would be represented with the value 1 for the trigrams mentioned above and 0 for all other features.

The point of encoding all instances according to a fixed, predefined set of features is that TiMBL compares a new instance, feature by feature, to all instances stored in memory. Similarity is defined by the so-called *k*-NN (*k* nearest neighbour) algorithm, where the value of *k* defines how many nearest neighbours a test instance must have in the training material for us to conclude that they are similar.

1. For technical reasons, word boundary markers were not included as part of the trigrams. Whether including them has an effect on the results will be investigated in our future work.

In our default setting, the *k* value is set to 1. Similarity itself is computed with the Dot Product measure (see Daelemans et al. 2007 for details). This measure is considered beneficial for binary values where only the value 1 contributes to establish similarity.

We use the default machine-learning algorithm in the TiMBL software package, IB1. As will be explained in the following, we employ binary features when encoding training and testing vectors, as recommended by Daelemans et al. (2007). We therefore use the Dot Product metric to compute the similarity between patterns. Conveniently, TiMBL has a built-in possibility of training and testing on the same material by so-called "leave-one-out", where the classifier trains successively on all training instances except one and uses this particular instance for testing, repeating this until all instances have been used once as test data. All our experiments are carried out using the leave-one-out classification method.

3.2 Lexical data

For our purposes we use two main lexical resources: Norwegian and English lexicon files originating from the SCARRIE project (De Smedt & Rosén 1999, 2000)[2] and the BNC corpus,[3] as well as Andersen's (2005, 2011) gold standard, which is a list of manually classified anglicisms and non-anglicisms from the NNC's neologism database. Words occurring in both lexicons have been removed, ensuring that all word forms are exclusively Norwegian or English. The "unique" lexicon files count 330,743 English and 358,162 Norwegian word forms, respectively. For control experiments, we held aside 5,000 English and 5,000 Norwegian words. The initial set of words thus counts 678,905 word forms, which in what follows will be referred to as "the full set" of words. Both lexicons include inflectional forms and compounds, and we kept special characters such as hyphens, assuming that they reflect language specific morphological patterns.

In addition to the 10,000 test words from the lexicon, we created a control set from Andersen's gold standard with 1,296 words consisting of 648 manually classified anglicisms and the same number of randomly selected non-anglicisms. Both test sets were used in the classification experiments to compare the results from training on the original set of words to the results achieved by training on previously unseen English words and anglicisms, respectively.

The non-anglicims in our material can be Norwegian words, but they may also be misspellings and loan words from other foreign languages than English

2. URL: http://ling.uib.no/desmedt/scarrie/lexdb.html

3. URL: http://www.natcorp.ox.ac.uk/corpus/index.xml

(Andersen 2005, 2011). Since they form such a heterogeneous group, it is less crucial whether the classifier is able to classify these words correctly. Like Andersen (2005) we thus aim for a system with *high anglicism precision.*

Given the two categories, the machine learning system has four classification options per instance (Table 1).

Table 1. Confusion matrix

	Anglicism	Non-anglicism
Anglicism	x	y
Non-anglicism	z	w

The leftmost column counts the number of words that the classifier has identified as anglicisms, while the rightmost column shows all instances classified as non-anglicisms. Thus, x is the number of correctly classified anglicisms, while z is the number of non-anglicisms incorrectly identified as anglicisms. Correspondingly, w is the correctly classified non-anglicisms, and y the number of anglicisms wrongly classified as non-anglicisms.

We define *anglicism precision* as the ratio between the words that are correctly classified as anglicisms and the sum of all words correctly and incorrectly labelled as such (1). The *overall accuracy* is the total number of correctly classified words, English and Norwegian, divided by the total number of words classified (2).

(1) $$\textit{Anglicism precision} = \frac{x}{x+y}$$

(2) $$\textit{Overall accuracy} = \frac{x+w}{x+y+z+w}$$

3.4 Building training vectors

As described in Section 3.1, building a vector with a chargram approach means that each position in the feature vector corresponds to a sequence of characters. The words in our training material are represented as instances of this fixed-length vector, encoded with binary values indicating the absence or presence of each feature in the vector. To keep the number of varying parameters as low as possible, we opted for three-character sequences (trigrams). We chose trigrams heuristically because a longer sequence would result in a very low frequency of occurrence for each sequence, whereas trigrams appear, intuitively, more informative than shorter n-grams (unigrams, bigrams). The training words were split into trigrams, which were added to the set of features while keeping track of the language origin and frequency.

Several studies have shown that machine learning benefits from selecting a subset of features that are maximally relevant for each class (Almuallim & Dietterich 1991; Mihalcea 2002; Hoste et al. 2002). Too many uninformative features may simply rule out the informative ones due to feature weighting in TiMBL. Based on Andersen's (2005) observations, we assume that trigrams occurring in both languages will be less predictive than trigrams unique to one of the languages. Therefore, we did not include trigrams occurring in both. Whether or not these features remain unique outside of our training material is of course an empirical question. We further pursued simple frequency (the *n* most frequent trigrams) and productivity (trigrams occurring more than *n* times) as two simple means of selecting the most informative features according to different thresholds.

3.5 Trigrams and frequencies

The full set of words generates a vector with 10,392 unique features. Of these, 7,578 are English and 2,814 are Norwegian trigrams. Table 2 shows the 15 most frequent uniquely English or Norwegian trigrams per language in our material. An obvious problem with feature selection is that it will necessarily lead to training instances that only have zero-valued features, because none of the features are present in that word.

Table 2. The 15 most frequent uniquely English or Norwegian trigrams

English trigrams		**Norwegian trigrams**	
ect	2,150	øre	3,059
oph	1,227	ære	2,362
row	823	kjø	2,255
hro	774	jør	2,089
iza	737	jøl	1,761
ics	713	ønn	1,679
chr	704	før	1,640
icu	678	stø	1,489
pec	664	ånd	1,471
icr	661	sjø	1,453
cus	598	løs	1,396
phy	594	øve	1,325
wit	585	åle	1,308
zat	553	øye	1,249
ext	552	løy	1,245

The most frequent English trigram in our material, ⟨*ect*⟩, occurs 2,150 times, and therefore has the binary value 1 for 2,150 words of the 30,743 English words in our training material (unless some words have more than one occurrence of the same trigram, something we have not accounted for but which we assume is a marginal phenomenon). This, then, gives a ratio of:

2,150/330,743 = 0.0065005155

In other words, the feature will be relevant in only six per thousand of all the English words in our training set. The top-tanked items show that the frequency decreases quite quickly, from more than 2,000 for the top-ranked English trigram to only a third (737) for the fifth most frequent.

Table 3 shows the number of unique trigrams in our material that occur above certain frequency thresholds: totally, for English, and for Norwegian.

Table 3. Frequency thresholds (f > n) and number of trigrams

Threshold (n)	Total no. of trigrams	No. of English trigrams	No. of Norw. trigrams
100	653	237	416
75	850	351	499
50	1,202	554	648
10	3,555	2,058	1,497
5	5,122	3,115	2,007
1	7,829	5,184	2,645
0	10,392	7,578	2,814

Notice that in our experiments, using a productivity threshold n, we built our vector without the trigrams occurring *n times or less* in the full data set. In an experiment with a given threshold n, all trigrams thus have frequencies *above* n (f > n). Consequently, productivity threshold 100 means that we kept all trigrams occurring 101 times or more (f > 100). Likewise, with threshold 1 (f > 1), we kept all trigrams in the vector occuring more than once. With threshold 0 all trigrams are kept, since all trigrams occur at least one time (f > 0).

Table 3 shows that removing the most low-frequent trigrams drastically reduces the number of features. From 10,392 trigrams in the entire set and 7,826 trigrams occurring two times or more (n=1), we find that 2,563 trigrams – 25 per cent – occur only once. Only 653 trigrams occur more than 100 times. With this in mind it is clear that our features will apply quite rarely and that many words in our training material (and also among new words to be classified) will only have zero-valued features. We will refer to such words as *zero-only instances*. As these instances do not provide the classifier with any clues as to whether the words are

English or Norwegian, we expected the classifier to achieve a higher overall accuracy if we left them out of the training material. In the following, the question is therefore how well the classifier performs in those cases where one or more trigram is present in the word.

4. Experiments and results

In the following we present three series of experiments. In Section 4.1, we report on our experiments with simple frequency as a criterion for feature selection; Section 4.2 accounts for productivity experiments; Section 4.3 presents an automatic, statistical approach to feature selection; and in Section 4.4 we give a brief discussion of the results. The simple frequency and productivity series can both be further divided into four sub-experiments: (a) a *baseline* experiment, (b) an *idealised baseline* experiment, (c) a *holdout* experiment and (d) a *gold standard* experiment. These are again sets of experiments with different frequency thresholds.

As explained in the previous section, we wanted to focus on the words that contained at least one of the trigrams in the feature vector. Experiment (a) is called the baseline because it allows for a comparison between training on the full set of words and training with an idealised set of words, i.e. without zero-only instances. In experiments (b) and (c) the classifier is trained without such instances, while the baseline shows how well we could expect the classifier to do when training with "noise" in the material.

Experiment (b), the idealised baseline, thus corresponds to the baseline, in that the trigrams are derived from the same set of words and that the same frequency tresholds have been applied, but differs from (a) in that the classifier is trained on a more informative subset of the words.

In experiment (c), we still trained the classifier with the same features, but on the "holdout" set of 10,000 words from the lexicon files (cf. Section 3.2). We did this in order to test the selected features on words that had not initially been used to derive the trigrams. In the final experiment (d), we tested our classifier on actual anglicisms and non-anglicisms from the gold standard.

The point of running these experiments was to indicate to which extent the features were applicable to new material. Since the words in experiments (c) and (d) did not contribute to generate the feature vector in the first place, they may be seen as control experiments, testing the predictive power of our sets of selected features. Experiment (c) shows classifier performance when training on unseen material of the same type (English and Norwegian word forms), while (d) tests how predictive English trigrams are in the classification of actual anglicisms. Like experiment (b), these are both idealised experiments.

In the simple frequency and producitivity series described in Sections 4.1–4.2, respectively, experiments (a)–(d) were carried out with four sub-experiments using different frequency thresholds. The same thresholds were applied throughout. In the gold standard series we only ran one experiment, using the threshold from the best performing set of features from the previous experiment. In Section 4.3, we describe another data-driven approach to feature selection: applying stastically based algorithms to identify the most predictive subset based on the encoding of the words as binary values representing the trigrams in the feature vector.

4.1 Simple frequency

In the simple frequency series of experiments we trained our classifier with the *n* most frequent features from each language in four experiments, varying *n* from 100 to 500, as seen in Table 4.

Table 4. Simple frequency baseline experiments (SFa)

Experiment	Language	Correct	Wrong	Precision	Recall	Overall accuracy
SFa-1 (n = 100)	English	34,487	0	100	11.00	57.10
	Norwegian	353,162	291,256			
SFa-2 (n = 200)	English	46,111	0	100	14.00	58.81
	Norwegian	353,162	279,632			
SFa 3 (n = 300)	English	53,572	0	100	16.00	59.91
	Norwegian	353,162	272,171			
SFa 4 (n = 500)	English	62,767	0	100	19.00	61.26
	Norwegian	353,162	262,976			

In the baseline experiment (Table 4) the classifier trained on the full set of words from the lexicon. Surprisingly, all the experiments yielded a maximal precision for English. However, both the overall accuracy and anglicism recall is quite low, meaning very few anglicisms were actually identified as such; only between 11 and 19 per cent. This indicates a strong overgeneralisation in favour of Norwegian. In fact, no Norwegian words were ever classified as English. As we shall see, overgeneralisation is a general trend throughout all our experiments. Experiment SFa-4, where the classifier trained with the most features, produced the best results in terms of both overall accuracy and anglicism recall.

The next experiment is the idealised baseline (Table 5), where we trained the classifier with the same trigrams as in the baseline but on the subset of words that contained one or more of the trigrams in the vector. Having weeded out the uninformative zero-only instances we expected fairly good results, and the results do indeed show that for these words, the classifier predicts the correct class every time (Table 5).

Table 5. Simple frequency idealised baseline experiments (SFb)

Experiment	Language	Correct	Wrong	Precision	Recall	Overall accuracy
SFb-1 (n = 100)	English	62,769	0	100	100	100
	Norwegian	67,036	0			
SFb-2 (n = 200)	English	53,572	0	100	100	100
	Norwegian	63,650	0			
SFb-3 (n = 300)	English	46,111	0	100	100	100
	Norwegian	60,053	0			
SFb-4 (n = 500)	English	34,487	0	100	100	100
	Norwegian	53,035	0			

Another interesting observation from the 'idealisation' of the training material is that by excluding zero-only words, the number of words in the training set is drastically reduced. The numbers compared to the initial pool of words used in the baseline are shown in Table 6. Only between 13 and 19 per cent of the initial set of 678,905 words contained one or more of our selected features, depending on the frequency threshold.

Table 6. Percentage of words in idealised baseline (SFb) compared to the baseline

Experiment (idealised baseline)	Number of English words	Number of Norwegian words	Total number of words	Total number of words in initial set	Per cent of baseline
SFb-1 (n = 100)	62,769	67,036	129,805	678,905	18.98
SFb-2 (n = 200)	53,572	63,650	117,222	678,905	17.27
SFb-3 (n = 300)	46,111	60,053	106,164	678,905	15.64
SFb-4 (n = 500)	34,487	53,035	87,522	678,905	12.89

The results from our holdout experiments (Table 7), training with the same features on a set of 10,000 previously unseen words from the lexicon, indicate that the features are also applicable to a broader set of English and Norwegian words. This series yielded a near-maximal or maximal anglicism precision in all experiments, and an overall accuracy between 97.88 and 99.42 per cent. Unlike in the baseline series, the recall for anglicisms was high in all of these experiments. Also here we found a tendency towards overgeneralisation; experiments SFc-1-3 were skewed towards Norwegian, as some English words were incorrectly identified as Norwegian but not the other way around; while SFc-4 was skewed towards English. With the high recall, the overgeneralisation tendency is nevertheless far smaller than in the baseline. The best results were achieved in experiment SFc-1, with a maximal anglicism precision and an overall accuracy of 99.42 per cent. Unlike the baseline, the experiment with fewer trigrams produced the best results. However, this seems to be more a consequence of the 'direction' of the overgeneralisation than evidence in support of the 200 most frequent features being more predictive. If we look closer at the series of sub-experiments, we see that they produced fairly consistent results, without much varation between the different frequency thresholds.

Table 7. Simple frequency holdout experiments (SFc)

Experiment	Language	Correct	Wrong	Precision	Recall	Overall accuracy
SFc-1 (n=100)	English	484	0	100	95.64	99.42
	Norwegian	720	7			
SFc-2 (n=200)	English	663	0	100	97.36	98.80
	Norwegian	821	18			
SFc-3 (n=300)	English	789	0	100	95.64	97.88
	Norwegian	875	36			
SFc-4 (n=500)	English	983	30	97.04	100	98.43
	Norwegian	899	0			

In our gold standard experiment, we trained the classifier with the same features on anglicisms and non-anglicisms from the NNC (Table 8). Since each series of sub experiments showed fairly consistent results with respect to the frequency thresholds, we only carried out one gold standard experiment, with the trigrams from the best holdout-experiment (SFc-1, n=100).

The classification yielded a quite high overall accuracy as most of the non-anglicisms were classified correctly, but with a low precision (43 per cent) and recall (32.89 per cent) for anglicisms. This in effect means that more than half of the manually classified anglicisms were not identified at all and that of the words identified as anglicisms by the classifier, only 40 per cent were classified correctly.

Table 8. Simple frequency gold standard experiment (SFd)

Experiment	Language	Correct	Wrong	Precision	Recall	Overall accuracy
SFd-1 (n=100)	Anglicism	25	33	43	32.89	95.83
	Non-angl.	1903	51			

4.2 Productivity

With productivity as a principle for feature selection, we tested different frequency thresholds by removing the most low-frequent trigrams from the feature vector. While Andersen (2005) used only trigrams with frequencies above 100, we tried different thresholds between 10 and 500, and observed that lowering the threshold produced slightly better overall classification results.

Like in the simple frequency series, the productivity baseline where we trained the classifier with the full set of words yielded a maximal precision for English (Table 9). Both the overall accuracy and the recall for English were higher compared to the baseline experiment in the simple frequency series, although still quite low. The results again indicate skewedness towards Norwegian, as no Norwegian words were ever classified as English.

Table 9. Productivity baseline experiments (Pa)

Experiment	Language	Correct	Wrong	Precision	Recall	Overall accuracy
Pa-1 (n = 10)	English	86,950	0	100	26.69	64.83
	Norwegian	353,162	238,793			
Pa-2 (n = 50)	English	67,003	0	100	20.57	61.89
	Norwegian	353,162	258,740			
Pa-3 (n = 75)	English	58,366	0	100	17.92	60.62
	Norwegian	353,162	267,377			
Pa-4 (n = 100)	English	51,550	0	100	16.00	59.61
	Norwegian	353,161	274,193			

In the idealised baseline experiments, presented in Table 10, the classifier predicted the right class for all instances except for the experiment with the lowest threshold (Pb-1), and accordingly the most features. This experiment yielded "only" 99.99 overall accuracy and recall, due to 12 out of 71,382 Norwegian words being wrongly classified as English.

Table 10. Productivity idealised experiments (Pb)

Experiment	Language	Correct	Wrong	Precision	Recall	Overall accuracy
Pb-1 (n = 10)	English	87,048	12	100	99.99	99.99
	Norwegian	71,370	0			
Pb-2 (n = 50)	English	67,007	0	100	100	100
	Norwegian	68,954	0			

(Continued)

Table 10. (Continued)

Experiment	Language	Correct	Wrong	Precision	Recall	Overall accuracy
Pb-3 (n=75)	English	58,367	0	100	100	100
	Norwegian	67,670	0			
Pb-4 (n=100)	English	51,550	0	100	100	100
	Norwegian	66,790	0			

Table 11 gives the productivity holdout results. The two experiments with the highest thresholds (and thus the lowest number of trigrams), Pc-3 and Pc-4, both yielded a maximal precision for English. No Norwegian words were classified as English. Conversely, in experiments Pc-1 and Pc-2, no English words were classified as Norwegian, upholding the trend of overgeneralisation in favour of one of the languages. The precision for English is a bit lower in these two experiments, but still above 90 per cent, and the recall is quite high.

Table 11. Productivity holdout experiments (Pc)

Experiment	Language	Correct	Wrong	Precision	Recall	Overall accuracy
Pc-1 (n=10)	English	1,354	134	90.99	100	94.27
	Norwegian	852	0			
Pc-2 (n=50)	English	1,036	60	94.53	100	96.99
	Norwegian	896	0			
Pc-3 (n=75)	English	840	0	100	93.54	96.84
	Norwegian	937	58			
Pc-4 (n=100)	English	758	0	100	96.07	*98.19*
	Norwegian	927	31			

The gold standard experiment, shown in Table 12, applies the 100-threshold as this yielded the best results in the holdout-series. The gold standard result is less skewed than the results in the baseline, idealised baseline and holdout series, but like the simple frequency gold standard experiment, it has significantly lower precision for English (41 per cent).

Table 12. Productivity gold standard experiments (Pd)

Experiment	Language	Correct	Wrong	Precision	Recall	Overall accuracy
P-1d (n=100)	English	36	52	40.91	35.64	95.31
	Norwegian	2,342	65			

4.3 Automatic feature selection

In our frequency-based approaches we have seen a maximal or close to maximal precision for anglicisms when training with English and Norwegian features on an idealised set of English and Norwegian words, but there are no obvious positive findings when applying the features to actual anglicisms. In this section, we test whether pruning the set of trigrams with statistics-based methods could improve classifier results.

For automatic feature selection we used the data mining system Weka (Waikato Environment for Knowledge Analysis).[4] Like TiMBL, this is a package of machine learning algorithms which is useful for data pre-processing and classification. We chose the search method BestFirst and evaluation measure CFsSubsetEval (Hall 1999; Bouckaert et al. 2009: 46). The automatic feature selection is built around the same strategies as the classification process itself; the algorithm assesses the relative weight of each feature based on the values realised for that feature in the encoding of the words.

Because selecting the most predictive trigrams from all words in our material proved too costly in terms of processing time and computer memory (the selection process timed out after seven days), we conducted these experiments with a smaller set of words. We prepared a dataset from 10,000 randomly selected word forms from the Norwegian and English lexicon files, which generated 4,043 unique trigrams. Next, we tested different thresholds using the productivity criterion, leaving out the trigrams with the lowest frequency. Since we did not know how many features Weka would select, we did not want to remove too many trigrams in advance. However, we wanted to see whether frequency is also a contributing factor in automatic classification, and thus tested the lower productivity thresholds 0–4. An f-value of 0 means that we did not remove any trigrams, while 1 means that we removed trigrams occurring only once, and 4 means that we removed trigrams occurring 4 times or less (as explained in Section 3.5).

Also here, we started with a baseline experiment (Table 13), training with the language-unique features derived from the set of 10,000 words and testing the different frequency thresholds. We then applied automatic feature selection before training our classifier with the potentially enhanced set of features (Table 14). We did not weed out zero-only instances from our training material; the classifier is trained on all 10,000 words.

4. URL: http://www.cs.waikato.ac.nz/ml/weka/

Table 13. Automatic feature selection baseline experiment (FSa)

Experiment	Language	Correct	Wrong	Precision	Recall	Overall accuracy
FSa-1 (f > 0)	English	2,397	0	100	47.94	73.97
	Norwegian	5,000	2,603			
FSa-2 (f > 1)	English	2,458	0	100	49.16	74.58
	Norwegian	5,000	2,542			
FSa-3 (f > 2)	English	2,379	0	100	47.11	73.79
	Norwegian	5,000	2,671			
FSa-4 (f > 3)	English	5,000	2,697	64.96	100	73.03
	Norwegian	2,303	0			
FSa-5 (f > 4)	English	5,000	2,812	63.10	100	71.88
	Norwegian	2,188	0			

The baseline yielded a maximum anglicism precision for the lowest thresholds in experiments FSa-1-3, and a low presicion but total recall for anglicisms in experiments FSa-3 and FSa-4. With the lower thresholds, the classifier seems to overgeneralise in favour of Norwegian, the other results are skewed towards English. The overall accuracy holds approximately the same level (between 71 and 75 per cent) for all experiments.

Training with the set of automatically selected features, both anglicism precision and overall accuracy were noticeably lower (Table 14), both compared to the baseline and to the results from our frequency-based approaches to feature selection described in the previous sections.

Table 14. Automatic feature selection: the selection experiment (FSb)

Experiment	Language	Correct	Wrong	Precision	Recall	Overall accuracy
FSb-1[5] (f > 0)	English	–	–	–	–	–
	Norwegian	–	–			
FSb-2 (f > 1)	English	5,000	3078	61.90	100	69.22
	Norwegian	1,922	0			
FSb-3 (f > 2)	English	5,000	3078	61.90	100	69.22
	Norwegian	1,922	0			
FSb-4 (f > 3)	English	5,000	3183	61.10	100	68.17
	Norwegian	1,817	0			
FSb-5 (f > 4)	English	5,000	3287	60.34	100	67.13
	Norwegian	1,713	0			

5. The feature selection timed out, probably due to the amount of features.

The best result was achieved in experiments FSb-2 and FSb-3, which yielded an overall precision of 69.22 per cent and 61.90 per cent presicion for anglicisms. No English words were wrongly classified as Norwegian, while more than half of the Norwegian words were classified as English.

Based on these results, frequency-based approaches to feature selection have proved more promising than automatic, statistics-based selection. This suggests that automatic feature selection is either not a suitable method for our material purposes, or that we need to refine our method.

4.4 Discussion of the results

From our results we see that the frequency-based approaches to feature selection produced very similar results throughout both series: a maximal precision for anglicisms, but a relatively low overall accuracy in the baseline experiments; a 100 per cent correct classification of all words in the idealised baseline experiments; close to a maximal anglicism precision and a high anglicism recall and overall accuracy in the holdout-experiments; and around 40 per cent anglicism precsion (and even lower recall), but a quite high overall accuracy in the gold standard experiments. Automatic feature selection led to a decreased classifier performance, compared to both the baseline and the frequency-based experiments.

We now account for some of the results in terms of frequency thresholds and the number of trigrams in the different experiments. If we compare the simple frequency and productivity experiments, the anglicism precision and overall accuracy were more or less the same. The recall was a bit higher in the productivity series; between 16 and 27 per cent compared to 11–19 per cent for simple frequency (cf. Tables 4 and 9). This could be due to some of the productivity experiments having more features in the feature vector. In the simple frequency baseline, the classifier trained with between 200 and 1,000 features (SFa-1-4, Table 15).

Table 15. The number of trigrams in the simple frequency (SF) and productivity (P) experiments

Experiment (threshold=n)	Total number of trigrams	English trigrams	Norwegian trigrams
SFa-1 (n=100)	200	100	100
SFa-2 (n=200)	400	200	400
SFa-3 (n=300)	600	300	300
SFa-4 (n=500)	1,000	500	500
Pa-4 (n=100)	733	268	465
Pa-3 (n=75)	944	392	552
Pa-2 (n=50)	1,342	629	713
Pa-1 (n=10)	3,919	2,360	1,559

In the productivity experiments, where we kept trigrams above certain thresholds, we find a higher number of features. Our chosen productivity thresholds 10, 50, 75 and 100 resulted in subsets of between 733 and 3,919 trigrams. The best experiments from both series were the ones with the highest number of trigrams in the vector: SFa-4 and Pa-1. The observation that more features lead to better classification results is further strengthened by the fact that the best experiment from the simple frequency baseline (with 1,000 features in total) yielded better results in terms of anglicism recall and overall accuracy than the productivity experiments that had less than 1,000 features (Pa-4 and Pa-3 with 733 and 944 features respectively, see Table 16).

Table 16. Classification results in relation to the number of features

Experiment	Number of trigrams	Anglicism precision	Anglisicm recall	Overall accuracy
Pa-4	733	100	16.00	59.61
Pa-3	944	100	17.92	60.62
SFa-4	1,000	100	19.00	61.26

However, the holdout experiments somewhat disrupts this picture, since here, the experiments with the most trigrams actually yielded a slightly lower precision for anglicisms: while the other frequencies yielded a maximum anglicism precision, experiment FSc-4 (n=500) yielded "only" a 97.04 per cent precision for anglicisms. Likewise, the two productivity experiments with fewer trigrams yielded a maximum anglicism precision, while the two experiments with the most trigrams yielded a 90.99 (Pc-1) and a 94.53 (Pc-2) per cent precision. It is therefore difficult to draw conclusions about any optimal threshold at this stage.

Regarding the control experiments, when training our classifier with the same features on new sets of words, we observe that they have a lower anglicism precision. The holdout results do not differ very much from the idealised baseline and are generally quite good; the worst classification result (Pc-1) yielded a more than 90 per cent anglicism precision, a total anglicism recall and a 94.27 per cent overall accuracy. As for the gold standard experiments, the selected features do not seem to have the same predictive power when applied to actual anglicisms as when applied to the set of words from which the trigrams were originally derived. When training the classifier on "real" anglicisms, precision for English decreases noticeably compared to the baseline.

In answer to our initial question – whether memory based learning can compete with or complement Andersen's (2005, 2011) hybrid tool – we are confident that it will provide a useful complementary method. Even if our selection methods partly suffer from low coverage and an overgeneralisation tendency (usually towards Norwegian), an obvious benefit of using data-driven methods is that we are able to derive large numbers of language-unique features, which in itself is a valuable resource. The frequency-based approaches are indeed worth pursuing further as a complement to the NNC hybrid classification tool.

5. Future work

This work represents the first effort to apply machine learning in the detection of anglicisms in Norwegian. We have pursued two frequency-based strategies for feature selection in memory based learning. Our strategies can be refined in several ways.

We have for practical reasons restricted our classification features to trigrams that have been extracted automatically from the words in our training material. In further work we could try to include chargrams of different lengths, such as two-character sequences (bigrams) and longer sequences. Further, our features have been selected by pertaining only to the criteria of uniqueness and productivity. Our selected method is in this sense completely data-driven, and disregards linguistic knowledge that could also prove useful in memory based learning experiments, such as typical English consonant and vowel clusters, word boundaries, and pre- and suffixes typical of one of the languages.

Andersen (Forthcoming) has made a closer examination of some of the words and trigrams from our experiments, and found that words which are erroneously not identified as anglicisms are often compounds with one Norwegian and one English part, where the Norwegian word has language specific characteristics (such as *åpningssynth* 'opening synth'). He further observes that the Norwegian characters *æ*, *ø* and *å* are prone to "override" English features. A possible enhancement of our model could thus be to include compound analysis. Further, the method could also benefit from including word boundary markers as part of the n-grams. A good place to start would be to add the features from Andersen's hybrid tool and train a classifier with the enhanced set of features. A further refinement would be to extend the set of features with knowledge-based information, e.g. by including the most typical English grapheme n-grams (uni- bi- and trigrams, marked for word boundaries) as described by Furiassi and Hofland (2007) and Furiassi (2008).

We should also consider testing other feature selection algorithms, and finally, although it requires a considerable effort in terms of manual classification, our method may benefit from using a larger set of actual anglicisms.

References

Abney, Steven. 2000. *Statistical methods*. London: Nature Publishing Group, Macmillian.

Almuallim, Hussein & Dietterich, Thomas G. 1991. Learning with many irrelevant features. In *Proceedings of the Ninth National Conference on Artificial Intelligence*. Menlo Park: AAAI Press, 547–552.

Andersen, Gisle. 2005. Assessing algorithms for automatic extraction of anglicisms in Norwegian texts. In *Proceedings of the International Conference on Corpus Linguistics (CL2005)*. <http://www.corpus.bham.ac.uk/PCLC>.

Andersen, Gisle. 2006. Engelske importord i norsk. *Språknytt* 3: 27–32.

Andersen, Gisle. 2011. Corpora as lexicographical basis: the case of anglicisms in Norwegian. *VARIENG – Studies in Variation, Contacts and Change in English* 6, <http://www.helsinki.fi/varieng/journal/index.html>.

Andersen, Gisle. Forthcoming. Corpus-based approaches to the study of anglicisms. In Virginia Pulcini and Cristiano Furiassi (eds). *The Anglicization of European Lexis*. To be published by John Benjamins.

Bouckaert, Remco R., Frank, Eibe, Hall, Mark, Richard, Kirkby, Reutemann, Peter, Seewald, Alex & Scuse, David. 2009. *WEKA Manual for Version 3-6-1*. University of Waikato, Hamilton, New Zealand. <http://ovh.dl.sourceforge.net/project/weka/documentation/3.6.x/-WekaManual-3- 6–1.pdf >.

Daelemans, Walter & van den Bosch, Antal. 2005. *Memory-based language processing*. Cambridge: Cambridge University Press.

Daelemans, Walter, Zavrel, Jakub, Van der Sloot, Ko & Van den Bosch, Antal. 2007. TiMBL: Tilburg Memory Based Learner, version 6.1, Reference Guide. *ILK Technical Report*. <http://ilk.uvt.nl/TiMBL>.

De Smedt, Koenraad & Rosén, Victoria. 1999. Datamaskinell skrivestøtte. In Lindgren, Birgitta (ed). *Språk i Norden 1999*. 20–32. Oslo: Novus.

De Smedt, Koenraad & Rosén Victoria. 2000. Automatic proofreading for Norwegian: The challenges of lexical and grammatical variation. In Nordgård, Torbjørn (ed) *NODALIDA'99: Proceedings from the 12th Nordiske datalingvistikkdager*, 206–215. Trondheim: Department of Linguistics NTNU.

Furiassi, Cristiano. 2008. What dictionaries leave out: new non-adapted Anglicisms in Italian. In *Investigating English with Corpora*, Aurelia Martelli & Virginia Pulcini (eds), 153–169. Monza: Polimetrica.

Furiassi, Cristiano & Hofland, Knut. 2007. The retrieval of false anglicisms in newspaper texts. In *Corpus Linguistics 25 Years on*, Roberta Facchinetti (ed), 347–363. Amsterdam: Rodopi.

Graedler, Anne-Line. 1998. *Morphological, semantic and functional aspects of English lexical borrowings in Norwegian*. Ph.D. dissertation, University of Oslo, Faculty of Arts. Oslo: Scandinavian University Press.

Görlach, Manfred. 2001. *A Dictionary of European anglicisms: a usage dictionary of anglicisms in sixteen European languages*. Oxford: Oxford University Press.

Johansson, Stig & Graedler, Anne-Line. 2002. *Rocka, hipt og snacksy: om engelsk i norsk språk og samfunn*. Kristiansand: Høyskoleforlaget.

Hall, Mark A. 1999. *Correlation-based Feature Selection for Machine Learning*. Ph.D. dissertation. The University of Wakato, Department of Computer Science.

Hoste, Véronique, Hendrickx, Iris, Daelemans, Walter & van den Bosch, Antal. 2002. Parameter Optimization for Machine-Learning of Word Sense Disambiguation. In *Natural Language Engineering* 8 (4), 311–325 Special Issue on Word Sense Disambiguation Systems.

Manning, Christopher & Schütze, Hinrich. 1999. *Foundations of Statistical Natural Language Processing*. Massachusetts: MIT Press.

Màrquez, L., Escudero, Gerard, Martinez, David & Rigau, German. 2006. Supervised corpus-based methods for WSD. In Eneko Agirre & Philip Edmonds (eds). *Word sense disambiguation: Algorithms and applications*, 167–207. Berlin: Springer.

Mihalcea, Rada. 2002. Word sense disambiguation with pattern learning and automatic feature selection. In *Natural Language Engineering* 8 (4): 343–358. Special Issue on Word Sense Disambiguation Systems.

Pedersen, Ted. 1999. Search techniques for learning probabilistic models of word sense disambiguation. *Working Notes of the AAAI Spring Symposium on Search Techniques for Problem Solving Under Uncertainty and Incomplete Information*, March 22–24, Palo Alto, CA. Unpublished.

Pedersen, Ted. 2002. Assessing system agreement and instance difficulty in the lexical sample tasks of SENSEVAL-2. *Proceedings of the ACL-02 workshop on Word sense disambiguation:* 40–46.

Stortingsmelding nr. 35 (2007–2008). 2008. *Mål og meining – ein heilskapleg norsk språkpolitikk*. Governmental White Paper. ⟨http://www.regjeringen.no/nb/dep/kud/dok/regpubl/stmeld/2007–2008/stmeld-nr-35- 2007-2008-.html?id=519923⟩.

Sæbø, Kjell Johan. Natural language corpus semantics: the Free Choice controversy. 2004. *Nordic Journal of Linguistics* 27(2): 197–218.

PART II

Corpus-based case studies

A corpus-based study of the adaptation of English import words in Norwegian*

Gisle Andersen
NHH Norwegian School of Economics

This paper focuses on English influence on Norwegian lexis and addresses the orthographic adaptation of import words, such as the change from *blog* to *blogg*, or *squash* to *skvåsj*. This adaptation can be viewed from a top-down perspective, by considering the effect of standardisation decisions made by the Norwegian Language Council, or from a bottom-up perspective, by considering unsolicited adaptation initiated by the language users themselves. Both types are observable in the 900 million word Norwegian Newspaper Corpus (NNC). The paper aims to show that the NNC lends itself easily to a large-scale investigation of either top-down or bottom-up adaptation. First of all, the corpus-based investigation illustrates the extent to which English-based import words are represented using original or adapted orthography. Secondly, the corpus provides empirical data that may shed significant light on the linguistic aspects of the adaptation process. Thus, through a quantitative and qualitative inspection of the data, I point to a set of linguistic and contextual factors that appear to have important bearings on the degree to which words undergo spelling adaptation. At the same time, the paper is intended to illustrate the usefulness of some of the facilities of the newly developed Corpuscle search engine and interface and to show its value when applied to a specific empirical research task.

1. Introduction

The influence of English is discernible at many levels of language. Clearly most notable is its influence on the general lexicon (e.g. *app, break even, image, smoothie*) and specialised terminology, not least in the business, financial and administrative domains (e.g. *controller, due diligence, subprime*; cf. also Kristiansen this volume). But contact-induced innovations are also observable at the discourse

* The bulk of this work was done during a Sabbatical stay at the Department of Linguistics and English Language at Lancaster University. I am very grateful to the department for its hospitality and to several members of staff for their generous and skillful evaluation of my work.

level, for instance in the emergence of new structures like the topic introducer *når det kommer til* 'when it comes to', and possibly also intonation, as seen from the emergent use of a high-rising tone as a givenness marker in narratives among young speakers of Western Norwegian dialects (Andersen forthcoming).

This chapter addresses a very specific aspect of English influence on Norwegian, namely the orthographic adaptation of import words, henceforth 'norwegification', as when *blog* becomes *blogg*, *fight* becomes *fait* and *squash* becomes *skvåsj*. (For simplicity, the respective forms are referred to as "E forms" and "N forms" in this chapter.) This is a process which can be viewed from a top-down perspective, by considering the effect of official normative decisions made by the Norwegian Language Council (*Språkrådet*) or from a bottom-up perspective, by considering unsolicited adaptation initiated by the language users themselves, which can be called spontaneous or 'folk' norwegification. Both types are observable in the Norwegian Newspaper Corpus (NNC; Andersen & Hofland this volume), and, as will be shown in this chapter, the NNC lends itself easily to a large-scale investigation of either top-down or bottom-up adaptation. The paper takes a strictly corpus-based approach and considers the extent to which English-based import words are written as E forms or N forms in the NNC. Thus the following research questions can be posed:

- to what extent have writers in the Norwegian Newspapers Corpus started using the norwegified spellings of import words recommended by the Norwegian Research Council?
- to what extent are recent import words in the Norwegian Newspapers Corpus characterised by unsolicited, user-initiated spelling adaptation?
- what can this tell us about the 'success criteria' for norwegification, that is, what characterises words that are frequently norwegified as supposed to those that are not, in terms of their orthographic complexity, phonological structure, collocational features, inflectional and derivational morphology or semantic features?

The influence of English is frequently deplored by people who fear for the future of the language or who find English-based neologisms to be unpleasant, unnecessary and a sign of sloppiness or undue anglomania (Winter-Froemel 2008; Fjeld and Nygaard this volume). It is not my wish to contribute to the language debate *per se*, or to lament the influence of English as a global language; neither will I in this context address the motivation for or attitudes towards anglicisms. Rather, my aim is to supply substantial empirical data that may shed light on the linguistic aspects of the adaptation process, and to point out a set of contextual factors that appear to have important bearings on the degree to which words undergo spelling adaptation. At the same time, this chapter will serve to illustrate the usefulness of some of the facilities of the newly developed Corpuscle search engine and interface (Meurer this volume) and to show its value when applied in a specific empirical research task.

2. Concepts and terminology

The influence of English on Norwegian lexis takes different shapes. Traditional lexicology makes a distinction between *domestic words* and *import words*, where the latter is variably defined according to their etymological origin (Hansen & Lund 1994) or lack of adaptation to the orthographical or phonetic structure of the target language (Sandøy 1997). Thus, the notion of import words in Norwegian can be used to denote words which are not part of the Germanic-based vocabulary of Old Norse but imported from Latin, Greek, Dutch, German, English or any other language, such as *fusjon* 'fusion, merger', or it may denote any imported word whose orthography or pronunciation has not been adapted to Norwegian, such as *fusion* (both of which occur in the NNC). It makes sense to single out words of foreign origin which are fully adapted to Norwegian, many of which are no longer perceived as foreign. In accordance with Sandøy (1997:13), these may be called *loan words* (*lånord*), such as *sjekk*. On the other hand, non-adapted words may be called *foreign words* (*fremmedord*) such as *checkout*. In this taxonomy *norwegification* refers to the process of domestication (Dunn 2008), i.e. adaptation of foreign words turning them into loan words in Norwegian.

Adaptation can affect morphology, phonology, orthography as well as semantics (cf. Section 6.5). Import words that are morphologically adapted take the same inflectional morphology as domestic Norwegian words, as with the recent word *app* whose inflectional forms *appen* 'the app', *apper* 'apps', *appene* 'the apps' readily occur in the NNC, albeit alongside *apps* used in the indefinite plural. Phonological adaptation means that foreign phonemes or phoneme combinations are replaced by equivalent domestic ones, as with *app* whose vowel is often changed from [æ] to [a]. However, only orthographic adaptation will be systematically addressed in this chapter, although there will be recurring reference to the other types. This adaptation involves the replacement of foreign graphemes or graphemic combinations with domestic ones in such a way that the connection between a word's phonology and orthography becomes more in line with the spelling norms of Norwegian. This categorically affects the foreign consonants c, q, w, x and z and clusters in which they occur, but also many other letter combinations. Norwegification entails a spelling that is in accordance with Norwegian graphotax (rules for acceptable letter sequences) and generally also increased orthophony on the part of the imported word (though not always: cf. Omdal 2008a: 95), as in the examples of complex vocalic graphemic combinations like *aw* which becomes *å* as in *trawl* → *trål* or diphthongal graphemic combinations like *igh* which becomes *ai* (*fight* → *fait*). However, some replacements involve the same level of graphemic complexity to represent a single phoneme, such as *sh* → *sj* for [ʃ] or *ch* → *sj* (*choke* → *sjåk*). Note also that unsolicited spelling adaptation may be partial, for instance in compounds like *jønkfood*, where the norwegification is restricted to the first component, or the form *krash*, which has a norwegified initial consonant but a foreign word-final consonant cluster. See Johansson and Graedler (2002: 164ff) for a survey of orthographic changes and Sandøy (1997) for a survey of the principles of norwegification. As will be shown in this chapter, adaptation is often gradual and variation occurs between non-adapted, partially adapted and fully adapted forms. The relation between foreign words and loan words should therefore be seen as a continuum rather than a dichotomy (Chrystal 1988; Piltingsrud 2001).

The English influence on lexis also comprises a number of phenomena that do not represent cases of morphemic importation or domestication of English-based lexical material. First, *replacement words* (*avløserord* 'calques') are morphemic substitutions based on target language material. This is a type of contact-induced innovation which is regarded as more language-politically acceptable than import words (e.g. Akselberg 2005). A pertinent and successful example is *varsler/varsling* for 'whistleblower/-ing'. Second, *loan translations* refer to the analogical replacement of each of the components of a foreign word with its domestic equivalents, as when *team building* becomes *lagbygging*. Third, contact-induced innovation is observable as *neosemanticism*, that is, emergent changes in the semantics of existing words (Fjeld & Nygaard this volume). A recent example is *karakter* 'character', which has taken on a new meaning of 'fictional character' in plays and movies etc., and which co-exists with its Norwegian synonym *rollefigur*. A type of contact-induced innovation which is rarely studied is the change in grammatical properties (valency) of individual words, as with the verb *snakke* 'talk', which has come to be used as a transitive verb whose complementation does not require the preposition *om* 'about', as seen from example (1):

(1) *Og da snakker vi business.* (FV01lgva)
And then we're talking business.

Moreover, imports from English may occur at levels other than the lexical, for instance the import of affixes, as seen from the highly productive *e-* prefix (cf. *e-faktura* 'e-invoice', *e-forbrytelse* 'e-crime', *e-handel*, 'e-shopping' etc.). Note that its productivity extends beyond the originally English import words, and many of the e-words are not imported wholesale. Besides, the influence may involve the use of a certain compound component with a particular meaning in the source language but innovative in the target language, as with *-factor* 'factor', which is equally productive; cf., *motivasjonsfaktor* 'motivation factor', *nerdefaktor* 'nerd factor', *rødvinsfaktor* 'red wine factor', etc. Finally, contact-induced innovation includes words and phrases at the level of discourse and pragmatics. This includes the import of interjections and discourse markers, such as *duh* or the irony marker *yeah right*, which are common in contemporary Norwegian (Andersen 2010a, forthcoming).

3. Previous research on norwegification

There is a rich literature on the international spread of anglicisms as a result of the role of English as a global language (Ljung 1985, 1988; Görlach 2001, 2003; Onysko 2007, 2009; Fischer & Pułaczewska 2008; Furiassi 2010). There is also a substantial amount of work on its influence on Norwegian (e.g. Stene 1945; Haugen 1953; Rand Schmidt 1982; Graedler & Johansson 1997; Graedler 1998; Johansson & Graedler 2002; Andersen 2005, 2010b, 2011). A notable recent effort is the project MIN "Modern import words in the Nordic countries", which has studied the effect of English on the six Nordic languages. This is documented in a 10-volume series (cf. e.g. Sandøy & Östman 2004; Jarvad & Sandøy 2007; Selback & Sandøy 2007; Omdal & Sandøy 2008). The main findings of the project are reproduced in a recent special issue in the *International Journal of the Sociology of Language* (Kristiansen & Sandøy 2010).

Work that specifically addresses spelling adaptation is not as frequent. Most notable is Sandøy (1997), whose account was initially written as a government white paper that establishes the language-political and linguistic principles for spelling adaptations to be applied by the Norwegian Language Council. Sandøy outlines the history of spelling reforms pertinent to norwegification and justifies the specific proposals for individual words suggested by the Norwegian Language Council's working group for standardisation. The standardised spellings listed in Sandøy's Annex 3 (1997: 141f) were officially recognised by the Norwegian Language Council in 1996 and approved by the Ministry of Culture (*Kulturdepartementet*), thereby becoming part of official Norwegian orthography. It is this set of words that constitutes the main dataset which will be investigated in this chapter. Importantly, when the Norwegian Language Council introduces spelling reforms of this kind, it is usually the case that the N and E forms become equal in status, so that both are part of official orthography.[1] However, according to their own

1. The exceptions to this from the 1996 reform are *breikdans*, *hipp*, *kaps*, *rafte*, *rapp(e)*, *snaksy* and *tilte*, which only have N forms as part of the written standard.

guidelines, the policy of the Norwegian Language Council is to use exclusively the N forms in their writings and to recommend this use when asked for advice about the spelling of anglicisms. Besides, the council is supposed to consider excluding the unadapted forms from the written standard after a norwegified form has been officially recognised for 20 years (Språkrådet 2011a).[2]

Also in a language planning context, Grønvik (1991) lists the formal requirements for import words in order to be considered as fully Norwegian. These include the phonology of an import word (containing no foreign phonemes or phonemic combinations), its orthography (containing no foreign graphemes or graphemic combinations), orthophony (correspondance of pronunciation and conventional Norwegian graphotax) and inflectional morphology (following the patterns of native Norwegian words). She adds that the norwegification of original spelling is generally considered an undesirable solution ('*naudløysing*' Grønvik 1991: 143) and that the preferable 'solution to the loan word problem' are translation loans or calques. She also describes briefly the principles of spelling adaptation, such as replacement of foreign consonants (c, q, w, x, z), elision of unpronounced consonants, unification of all foreign letter combinations representing [ʃ] to sj, consonant doubling, etc.

Masvie (1992) uses a questionnaire to chart co-variation between social categories and linguistic behaviour. She investigates the use of and attitudes towards English, and informants are asked to give their preference for either the original or adapted form of 12 anglicisms. So her findings are based on self-reported rather than actual usage. There are only minor preferential differences between user groups, but the adapted forms are preferred slightly more often by young female users from Farsund (vs. Oslo). There are notable differences, however, in the figures for individual words, between the well-established anglicisms *gear/gir*, *lunch/lunsj*, *mix/miks*, *hike/haike* and *peanut/peanøtt*, for which there is an overwhelming preference for the N forms (these have been part of the spelling norm since 1940 or earlier; cf. Sandøy 1997: 67) and the newer anglicisms *tape/teip*, *crawl/krål*, *striptease/striptis*, *clutch/kløtsj* and *guide/gaid*, where the informants have a clear preference for the E forms (these were not part of the official norm at the time of her study, with the exception of *teip*).

Piltingsrud (2001) is the work that is closest in focus and methodology to the current one, as she also investigates the inventory of words from the 1996 spelling reform. Her data are drawn from what she refers to as *Bergenskorpuset* 'the Bergen corpus', which essentially is the NNC in its initial phase, including the first two years of the harvesting period, at a time where there were only 8 newspapers

2. A short overview of the norwegification principles is also found in Sandøy (2004).

in the corpus. Another important difference is that her study strictly considers the lemmas specifically listed in the spelling reform document, thus she ignored any derived forms such as the verb *kick* or the noun *rapper*, but she does include inflected forms and compounds containing the anglicisms. She emphasises the problematic nature of certain types of orthographic change, such as *squash* and *know-how*. She observes generally very low scores for the norwegified forms four years after the spelling of these anglicisms was standardised, with a few notable exceptions (cf. Section 5.2 below). Her study also supplies valuable information by means of dates for the first registration in *Nyordsmaterialet*, a lexical database of neologisms (cf. Fjeld & Nygaard this volume), showing that some of the E forms are registered as early as the 1920s (*clinch*, *fighter*), while most of them date from the 1960s and 1970s.

In their thorough diachronic and synchronic account of English and its influence on Norwegian, Johansson and Graedler (2002) devote some attention to spelling adaptation (2002: 162ff). They stress that Norwegian has more orthophonic spelling norms than English and that most anglicisms retain their original orthography, despite a long tradition for orthographic adaptation of import words. They comment on the 1997 spelling reform and the reactions it triggered in the media, and point out the co-existence of official standardisation and unsolicited norwegification. Most importantly for the current research is their survey of orthographic changes (cf. Section 6.1). They also present usage statistics from the 1990s of some of the words from the 1997 reform, showing a limited use of the N forms. However, they have restricted their counts to number of articles in which a form occurs and have not checked individual tokens or corrected for metalinguistic use, use in titles, quotations or the like (cf. Section 4.3).

Within the framework of the MIN project, Omdal (2008a, b, c) addresses morphological and orthographical adaptation of import words (not exclusively anglicisms) in Norwegian. The study is based on 1,822 tokens of 813 word forms that were manually retrieved from five newspaper editions from 1975 and 2000. Many of the tokens are drawn from advertisements, and Omdal points out that one must be careful when making generalisations beyond this material (Omdal 2008: 102). Selback (2007) notes that the proportion of import words in the Norwegian MIN corpus is less than 1 per cent, and that the figure is higher in advertisements than in journalistic text (1.7 vs. 0.7 per cent, respectively). She also observes that anglicisms are more frequent in reviews and articles concerning leisure activities (*cruise*, *charter* etc.). In Omdal's study, each token was classified for its type of consonant and vowel adaptations in terms of 37 orthographic features outlined by Johannson and Graedler (2002: 164–166). Norwegian has a relatively strong tradition of normative spelling adaptation, especially when compared to Danish (Omdal 2008c: 164). This is reflected in the fact that the degree of observed adaptation is higher in Norwegian and Icelandic than in the other Nordic languages, with Danish showing the lowest degree of adaptation. Omdal reports a ratio of adapted vs. unadapted forms that is almost even, with 44 vs. 42 per cent of the total, respectively.[3] This is a much higher adaptation ratio than the findings of the current study, to be reported below. In all likelihood this difference is due to the inventory of forms investigated, which include well established anglicisms such as *attraktiv* 'attractive', *mobil* 'mobile', *senter* 'centre' and *stress*, as opposed to the much more recent anglicisms to be investigated in the current study, based on some 338,000 tokens. The findings of Omdal and his Nordic colleagues in the MIN project are discussed by Graedler and Kvaran (2010), who rightly observe that "there is a tendency for the most recent import word to be less often adapted in the spelling than the older, established words" (Graedler & Kvaran 2010: 35f). It is not unlikely that the adaptation ratio would have been different in a larger dataset. Especially the diphthongs of words like *e-mail*, *stayer*, *drive-in* and *design* are unadapted, as well as the vowels of *scooter* and *cruise*. For consonants, the vast majority of unadapted forms are due to c and x in words like *cruise* and *sex* (86 %).

Finally, taking a historical perspective on the issue of lexical purism in the Nordic countries, Vikør (2010) notes that the written standard Bokmål is a relatively anti-purist variety, even in spelling matters, while Nynorsk is more purist. The development of replacement words has been problematic because international vocabulary is often indispensible and "new Norwegian coinages for well-known international words hampered communication" (Vikør 2010: 22). Importantly, he reports the general success of norwegification practises in the pre-WWII era: "while lexical purism failed, orthographical purism triumphed" (Vikør 2010: 21). This has changed radically with the modern influx of anglicisms, and now the norwegification proposals are generally met with considerable resistance in the population.

4. Inventory, data and methods

The current study explores the NNC via the new Corpuscle search engine and interface (Meurer this volume). At the time of retrieval (July 2010), the corpus consisted of approximately 938 million running words. The investigation incorporates three word sets which have been subjected to the same type of quantitative

3. The remaining 14 per cent are classified as 'neutral', i.e. words such as *sponsor* "that have an English spelling which fits well into the national orthographic system, thus making their status as either foreign or integrated hard to determine" (Graedler & Kvaran 2010: 35).

and qualitative analysis. Each word set consists of a list of anglicisms represented as word pairs with minimally one orthographically adapted N form (e.g. *taiming*) and an unadapted E form (*timing*). I consider these as sociolinguistic variables, with the N and E forms constituting possible variants. Occasionally, more than one N variant may be possible; this applies specifically to anglicisms which are realised differently in the two written standards Nynorsk and Bokmål, such as *entertainer* → *enterteinar/enterteiner*, where the *-ar* forms represent Nynorsk morphology. In some cases I have collapsed several word pairs into one variable due to their common morphological stem; cf. Tables 1–2 below, where all these groupings can be found. Although hybrid forms consisting of an adapted and an unadapted component may theoretically occur – such as *breikdance* 'breakdance', I have not searched specifically for these, but restricted the set of variants to the spellings proposed by the Norwegian Language Council, which would not allow such hybrid forms. Neither have I included unsolicited forms such as *ræpp* for *rap/rapp*, which is not among the realisations recognised by the Norwegian Language Council (but see Section 4.3).

4.1 The three datasets

The first and largest set of words, and the one which will receive the most attention in the study, is the list of words from the comprehensive spelling reform in 1996 (Sandøy 1997: 141f). The original list contains 49 word pairs.[4] Since my primary focus is English influence, I decided to ignore three lexemes from French, such as *bulletin* → *bulleteng* and *pauvre* → *påver*. Moreover, many of the words could be collapsed into the same lexical variable, e.g. *guide* → *gaid* (n)/*gaid* (v), which were listed as separate entries. One word pair did not contain any orthographic difference because the N and E forms coincide, namely *raft* → *raft*, where the domestication is restricted to regular morphological affixation by which the stem takes verbal endings *-e*/*-er* or the nominal *-ing*. These inflected/derived forms are not a distinguishing feature of E vs. N forms but characteristic of anglicisms generally. Having performed these operations, the word set was reduced to 36 word pairs (cf. Table 2 below). Note that one anglicism, *snacksy*[5] → *snaksy*, is a pseudo-anglicism, i.e. an English-looking form that does not occur in English (Johansson & Graedler 2002; Dunn 2008).

4. For some reason, the first word *breikdans* is not represented with its E form *breakdance* in Sandøy's (1997: 141) table.

5. The E form is incorrectly spelt *snacsy* in Sandøy's (1997: 141) table.

The second word set comprises relevant word pairs from the next stage of reform proposed in 2004 (Språkrådet 2011b), which includes *coil* → *koil*, *hickory* → *hikkori* etc. Applying the same principles as above, I set aside the non-English import words *accessoirer* 'accessories' and *nonchalant* (Fr.), *bacalao* (Sp./Pg.), *dachs* and *(sado)masochist/m* (Ge.) and *maracas* (Pg.). I also chose to ignore the word pair *commando* → *kommando*, which – according to the standardisation document – in its E form refers to a specific type of military troop (cf. Oxford English Dictionary (OED) *commando*: '[a] party commanded or called out for military purposes'), but whose N form coincides with the more general word meaning 'command'. The N form is massively recurrent in the corpus, but no traces of the specific meaning inherent in the anglicism were found. Hence, the tokens cannot be said to represent domestication of this anglicism. These operations reduced the set to 13 word pairs.

Finally, I compiled a word set consisting of six relatively recent anglicisms, most of which are associated with youth language or slang, specifically *blog* → *blogg*, *crazy* → *kreisi*, *date* → *deit*, *dull* → *døll*, *nerd* → *nørd* and *ugly* → øgli. The purpose of incorporating these in the investigation is to see if the process of unsolicited norwegification appears to be governed by the same principles as the normative process, and to see whether this type is more or less successful than the norwegification which is recommended by the regulatory body.

4.2 The Corpuscle interface to the Norwegian Newspaper Corpus

The NNC is a good resource for the investigation of neologisms and anglicisms. It is very large and represents a consistent text category of web-based newspapers, and it includes an unbroken flow of text covering the period from 1998 to the present (Andersen and Hofland this volume). In this study, the investigation of each word set is based on systematic searching using the Corpuscle interface and search engine (Meurer this volume). The system is both fast and flexible, and it allows for complex truncated searches. This is ideal for the current purposes, since the retrieval of relevant tokens amounts to looking for a long list of word stems which undergo various morphological processes. A concordance view from the Corpuscle system is shown in Figure 1.

The Corpuscle search system allows for complex searches based on conventional regular expressions typed in the search window. I therefore created a complex search expression by means of perl script which transforms a list into a search expression of truncated forms separated by the OR operator (|). The system is robust enough to retrieve a complex search like the following in one go (where "..." indicates the remaining words from the 1997 reform).

```
.*(breikdans|breakdance|enterteinar|…|outsider).*
```

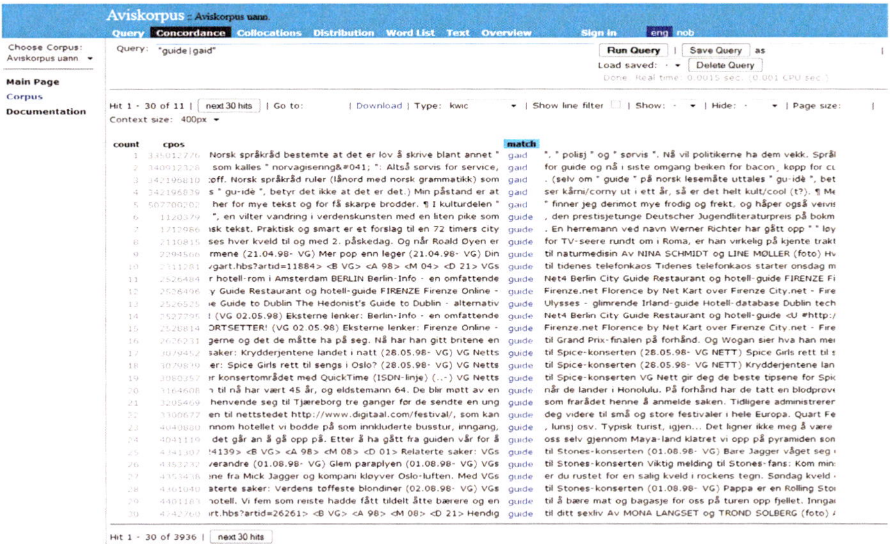

Figure 1. Corpuscle concordance of the word pair *guide* → *gaid*

This robustness simplified the retrieval process radically. Having a generalised query language allowing for UNIX-compatible regular expressions is advantageous for the linguist who is familiar with basic programming, as there is no need to study a specific/proprietary corpus query language. Where needed, additional disambiguating lexeme-specific searches were carried out, for instance by using. `*hip[^p].*` to search for *hip*, and not *hipp*, etc. Another very useful feature of Corpuscle is the word list mode, as illustrated in Figure 2.

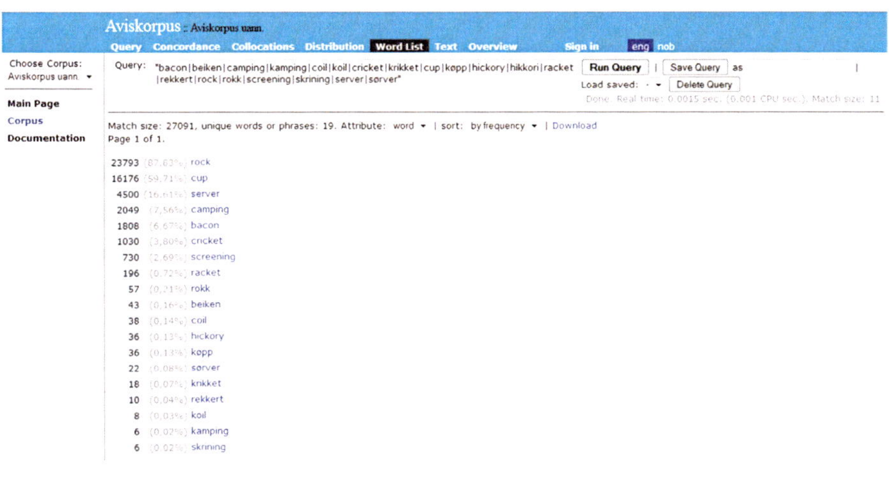

Figure 2. Corpuscle word list view of anglicisms from the 2004 reform (top of list)

This word list view gives the statistics for all unique word forms retrieved in a specific search, and this is useful for the analysis of many different lexemes based on a complex search. Besides, it is equally convenient for the analysis of the variability and morphological complexity of individual words, as seen in Figure 3.

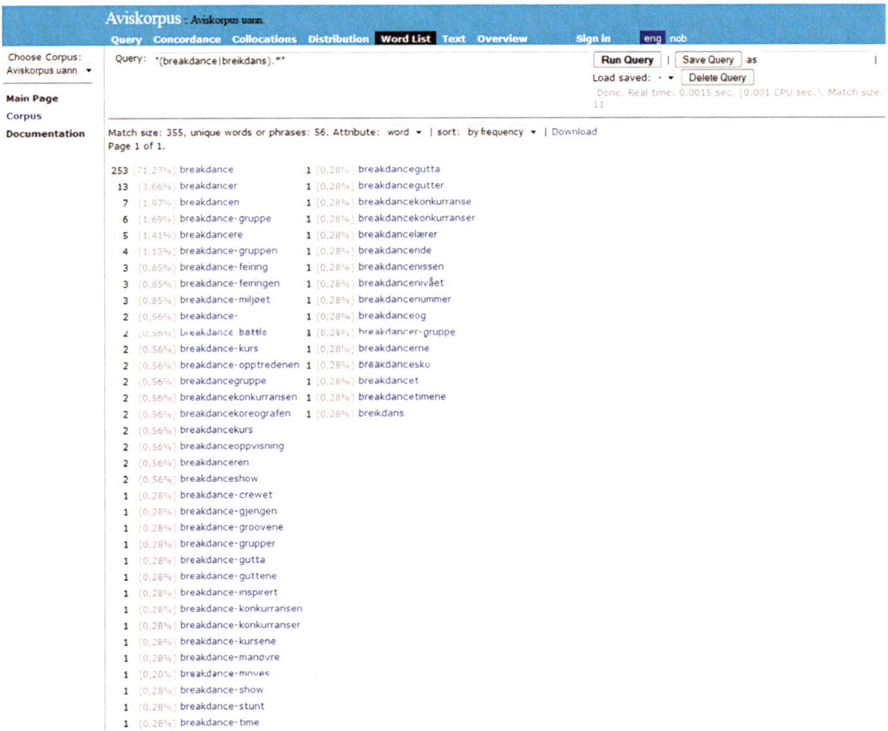

Figure 3. Corpuscle word list of morphological variability of the word pair *breakdance → breikdans*

4.3 Step-by-step analysis

The first step of my data retrieval, then, amounted to performing the necessary searches in Corpuscle using a combination of truncated searches for individual word pairs as well as regular expressions retrieving all the tokens relevant to one of the three word sets mentioned above. These searches retrieved all the instances of adapted and unadapted anglicisms, including all inflectional and derivational forms (compounds etc.) in which they occur.

In the second step, there was a need for semi-automatic postprocessing of the retrieved data. For instance I had to remove irrelevant items such as *manuskript* 'manuscript', which is an already norwegified import word and not relevant for the *script* → *skript* word pair. Such editing was mostly done directly in the exported text file by means of regular expressions in the text editor TextPad, or it was done by means of a perl script which I developed to remove duplicate instances automatically.

Third, there was a need for a manual inspection of all the retrieved tokens in order to remove instances resulting from spelling errors and tokens representing metalinguistic use or other lexemes than the anglicisms in question. This can be illustrated with the example of a specific form, *sørver*, whose concordance is seen in Figure 4.

Figure 4. Corpuscle collocation of *sørver*

One token of *sørver*, no. 11 (cf. leftmost column) must be ignored, being a spelling error of *sørover* 'southwards'. The three tokens 8–10 must be reduced to one instance, since two of them are the result of duplication. Tokens 2, 3, 5 and 6 represent metalinguistic use resulting from description of the 2004 spelling reform in newspaper articles; cf. example (2).

(2) *og datafolk kan fremdeles skrive server i stedet for sørver* (VG02xx13)
and computer people can still write server instead of sørver

(3) *Unge mennesker skriver allerede streit for straight, og de deiter fra engelsk date for stevnemøte.* (DB02xx14)
young people are already writing streit for straight, and they deit from English date for *stevnemøte* ('date')

I have consistently ruled out these types of metalinguistic use in the statistics, as they are not true instantiations of authentic use of either the adapted or unadapted forms. Note that the form *server/sørver* is actually ambiguous between a noun stem [*server/sørver*] and the inflected form [[*serv/sørv*]*er*], which can have either a nominal (plural) or verbal (present tense) reading. Since all three words derive from English words with a common stem – 'server', 'to serve' or 'a serve', respectively – all such tokens are included in the analysis. However, Norwegian has a homographic domestic word *sørv* denoting a small fish, which occurs in the uninflected form in the corpus, but not in the plural. Naturally, this was excluded from the analysis since it represents a different lexeme. In fact, many of the words in the study are ambiguous in this way, and separating relevant from irrelevant tokens on lexical grounds was quite a substantial task, to be described in more detail in the qualitative discussion below. Furthermore, the manual check involved the removal of E tokens used in code-switching or wholly-English citations as in example (3).

(3) *"Ambitions are already starting to fade", synger de.* (VG090813)
"Ambitions are already starting to fade", they sing.

The final step of the analysis involved statistical operations, namely the calculation of the ratio between N and E forms for each dataset, which will be shown in the next section.

5. Degree of norwegification in the three datasets

In this section, I give an overview of the quantitative results of this investigation. I first present the statistical results for the three datasets (Section 5.1), before I present each of the datasets in more detail (Sections 5.2–5.4).

5.1 Overall results for the three datasets

As mentioned in Section 4, I have investigated words from the comprehensive spelling reform in 1996, words from the less comprehensive reform proposed in 2004, and a set of unsolicited norwegifications. The overall results of these three datasets are seen in Table 1.

Table 1. Overall results of norwegification of anglicisms in the NNC

Dataset	N form	E form	Sum	% N form
1997 spelling reform	17,736	245,093	262,829	6.7%
2004 spelling reform	67	14,085	14,152	0.5%
Unsolicited normalisation	53,362	7,624	60,986	87.5%

These average figures show that the N forms are massively disfavoured against the E forms of the anglicisms investigated. The 1997 spelling reform appears to have had a slightly stronger effect than the more recent 2004 reform, but it would be wrong to claim that any of the spelling reforms have had any significant impact on the spelling used in newspapers. However, as will become evident in the following sections, there are considerable differences to be noted between the individual word pairs in terms of their degree of normalisation, and the high ratio of norwegified words in the third dataset is due to a few very frequent words.

5.2 A more detailed look at the words from the 1997 spelling reform

The full list of relevant word pairs from the 1997 reform is given in Table 2. The table shows the N and E forms and their frequencies, as well as the percentage of forms that have a normalised spelling (rightmost column). The data are sorted by degree of norwegification.

Table 2. Percentage of norwegification of words from the 1997 reform

N form	E form	N tokens	E tokens	Sum	% N form
keitering	catering	0	996	996	0.0%
overhedd	overhead	0	200	200	0.0%
sjåk	choke	0	31	31	0.0%
snaksy	snacksy	0	23	23	0.0%
sjarter	charter	0	10,450	10,450	0.0%
breikdans	breakdance	0	357	357	0.0%
polisj	polish	0	104	104	0.0%
hedde	heade	2	14,619	14,621	0.0%
gaid/e	guide	11	69,754	69,765	0.0%
fait/faite	fight	2	3,644	3,646	0.1%
sørvis	service	66	82,061	82,127	0.1%
finisj	finish	3	2,446	2,449	0.1%
utsidar/-er	outsider	7	3,955	3,962	0.2%
skvåsj	squash	2	1,071	1,073	0.2%
enterteinar/-er	entertainer	5	1,022	1,027	0.5%
kikk	kick	17	3,295	3,312	0.5%
taime	time	31	4,568	4,599	0.7%
seif/-e	safe	59	4,249	4,308	1.4%

(Continued)

Table 2. Percentage of norwegification of words from the 1997 reform (Continued)

N form	E form	N tokens	E tokens	Sum	% N form
innputt	input	5	265	270	1.9%
utputt	output	1	39	40	2.5%
feide/-er/-ar/-ing	fade	5	125	130	3.8%
konteinar/-er	container	570	10,086	10,656	5.3%
kaps	caps	189	1,954	2,143	8.8%
skup	scoop	132	695	827	16.0%
ketsjup	ketchup	250	1,075	1,325	18.9%
hipp	hip	2,740	10,786	13,526	20.3%
skript	script	52	191	243	21.4%
pønk/-ar/-er	punk/-ar/-er	1,794	3,201	4,995	35.9%
rapp/-e	rap	7,810	3,854	11,664	67.0%
innsidar/-er	insider	1,313	346	1,659	79.1%
pins	pin	227	53	280	81.1%
klinsj/-e	clinch	420	64	484	86.8%
streit/-e	straight	1,407	181	1,588	88.6%
		17,736	245,093	262,829	6.7%

As mentioned, I have ignored a few of the 1997 word pairs since there is no variation in their word stem (*raft*), or since they are not of English origin (*pauvre*). Note also that the N forms *breikdans*, *sjarter* and *polisj* in fact do occur once, but this is not reflected in Table 1 since the uses are metalinguistic. The same applies to one token of *entertainer*. Three other anglicisms are also never norwegified, namely *keitering overhedd* and *sjåk*.

A great many words are norwegified in less than five per cent of the cases, namely the 14 word pairs from *hedde* to *feide* in Table 1. Yet, we observe that the Norwegian Language Council's proposed spelling has had some effect even among these words, most notable in *sørvis* (66 tokens), *taime* (31) and *seif* (59).

A smaller group of six words, *kaps*, *skup*, *ketsjup*, *hipp*, *skript* and *pønk*, are slightly more often norwegified, ranging from 8 to 36 per cent of the cases.

Very noticeable from these statistics is the gap in norwegification ratio in the range between 36 per cent and 67 per cent. None of the word pairs have a norwegification ratio which is around 50 per cent of the cases. In other words, norwegification seems to be an 'either/or': that is, generally speaking language users either massively favour the adapted form of a word, or they favour the unadapted form, and the two forms are never equally distributed.

Finally, the five N forms *rapp*, *innsidar/-er*, *pins*, *klinsj* and *streit* emerge as the success stories from the 1997 reform. This is to some degree consistent with the observations made by Piltingsrud (2001:67), whose data indicates that these words were among the frequent norwegifications as early as 2000. This raises the question, what is it about these words which make them susceptible to adoption by writers? This question is addressed in Section 6. But first, I will consider the two other datasets.

5.3 Degree of norwegification of words from the 2004 spelling reform

The full list of relevant word pairs from the 2004 reform is given in Table 3, sorted by degree of norwegification.

Table 3. Percentage of norwegification of words from the 2004 reform

N form	E form	N tokens	E tokens	Sum	% N form
koil	coil	0	32	32	0.0%
hikkory	hickory	0	33	33	0.0%
kannabis	cannabis	1	4,431	4,432	0.0%
sørver	server	3	5,420	5,423	0.1%
snaks	snacks	5	1,311	1,316	0.4%
sørve/sørv	serve	3	746	749	0.4%
gimmik	gimmick	4	752	756	0,5%
karving	carving	2	227	229	0.9%
rekkert	racket	10	716	726	1.4%
karavan	caravan	5	237	242	2.1%
korny	corny	7	178	185	3.8%
karting	carting	27	2	29	93.1%
		67	14,085	14,152	0.5%

In addition to the N tokens reported in the table, most of the words occur with at least one metalinguistic occurrence in a newspaper article that describes the spelling reform. We note from the table that two of the words are never norwegified, while the remaining words – bar one – have norwegified forms only in up to 3.8 per cent of the cases. The odd one out is *carting* → *karting*, which is mostly used with the domestic form. However, and importantly, this word pair is not a norwegification in the ordinary sense, because both the forms *carting* and *karting* occur in English and they denote different concepts. While *carting* "is a dog sport or activity in which a dog … pulls a dogcart filled with supplies"

(Wikipedia *carting*), *karting* "is a variant of open-wheel motor sport with small, open, four-wheeled vehicles called karts, go-karts, or gearbox/shifter karts" (Wikipedia *karting*). This conceptual difference seems to have gone unnoticed by the spelling reformists, who are presenting *carting* → *karting* as an ordinary replacement of a foreign consonant, without specifying that the two forms have different designations in the source language. The 27 *karting* tokens seem to refer exclusively to the 'karting' sense and are thus not the result of norwegification of *carting*. If we correct for this error, the overall norwegification ratio of words from the 2004 reform is reduced from 0.5 to 0.3 per cent.

5.4 Degree of unsolicited norwegification

The degree of norwegification of the selected anglicisms observed in the corpus that have not (yet) been standardised by the Norwegian Language Council is shown in Table 4.

Table 4. Percentage of norwegification of words not normalised by any spelling reform

N form	E form	N tokens	E tokens	Sum	% N form
nørd	nerd	15	4,481	4,496	0.3%
kreisi	crazy	6	540	546	1.1%
deit	date	55	2,505	2,560	2.1%
øgli	ugly	4	20	24	16.7%
døll	dull	185	2	187	98.9%
blogg	blog	53,097	76	53,173	99.9%
		53,362	**7,624**	**60,986**	**87.5%**

We note that there are greatly different ratios for these words. Most of them are rarely norwegified, specifically *nerd, date* and *crazy*. It should be pointed out that *nerd* is very often adapted phonologically and pronounced with a domestic vowel [æ] rather than with the unadapted [ɜ] or semi-adapted [øː]. This is likely to account at least partly for the low norwegification ratio of this word, since the unadapted E form *nerd* accords with the common adapted pronunciation. We also note that two words, *blog* → *blogg* and the adjective *dull* → *døll*, are remarkably often norwegified. I shall have more to say in Section 6 about possible explanations for their success, which is partly related to homography and potential meaning differences between the two forms *dull* and *døll*. Note that the 'either/or' principle also seems to hold true for these data, as none of the E vs. N forms are evenly distributed.

6. Towards an analysis of factors affecting the variation between N/E forms

In this section I shall take a closer qualitative look at some of the individual word pairs above, with a view to pointing out some general tendencies. The aim is to lay out a number of linguistic factors that may have a bearing on the degree to which anglicisms are norwegified. I wish to consider the degree to which factors such as orthographic complexity, collocations, morphology, homography and semantic features may affect the adaptation process. The discussion will hopefully also shed light on problematic aspects of some of the N forms proposed by the Norwegian Language Council, and may account for their low norwegification ratio. The account is meant to be hypothesis-generating rather than hypothesis-testing.

6.1 Complexity of the orthographic change

It is obvious from the discussion above that the spelling adaptation of individual words varies greatly in the degree of orthographic complexity inherent in the change. At one end, we find words whose adaptation is restricted to a mere doubling of a consonant, in line with the Norwegian norm for indicating a short vowel, as seen in a word pair like *hip* → *hipp*. Slightly more substantial is the replacement of a foreign single consonant, individually as in *script* → *skript* or as part of a cluster as in *polish* → *polisj*, or a single vowel grapheme as in *server* → *sørver* or in diphthongs as in *entertainer* → *enterteiner*. More complex are the consonant changes that involve the reduction of a consonant in a cluster, as in *snacks* → *snaks*, and words where a consonant cluster representing a single phoneme is replaced by its Norwegian equivalent, as in *ketchup* → *ketsjup*. At the same complexity level are the vowel changes that involve the reduction from a two letter combination to a single one (*heade* → *hedde*) or vice versa (*time* → *taime*), and further the reduction of an orthographic vowel-consonant combination to an orthographic diphthong, as in *fight* → *fait* and the even more complex *straight* → *streit*. At the most complex end of the scale, we find words whose norwegification involves a combination of several of these changes, such as *squash* → *skvåsj*, where everything but the two s-es is changed.

Why would this be a relevant factor? We know for a fact that the norwegification of recent import words meets considerable resistance in the population.[6] As Vikør points out, the Norwegian Language Council's attempts at norwegification

6. Circumstantial evidence can be found in readers' comments to media coverage about the reforms, and, indeed, reactions to reports about the current research project, where the proposed N forms are often characterised in negative terms; cf. e.g. Aftenposten (2010)

"of more recent English loanwords have met … more resistance than the earlier instances" (Vikør 2010: 21); indeed many of the N forms from the 1996 reform were seen as "undignified and therefore ridiculous" (Vikør 1998: 106, quoted in Piltingsrud 2001). It seems reasonable to assume, *ceteris paribus*, that the more an N form differs from its E equivalent, the greater the resistance, due to writers' and readers' unfamiliarity with the graphical image of the adapted word. Arguably, then, the simplest of these changes have the lowest threshold of acceptance among the language users and the more radical changes to the graphical image are harder for readers and writers to accept, presumably for esthetic reasons (Grønvik 1991: 155). In sum, this leads to the following postulates:

[P1] The greater the orthographic difference between the N and E forms, the lower the frequency of norwegification.

[P2] The smaller the orthographic difference between the N and E forms, the higher the frequency of norwegification.

There is some support for these postulates observable from the patterns that emerge from Omdal's rather sparse data (2008a: 99). For consonants it is indeed consonant doubling and the replacements c → k and sh → sj which are among the most common adaptations, while there is more resistance towards cluster changes such as th → t and ch → tch and gh → f. For vowels, we note a tendency to norwegify u → ø, while ee/ie/ey → i and oo/ui/iew → u are less susceptible. Similarly, comments by Chrystal (1988), Graedler (1996) and Piltingsrud (2001) suggest that consonant doubling and the c → k and ch → sj changes are early and "undramatic" adaptations, while Grønvik briefly suggests that vowel changes may be more radical than consonant changes (Grønvik 1991: 152). The findings from my own data support these postulates only to a certain extent. Indeed, among the more successful norwegifications we do find words like *blogg* and *rapp* which are of the simplest type. On the other hand, many other simple norwegifications are unsuccessful, such as *hipp* and *hikkory*. As regards orthographically complex norwegifications we indeed find *choke* → *sjåk* and *squash* → *skvåsj* to be very unsuccessful, but at the same time the two most frequently norwegified words from the 1997 reform are relatively complex, namely *clinch* → *klinsj* and *straight* → *streit*. Hence, there is no clear pattern to be observed regarding orthographic complexity and degree of norwegification, although the two postulates seem intuitively correct. More conspicuous support for these assumptions would require a thorough statistical analysis of each of the orthographic features, for instance with a basis in the categories outlined by Johansson and Graedler (2002: 164ff). Unfortunately, such an analysis goes beyond the scope of the current chapter.

6.2 Collocations

While orthographic complexity may be a dubious factor, the collocational environment of an anglicism seems to have a more consistent impact on whether it is realised as an N form or an E form. As mentioned, certain contexts are irrelevant for this variation since the anglicism is part of a code-switching sequence or a quotation (cf. (3) above), or since the candidate form is a different lexeme, which applies for instance to *hipp* as part of idiomatic multiword expressions *hipp hurra* 'hip horray' or *hipp som happ* 'of equal value or importance'. These aside, inspection of the data seems to justify a generalisation about the linguistic impact of context, *ceteris paribus*. The following postulate seems to apply:

[P3] An English collocational context decreases the likelihood of norwegification.

This can be illustrated with reference to the collocational pattern of the successful norwegification *straight* → *streit*. We note from Table 2 above that 181 of the 1,407 tokens are E realisations. It is clear from the data that many of the E forms occur in contextual environments where the preceding or following word is also of English origin. These tokens are often collocations that have been imported wholesale as various types of multiword expressions, as illustrated in [4–8].

(4) *Samtidig kom straight edge-bølgen til Norge.* (AP080819)
At the same time the straight edge wave came to Norway.

(5) *Vi må nok erkjenne at det ikke er noe "**straight forward-krav**"* (DN011102)
We must (mod-prt) acknowledge that it is not a straight forward requirement

(6) *Dialektrapping med suveren flow og karisma* ***straight outta*** *Hovdebygda.* (DBxx0212)
Dialect rapping with unprecedented flow and charisma straight outta Hovdebygda.

(7) *Rå funk, bluegrass, køntrimelankoli og* ***straight ahead jazz.*** (DN050820)
Raw funk, bluegrass, country melancholia and straight ahead jazz.

(8) *så jeg bruker mer enn gjerne noen uker på å "**get things straight**".* (FV040115)
so I am more than happy to spend a few weeks in order to get things straight

As can be seen from the examples, such collocations may be compounds, phrases or clauses that are imported wholesale. A compound such as the hardcore punk musical genre *straight edge* (4) usually retains its spelling as two words, contrary to the Norwegian convention for compounds. The collocations also include repeated instances of more or less lexicalised phrases such as *straight forward*, *straight ahead* and *straight outta* [5–7], and also the poker expression *straight flush*. I consider an example like the clausal *get things straight* in (8) to be a case of code-switching and not an import word, although this distinction may be difficult to draw.

In fact, collocations like *straight forward*,[7] *straight flush* and *straight pool* categorically take the E form in the data. It could be argued, then, that [P3] should be formulated more strongly to rule out the possibility of an N realisation in cases such as [4–7]. However, this would seem to go beyond what is justifiable, since there are several examples of N forms with an English neighbouring word, as in *streit americana*, *streit image*, *streit r&b* etc. These are perhaps less lexicalised than the forms in [4–7] and not necessarily imported wholesale as phrases, but it seems unjustified to rule out the possibility of hybrid realisations such as *streit flush*, especially given that a hybrid compound such as *jazzstreit* does occur in the data. At any rate, it seems that we can safely assume that an English collocational context increases the likelihood of an E form.

6.3 Morphology

The morphological processes that may affect import words include inflection, affixal derivation and compounding. One of the most remarkable features that can be observed in a large newspaper corpus such as the NNC is the morphological productivity of many words (de Smedt this volume), including anglicisms. This productivity can be seen both in anglicisms that are commonly norwegified as well as those that are not. Most notably, the E form *hip* occurs in as many as 1,317 distinct forms while its N equivalent *hipp* occurs in 163 distinct forms. Whether or not intended by the Norwegian Language Council, the norwegification of *hip* → *hipp* incorporates the musical genre *hiphop*, commonly spelt *hipphopp*, *hipp-hopp* or *hip-hop*, and this lexeme is thus included in the statistics for *hip* → *hipp*.

Note that inflectional, derivational and compositional developments may occur as N or E forms, and the morphological productivity of each realisation seems to concur with the overall degree of norwegification of the lexeme. To illustrate, *finish* → *finisj* is rarely norwegified (0.1%) and its E form occurs in 91 distinct forms including *metallic-finish*, *thriller-finish* and *tre-finish* 'wood finish', while only one compound with the N form occurs, specifically *pianolakkfinisj* 'piano

7. Note that the form *straightforward* does not occur in the corpus.

varnish finish'. Conversely, for *straight* → *streit*, which is frequently norwegified (88.6 %), the N form is considerably more productive than the E form, with 67 versus 19 distinct forms.

Regarding compounds, both hybrid and non-hybrid forms occur, as seen from forms such as *halvstreit* 'semi-straight' (N+N), *knall-straight* 'very straight' (N+E), *jazzstreit* (E+N) and *indiestreite* 'indie straight' (pl./def., E+E). Note also that the forms *photofinish* and *fotofinish* both occur in the data (but never *photofinisj*). This tells us that when an imported compound consists of an already existing and norwegified import word, language users may on occasion choose between a hybrid or a non-hybrid realisation, and, more generally, the E realisation of a compound component (*-finish*) does not rule out an N realisation of another compound component (*foto-*).

I wish to argue that this variation is not random, but, as with collocations described above, the E/N variability of anglicisms in compounds is likely to be affected by the linguistic properties of the neighbouring compound components. In other words, the following may be postulated:

[P4] Co-occurrence with an English compound component decreases the likelihood of norwegification.

The anglicism *kick* → *kikk* provides an illustrative case. There are many compounds which categorically take the E form such as *ass-kicking, dropkick, kickback, kick-off/kickoff, kickflips* and *sidekick*, all of which have been imported wholesale as compounds. An interesting case is *kickboxing/kickboksing*, which categorically takes the E form in the first compound component, but shows variation in the second. This is presumably due to the fact that *boksing* 'boxing' has long existed as a norwegified form, on a par with *foto* above, and is probably no longer perceived as an anglicism by most users. Although one could theoretically, then, also find the fully norwegified form *kikkboksing*, this never occurs. Incidentally, another explanatory factor here may be the homography of *kikk*, to be described in Section 6.4 below.

The inspection of inflections and affixal derivations shows first of all that inflections by far outnumber derivations. For frequent anglicisms, we do find derivations like *uhipp* 'unhip', *hipphet* 'hipness' and *streitifisert* 'straightified' but the most common derivation seems to be deverbal nouns following the patterns of *dating* and *fighter*, so-called *nomina actionis* and *nomina agentis* (Graedler 1998: 175). Here, the affixal forms coincide with the source language equivalent, and we cannot really say whether or not they represent *post hoc* word formation. A notable derivation is the fixed phrase *på deiteren/dateren*, lit. 'on the dater', meaning 'engaged in dating', which follows analogously from the similar pattern of the domestic idiom *på sjekkeren*, meaning 'engaged in courtship, wooing'.

Table 5. Non-compositional derived and inflected forms of *streit/straight*

N form	E form	Morphological category	Meaning	N tokens	E tokens	Sum	% N form
streit	straight	adjectival stem	straight	672	128	800	84.0%
streita	straighta	past tense verb	straightened	4	1	5	80.0%
streite	straighte	adj. def./pl.	(the) straight	412	28	440	93.6%
streiter	–	pres. tense verb	straighten(s)	3	0	3	100.0%
streitere	straightere	adj. comp.	straighter	77	3	80	96.3%
streitest	–	adj. sup.	straightest	2	0	2	100.0%
streiteste	straighteste	adj. sup. def.	the straightest	43	2	45	95.6%
streitet	–	past tense verb	straightened	1	0	1	100.0%
streithet	–	derived noun	straightness	1	0	1	100.0%
streiting	–	derived noun	straighting (straight person)	10	0	10	100.0%
streitingen	straightingen	noun def. sg.	the straighting	6	2	8	75.0%
streitingene	–	noun def. pl.	the straightings	14	0	14	100.0%
streitingenes	–	noun def. pl. gen.	the straightings'/'s	1	0	1	100.0%
streitinger	–	noun indef. pl.	straightings	91	0	91	100.0%
streitingers	–	noun indef. pl. gen.	straightings'	1	0	1	100.0%
streitifiseringen	–	deverbal noun	the straightification	1	0	1	100.0%
streitifisert	–	derived verb past tense	straightified	1	0	1	100.0%
ustreit	–	derived adj.	unstraight	4	0	4	100.0%
ustreite	–	derived adj. def./pl.	(the) unstraight	3	0	3	100.0%

Much more frequent are inflectional forms, which thrive in the data. The productivity of inflectional and derivational forms can be illustrated with reference to *straight* → *streit*, as shown in Table 5.

Table 5 shows that the N form has a much wider range of derived and inflected forms than the E form, that there is a clear preference for using the N form with domestic inflectional affixation, and – with the exception of two tokens of *straightingen* – that the derivational forms *streithet*, *streiting*, *streitifisering/-e* and *ustreit* categorically take the N form. In fact, there seems to be a general tendency that words containing a domestic affix contain the N form, *ceteris paribus*. This is supported by the figures for *dull* → *døll*. The uninflected E form *dull* only occurs twice (cf. 6.4 on the homography of this form), as opposed to the uninflected N stem which occurs 69 times. The form *dulle* does not occur as an E form of this anglicism; hence the form *dølle* is categorically used for the definite and plural form of this adjective. Only the N forms occur as comparative or superlative inflections of the adjective, with 13 and 16 tokens respectively. In other words, the inflectional forms of this lexeme categorically take the N form. Given these observations it makes sense to postulate the following:

[P5] Co-occurrence with a Norwegian inflectional or derivational affix increases the likelihood of norwegification.

This connection between spelling and morphology is supported by similar observations made for Danish by Bønlykke Olsen (2003, also reported in Jarvad 2007) and for Norwegian by Grønvik (1991:145) and Graedler (1996), who remarks that "it may be difficult to establish what is the cause and effect" (Graedler 1996:78) in this connection.

Postulates [P3–P5] are in effect saying the same thing, namely that a general *principle of attraction* applies, in that neighbouring collocations, compound components or inflectional or derivational affixes have an effect on the realisation of anglicisms, in such a way that a neighbouring source language morpheme increases the likelihood of an unadapted realisation, and conversely that a neighbouring target language morpheme decreases the likelihood of an unadapted realisation.

6.4 Homography

Imported words from English may in their original or adapted form have homographic forms in the target language. It is conceivable that homographic forms may interfere with the adoption of the N forms in different ways, and it is of interest to find out if such homography has a bearing on the distribution of E and N forms.

By way of example, the norwegification *fight* → *fait* is problematic due to homography of the N form. The orthographic pattern *fait* occurs in many disregarded contexts in French-based borrowings, such as *parfait*. A total of 60 tokens of the non-compositional forms *fait/faits/faiting* were identified in the corpus. All non-quotational tokens of *fait* and *faits* occurred in the singular or plural form or of the French multiword *fait accompli* and hence were irrelevant for this anglicism. The two tokens of *faiting* turned out to be misspellings of the multiword *fainting game*. The only sign of norwegification of this anglicism is seen in two tokens of *faiter*, massively outnumbered by its E equivalent. The form *faiter* can represent either the inflected present tense verb form [[*fait*]*er*] 'fight(s)' as well as the deverbal noun [*faiter*] 'a fighter', and in fact the two tokens represent both categories. It should be noted that the deverbal noun was not included in the Norwegian Language Council's list of forms that the spelling reform was meant to cover.

Similarly, the N form *feide* for *fade* turns out to be an exceptionally problematic norwegification. This is due to the existing domestic noun *feide* 'feud'. All compounds containing the pattern *-feid-* were indeed realisations of this latter noun.[8] In addition, the form *feide* is homographic with the past tense form of a domestic verb *feie* 'broom, sweep'. There are many tokens of the form *feide*, but virtually all are past tense forms of the domestic verb and not the N form of the anglicism. In fact, even the collocation *feide ut*, is ambiguous between 'fade out' and 'broomed/swept out', and all but one of its 23 tokens are used in the domestic sense 'were swept out'.

The analysis of *kick* → *kikk* required considerable post-processing and manual work, since the form *kikk* also represents the neuter/masculine noun meaning 'look, peek', which outnumbers the N form *kikk* with 1,033 versus 5 tokens respectively. An example of the N realisation is (10).

(10) *og fortalte at han hadde fått et kikk og skulle teste hvor fort den gikk, sier Jensen.* (AP091017)
and told that he had got a kick and was going to test how fast it could go, Jensen says.

The ambiguous inflected forms *kikka*, *kikket* etc. also generally do not represent the N form of the anglicism. Note also that the anglicism includes a phrasal verb *kicke på*, which has a different meaning from the noun observed by the Norwegian Language Council, as seen in example (11).

8. I also ignored one special case of fade used as dialectal representation of *fatet* 'the plate': [i] *dårr e prim på di pannekagene så ligge på høyra siå av fade, å smør å sokker på di te venstre.*

(11) *Jeg tror folk* ***kicka på*** *at han var svensk, kommenterer Bjørn.* (DB991001)
I think people **disapproved of** the fact that he was Swedish, Bjørn comments.

(12) *Politiet reagerte på at lasten var for tung. Da de* ***kikka på*** *innholdet oppdaga de den forbudte fangsten.* (NL010422)
The police noticed that the cargo was too heavy. When they **looked at** the contents they noticed the illegal catch.

While (12) is ambiguous between the readings 'took a peek at' and 'disapproved of/ talked negative about', (11) is not. In the examples analysed, the phrasal verb [*kikke på*] is reserved for the old meaning 'look at', while [*kicke på*] is reserved for the new meaning of the anglicism.

The implication of these observations is not that homography is inherently problematic; after all, all users will be able to disambiguate *kikke på* in the context of (12) and to distinguish the two senses of *feide* above on the basis of tense. But my claim is that homography may affect writers' willingness to adopt a norwegified spelling in cases where the N form already exists as a different lexeme. Given the apparent reluctance to use the N forms of these anglicisms (Table 2 above), it does not seem unlikely that the adaptation of N forms like *fait*, *feide* and *kikk* is obstructed by their existing homographs. Taken further, we may even argue that orthography may be used in a disambiguation strategy, in that the form *kikk* (and its affixations) is generally reserved for the meaning of the domestic word, while *kick* is reserved for the new imported meaning, which the examples [11–12], and indeed the data more generally, seem to suggest. These considerations lead to the following postulate regarding homography:

[P6] If the N form of an anglicism competes with an existing homograph, this has a disfavouring effect on norwegification.

Conversely, there are cases where it is the E form that has an existing homograph in Norwegian. This applies to *time* → *taime*, whose E form can also mean 'hour', and to *dull* → *døll*, whose stem and inflected form *dulle* (pl./def.) are both ambiguous. The form *dull* occurs 24 times, of which only two represent E forms of the anglicism (as opposed to the uninflected N stem which occurs 69 times), while other non-quotational tokens represent a noun meaning 'cuddle' or are part of the idiomatic phrase *i dull med* 'in relaxed conversation with'. Similarly, the form *dulle* occurs in the corpus but only as the infinitive of a verb meaning 'to cuddle'. It would therefore not be unjustified to claim that the existence of a homographic E form could have a favouring effect on the adaptation process, since the choice of the N form would have a disambiguating effect. However, for *time* → *taime*, no such effect is observable in the data, since the N forms are consistently outnumbered by the E forms for this lexeme. Nevertheless, these considerations lead to the following postulate regarding homography, given the high frequency of *døll* and its inflections:

[P7] If the E form of an anglicism competes with an existing homograph, this has a favouring effect on norwegification.

That homography may be a relevant factor is noted in passing by Grønvik, who suggest that homographs may be "confusing" (Grønvik 1991: 155), and Piltingsrud (2001) suggests that "decisions that lead to Norwegian homography with established Norwegian words are unsuccessful" (Piltingsrud 2001: 71). It was observed by Omdal (2008) that *sex* is among the most frequent unadapted forms in the MINS material. I would argue strongly that this is due to the virtual impossibility of norwegifying this word, since it would introduce a very salient homography with the numeral *seks* 'six'. This point seems to have gone unnoticed by Omdal, since *sex* is calculated among the other E realisations of the x → ks variable.

The above observations regarding homography can be summarised as in Table 6.

Table 6. Survey of homographic categories

Homographic category	Ambiguous homograph	Disambiguating alternative	Meaning of homograph	Presumed effect on use of N form
unadapted (E) stem	*time*	*taime*	'hour'	favouring
adapted (N) stem	*feide*	*fade*	'feud/swept'	disfavouring
unadapted (E) inflection	*dulle*	*dølle*	'cuddle'	favouring
adapted (N) inflection	*kikke (på)*	*kicke (på)*	'take a peak at'	disfavouring

These are the basic types, but the picture may be even more complex. Especially short and monomorphemic anglicisms are likely to have homographic forms. The word *rap* → *rapp* is particularly intriguing, as both the stem and several inflected forms are multiply ambiguous. The form *rap* could mean 'burp', *rapp* could mean 'a flogging' or 'quick' *rappe* could mean 'flog', 'steal' or 'quick', etc. As it happens, the inflected forms of *rap* show a strong tendency towards N realisations such as *rappe* '(to) rap', *rappa* 'rapped' *rappen* 'the rap', *rapper* 'rap(s)' (v), and *rappet* 'rapped'. All of these forms avoid the reading of 'burp', but not unambiguously since they introduce the ambiguity with the 'flog' or 'steal' readings. As Table 2 shows, *rapp* is nevertheless among the successful norwegification proposals with 67.0 per cent. This would suggest that in multiply ambiguous anglicisms, orthophony considerations overrule ambiguity, as writers – caught between the devil and the deep blue sea – tend to opt for those ambiguous forms which also conform with Norwegian orthophony and therefore prefer the consonant doubling forms in this case.[9] At any rate, it seems that the conjecture of a *disambiguation strategy* – by which writers prefer N forms to avoid the alternative reading of ambiguous E forms, or vice versa – seems to have a lot to offer as an explanation of why writers choose the forms that they do.

6.5 Semantic factors

The scope of a single chapter does not allow for a full account of semantic factors, but I wish to propose that they may also have a bearing on the distribution of E versus N forms of anglicisms. This will be done primarily with reference to the frequently norwegified word *straight* → *streit*. Several previous studies have observed that import words may be characterised by *post hoc* specialisation in meaning (e.g. Görlach 2001, 2003; Alexieva 2008; Winter-Froemel 2008; Dunn 2008). It is possible that the frequently norwegified anglicisms concur with emergent semantic shifts. In this connection, several questions arise: Are the N and E forms necessarily synonymous? Can the high ratio of N forms of certain words be explained by emergent changes in their semantic reference? Does one form co-occur with particular meanings? It is not possible to account fully for this here, as this would require a more detailed qualitative analysis, but I will present some findings that may suggest that semantic factors do play a role. The findings are largely based on collocational statistics and mutual information scores, which are directly retrievable from the Corpuscle interface.

For *straight* → *streit* it is noticeable that certain senses appear to be confined to one particular spelling.

[14] *Her drikkes det øl, her nytes whisky straight og her rocker Jack Knife* (BT060309)
Here people drink beer, here they drink whisky straight and here Jack Knife rocks

[15] *torsdag kveld var lokalet fylt av stort sett streit utseende gutter og jenter på den nedre siden av 30-årsalder* (SA020413)
Thursday evening the venue was filled with mainly straight looking boys and girls in their early 30s

No examples of *streit* in the sense "without adornment, admixture, or dilution" (OED straight) in connection with spirits were found, but the E form readily collocates with *whisky* and *vodka*. On the other hand, *streit* is the only form that

9. Note that unsolicited forms *ræp*, *ræpper* and *ræpping* also occur in the corpus, but they are massively outnumbered by the standardised N forms.

occurs in the two idioms *streit nok* 'straight enough', which seem equivalent to 'fair enough', and the phrasal verb *se streit ut* 'look straight', as well as *streit utseende* 'straight looking/looks' in [15]. These findings are indicative of a semantic specialisation that may be ongoing. Moreover, the form *streit* is particularly frequent as a modifier of nouns referring to aspects of popular culture, especially music (*rock, pop, blues, heavy, musikk* 'music', *thriller, film, såpeopera* 'soap opera', *låt* 'song', *produsert* 'produced', *komp* 'accompaniment'), denoting a sense of 'mainstream' or 'in accordance with the genre conventions'. It is clear that the closest metaphorical sense recorded in the OED is not fitting to describe this new meaning of *streit*:

> d. Mus. Applied to a kind of jazz characterized by adherence to a score or set orchestration and a lack of improvisation, or to a player of this kind of jazz. Also, of music or a musician: 'serious' or dance-band as opposed to jazz; = legitimate (OED *straight*).

Streit is also common with nouns that denote a verbal account of something (*budskap* 'message', *historie* 'story', *forklaring* 'account', *fortelling* 'story', *definisjoner* 'definitions'), in the sense 'credible, trustworthy'. The closest sense recorded in the OED is probably the following (cf. *straight talk/answer*):

> e. colloq. Of an utterance: Outspoken, unreserved. Also, straightforward, not evasive. straight talk: a piece of plain speaking. (OED *straight*).

But the OED definition does not really fit the collocations above. In other words, there seem to be ongoing metonymic shifts towards meanings such as 'mainstream' and 'trustworthy' which have occurred *post hoc*. For other senses such as *straight/streit* referring to heterosexuality, abstinence from drugs and social acceptability, no meaning shift can be observed, but the uses of *straight/streit* seem generally to conform with those listed in OED.

> d. slang (orig. U.S.). Conventional, respectable, socially acceptable. Also spec.
> (a) heterosexual; not practising sexual perversions;.
> (b) not using or under influence of drugs; sober, abstinent. (OED *straight*).

It may be speculative to claim that there should be a systematic correlation between a particular sense and a particular spelling, but I wish to suggest that there is at least a potential for the N form to function as a marker that a meaning shift has taken place or is emergent. It is conceivable that writers use the orthography of the respective E vs. N forms as markers of potential semantic differences and that the choice of a form *streit* contributes to underlining that the word has a new sense that has developed after borrowing. At any rate, it seems justified to make the following postulate regarding semantic change.

[P8] If an anglicism has a sense that has developed *post hoc*, this increases the likelihood of norwegification.

I also investigated the semantics of the other most frequently norwegified anglicism, namely *dull* → *døll*. However, I found no evidence that its use does not conform well to the OED-recorded meanings of *dull* such as 'not lively, tedious, uninteresting, uneventful' etc. However, an audience member at a presentation I gave commented that young people no longer perceive of *døll* as a counterpart to *dull*, or perhaps not even as originating in English, but as a fully integrated Norwegian adjective with a meaning which is not necessarily synonymous with its domestic counterpart *kjedelig*.

7. Conclusion and further work

This paper has been concerned with developing hypotheses rather than testing them. On the basis of the Norwegian Newspaper Corpus, I have shown that most new anglicisms are rarely norwegified. I have argued that the degree of norwegification of individual words is not coincidental, but that factors such as orthographic complexity, collocations, morphology, homography and semantic features may affect the adaptation process. The principles that seem to apply have been formulated as postulates, restated below.

[P1] The greater the orthographic difference between the N and E forms, the lower the frequency of norwegification.

[P2] The smaller the orthographic difference between the N and E forms, the higher the frequency of norwegification.

[P3] An English collocational context decreases the likelihood of norwegification.

[P4] Co-occurrence with an English compound component decreases the likelihood of norwegification.

[P5] Co-occurrence with a Norwegian inflectional or derivational affix increases the likelihood of norwegification.

[P6] If the N form of an anglicism competes with an existing homograph, this has a disfavouring effect on norwegification.

[P7] If the E form of an anglicism competes with an existing homograph, this has a favouring effect on norwegification.

[P8] If an anglicism has a reference that has developed *post hoc*, this increases the likelihood of norwegification.

Though these may seem like plausible principles, I do not necessarily consider each of them to be of equal importance. There is a need to investigate further which of the factors play a significant role, and which are less crucial. I have suggested that orthography, for example, may have less of a systematic effect than homography, perhaps with the modification that the very simplest norwegifications – which involve a minor change to the orthographic image of a word such as the doubling of a consonant – are likely to be readily accepted by writers and readers. This would explain the success of *rapp* and *blogg*. However, the descriptions of relevant orthographical and other factors made in the previous literature are largely anecdotal and impressionistic and not sufficiently empirically based. What is needed is for these hypotheses to be rigorously tested using more sophisticated statistical measures than applied here. This would require coding each token in terms of all of relevant variables and subjecting the data to a multifactorial analysis.

The findings of the current study may have implications for the normative work of the Norwegian Language Council, who may take an interest in finding out why *streit* is such a successful norwegification, while most other proposals are not. I have pointed out that there are serious problems with several of the norwegifications proposed by the Norwegian Language Council. Especially cases where a homograph of the N form exists seem to have little success. Disambiguation seems to be a key principle, and it works both ways, as seen from homographic words such as *kikk*, which seem to obstruct norwegification, and words like *døll*, where the homography seems to have a favouring effect. In passing, one might question on what grounds the Norwegian Language Council choose to promote forms such as *hedde* 'head', v. and *overhedd* 'overhead' but disregard the norwegification of other common words with the same stem, such as *skinhead*. It is also difficult to understand why the norwegification is meant to include the noun and verb *rap* but not its derived *nomen agentis rapper* or its *nomen actionis rapping*, etc. Similar inconsistencies have been pointed out by Papazian (1991), Vinje (1996) and Piltingsrud (2001).

Other related tasks merit further investigation. The Nynorsk/Bokmål dimension remains to be explored. We may hypothesise that Nynorsk, being the more puristic of the two varieties (Vikør 2010: 23), accepts a higher degree of norwegified forms, and the Norwegian Newspaper Corpus data may be used to investigate different degrees of norwegification in the two written varieties. It should also be investigated whether the principles above have a cross-linguistic application or if they are specific to English import words into Norwegian. Moreover, I have exclusively relied on written data in this study, while some earlier studies have investigated phonological adaptation based on speech data. A recent study, Svavarsdóttir et al. (2010), relies on questionnaires for the purpose of studying phonological adaptation, and the work of the MIN project used interviews and elicitation methods to study phonological adaptation (Jarvad 2007), showing some degree of correlation between its age as an anglicism and degree of adaptation (Johansen 2007). However, we have yet to explore the relation and possible correlation between phonological and orthographical adaptation. Having suggested, impressionistically, that the high frequency of *nerd* is likely due to its common adapted pronunciation to [nærd], I have merely scratched the surface of this topic. The availability of spoken corpora of Norwegian facilitates a complementary approach investigating adaptation in both speech and writing.

References

Aftenposten. 2010. Ingen vil skrive sjarter og sjåk. ⟨http://www.aftenposten.no/kul_und/article3858198.ece⟩ (15 September, 2010).

Akselberg, Gunnstein. 2005. Trends in the linguistic developments since 1945. III: Norwegian. In *The Nordic Languages: An International Handbook of the History of the North Germanic Languages*, Vol. 2, Oskar, Bandle, Kurt Braunmuller, Ernst Hakon Jahr, Allan Karker, Hans-Peter Naumann, Ulf Teleman, Lennart Elmevik & Gun Widmark (eds), 1823–1831. Berlin: Walter de Gruyter.

Alexieva, Nevena. 2008. How and why are anglicisms often lexically different from their English etymons? In *Anglicisms in Europe: Linguistic Diversity in a Global Context*, Roswhitha Fischer & Hanna Pułaczewska, 16–41. Newcastle upon Tyne: Cambridge Scholars.

Andersen, Gisle. 2005. Assessing algorithms for automatic extraction of anglicisms in Norwegian texts. Paper presented at Corpus Linguistics 2005, Birmingham, July 2005.

Andersen, Gisle. 2010a. A pragmatic perspective on English-to-Norwegian borrowing of discourse markers. Paper presented at the 4th International Conference on Intercultural Pragmatics and Communication, Madrid, November 2010.

Andersen, Gisle. 2010b. Halvautomatisk ekserpering av anglisismer i norsk (Semi-automatic extraction of anglicisms in Norwegian). *Nordiska Studier i Lexikografi* 10: 72–85.

Andersen, Gisle. 2011. Finisj eller finish? – Norvagisering femten år etter normeringsvedtaket. *Språknytt* 2011(1): 27–29.

Andersen, Gisle. Forthcoming. Pragmatics and relevance. To appear in *Corpus Pragmatics*, Rühlemann, Christoph & Karin Aijmer (eds). Cambridge: CUP.

Bønlykke Olsen, Katrine. 2003. Om bøjning af engelske ord i dansk. *Nyt fra Sprognævnet* 2003(2): 6–11.

Chrystal, Judith-Ann. 1988. Engelskan i svensk dagspress. *Skrifter Utgivna av Svenska Språknämnden* 74. Göteborg: Esselte Studium.

Dunn, John. 2008. Face control, electronic soap and the four-storey cottage with a jacuzzi: Anglicisation, globalisation and the creation of linguistic difference. In *Anglicisms in Europe: Linguistic Diversity in a Global Context*, Roswitha Fischer & Hanna Pułaczewska (eds), 52–68. Newcastle upon Tyne: Cambridge Scholars.

Fischer, Roswitha & Pułaczewska, Hanna (eds). 2008. *Anglicisms in Europe: Linguistic Diversity in a Global Context*. Newcastle upon Tyne: Cambridge Scholars.

Furiassi, Cristiano. 2010. *False Anglicisms in Italian*. Milano: Polimetrica.

Görlach, Manfred (ed). 2001. *A Dictionary of European Anglicisms: A Usage Dictionary of Anglicisms in Sixteen Selected European Languages*. Oxford: OUP.

Görlach, Manfred. 2003. *English Words Abroad* (Terminology and Lexicography Research and Practice 7). Amsterdam: John Benjamins.

Graedler, Anne-Line & Kvaran, Gudrún. 2010. Foreign influence on the written language in the Nordic language communities. *International Journal of the Sociology of Language* 204: 31–42.

Graedler, Anne-Line & Johansson, Stig. 1997. *Anglisismeordboka: Engelske lånord i norsk.* Oslo: Universitetsforlaget.

Graedler, Anne-Line. 1996. Forholdet mellom stavemåte og bøyning i engelske lånord. In *Engelske ord med norsk rettskriving? Seks seminarforedrag 1996*, Knud Blauw et al. (eds), 67–80. Bergen: Bergens Riksmålsforening, Riksmålsforbundet and Det norske Akademi for Sprog og Litteratur.

Graedler, Anne-Line. 1998. *Morphological, Semantic and Functional Aspects of English Lexical Borrowings in Norwegian.* Oslo: Scandinavian University Press.

Grønvik, Oddrun. 1991. Lånordproblemet i norsk. Gruppering og systematisering av lånorda og ulike måtar å ta stiling til dei i normeringa. In *Språkideologi og språkplanlegging i Noreg*, Helge Sandøy, Arne Torp, Kjell Ivar Vannebo & Lars Sigurdsson Vikør (eds), 141–162. Bergen: Nordisk institutt, Universitetet i Bergen.

Hansen, Erik & Lund, Jørn. 1994. *Kulturens Gesandter. Fremmedordene i dansk.* Copenhagen: Munksgaard.

Haugen, Einar. 1953. *The Norwegian Language in America: A Study in Bilingual Behavior.*

Jarvad, Pia & Sandøy, Helge (eds). 2007. Stuntman *og andre importord i Norden: Om udtale og bøjning* [Moderne importord i språka i Norden 7]. Oslo: Novus.

Jarvad, Pia. 2007. Tilpasning af engelske ord i bøyning og udtale i de nordiske sprog. In Stuntman *og andre importord i Norden: Om udtale og bøjning* [Moderne importord i språka i Norden 7], Pia Jarvad & Helge Sandøy (eds), 9–26 Oslo: Novus.

Johansen, Roy. 2007. Tilpassing av importord i norsk talemål. In Stuntman *og andre importord i Norden: Om udtale og bøjning* [Moderne importord i språka i Norden 7], Pia Jarvad & Helge Sandøy (eds). Oslo: Novus.

Johansson, Stig & Graedler, Anne-Line. 2002. *Rocka, hipt og snacksy: Om engelsk i norsk språk og samfunn.* Kristiansand: Høyskoleforlaget.

Kristiansen, Tore & Sandøy, Helge. 2010. Introduction: The linguistic consequences of globalization: The Nordic laboratory. *International Journal of the Sociology of Language* 204: 1–8.

Ljung, Magnus 1985. *Lam anka – ett måste? En undersökning av engelskan i svenskan, dess mottagande och spridning* [EIS Report No. 8]. Stockholm: University of Stockholm.

Ljung, Magnus 1988. *Skinheads, Hackers & Lama Ankor. Engelskan i 80-talets svenska.* Stockholm: Trevi.

Masvie, Inger-Lise 1992. English in Norway. A Sociolinguistic Study. MA thesis, Institutt for britiske og amerikanske studiar, University of Oslo.

Omdal, Helge & Sandøy, Helge (eds). 2008. *Nasjonal eller internasjonal skrivemåte?: Om importord i seks nordiske språksamfunn*[Moderne importord i språka i Norden 8]. Oslo: Novus.

Omdal, Helge. 2008a. *Bacon* eller *beiken*? Tilpassing av moderne importord i norsk. In *Nasjonal eller internasjonal skrivemåte?: Om importord i seks nordiske språksamfunn* [Moderne importord i språka i Norden 8], Helge Omdal & Helge Sandoy (eds), 77–103. Oslo: Novus.

Omdal, Helge. 2008b. Tilpassing eller ikke tilpassing? Sammenlikning av resultater. In *Nasjonal eller internasjonal skrivemåte?: Om importord i seks nordiske språksamfunn* [Moderne importord i språka i Norden 8], Helge Omdal & Helge Sandoy (eds), 163–186. Oslo: Novus.

Omdal, Helge. 2008c. Undersøkelse av tilpassing av moderne importord i nordiske språk. In *Nasjonal eller internasjonal skrivemåte?: Om importord i seks nordiske språksamfunn* [Moderne importord i språka i Norden 8], Helge Omdal & Helge Sandoy (eds), 9–20. Oslo: Novus.

Onysko, Alexander. 2007. *Anglicisms in German: Borrowing, lexical productivity, and written codeswitching*. Berlin: Mouton de Gruyter.

Onysko, Alexander. 2009. Exploring discourse on globalizing English. *English Today* 25(1): 25–35.

Oxford English Dictionary Online. 2011a. Commando. ⟨http://www.oed.com/viewdictionaryentry:showfullentry/true?t:ac=Entry/36974⟩ (14 February, 2011).

Oxford English Dictionary Online. 2011b. Straight. ⟨http://www.oed.com/viewdictionaryentry:showfullentry/true?t:ac=Entry/191142⟩ (14 February, 2011).

Papazian, Eric. 1991. Norsk språknormering i dag. In *Språkideologi og språkplanlegging i Noreg*, Helge Sandøy, Arne Torp, Kjell Ivar Vannebo & Lars Sigurdsson Vikør (eds), 86–109. Bergen: Nordisk institutt, Universitetet i Bergen.

Piltingsrud, Kirsten. 2001. Feida fait?: En analyse av Norsk språkråds norvagiseringspraksis med utgangspunkt i vedtaket fra 1996. MA thesis, University of Oslo.

Rand Schmidt, Kari Anne. 1982. The adaptation of English loan words in Norwegian. In *The English Element in European Languages*, Vol 2, R. Filipovic (ed), 338–377. Zagreb: Institute of Linguistics, University of Zagreb.

Sandøy, Helge & Östman, Jan-Ola (eds). 2004. *"Det främmande" i nordisk språkpolitik: Om normering av utländska ord* [Moderne importord i språka i Norden 2]. Oslo: Novus.

Sandøy, Helge. 1997. *Lånte fjører eller bunad? Om norsk skrivemåte av importord*. Utgreiing for Kulturdepartementet og Norsk språkråd. ⟨http://www.sprakrad.no/upload/567NORVb.pdf⟩ (12 July, 2010).

Sandøy, Helge. 2004. Norvagisering og fornorsking. In *"Det främmande" i nordisk språkpolitik: Om normering av utländska ord* [Moderne importord i språka i Norden 2], Helge Sandøy & Jan Ola Östman (eds), 107–141. Oslo: Novus.

Selback, Bente & Sandøy, Helge (eds). 2007. Fire dagar i nordiske aviser: Ei jamføring av påverknaden i ordforrådet i sju språksamfunn [Moderne importord i språka i Norden 3]. Oslo: Novus.

Selback, Bente. 2007. Norsk. In *Fire dagar i nordiske aviser: Ei jamføring av påverknaden i ordforrådet i sju språksamfunn* [Moderne importord i språka i Norden 3], Bente Selback & Helge Sandøy (eds), 49–66. Oslo: Novus.

Språkrådet [The Norwegian Language Council]. 2011a. Importord – fornorsking eller norvagisering? ⟨http://www.sprakradet.no/Sprakhjelp/Raad/Norsk-for-engelsk/Importord/Importord_fornorsking_eller/⟩ (10 January, 2011).

Språkrådet [The Norwegian Language Council]. 2011b. Rettskrivingsvedtak frå Norsk språkråd 2004. ⟨http://www.sprakrad.no/upload/8181/KKDframlegg04a.pdf⟩ (10 January, 2011).

Stene, Aasta. 1945. *English Loan-words in Modern Norwegian: A Study of Linguistic Borrowing in the Process*. Oslo: Tanum.

Svavarsdóttir, Ásta, Paatola, Ulla & Sandøy, Helge. 2010. English influence on the spoken language – with a special focus on its social, semantic and functional conditioning. *International Journal of the Sociology of Language* 204: 43–58.

Vikør, Lars S. 1998. Normering av fremmendord i internasjonalt perspektiv. In *Normer og regler – Festskrift til Dag Gundersen 15. januar 1998*, Ruth Vatvedt Fjeld & Boye Wangensteen (eds). Oslo: Kunnskapsforlaget.

Vikør, Lars S. 2010. Language purism in the Nordic countries. *International Journal of the Sociology of Language* 204: 9–30.

Vinje, Finn-Erik. 1996. Om staving av fremmedord i norsk og nordisk. In *Engelske ord med norsk rettskriving? Seks seminarforedrag 1996*, Knud Blauw et al. (eds). Bergen: Bergens Riksmålsforening, Riksmålsforbundet and Det norske Akademi for Sprog og Litteratur.

Wikipedia. 2011a. Carting. ⟨ http://en.wikipedia.org/wiki/Carting ⟩ (11 January, 2011).

Wikipedia. 2011b. Karting. ⟨ http://en.wikipedia.org/wiki/Karting ⟩ (11 January, 2011).

Winter-Froemel, Esme. 2008. Unpleasant, unnecessary, unintelligible? Cognitive and communicative criteria for evaluating borrowings and alternative strategies. In *Anglicisms in Europe: Linguistic Diversity in a Global Context*, Roswitha Fischer & Hanna Pułaczewska, 16–41. Newcastle upon Tyne: Cambridge Scholars.

Norm clusters in written Norwegian

Helge Dyvik
University of Bergen

Written Norwegian comes in two standards, Bokmål and Nynorsk, each allowing much variation in stem forms and inflections. Actual texts show intricate interdependencies among the alternative options. This chapter reports on the use of correspondence analysis and implicational analysis applied to a newspaper corpus in order to chart the patterns of variation. The aim is to test the utility of the method itself, and the study therefore concentrates on a small selection of phenomena. The long-term aim of a future extended project is to monitor actual usage in relation to the official standards, thereby identifying possible emerging subvarieties. This will be of value in the maintenance of the official written standards. The results indicate that the approach can yield valuable insights.

1. Introduction[1]

The two written standards for Norwegian, Bokmål and Nynorsk, are linguistically exceptional, not only because there are two of them, but also because each of them allows an unusual amount of variation among alternative stem forms[2] and inflectional endings. This is a result of the official language policy of the 20th century, where the original idea was to pave the way for the merger of the two standards by allowing extensive variation while excluding many traditional forms. This policy failed and has been abandoned, and much of the variation that was allowed in the official norms, but never taken up in actual usage, has been removed. But still the policy has left its mark on the language as it is actually written, in the form of a fair amount of variation. The variation is correlated in rather complex

1. I am grateful to the Norwegian Language Council and the Faculty of Humanities, University of Bergen, for funding the research reported here. About 90% of the funding came from the Language Council.

2. The variations in stem forms, such as *hånd* vs. *hand* 'hand', are frequently referred to as 'spelling variants'. This is slightly misleading since they are not alternative ways of spelling the same sequence of phonemes, but rather capture alternative spoken variants.

ways with stylistic and sociolinguistic variables, e.g. on a scale from 'traditional' or 'moderate' to 'radical', or on a scale from 'high style' to 'folksy'. The choice between those two scales for classification may also be politically loaded, since some would claim that 'radical' forms should not be seen as confined to 'folksy' style. Also, the stylistic perceptions change over time; thus, to some the stylistic effect of extensive use of 'radical' forms in Bokmål today (e.g. extensive feminine gender), at least in texts of an abstract, discursive nature, may be to make the text look quaint and oldfashioned rather than modern, reminiscent of the social-democratic, reform-optimistic fifties.

Present language policy is to base the official norms for Bokmål and Nynorsk, not on a future goal, but on developments in observed usage, which hence needs to be systematically examined. One important difference between the official, prescribed norms and the operative norms of actual usage is that while the former impose few constraints on how alternative forms are combined in a text, actual usage displays intricate patterns of dependency among the alternatives.[3] These dependencies frequently seem to take the form of unilateral or bilateral implications. For example, one dimension of variation in Bokmål concerns the past and past participle endings in a subclass of weak verbs, which may be either *-et* (traditional, moderate) or *-a* (radical): *kastet* or *kasta* 'threw', 'thrown'. Similarly, while Bokmål has three grammatical genders, a two-gender option is possible, since all feminine nouns may optionally (and individually) be masculine. Apart from agreement, gender is reflected in the ending of the definite singular. Thus a noun like *hytte* 'cabin' in the definite singular may have either the form *hytten* masc. (traditional, moderate) or *hytta* fem. (radical, or in the case of this word, neutral).[4] A Bokmål dictionary describes these options on a word-by-word level, thereby imposing no constraints on the combination of choices across lemmas in a text. However, in actual usage the choice of *a*-forms

3. In practical teaching of the norm, however, there tends to be a strong emphasis on conveying information about a number of such dependencies, in order to achieve consistency within a subnorm.

4. Since gender per definition is a matter of agreement, the use of the ending *-a* does not imply feminine gender with absolute necessity. There is a common variety of Bokmål where *-a* occurs on some nouns, while there is no masculine/feminine distinction in the agreeing forms (e.g. the indefinite article *en*(m) in *en jente* 'a girl' occurs together with *jenta* 'the girl'), and constructions that would force such agreement are avoided (e.g. postposed possessive in phrases like *jenta mi*(f) 'my girl', *min*(m) *jente* with preposed possessive being used instead). In this variety the *-en*/*-a* variation is simply a case of allomorphy within common gender. However, this fact does not reduce the value of the *-en*/*-a* variation as an indicator of subnorm. For simplicity, we will continue to refer to the *-a*-forms as 'feminines' in this chapter.

of weak verbs is generally perceived as more radical than the choice of feminine forms of most nouns. A pattern resulting from this is that a text using the form *kasta* will very probably use the feminine form *hytta* as well, while *hytta* is perceived as stylistically compatible with both *kasta* and *kastet*. If this turns out to be the actual pattern, then there is a unilateral implication between *kasta* and *hytta*: in the domain of Bokmål texts, *kasta* implies *hytta*, but not vice versa. Conversely, the more traditional masculine *hytten* will then imply the traditional *kastet*, but not vice versa. In a pattern like this, then, the implying, mutually exclusive, forms – *kasta* and *hytten* – emerge as more 'marked' or 'special', while the implied forms – *kastet* and *hytta* – emerge as more 'unmarked' or 'neutral', typical of more texts.

The research questions addressed in the present chapter concern the extent to which the form choices in actual texts display implicational patterns of this kind, and, as a corollary, the extent to which more or less well-defined subvarieties of Bokmål and Nynorsk may be identified.[5] Among earlier attempts to specify the properties of subvarieties of Bokmål is the work of Koenraad De Smedt and Victoria Rosén (Rosén & De Smedt 2000, De Smedt & Rosén 2000) in connection with the SCARRIE proofreading project. Their experimental system allowed users to choose among five subvarieties, thus constraining the set of proposals made by the system. While De Smedt and Rosén's individuation of subvarieties was informant-based, the aim of the present project is to derive information about subvarieties from corpus data.

2. A pilot study

A 'morphosyntactic word' (MSW) is taken to be a combination of a lemma form and a set of values of morphological categories which the lemma can realize. Thus, ⟨`hytte +Noun +Def +Sg`⟩ is the MSW which can be realized as either *hytta* or *hytten* in Bokmål. A MSW with more than one possible realization may be called a 'variable MSW'. Each variable MSW may be seen as a 'dimension' along which texts may vary (the ordering of forms within each dimension is not important – it may be taken to be alphabetical). The official norms for Bokmål and Nynorsk (in conjunction with possible non-official forms in actual usage) will then define a multidimensional space, and a given text will be located as a point within the

5. The phenomena studied here are confined to cases of variation in inflectional endings, although the approach is easily extended to form variation in general, such as the variation between the stem forms *hånd* and *hand* 'hand', etc.

subspace defined by the variable MSWs occurring within it (or as a set of points if at least one variable MSW is inconsistently realized).[6]

Since the official norms involve few constraints on the combination of possible forms within a text, they suggest as a null hypothesis that texts will spread out approximately evenly throughout the space. However, experience tells us that this is not the case, as indicated above. To the extent that implicational relations of the exemplified kind hold, certain combinations of forms will not occur, thus leaving the space empty in certain regions, e.g. in the region where the forms *hytten* and *kasta* are combined. Consequently our expectation is that the texts will tend to form more or less clearly defined clusters within the space. I will refer to such clusters as 'norm clusters'. Relatively clearly defined norm clusters within the total text universe will then approach the status of emerging subvarieties of Bokmål and Nynorsk. Hence empirically based charting of norm clusters will provide important information for further work towards the standardization of written Norwegian.

I have conducted a pilot study based on newspaper texts in order to investigate the viability of an approach along the lines suggested. In the preliminary investigation reported here I concentrate on a small set of linguistic phenomena, subjecting the extracted material to two kinds of analysis: *correspondence analysis* in order to visualize the clustering of forms and texts, and a more direct analysis of the *implicational relations* among the forms, visualized as directed graphs.

3. The texts

The pilot study is based on texts extracted from the web editions of four Bokmål and six Nynorsk newspapers.[7] Two newspapers, *Bergens Tidende* and

6. A multidimensional space may be an unaccustomed concept to some readers. Since three dimensions are as many as we can easily visualize, we may exemplify with an imagined cube *c* whose breadth dimension has the points *handa – handen – hånda – hånden*, whose depth dimension has the points *framtida – framtiden – fremtida – fremtiden*, and whose height dimension has the points *kona – konen*. A text with the forms *framtida, hånda, kona* will then correspond to a given point within *c*, a text with *fremtiden, hånden, kona* to another point, etc. while we will expect certain other locations in *c* not to be filled by any texts, e.g. the location of the combination *framtida, handen, konen*.

7. I am indebted to Knut Hofland, Uni Digital, for collecting, structuring and morphologically tagging the corpus, and for organizing it into texts according to the criteria described below.

Klassekampen, occur in both lists because they contain articles in both language varieties.[8] The Bokmål newspapers are:

- *Aftenposten*, an Oslo-based daily newspaper of nation-wide distribution, and one of Norway's two largest newspapers in terms of circulation.
- *Bergens Tidende*, a Bergen-based daily newspaper and the major newspaper in Western Norway, with about 35% of *Aftenposten*'s circulation.
- *Dagbladet*, an Oslo-based daily newspaper of nation-wide distribution and about 45% of *Aftenposten*'s circulation.
- *Klassekampen*, an Oslo-based daily newspaper of nation-wide distribution and around 5% of *Aftenposten*'s circulation.

The Nynorsk newspapers are:

- *Bergens Tidende* (see above).
- *Dag og Tid*, an Oslo-based weekly newspaper of nation-wide distribution and around 3% of *Aftenposten*'s circulation.
- *Hallingdølen*, a local newspaper published in Ål in Hallingdal, with about 4% of *Aftenposten*'s circulation.
- *Klassekampen* (see above).
- *Nationen*, an Oslo-based daily newspaper of nation-wide distribution and around 6% of *Aftenposten*'s circulation.
- *Sogn Avis*, a local newspaper published in Leikanger in Sogn, with about 4% of *Aftenposten*'s circulation.

The higher number of Nynorsk newspapers was chosen in order to compensate to some extent for the smaller text volume in the Nynorsk sources. According to the criteria specified below a selection of 55,000 Bokmål articles and 35,000 Nynorsk articles was made, yielding a Bokmål corpus of 22 million words and a Nynorsk corpus of 12 million words. The articles are taken from the period between the years 2000 and 2009, but the overwhelming majority is from 2008 and 2009.

As the aim of the project is to study the clustering of texts in the space defined by the variable MSWs, an appropriate 'text' concept had to be defined. The individual newspaper article is too small to yield sufficient data for informative comparison with other texts. Therefore, based on the assumption that the two most important determinants of the form options chosen are the journalist/author and the newspaper, a 'text' is defined for present purposes as the sum of

8. This is also true of *Nationen*, although only the Nynorsk parts have been sampled in this project.

what a given author has written in a given newspaper. For each newspaper (or for the Bokmål and Nynorsk parts of the paper, respectively, in the case of newspapers using both Bokmål and Nynorsk) the 20 most productive authors were then selected, yielding a text inventory of 80 Bokmål and 120 Nynorsk texts. These are the texts that constitute the corpus of 22 + 12 = 34 million words mentioned above. In the graphs each text is coded by an index identifying the author, with the initials of the newspaper suffixed. Thus, '71KK' is the text consisting of what author no. 71 has written in the *Klassekampen* part of the corpus. The texts were automatically tagged with lemma forms and morphological categories by means of the *Oslo-Bergen Tagger*.[9]

4. Data extraction and processing

The lexical database *Norsk Ordbank*, in which (officially and non-officially) possible inflectional forms are registered, allows the automatic identification of variable MSWs in a text. Based on this information, for each phenomenon studied all forms of variable MSWs in each text – i.e. all word forms that could have been different according to *Norsk Ordbank* – were registered in a table with the text ids along one axis and the forms along the other.[10] Distances between texts based on the differences between their rows of forms, and distances between forms based on the differences between their columns of texts, could now be calculated by means of correspondence analysis, of which the implementation in the program *R* (Baayen 2008: 128 ff.) was used, or more precisely the method *corres.fnc* in the module *languageR*.[11] In correspondence analysis the row and column maps (i.e. the plottings of texts and word forms, respectively) are superimposed on each other. The result is represented as a common multidimensional space in which both texts and word forms are distributed. The necessarily two-dimensional diagrams below show the projection of this space on its two most informative dimensions, i.e. the two dimensions responsible for most of the information about distances within the multidimensional space. The most common forms, typical of most texts, will tend to occur close to the centre of the diagram, while more rare forms tend to occur more peripherally, and near opposite edges to

9. See Johannesen et al. this volume.

10. Second elements of compounds that are listed in the lexical resources are also included in the data.

11. I am indebted to Øystein Reigem, Uni Digital, and Christer Johansson, University of Bergen, for help in carrying out the correspondence analysis.

the extent that they tend to be mutually exclusive. Therefore, as we move from a peripheral form towards the centre, the sequence of forms which we pass on our way roughly suggests an implicational relation holding between peripheral, rare forms and more central and widespread forms, which are 'implied' in the sense that choice of a more peripheral form (usually) implies the choice of a more central form along the same line, but not vice versa.

Several caveats are in order here. In the first place, it is important to bear in mind that much information about distances may be hidden in non-projected dimensions, somewhat like the actual distances between the visible stars in a night sky. In the second place, the dimensions of the space calculated are the result of the correspondence analysis' attempt to structure the information about distances as simply as possible, which means that the dimensions do not correspond exactly to the imagined dimensions defined by the MSWs, as briefly discussed in 2 above. In the third place, and as a corollary of this, the clustering of forms and texts will not only be influenced by the strictly linguistic parameters of choice among a set of alternative inflectional forms, but also by corresponding vocabulary: texts with a shared topic, and hence a shared vocabulary, will tend to be closer together than texts with different topics, other things being equal. However, the latter problem is to some extent counteracted by limiting the analysis to high-frequency items.

Since the positions of the forms in the correspondence analysis diagrams only give rough hints about implicational relations among the forms, primarily because differences in vocabulary across texts also influence the plots of texts and forms, some of the implicational relations (IRs) have in addition been subjected to a more precise analysis whose results are represented as directed graphs.[12] The IR-analysis is based on the following normalizations and assumptions:

1. Quite a few texts are 'inconsistent' in the sense that for some MSW, more than one of its alternative forms occur in the text. This may partly be the result of tagging errors, partly the result of quotations in the text, and partly real inconsistencies. In such cases the alternatives tend to have clearly different frequencies of occurrence, and I have therefore made the simplifying move of disregarding the form with the lowest frequency of occurrence in such cases, classifying the texts according to the most frequent form expressing a given MSW. Thus, an '*a*-text' will be a text in which *a* is the most frequent expression of the relevant MSW.

12. I am indebted to Øystein Reigem, Uni Digital, for implementing the implication analysis and its graphics according to gradually developing specifications.

2. A form *a* is said to imply a form *b* if all *a*-texts which contain some form of the MSW of which *b* is a possible expression, are also *b*-texts. For example, consider MSW1 ⟨`hytte +Noun +Def +Sg`⟩ ('cabin') with the possible forms *hytten* masc. and *hytta* fem., and MSW2 ⟨`gate +Noun +Def +Sg`⟩ ('street') with the possible forms *gaten* masc. and *gata* fem. *hytten* is said to imply *gaten* if and only if all *hytten*-texts containing MSW2 are also *gaten*-texts. This is compatible with the converse not holding, i.e. that some *gaten*-texts which also contain MSW1 are *hytta*-texts. If so, the implication is unilateral; if not, it is bilateral.
3. I assume that the implicational relation is transitive, i.e. that if *a* implies *b* and *b* implies *c*, then *a* implies *c*. This extends the relation to form pairs which never occur together in the same text in the corpus, and it is hence somewhat risky and probably leads to some spurious properties of the graphs, in particular given the sparseness of some of the relevant data. Nevertheless I find reason to assume that the graphs generally give a valid picture of the situation.

It should be stressed that these normalizations and assumptions apply to the IR-analysis only, and not to the correspondence analysis.

5. Case I: Feminine nouns in Bokmål

I first consider the choice of feminine vs. masculine gender[13] for the set of Bokmål nouns allowing this option. This set comprises all nouns that may be feminine in the language, i.e. feminine gender is optional in Bokmål. From this set I select the subset whose lemmas have a frequency of 500 or above in the 22 mill word Bokmål part of the corpus. This yields an inventory of 60 lemmas.

5.1 Correspondence analysis

Figure 1, in which the individual items are too small to be readable, is included in order to show the shape of the 'cloud' resulting from a correspondence analysis of the varying definite singular forms of the 60 nouns and the texts in which they occur. The two maximally informative dimensions are shown in Figure 1, but they give only 33.9% of the total information about distances in the multidimensional space (*x*-axis: 21%, *y*-axis: 12.9%). Still, some clear patterns emerge. As later figures zooming in on parts of the plot show, the radical feminine *a*-forms distribute towards the left in the plot, while the moderate masculine *en*-forms distribute

13. See Footnote 4 above.

towards the right. Furthermore, with some overlaps we find the texts from the four newspapers distributed from left to right in the order *Klassekampen – Dagbladet – Aftenposten – Bergens Tidende*.

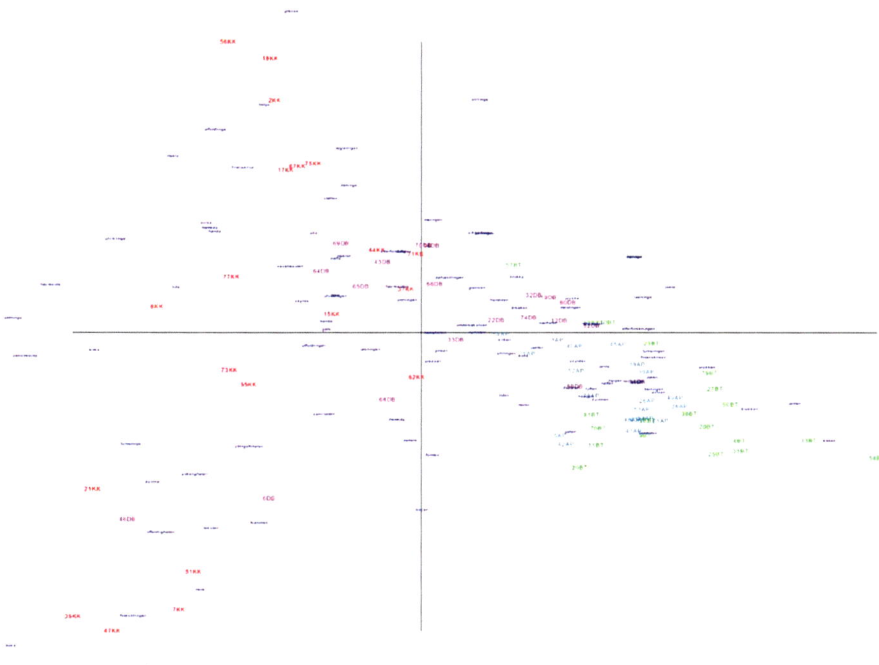

Figure 1. The 'cloud' displaying the distribution of masc. and fem. noun forms

The pointed shape of the 'cloud' towards the right is noteworthy. Dense clusters occur when relatively many texts share a number of choices; this is the intended meaning of the term 'norm cluster'. Choices which less consistently are correlated with other choices across texts lead to a more diffuse distribution. A claim which is sometimes made is that moderate Bokmål is more of a real, identifiable subvariety of Bokmål than radical Bokmål, which may be more of an abstraction in the sense that it refers to the sum of possible departures from moderate Bokmål without itself being a subvariety about which language users tend to have consistent intuitions. The pointed shape towards the moderate *-en* end of the plot, and the higher density within it, is compatible with such a claim, although it must of course be borne in mind that the plot covers only one phenomenon and considers only a limited number of texts. It should also be noted that low frequency in itself typically leads to a more sparse distribution because there will be fewer shared cooccurrence partners across texts among low-frequency forms. This is therefore an alternative possible explanation of the sparseness in the left-hand *-a* end of the plot.

Figure 2 is a close-up of the right-hand side of the plot, in which we find texts form *Bergens Tidende* (BT), *Aftenposten* (AP) and a few from *Dagbladet* (DB).

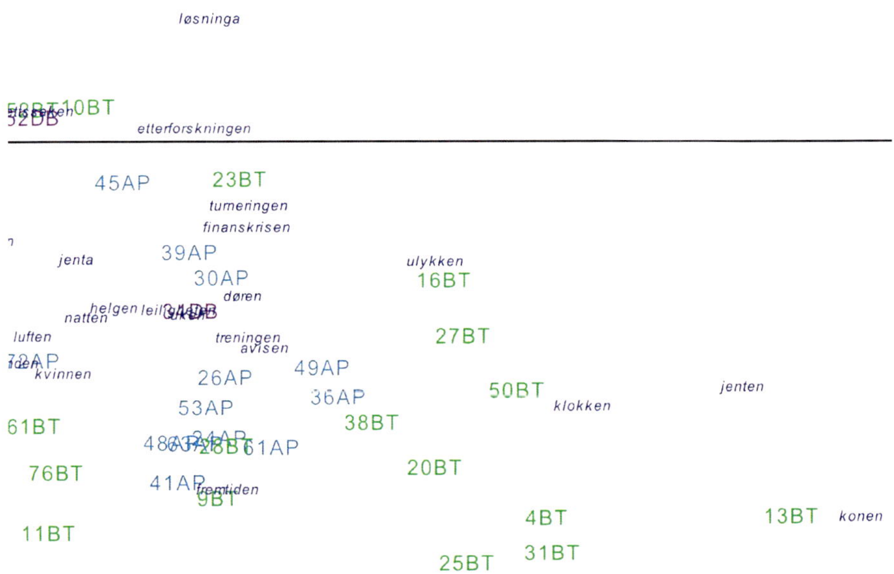

Figure 2. The rightmost part of the plot in Figure 1

At the far right we see the forms *jenten* 'the girl' masc. and *konen* 'the wife'/'the woman' masc. These are special for *Bergens Tidende* and reflect a consistent two-gender variety of Bokmål (which means that the gender here should properly be called 'common' rather than 'masculine'). As we move leftwards towards the centre, we find the feminine alternative *jenta* among the first *a*-forms to show up. *kona* and *klokka* 'the clock' also occur to the right of the centre, in the denser part of the plot (but outside Figure 2; see, however, Figure 4). This suggests that *konen* and *jenten* are marked forms at the top of the implicational scale: a text with these forms will most probably have all the other relevant nouns in the masculine, too. Within the denser norm cluster we find the *a*-forms *jenta* and *kona* occurring together with mostly *en*-forms of other nouns, such as *ulykken* 'the accident', *etterforskningen* 'the investigation', *turneringen* 'the tournament', *finanskrisen* 'the financial crisis', *døren* 'the door', *avisen* 'the newspaper', *natten* 'the night', *luften* 'the air', *kvinnen* 'the woman' etc. The last noun is worth noticing, since it shows that biological gender has limited relevance here. The nouns *kvinne* and *kone* have different stylistic properties, and the feminine form *kvinna* is perceived as markedly more radical than *kona*. The form *kvinna* occurs near the middle of the bottom left quadrant in Figure 1. It should also be noted that the total frequency of the form *kvinna* in the corpus is 14, as against 3,049 for *kvinnen*. The numbers for the forms of 'kone' are 80 for *konen* and 934 for *kona*.

Figure 3 is a close-up of a region in the far left of the plot.

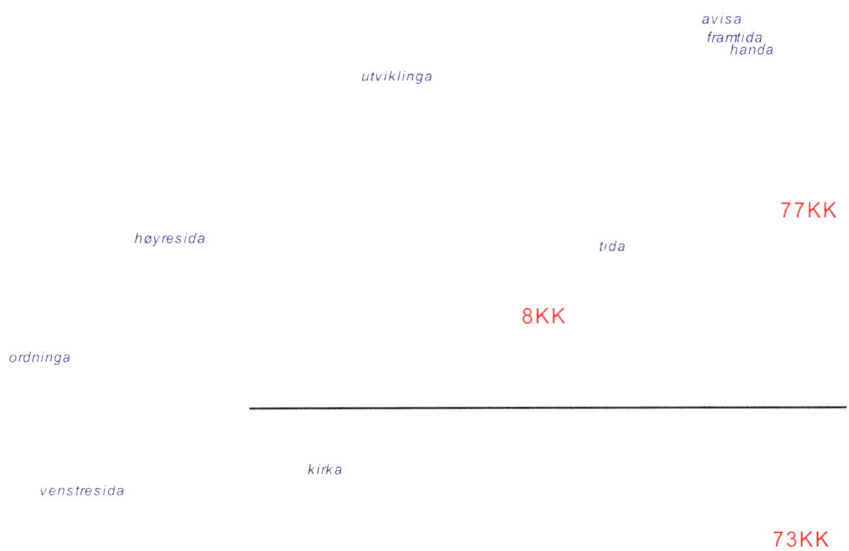

Figure 3. The leftmost part of the plot in Figure 1

In this part of the plot only the newspaper *Klassekampen* is represented.[14] At the left edge we expect to find marked forms, typical of relatively few texts, and probably implying *a*-forms of other relevant nouns as well. However, the sparseness of this part of the plot indicates that there is less consistency in the choice of *a*-forms across the texts departing from the norm in the direction of -*a* than there is in the choice of *en*-forms across the texts near the other edge (Figure 2). The nouns in Figure 3 are *ordninga* 'the arrangement', *venstresida* 'the (political) left', *høyresida* 'the (political) right', *kirka* 'the church', *utviklinga* 'the development', *tida* 'the time', *avisa* 'the newspaper', *framtida* 'the future', *handa* 'the hand', where the leftmost members tend to denote abstract concepts typical of texts of discursive type, which is compatible with the common impression that these are the last nouns to get the radical *a*-forms.

14. This does not preclude that the forms may occur in the other newspapers as well, but other choices pull those texts further to the right in the plot.

Figure 4 is a close-up of the central region of the plot in Figure 1.

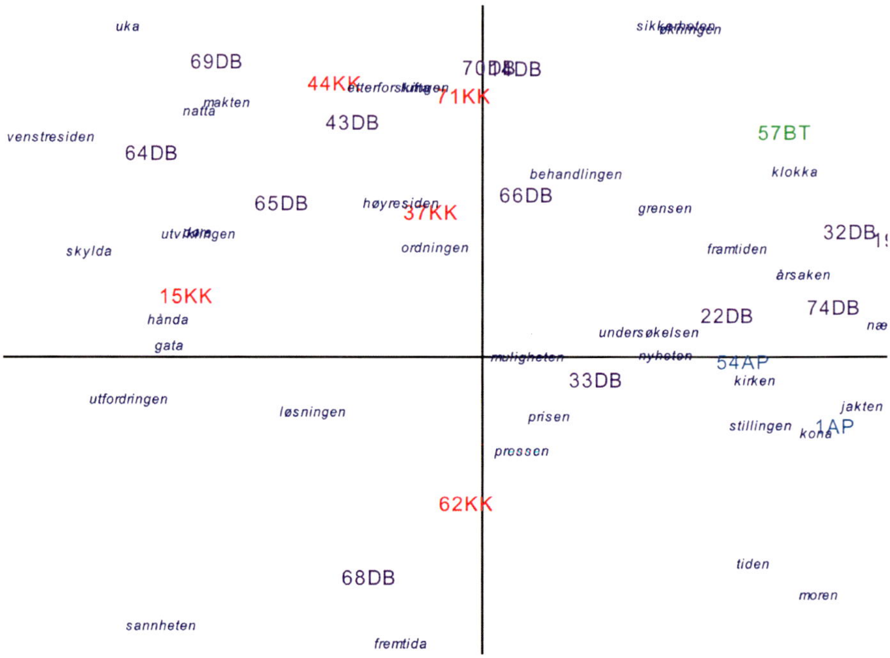

Figure 4. The central part of the plot in Figure 1

It is noticable that the *Klassekampen* texts occur exclusively on the left-hand side of the middle line, although also quite close to it, while the *Aftenposten* and *Bergens Tidende* texts occur exclusively on the right-hand side. Only *Dagbladet* distributes on both sides, placing the newspaper in the central region where we expect to find the forms that are typical of most of the texts. However, the central part of the plot is not the maximally dense part, indicating that the texts deviating to the right are more consistent in their choices than the others are, thus forming a norm cluster.

The nouns with *a*-forms in the central region are typically concretes or other words characteristic of everyday language, such as *skylda* 'the blame', *uka* 'the week', *hånda* 'the hand', *gata* 'the street', *natta* 'the night', *døra* 'the door', *klokka* 'the clock' and *kona* 'the wife'. *en*-forms in Figure 4 comprise abstracts typical of discursive prose stretching into the left part, such as *venstresiden* 'the (political) left', *utfordringen* 'the challenge', *sannheten* 'the truth', *utviklingen* 'the development', *makten* 'the power', *løsningen* 'the solution', *etterforskningen* 'the investigation', *høyresiden* 'the (political) right', *ordningen* 'the arrangement' (corroborating the impression that the *en*-form is most persistent in such words even in texts where other nouns get *-a*), and further to the right *muligheten* 'the possibility', *pressen* 'the press', *behandlingen* 'the treatment', *undersøkelsen* 'the investigation', *nyheten* ' the piece of news', *framtiden* 'the future', *kirken* 'the church', *stillingen* 'the position', *tiden* 'the time', årsaken 'the cause', *moren* 'the mother' and *jakten* 'the hunt'.

en-forms even further to the left than the area shown in Figure 4, in the bottom left quadrant, are *historien* 'the history', *ytringsfriheten* 'the freedom of expression', *teksten* 'the text', *virkeligheten* 'the reality', *offentligheten* 'the public sphere' and *forestillingen* 'the performance'/'the idea'. For *ytringsfriheten, teksten* and *virkeligheten* the corresponding *a*-forms do not occur at all in the corpus, while the numbers of occurrences in the other three cases are: *forestillingen*: 757, *forestillinga*: 7, *historien*: 2,540, *historia*: 16, *offentligheten*: 828, *offentligheta*: 2. The reason why the strongly dominant *en*-forms in these cases still do not occur more centrally in the diagram is probably related to vocabulary: these 'intellectual' concepts seem to be more typical of the *Klassekampen* and *Dagbladet* journalists in their vicinity than they are of the writers in *Aftenposten* and *Bergens Tidende*.

5.2 Implication analysis

As described in Section 4 above I have performed a more direct analysis of the implicational relations between the form choices in the corpus as a whole, disregarding the distribution across different newspapers. In the graphs that follow, the forms which imply each other mutually according to the criteria in Section 4 are placed within the same oval, while unilateral implications are marked with arrows between ovals. The frequency of the forms is roughly indicated by the thickness of the oval line, according to a logarithmic scale ($\log_5$). When the oval contains more than one form, the thickness of the line indicates average frequency.

Figure 5 shows the bottom of the implicational graph, directly or indirectly dominated by all other forms, both *a*-forms and *en*-forms. These forms, then, emerge as the maximally 'unmarked' forms, expected to occur across the text universe.

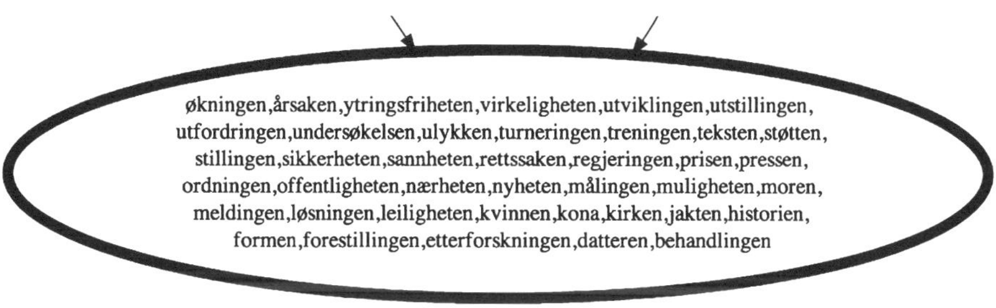

Figure 5. The bottom of the implicational graph with maximally 'unmarked' forms

The forms in Figure 5 are all *en*-forms, with the exception of *kona*. Also, many of them denote abstracts typical of discursive prose.

As indicated in Section 4 the graph has a few spurious properties resulting from the low frequency of some forms in combination with our assumption of transitivity of the implicational relation. For example, the rare forms *utfordringa* and *konen* occur high up in the graph (see Figures 7 and 8), and hence appear to imply their alternatives *utfordringen* and *kona* in Figure 5, which obviously is not actually the case. The same is the case with the forms *utstillingen, treningen, stillingen, kirken, kvinnen* and *datteren* in Figure 5, whose alternatives also occur higher up in the graph. I assume that less sparse data would have moved these forms out of the bottom oval into positions dominated by only subsets of the rest of the forms.

Figure 6 shows the left part of the graph, with *kvinna* 'the woman' at the top, indicating its position as a strongly marked choice implying most other *a*-forms. Unexpectedly it also dominates the *en*-forms *natten* 'the night' and *tiden* 'the time' (which could have been seen more easily in the undivided version of the graph divided up between Figures 6, 7 and 8 for reasons of space), which indicates that the implicational relations found for low-frequency items (*kvinna* has

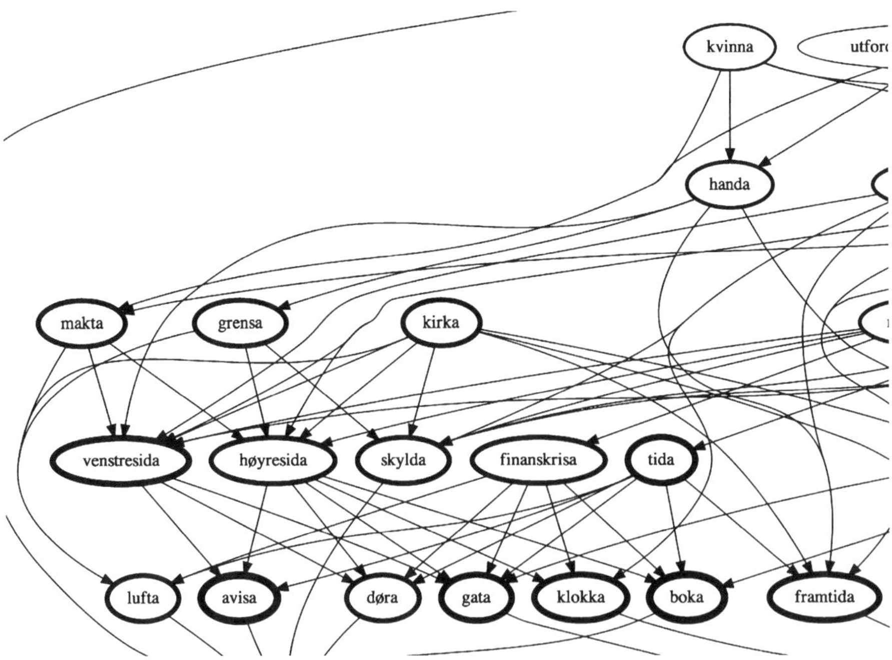

Figure 6. The left part of the implication graph

14 occurrences) must be taken with a grain of salt – there is exactly one text in which the form *kvinna* cooccurs with *natten*, and the same is the case with *kvinna* and *tiden*. Similar probably spurious implications occur with *løsninga* 'the solution', *utfordringa* 'the challenge', *stillinga* 'the position', *utstillinga* 'the exhibition', *målinga* 'the measuring', *meldinga* 'the message', *treninga* 'the exercise' and *dattera* 'the daughter' in Figure 7. For the more frequent and hence more reliable *a*-cases in Figures 6 and 7 we notice that *a*-forms of more abstract words tend to imply *a*-forms of more concrete or everyday words. Thus, *makta* 'the power', *grensa* 'the limit'/'the border', *kirka* 'the church', and further down *venstresida* 'the left', *høyresida* 'the right', *skylda* 'the blame' and *finanskrisa* 'the financial crisis' dominate the

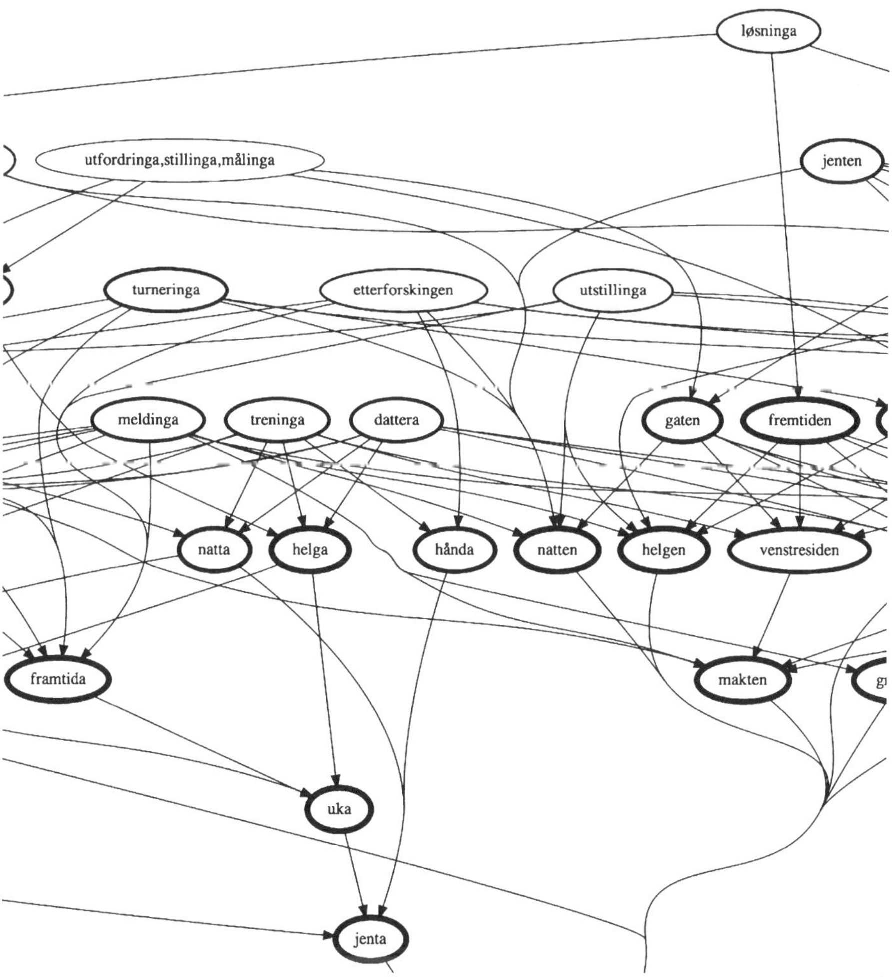

Figure 7. The middle part of the implication graph

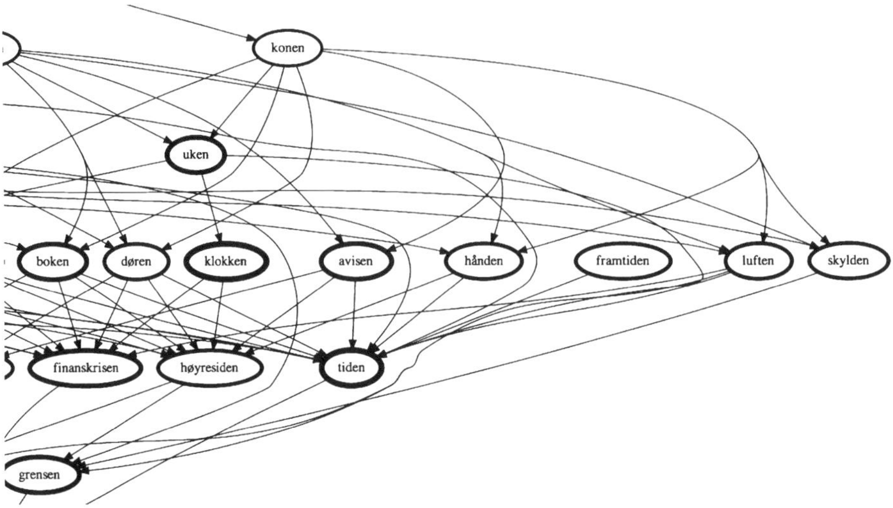

Figure 8. The right part of the implication graph

more everyday concepts *lufta* 'the air', *avisa* 'the newspaper', *døra* 'the door', *gata* 'the street', *boka* 'the book', *framtida* 'the future', and even further down *uka* 'the week' and *jenta* 'the girl'. Some of the exceptions to this pattern should probably be attributed to stylistic properties associated with individual words. We may notice that some of the *a*-forms of concretes that occur higher up and hence appear to be more marked choices denote female humans, such as *kvinna* 'the woman' and *dattera* 'the daughter'. Another example is *mora* 'the mother', which does not occur in the graph because it does not seem to cooccur with any of the other 59 nouns considered.

Figures 7 and 8 show the *en*-forms, which, as expected, tend to display the same implicational hierarchy as the *a*-forms, but turned upside-down. On the *en*-side the everyday words are on top: if you choose the *en*-form of concretes like *gaten* 'the street', *boken* 'the book', *døren* 'the door', *klokken* 'the clock', *avisen* 'the newspaper' *luften* 'the air' etc. then you are likely to choose also the *en*-forms of more abstract nouns like *venstresiden* 'the left', *høyresiden* 'the right', *finanskrisen* 'the financial crisis', *makten* 'the power', *grensen* 'the limit'/'the border', etc. At the very top (apart from the spurious *løsninga*) we find the rare forms *jenten* 'the girl' and *konen* 'the wife'. It is interesting that nouns denoting female humans stand apart from other concretes, but in two diametrically opposed ways. There are two subclasses of them, each occurring high up in its own implicational hierarchy: those whose *en*-forms are clearly marked choices (*jenten, konen*), and those whose *a*-forms are clearly marked choices (*kvinna, dattera, mora*).

6. Case II: Weak verbs in Bokmål

The largest and most productive class of weak verbs in Bokmål has the alternative endings *-et* (traditional, moderate) and *-a* (radical) in past and past participle forms. Thus, the MSWs ⟨`kaste +Verb +Past`⟩ and ⟨`kaste +Verb +PastPart`⟩ both have the alternative forms *kastet* and *kasta*. I have registered all past and past participle forms of verbs of this class whose lemmas have a frequency of occurrence equal to or greater than 500 in the 22 million word Bokmål part of the corpus. This yields an inventory of 58 verbs.

Figure 9 shows the shape of the 'cloud' resulting from a correspondence analysis of this material projected on the two most informative dimensions, which are jointly responsible for 31% of the information about distances in the space (x-axis: 18.6%; y-axis: 12.4%).

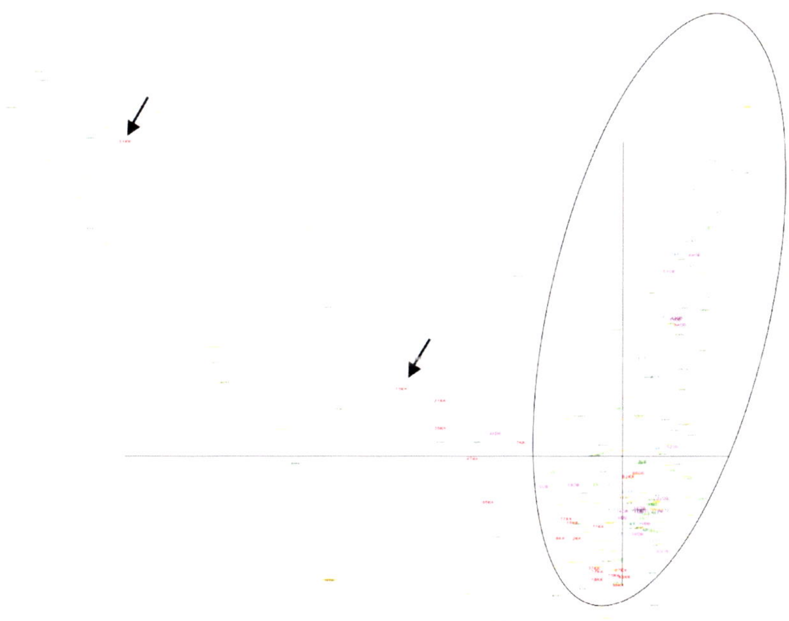

Figure 9. The 'cloud' displaying the distribution of *et*- and *a*-forms of weak verbs

In the plot in Figure 9, unlike in the masculine/feminine case, there is no transitional area where the two form categories mingle. The oval encloses only *et*-forms (with the exception of the form *rykka* 'moved quickly' and a couple of peripheral forms mentioned below), while all the forms outside the oval are *a*-forms (except a few forms which are neither, for verbs which allow further options, such as *lagde*, past tense of *lage* 'make'). This suggests that there may be less of an implicational hierarchy among the verbal *et*-forms or *a*-forms than there was in the case of the nouns: the tendency is to use either one or the other ending consistently, irrespective of verb. Still the *a*-forms spread out much more sparsely than the *et*-forms. This sparseness is probably not the result of less consistency in the choice of *a*-forms as against *et*-forms across the texts, then, but rather the result of the extremely low frequency of the *a*-forms. The strong tendency is that the *a*-forms have less than ten occurrences, while the *et*-forms have a three-digit number of occurrences in the corpus. Therefore the *a*-forms cooccur with a much lower number of the other forms than do the *et*-forms, a circumstance which gives rise to a greater distance between them in the plot, since the *a*-forms will share fewer cooccurrence partners than the *et*-forms.

With one exception – one *Dagbladet* text – *Klassekampen* is the only newspaper whose texts occur outside the oval.[15] Among the *Klassekampen* texts, only one is located near the upper left corner, as indicated by the leftmost arrow in Figure 9. The next *Klassekampen* text is located at the rightmost arrow. The forms in the sparse area from the left inwards are: *jobba* 'worked', *laga* 'made', *bekrefta* 'confirmed', *handla* 'shopped'/'acted', *henta* 'fetched', *snakka* 'talked', *venta* 'waited'/'expected', *samla* 'collected', *overraska* 'surprised', *mista* 'lost', *endra* 'changed', *regna* 'calculated'/'rained', *sikra* 'secured', *flytta* 'moved', *varsla* 'notified', *fjerna* 'removed'. Thus the indications are that one single writer among the 80 Bokmål writers is mainly responsible for this *a*-form protuberance from the central area in the plot.

Figure 10 shows the central and densest part of the plot in Figure 9.[16] All the four newspapers are densely represented in this region (although with *Klassekampen* near the edge of the *et*-area), indicating that the *et*-forms constitute a clear norm cluster for this corpus, and the only cluster in the verbal *-et*/*-a* space.

As shown in Figure 9 the *et*-forms (and two *a*-forms) also have a protuberance into the top right quadrant. All three newspapers *Aftenposten, Bergens Tidende* and *Dagbladet* are represented here, but not *Klassekampen*. Apparently this departure from the main cluster is not explained by the choice of inflectional forms, but by vocabulary. The forms from the top down are *scoret*, *scora* 'scored',

15. This does not exclude the possibility of *a*-forms in other texts, but if so, the preponderance of other forms still place such texts within the oval.

16. When a form occurs twice in the plot, one occurrence is the past tense form and the other the past participle form. The past tense forms are printed in bolder type.

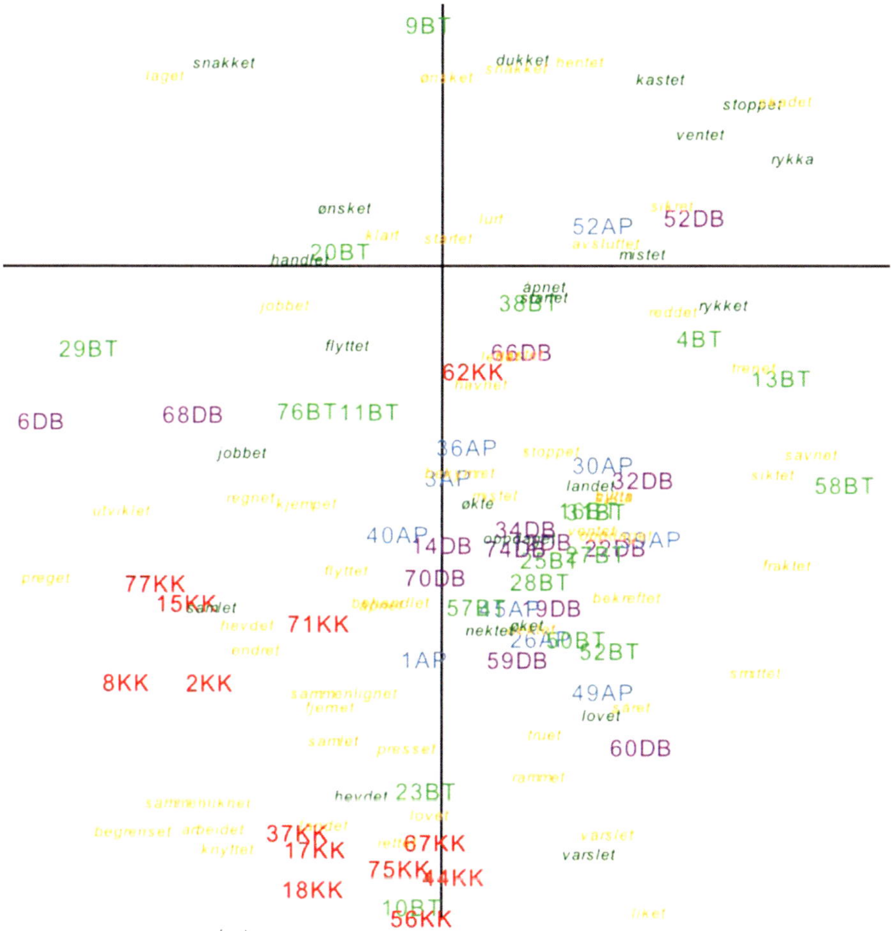

Figure 10. The central region of the plot in Figure 9

mista 'lost', *trent* 'exercised', *rykte* 'moved quickly',[17] *byttet* 'changed', *laget* 'made', *reddet* 'saved', *sørget* 'secured'/'grieved', *virket* 'worked'/'seemed', *skuffet* 'disappointed', *klarte* 'managed', *sikret* 'secured', *havnet* 'ended up', *hentet* 'fetched' and *ledet* 'led'. As this vocabulary already suggests, the writers represented in this area are sports journalists. The absence of *Klassekampen* fits well with the fact that this newspaper does not have sports pages. The reason why the sports terminology

17. The forms *trent* and *rykte*, a past participle and a past tense form, respectively, do not end in *-a* or *-et*, but are included because the verbs in question also allow the *-a*/*-et* inflection.

leads to this kind of departure from the main cluster may be that the sports pages use comparatively little of the rest of the vocabulary of the language, and possibly also, conversely, that the verbs typical of the sports pages are not frequent in other text types.

As expected from the fact that *et*- and *a*-forms hardly mingle at all in the plot, the implicational analysis of this material indicates no clear implicational hierarchy among these forms across different verbs. The tendency is for a text to use one or the other ending consistently across verbs.

In order to inspect patterns of cooccurrence across the noun and verb forms of cases I and II the two tables were combined into one and the result subjected to correspondence analysis again. The resulting plot has the same general shape as Figure 1, with roughly the same distribution of the noun forms, but now with the verb forms interspersed. All the verbal *a*-forms occur peripherally, and the vast majority on the left side, in the general area of the more marked nominal *a*-forms (*kvinna, mora* etc.). As we move towards the centre, the *et*-forms start showing up at the same time as the nominal *a*-forms typical of everyday language (*gata, uka, natta, skylda* etc.), i.e. as we enter the area shown in Figure 4. This supports the impression that the choice of verbal *a*-forms clusters with the choice of the most markedly 'radical' nominal *a*-forms.

7. Case III: Infinitives in Nynorsk

Infinitives in Nynorsk may end in *-a* or in *-e*. Unlike the case of feminine and masculine nouns in Bokmål, in this case the official norm to some extent prescribes the distribution of the two endings across verbs, according to three options: (i) consistent *-a* in all verbs, (ii) consistent *-e* in all verbs, (iii) 'split infinitive' ('kløyvd infinitiv'). Option (iii) involves *-a* in some infinitives and *-e* in others based on historically rooted patterns of variation in certain dialects in the Eastern and middle part of Norway, excluding most of North Norway (see e.g. Faarlund et al. 1997:476 f.; Skjekkeland 1997:69). The historical explanation is related to syllable quantity. In Modern Norwegian, with the exception of a small dialectal area in Gudbrandsdalen, accented syllables are always long, i.e. they have a long vowel, or a short vowel plus a long consonant or consonant cluster.[18] Accented syllables in Old Norse could also be short, with a short

18. This is the traditional analysis. There are alternative phonological analyses of these phenomena which I will not go into for present purposes.

vowel plus a short consonant. In modern dialects such syllables generally have been lengthened either by lengthening of the vowel (typical of the West) or by lengthening of the consonant (typical of the East). But already in late Old Norse, before the changes in syllable quantity, we see evidence that unstressed [a] was reduced to an [e]- or [æ]-like sound after long syllables, but not after short ones, in manuscripts from the Eastern part of the country. The split infinitive is a reflex in modern dialects of this quantitatively conditioned reduction. However, after the lengthening of the old short accented syllables there is no quantitative conditioning of this variation from a synchronic point of view. This means that unless you have either split infinitive in your own dialect or expert knowledge of Old Norse and language history, there is no way to predict that *bite* = 'bite' (with originally long /i:/) should have *-e* while *vita* = 'know' (with originally short /i/) should have *-a* according to the rules of the split infinitive. As a consequence, the split infinitive option in written Nynorsk is recommended only for people who have this phenomenon in their own dialect. As long as such writers distribute the *-a* and the *-e* according to their own dialect they are within the official norm. This still opens up for some variation, since the split infinitive dialects are not consistent among themselves as to how many of the originally short-syllabic verbs get *-a* rather than *-e* in the infinitive. Hence charting the variation in Nynorsk infinitives is also of some interest.

7.1 Correspondence analysis

I have registered all infinitival forms of verbs of this class whose lemmas have a frequency of occurrence equal to or greater than 500 in the 12 million word Nynorsk part of the corpus. This yields an inventory of 83 verb lemmas. Figure 11 shows the shape of the 'cloud' plotting the *e*- and *a*-infinitives in the six Nynorsk newspapers. The two dimensions in the graph contain 48.7% of the information about distances in the space (*x*-axis: 41.9%, *y*-axis: 6.8%).

In Figure 11 most of the *a*-infinitives cluster densely in the far left, while most of the *e*-infinitives spread out vertically in the far right. In the left-hand *a*-cluster we find all the writers of *Sogn Avis*, exactly half of the writers of *Dag og Tid*, 8 out of the 20 writers of *Bergens Tidende*, 6 out of the 20 writers of *Klassekampen*, 2 out of the 20 writers of *Nationen*, and none from *Hallingdølen*. Thus, across the six newspapers 38% of the writers use consistent *a*-infinitives.

The remaining writers mostly cluster with the *e*-forms, the most notable exception being *Hallingdølen*. Figure 12 shows part of the lower right quadrant of Figure 11, with most of the *Hallingdølen* writers spreading out between the two clusters.

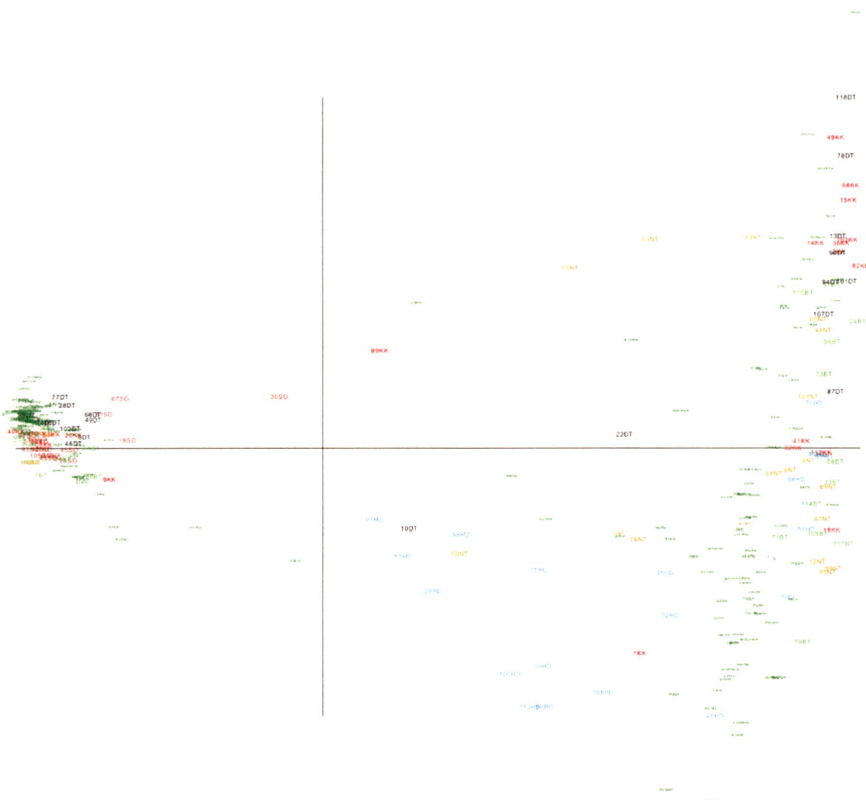

Figure 11. The 'cloud' displaying the distribution of *e-* and *a*-infinitives

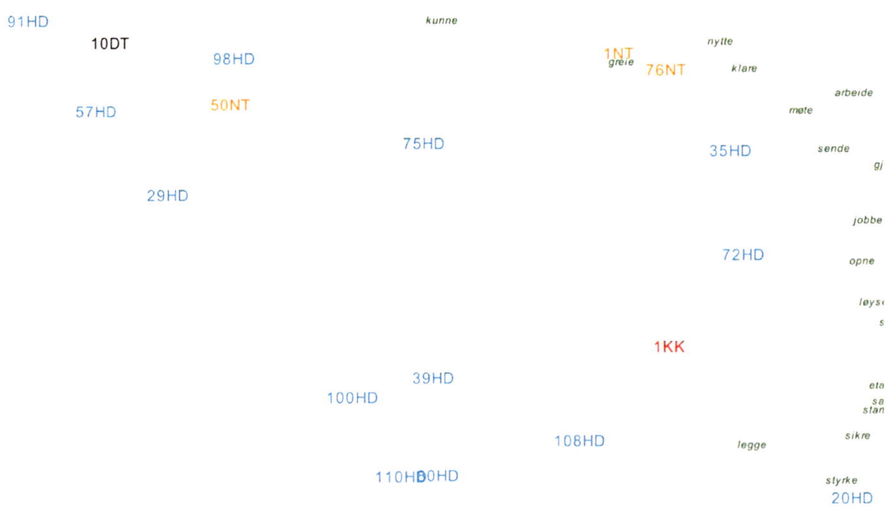

Figure 12. Part of the lower right quadrant of Figure 11, showing writers between the main clusters

Hallingdølen is published in an area where the dialects use split infinitive, but the newspaper does not impose the use of split infinitive on its journalists. The plot indicates that the writers of *Hallingdølen*, plus a couple from *Nationen* and *Dag og Tid*, use split infinitive to varying degrees, from almost consistent *e*-forms through a gradually increasing number of *a*-forms.

The rules of the split infinitive, prescribing *-a* in originally short-syllabic verbs, have consequences for the vertical distribution of the forms. Thus the lower left quadrant of Figure 11, shown in Figure 13 shows a 'tail' of *a*-forms departing from the main cluster in the direction of the *Hallingdølen* writers, and they are all short-syllabic with the single exception of *styrka* 'strengthen'.

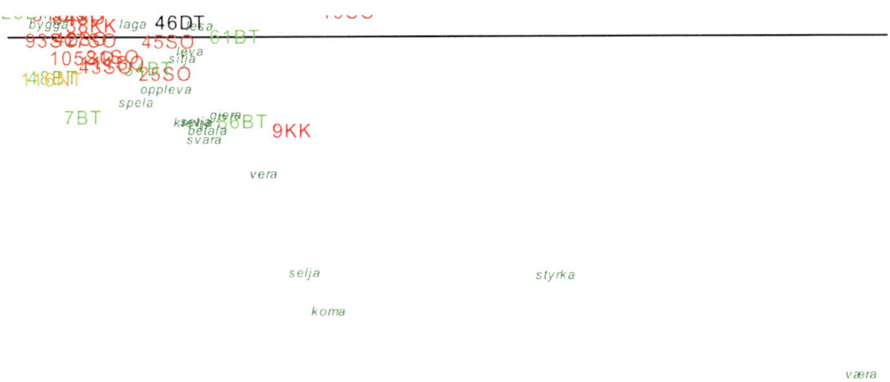

Figure 13. The lower left quadrant of Figure 11; a tail of the *a*-cluster

There are two forms of the infinitive *vera* = 'be', *vera* and *væra*, shown in Figure 13, with the latter apparently mostly restricted to the users of split infinitive, as appears from its position near the centre of the graph.

On the right-hand side the split infinitive writers lead to a corresponding preponderance of long-syllabic forms in the lower half of the *e*-cluster, with most of the short-syllabic forms in the upper half. However, it seems that other factors also influence the distribution of the *e*-forms. It is not immediately clear why the *e*-forms spread out so much more in the vertical dimension than the *a*-forms (see Figure 11), but it seems likely that it is related to the distribution of vocabulary across writers. There is a noticable tendency for the *e*-infinitives in the upper and lower halves to belong to different semantic fields. The verbs in the upper region, from the top, are (with originally long-syllabic forms marked with an asterisk, since the split infinitive favours short-syllabic forms in this region, making long-syllabic forms more marked): *lese* 'read', **skrive* 'write', **snakke* 'talk', *leve* 'live', **kjenne* 'feel', *fortelje* 'tell', **tenkje* 'think', *spele* 'play', *spørje* 'ask', *vite* 'know', *vere* 'be', **lære* 'learn'/'teach', **kalle* 'call', *gjere* 'do', *lage* 'make', *tene* 'earn'/'serve', *komme* 'come', **vise* 'show', **høyre* 'hear', *sitje* 'sit', *velje* 'choose', *oppleve* 'experience', *seie* 'say'. Thus, the majority of these verbs are related to the general sphere of communication or intellectual activities. The verbs in the lower three quarters of the lower half, on the other hand, are, from the bottom upwards (this time with originally short-syllabic forms asterisked): *køyre* 'drive', *bygge* 'build', *koste* 'cost', *vurdere* 'evaluate', *styrke* 'strengthen', *legge* 'lay', *sikre* 'secure', *starte* 'start', *innføre* 'import'/'introduce', *byggje* 'build', *satse* 'invest', *etablere* 'establish', *melde* 'report', *søkje* 'apply', *auke* 'increase', *redusere* 'reduce', *løyse* 'solve', *rekne* 'calculate', **betale* 'pay', *opne* 'open', *kjøpe* 'buy', *hente* 'fetch', *flytte* 'move', *jobbe* 'work' **selje* 'sell', *liggje* 'lie' (in a position) *vente* 'wait'/'expect', *samle* 'collect', *gjennomføre* 'carry through', *drive* 'run' (transitive), *sende* 'send', *leggje* 'lay', *følgje* 'follow', *skaffe* 'provide', *møte* 'meet', *bruke* 'use', *arbeide* 'work', **klare* 'manage', *greie* 'manage', *utvikle* 'develop'. Thus, the general sphere here seems to be industry, trade and economy.

The vertical distribution distinguishing two semantic fields among the *e*-forms indicates that the writers tend to specialize in certain domains, such as culture vs. economic news. This accords well with the fact that all the *Dag og Tid* writers and most of the *Klassekampen* writers within the *e*-cluster are located in its upper half. Both these newspapers have an emphasis on culture and political commentary. The majority *e*-cluster writers of *Nationen*, a newspaper with an emphasis on regional politics and agriculture, are located in the lower region, while the *Bergens Tidende* writers within the *e*-cluster spread out evenly between the two regions. This indicates that the journalists of this major newspaper can be more specialized than what is possible for the journalists of the much smaller *Sogn Avis*, which dominates the left-hand *a*-cluster. This circumstance may be the reason why we do not see a corresponding division of the *a*-cluster into semantically motivated subregions: each journalist in a small newspaper has to cover several domains, and some domains may also be covered to a lesser extent.

7.2 Implication analysis

The semantic factors discussed above to some extent obscure the patterns of variation within the choices of *e*-forms and *a*-forms of the infinitives. We have therefore subjected the data to an implication analysis of the kind described in 4 above. The analysis reveals an implicational pattern among the users of split infinitive concerning the choice of infinitive forms. Figure 14 shows the right half of the resulting graph, comprising the *a*-forms. The left half, comprising the *e*-forms, is almost exactly like the right half turned upside down.

Most of the originally short-syllabic *a*-forms occur below the large set of *a*-forms with mutual implications. The pattern indicates a relatively clear ranking of the short-syllabic *a*-forms used by writers which use split infinitive. *vera* 'be' at the bottom indicates that at least this form is used by all such writers, and some

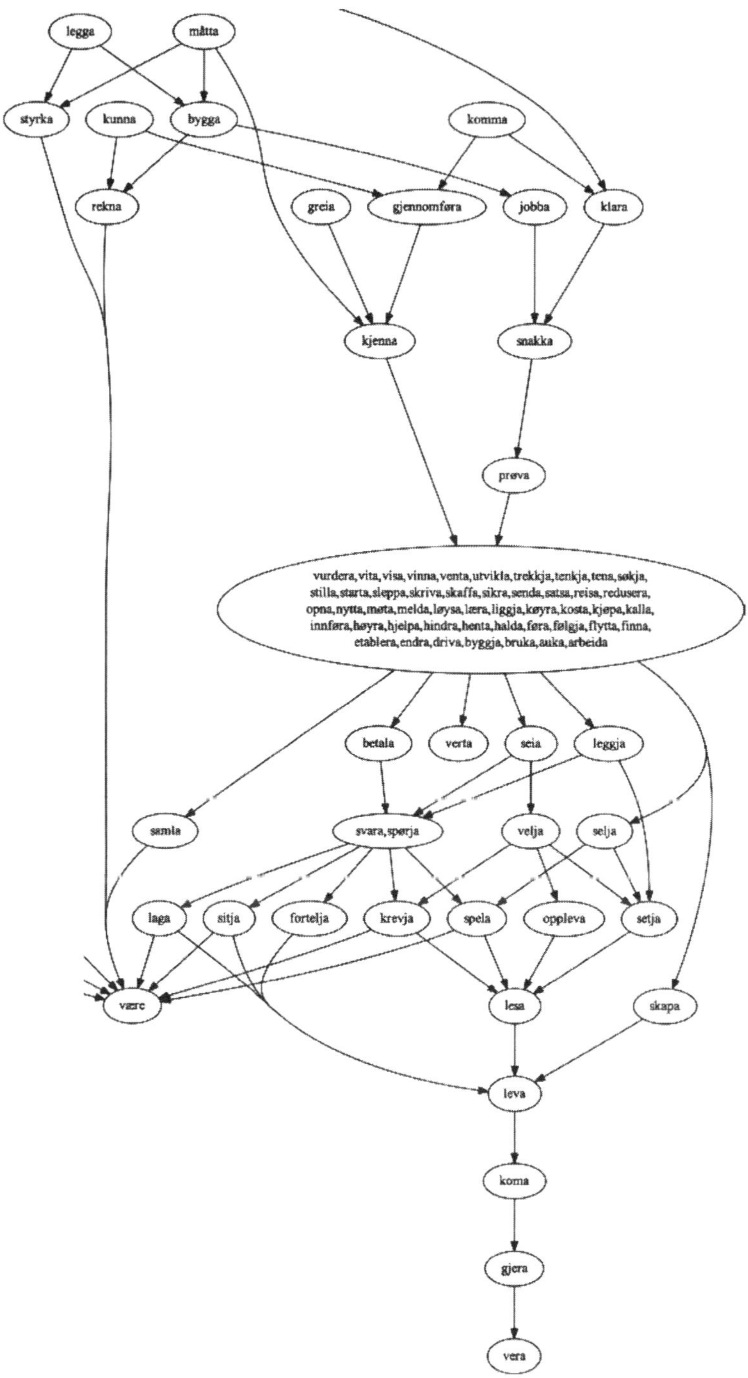

Figure 14. Implicational relations among the *a*-infinitives

will use only this *a*-form while using *-e* in all other infinitives. *gjera* 'do' above it indicates that some will use only these two *a*-forms, etc. This is matched by the fact that *vere* dominates *gjere* etc. at the top of the other half of the graph (not shown here) – i.e. if a writer chooses *vere*, then all infinitives are *e*-forms.

The graph must be read with the caveats mentioned in Sections 4 and 5.2 above. Still, it strongly suggests a rather consistent pattern of implications across split-infinitive writers with regard to the most frequent verbs. Breaking this pattern would then probably be perceived as a violation of the operative norm for nynorsk. At the same time it is clearly unrealistic to expect non-expert writers without this phenomenon in their own dialects to acquire mastery of this system, including the implicational relationships. This might be taken as an argument against keeping the split infinitive option as part of the standard language, assuming that a standard in a strict sense is the aim.

8. Conclusion

The primary goal of the pilot project reported here was to test the utility of correspondence analysis and implication analysis in the investigation of norm clusters in Bokmål and Nynorsk. The techniques will have to be applied to a much larger and more representative corpus, and to a much wider range of linguistic phenomena, before fairly safe conclusions about the situation of written Norwegian and its possible emergent subvarieties can be reached. Still, the analyses indicate that the approach is able to yield plausible insights about clusterings and implicational relationships. The following tendencies were among the ones indicated:

- In the alternation between masculine and feminine gender (in the sense of Footnote 4) of nouns in Bokmål, the choice of masculine gender forms the densest cluster, indicating that this choice may be correlated with more consistency across texts, i.e. a more clearly defined subnorm, than the alternative choice.
- There is an implicational relationship between the choice of feminine gender for nouns denoting abstract concepts from the academic sphere and the choice of feminine gender for concretes and everyday words, where the former choice implies the latter, but not vice versa.
- In the alternation between *-et* and *-a* in weak verbs in Bokmål the *et*-forms form a solid norm cluster, while pervasive use of *a*-forms seems to be typical of a tiny fraction of the writers involved.
- The use of *a*-forms of weak verbs clusters with the choice of feminine gender for abstract words from the academic sphere.

- In the alternation between *-a* and *-e* in infinitives in Nynorsk the writers using the split infinitive show a fair amount of variation, but still display a comparatively clear implicational relationship in their choice of ending for individual verbs. The complexity of this system is not conducive to having it captured by clear normative rules.

These results in themselves are not very novel or surprising. But they corroborate and provide a further articulation of common existing assumptions, and this is done on the basis of empirical corpus data rather than on that of intuitive judgments. This supports the conclusion that the approach tested here, applied to a much larger corpus, may provide useful information about emerging norm patterns for the long-term work towards the adaptation of the written standards to developments in the operative norms revealed in real texts.

References

Baayen, R. Harald 2008. *Analyzing Linguistic Data. A Practical Introduction to Statistics Using R*. Cambridge: CUP.

Faarlund, Jan Terje, Lie, Svein & Vannebo, Kjell Ivar. 1997. *Norsk referansegrammatikk*. Oslo: Universitetsforlaget.

Rosén, Victoria & De Smedt, Koenraad 2000. *Er korrekturlesningsevnen di god? Resultater fra SCARRIE. In *Nordlyd: Tromsø University Working Papers on Language and Linguistics* 28, Olaf Jansen Westvik, Toril Swan, Endre Mørck & Ove Lorentz (eds), 214–228. Tromsø: University of Tromsø.

De Smedt, Koenraad & Rosén, Victoria. 2000. Automatic proofreading for Norwegian: The challenges of lexical and grammatical variation. In *NODALIDA'99: Proceedings from the* 12th *"Nordiske datalingvistikkdager", Trondheim, December 9–10, 1999*, Torbjørn Nordgård (ed), 206–215. Trondheim: NTNU.

Norsk Ordbank. ⟨http://www.hf.uio.no/iln/om/organisasjon/edd/forsking/norsk-ordbank/⟩ (20 March, 2011).

SCARRIE. ⟨http//ling.b.uib.no/projects/scarrie/⟩ (19 March, 2011).

Skjekkeland, Martin. 1997. *Dei norske dialektane*. Kristiansand: Høyskoleforlaget.

Lexical neography in modern Norwegian

Ruth Vatvedt Fjeld & Lars Nygaard
University of Oslo / Kaldera language technology

This article presents a short history of Norwegian neography and some of the problems in the field of lexical development. Norwegian linguistic purism has unfortunately led to a negative perspective on loanwords, and for a long time there was little neography in Norwegian lexicography. When registration of neologisms was initiated, the methodology and coverage was insufficient. This article presents a classification of neologisms and a new method of semi-automatic identification of neologisms from the Norwegian Newspaper Corpus (NNC). Some of the results show that the overwhelming amount of new words in Norwegian are inherited words, mostly compounds, and that genuinely new words are fairly rare.

1. Introduction

The vocabulary in a language will normally change much more rapidly than syntax and morphology. During a period of 20 years, a number of lexical changes take place in a living language. The fact that a language acquires new words is a sign that it is alive and able to adapt to new cultural and social conditions and situations. Studies and registration of lexical changes are called lexical neography. Such studies might predict linguistic changes in general, since new words and expressions and how lexical items are used also reflect how lexical change has taken place inside the structure of a particular language. Since lexical neography also implies a survey of general cultural changes in a language community, the study of neologisms has two sides, one purely linguistic, and one cultural, which makes this field quite attractive and leads to a considerable amount of publicity.

Neography was for a long time neglected in Nordic lexicography. That is no coincidence, since linguistic research and language counseling in the Nordic countries has been quite puristic, which has led to the rejection of new loan words or word constituents or derivations that did not follow traditional patterns of word formation (Sandøy 2000). This policy has been most outspoken in Iceland and the Faeroe Islands (cf. e.g. Thomsen 2002: 107), and has lead to differences between the vocabulary in use and the words listed in dictionaries and used in official documents.

Lexical purism has been prominent not only in the Nordic region. Depending on national efforts in language planning, adoption of new words varies greatly from language to language and time to time. For a long time, German language planning was quite puristic, but there has been a dramatic change in the linguistic climate in Germany since the 1960s, and modern German is now receptive of borrowings, mainly from English, like many other contemporary languages. The same has happened to the modern Danish language (Sørensen 1995).

During the late Middle Ages, the Norwegian language was flooded by Low German loan words that altered more than 50 per cent of the Norwegian vocabulary (Simensen 1995). This is not a unique event in language history. Many languages have at times been so open to loans after strong cultural and linguistic influence from the outside that they might be regarded as mixed languages. English is often mentioned as an example; Norwegian and other Scandinavian languages may also be included here. Nevertheless, these languages survive and build up their own identity after a period of political peace and stability. After some hundred years of Danish supremacy and strong linguistic influence from the Danish language, a new Norwegian nation was established in 1814. As a consequence it was deemed necessary to create a modern Norwegian language and to protect it against foreign intrusion. That has lead to a protectionism in language policy and might be some of the reason that lexical neography has been neglected.

This article presents a new definition of lexical neologisms and a classification of different types of neologisms as well as a survey of previous investigations of Norwegian neologisms. The final part of the article describes a modern, statistical method of retrieving lexical neologisms semi-automatically from large newspaper corpora. Some results from this study indicate that the general fear of intrusion from foreign languages into Norwegian might be an overstatement and that national linguistic protection is unnecessary.

2. What is a lexical neologism?

It can be quite difficult to establish a good definition of a neologism. Most definitions presented are quite broad, imprecise or circular, such as "a lexical element that is considered a lexical innovation or a new lexical sense at some point" (NLO 1997: 188). An exception is Hargraves (2004) who defines neologisms as "letters in combinations hitherto unseen in a language" as a starting point. He completes this definition by a question relating to dictionaries: "is there something genuinely innovative about the word hitherto unnoted in dictionaries?" To answer that question one has to study all dictionaries and then add human assessment to decide what is genuinely innovative. Herberg and Steffens (2004) give an extensive definition in the introduction to their dictionary *Neuer Wortschatz. Neologismen der neunziger jahre im Deutschland*:

> Ein Neologismus ist eine lexikalische Einheit bzw. eine Bedeutung, die in einen bestimmten Abschnitt der Sprachentwicklung in einer Komunikations-gemeinschaft aufkommt, sich ausbreitet, als sprachliche Norm allgemein akzeptiert und in diesem Entwicklungsabschnitt von der Mehrheit der Sprachbenutzer über eine gewisse Zeit hin als neu empfunden wird.[1]

One problem with definitions related to existing dictionaries is that the newly discovered word might represent a lacuna in the recording of the language's vocabulary, which means that the lemma coverage of a dictionary has failed to document all actual words in use in a language. Another problem is the relativity of an adjective like *new*: it is by nature a transitional phenomenon. Existing, but rarely used words that have a sudden increased frequency might be counted as neologisms. An example of such a change of use is the word *klima* 'climate', which was borrowed from Greek long time ago for use in expert's language. Today it is used in newspaper texts almost every day; the word has become a general word in modern Norwegian, and is to be counted as a neologism. Strange and specialized technical terms can get new life and generalized meaning if they denote a special phenomenon or subject that becomes relevant or give consequences for people in general.

We believe that a definition of lexical neologisms should account for several types of changes: new words or **neoformatives**, new meaning of existing words or **neosemanticisms** and new phrases or **neophrasemes**. Since lexicon and syntax never can be kept totally apart in language in use, we consider the two last types as results of lexico-syntactic changes. In the following we describe these categories in turn.

2.1 Neoformatives

Neoformatives are what most people think of when talking about new words, and consist of letters in a combination that is new in a language (cf. Hargraves 2004). Related to Herbert and Steffens' definition above, a neoformative is a lexical element that has not been used in the actual language before its appearance. Most neoformatives are loan words from other cultures, such as *hijab* or *freeware* in

1. A neologism is a lexical element or a lexical sense which has come into existence in a certain period of the linguistic development of a language community, and which spreads into the language and becomes generally accepted as a linguistic norm. The neologism is perceived as new by most of its users for a certain period of time. (Authors' translation)

modern Norwegian, more seldom new inventions of hereditary material, such as *pingle* (Brunstad 2005: 78) or *lættis* (Fjeld 2008: 18), mostly used in modern slang.

2.2 Neosemanticisms

When an existing word is used in a new way and with a new meaning, it is counted as a neosemanticism. Such change is happening to a certain degree with most words, since the culture where the word is used also changes. The definition of a common word such as *bed* would probably be slightly different today than hundred years ago, since the culture of sleeping has changed. However, such changes happen quite slowly and should not be counted as neosemanticism.

The phenomenon of neosemanticisms can be illustrated by words which have existed in a special subject field for a long time, and suddenly find their way into modern culture, such as the already mentioned word *klima,* and the even more recent *tsunami*. The word is borrowed from Japanese and was a technical term in the field of meteorology before its increased use after a major natural disaster in Thailand on the 25th December 2004. After few weeks it became a fairly general word and took on a figurative use in modern Norwegian, meaning 'sudden and unexpected disaster', in contrast to the meteorologist term 'great sea waves caused by underground earthquakes'. The NNC shows that the word was used only 2 times in Norwegian electronic newspapers in 2003, 71 times in 2004 and 427 times in 2005. For a while such words function as buzz words or vogue words; *tsunami* was for a period used for all kinds of surprising and sudden changes. Such neosemanticisms can be found by statistical methods, since it is all of a sudden much more frequently used. A clear change in a word's frequency of use is evidence of a novelty in the vocabulary of a language. A neologism is a lexical element or a lexical sense which has come into existence in a certain period of the linguistic development of a language community, and which spreads into the language and becomes generally accepted as a linguistic norm. The neologism is perceived as new by most of its users for a certain period of time. After the big disaster in Japan in March 2011 the word probably will only be used as a technical word again in respect of all those suffering after the tsunami catastrophe in Japan. Such semantic development is easy to follow from the statistics of a dynamic corpus like the NNC.

Neosemanticisms might be the result of abbreviation. Among most Norwegians today, a text message sent via cell phone is called just *melding* 'message', but is automatically understood as an 'SMS-message'. This reaction seems to be a protective mechanism in languages to avoid too large a vocabulary. All in all, new words that remain in a language are relatively rare.

Another kind of neosemanticism is the result of sense division when a special form of an existing word gets a specialized meaning. The Norwegian orthography often allows variant forms in spelling, to cover the different dialects as well as possible. Some of these variant forms also develop different meanings, mostly through slang, like the word *feit/fet* 'fat', where the form *feit* has the traditional meaning, and *fet* is mostly used in a metaphorical meaning 'good' (Fjeld 2008: 23).

2.3 Neophrasemes

Neophrasemes are new expressions that consist of more than one word. They either contain neoformatives or consist of an existing phrase with a new meaning, as a special kind of neosemanticisms. Neophrasemes may either be borrowed multi-word phrases such as *sudden death* and *hard core* (cf. G. Andersen this volume) or a mix of loan and inherited words, such as *printe ut* 'print out', or they may consist of existing words with a new meaning, like the new routine formula *ha det/hadet* 'goodbye' or *være på nett* 'be online' in the sense of 'have contact, be present-minded'. A neophraseme that recently entered written Norwegian is the prepositional phrase *rundt forbi* 'around, here and there' as an alternative to *rundt omkring*, probably borrowed from dialects in southern Norway. Other changes of this kind have unknown origin, like the double construction *for – siden* 'ago' which often is changed into *for – tilbake* with the same meaning and function as the traditional one. Such neophrasemes are rarely documented in dictionaries or grammars, they are not interesting as patterns in word formation, and have frequently been regarded as incorrect usage instead of new development. However, even if they are considered as slang or unidiomatic, when they occur with a rapidly increasing frequency for instance in Norwegian newspaper texts, sooner or later they have to be counted as parts of the general vocabulary. Several of these phrases have a grammatical function in addition to the lexical one, and they are also signs of linguistic change that often implies syntactic changes, for instance in argument structure. The neophraseme *tenke til å* 'plan to' (NNC 1339)[2] instead of the traditional *tenke å* is not yet counted as correct Norwegian, probably because it is poorly documented. Often neophrasemes are signs of more general lexico-syntactic changes, like loss of case or change in argument structure, and is a part of the lexical documentation of modern Norwegian. Investigation of neophrasemes also includes phrases with idiomatic content, such as *høy sigarføring* 'boastful and smug lifestyle' and *på trynet* 'stupid, pointless', that come into general use after a good formulation for instance by a well known politician or entertainer, and may become part of the general vocabulary (Lyse & Andersen this volume). Therefore such idiomatic phrases should not be left to specialized citation dictionaries.

2. Result from search in the Norwegian Newspaper Corpus of 900 mill words 25.3.2011.

2.4 A new definition of neologisms

We define a neologism as a lexico-syntactic phenomenon which has recently entered into general usage as a neoformative, neosemanticism or neophrasem and which acquires a certain degree of stability in language use.

This definition does not depend on registration in any particular dictionary or database, nor normative valuation, only on attestation in corpora or other sources documenting language use. The definition of 'recently' must be specified from case to case, according to the resources available for attestation and the purpose of the documentation, since neologisms are transitional.

3. Neologisms as a transitional phenomenon

Most neologisms that appear in a language disappear quite rapidly and remain historical linguistic phenomena called **occasionalisms**, i.e. new words that occur in particular situations or cases and are understandable only in contexts from such situations. An example is the word *annonseboikott* 'advertisement boycott', which came into use in 2007 when a political newspaper rejected publishing advertisements for some issue they did not accept. They are not to be counted as real new words by our definition. On the other hand, new words and phrases are no longer to be considered neologisms when they have come into use as parts of the general vocabulary of a language and are to be integrated in regular dictionaries. Neologisms are thus transitional phenomena. At which point a word is to be considered a regular word, is difficult to decide, since all new words must be perceived as potential occasionalisms. Neography does, in fact, depend on longitudinal studies.

Some occasionalisms live for a few years before they disappear. A typical example is *tastafon* 'push button phone', for telephones without a call disc. This kind of telephone quickly became very popular and the word was coined through a contest in the newspapers. A few years later, however, all phones were push button phones, and the traditional term *telephone* was used for push button phones also. In new editions of general dictionaries the word *tastafon* should be marked as obsolete or characteristic of a particular period, if not deleted altogether. Such words might be called **guest words**, since they are relatively short-lived neologisms that become superfluous because of technical changes or the like.

Another example from the same semantic field is *fasttelefon* 'landline phone'. Since most phones now are wireless and personal, such as *mobiltelefon* 'cell phone', we have to indicate when they are not, which has given the possible guest word *fasttelefon*. This word will probably disappear if all phones become personal phones like cell phones. In cases like this, we often see that the semantic negation of an established word (its complement or alternative) becomes the new word whenever a new phenomenon occurs or a new gadget is invented. After a while, the former denotation often takes over the meaning of the new concept, as if *mobiltelefon* is just called *telefon*.

The third type of neologisms consists of new words that remain in a language and hence are a real augmentation of the lexical inventory of a language. In this article we will call them **stayer words**.

To sum up, we distinguish between three types of neologisms, occasionalisms, guest words and stayer words, where the final category comprises real neologisms. In investigations of large text corpora, most new combinations of letters are either noise, occasionalisms or guest words. The main task is to separate them from the new stayer words.

4. How are new words coined?

The most common way to create new words in Norwegian, as in most Germanic languages, is to establish compounds of simple word forms, like *fjern* 'distant' + *syn* 'vision' for the once new invention TV. Further, the words *fjernsyn* 'television' and *skjerm* 'screen' are used to coin the new compound *fjernsynsskjerm*. The first time the word appeared in newspapers or on sale adverts for televisions, it was fully understandable for everyone, even if it had never occurred before. In principle, this mechanism of making new compounds should cover all needs for new words by means of new combinations of the words in the existing Norwegian vocabulary. Despite this possibility, Norwegian language users tend to borrow a lot of words and phrases from other languages, or even make up pseudoloan such as *mobil* 'cell phone' and *snacksy* 'yummy' (Graedler & Johansson 1997).

New simple words can be made of existing word formation elements, but it is relatively rare; an example is the slang word *lættis* 'hysterics', which is derived from the stem of the adjective *latterlig* 'ridiculous' and the suffix *-is*. This suffix is used in several Norwegian slang expressions (probably borrowed from Swedish slang). A few neologisms are made of peculiar material, such as the window cleaning utensil *nal* 'squeegee', which is an appellativization of a trade mark (coined by reverse spelling of the inventor's name *Lahn*), and has become a regular appellative in Norwegian. Proper names and trademarks ending up as general words are not as rare as one might think. Words like *skai* for artificial leather, *farris* for bottled water, *helsetrøye* for a special type of underwear are of that kind; most people do not know that such words once were brands for new products. Companies often spend large sums on establishing these trademarks, and lexicographers can by mere accident get into legal problems simply by describing registered trademarks as general words. One example is the popular product Walkman from Sony, who first launched a portable radio and disc-player, which became very popular in Norway in the 1980s. Hence the word *walkman* was taken into the first edition of *Bokmålsordboka* (1986), but had to be replaced by the self coined word *lommedisco* 'pocket disco' after protests from Sony.

But most lexical novelties are borrowed from other languages and represent new inventions or phenomena from other cultures, such as *coach, mafia* or *moské* 'mosque'. Quite often the names of cultural products or events are borrowed, such as food names. A typical example is *pizza* which is now one of the most common Norwegian dishes. The word was borrowed from Italian in the 1960s, probably through American English. The United States has had a particularly strong cultural influence after World War II, and many words have been borrowed from American English in that period.

New words or phrases borrowed from English are not always genuinely English; many stem from a different language but have come into Norwegian via English and have been adapted phonologically and morphologically to that language before being adapted to Norwegian. These words are in particular the so-called **internationalisms**, which stem from classical languages such as Greek and Latin. Such words are generally borrowed and used in most modern languages. A typical example is *karakter* 'mark, grade', which has a traditional Norwegian sense as an evaluative result of school work, in addition to that of 'nature' and 'distinctive feature'. Recently a new meaning of 'letter, sign' borrowed from English has come into Norwegian as a neosemanticism, as well as the partly misunderstood meaning 'fictional character', making the word even more polysemous than before. Such influence occurs relatively often, since most Norwegians have learnt to read and speak English. These neosemanticisms are not the result of a denotation need; it is more a result of general cultural influence. Now and then words are borrowed from other languages, like *tsunami* from Japanese and *kajal* from Hindi.

A very special way to coin new words is by word campaigns, often against an existing word. In Norway there was an ongoing campaign against the word *baksnakk* 'backbiting' and for the promotion of the construct *framsnakk* 'frontbiting/praise' on Facebook in the summer of 2010, and there are many thousands supporters voting for that coinage. They want to draw attention to the negative side of talking behind somebody's back, which is praiseworthy, but such campaigns rarely lead to augmentation of the vocabulary of a language.

5. Why do we need new words?

It is said that a need for a new word usually arises from a new idea or invention that needs a designation. Most words coined for an existing concept are made for a stylistic, euphemistic or puristic purpose. Coining new words is one of the most typical means to establish slang, and some slang words spread into the common language. For instance, the traditional word *moro* 'fun' was called *gøy* (cf. English 'guy') in urban slang in the early 1900s and later spread to the common vocabulary as an alternative to the traditional one, an now is found in most dictionaries of Norwegian.

Other reasons for an existing word to be replaced by a neologism may be the result of language planning. Dislike of foreign words and desire to preserve the national language has been strong in the official policy regarding the Norwegian language. The Norwegian Language Council has an official policy to find domestic substitutes for loan words, so-called **avløserord** 'substitute word', like *snøbrett* instead of *snowboard*. Thus new lexemes have been coined according to traditional word formation rules with inherited word formation elements to replace the unwanted borrowing. Linguistic purism and nationalism has been perceived as allies, aiming to establish a modern national language that required protection against outside influence. Instead of accepting the neologisms, Norwegians have been encouraged to use "good old words" in a patriotic purpose. However, lexical neography shows that this work is often futile.

Coined substitute words with borrowed meaning often live in parallel with the original loan, as is the case with *mail* and *e-post*, which are both commonly used, *e-post* more often (64,241 tokens in the NNC) than *mail* (15,761 tokens), and with *snowboard* (2,429) and *snøbrett* (1,207), where the loan is used twice as often at the substitute. Other examples are *backup* (1,072) vs. *reservekopi* (1) and *backpacker* (1,024) vs. *ryggsekkturist* (448). All examples are replacement words launched by the Norwegian Language Council. Often language planners are coining these translation loans too long after the borrowed lexemes have come into common use. This leads to a special kind of synonymy, namely parallel neologisms for the same concept, where only one is recommended for official use. After some years of co-existence, one form may win over the other, usually the shortest, or the one that becomes abbreviated. A typical example is *televisjon* 'television', with the common abbreviation *TV*. The substitute word was *fjernsyn*, and as the Norwegian translation in this case is missing a straightforward acronym, the dominant expression for television in modern Norwegian is *TV*. The term *fjernsyn* is in principle self-explanatory for most Norwegians, but the clarity and transparency often have to give up for shorter forms.

A new word for an established concept can also be introduced with a euphemistic or political purpose, such as *renholder* (NNC 366) 'cleaner' for *vaskekone* (52) 'charwoman'. This neoformative has other connotations than the established word and a more politically correct meaning without sexual discrimination, since it does not take for granted that only women can do cleaning work. Several designations for occupations and positions have undergone this change the last thirty years.

Several neologisms are coined by experts and semi-experts. In particular, information technology has given rise to many such words, like *backup* instead of *kopi* 'copy', often more to impress than out of a real need for a new word.

Politicians and other celebrities who coin new words in a successful way are another source of lexical neologisms. A typical example of contemporary Norwegian is when the Norwegian Crown Prince used the compound *adrenalinsint* 'adrenaline angry' (NNC 6) in his speech to his bride in 2001, or when the leader of the right wing Progress Party in February 2009 warned the Norwegian people against *snikislamisering* 'hidden islamization' (NNC 275) and its variant form *snikislamifisering* (NNC 16), which is more derogative. During 2009 the word *snik-* 'hidden, stealth' has become a widely used first element in compounds with the pejorative connotation 'in hiding' (NNC 12,848), partly synonymous with the first element *skap-* 'closet' (cf. Jarvad 1995) but with even more negative connotations.

Elsen (2004) points out that new words are often made up to achieve special effects in a text. In particular, new words are made by new derivation rules, cf. *kneskure* and *køe* below, as well as new combinations of sounds or morphemes. Such new derivations can give special sound effects or image-related associations, or other effects that have not existed in the language; they function as exotisms or associative words. A relatively recent Norwegian example is *gruff*, which may be a combination of *grue* 'dread' and the interjection *uff* 'bah', a vague designation for something bad or unpleasant. The word was coined in an advertisement for coffee in the 1960s, and is now established as a conventional word in modern Norwegian. Furthermore, new combinations of words in compounds are a typical way of achieving new effects, like *monstermast* 'monster mast', created by political activists who were against the construction of a new electric cable leading electricity over a nature reserve area. Such words are coined deliberately by authors or copywriters. On the other hand, a new word can be coined because it is easier to pronounce than an older expression, or it may be easier to understand, and thereby replace a previously established word. This is precisely what is happening to the word *forfordele*, which is a borrowing from German meaning that you get less than what you are entitled to in a sharing process. This word is frequently used in its opposite meaning, and this should be accepted as its second sense. Such coinage is often done unconsciously and unintentionally by language users. The reason why new words and expressions occur, can therefore be quite numerous, and quite different. New words reflect actual preferences in word formation related to users' needs.

6. Previous registration of neologisms in Norwegian

German loan words in Norwegian have been registered and well studied through the history of Norwegian philology (cf. Simensen 1995). In the years before and during World War II, Aasta Stene registered and documented English loans in Norwegian (Stene 1945). Her work was followed up by Graedler and Johansson (1997) in an extensive study of anglisisms in modern Norwegian. But investigations and recording of loan words from other languages as well as lexical neologisms in general have not been seen as a task for linguistics until the mid 1950s. The first study to identify and describe neologisms in modern Norwegian was part of a Nordic project initiated by the Nordic language councils. Their yearbooks *Nordiske språkspørsmål* (Questions in Nordic linguistics) were published in the period 1955–1967, each volume had lists of registered new words in Danish, Norwegian and Swedish. The goal of this project was to study neologisms in the Nordic languages to describe the tendencies in modern word formation, and, if possible, coordinate the new terms in the languages in question, to keep the Nordic languages as mutually understandable as possible. The recommendation was to replace loan words with substitute words or word elements of Nordic heritage and to keep them as similar as possible across the Nordic languages. The success of the project was quite limited. This might be illustrated by the Nordic words for *computer,* an important and much debated issue in the yearbooks in the 1970s. The result was *datamaskin* in Norwegian, *dator* in Swedish and *datamat* in Danish, despite persistent efforts by the Nordic language councils to find a common term of this technological invention. In the first issue of the Yearbook it was stated that the Norwegian neologisms had been excerpted in the period May 1955 – September 1956. The result was listed systematically in four groups or types, presented here with examples:

1. New single word: **friskus** 'tough nut' (1955), **krashe** 'crash' (1955)
2. New derivations of previously known words, **gisper** 'horror movie' (1955), **spreking** 'fit and active person' (1955)
3. New verbs derived from nouns: **kneskure** 'scrub kneeling' (1955), **køe** 'queue up' (1955)
4. Compounds – new or previously rarely used: **hjemmehjelp** 'home help' (1955), **innsmett** 'shelter' (1955), **samrør** 'intermingling' (1955) **skumplast** 'foam plastic' (1955)

These words excerpted from newspaper texts by staff at the Norwegian Language Council. It has not been possible to find any documentation on the methods or goals for this compilation of neologisms; it seems that the words were recorded unsystematically by those who felt an interest for the topic when they read their own newspaper.

As a result of the Nordic cooperation, the first Norwegian dictionary of new words was published by the Norwegian Language Council in 1982, *Nye ord i norsk 1945–1975,* edited by Vigleik Leira (The Norwegian Language Council 1982). The book was meant to be descriptive, yet it should also be normative and advisory for future language planning. From 1975 until 2001, Leira systematically collected neologisms from a representative sample of newspapers and built up his own archive of new words in Norwegian. This archive contains more than 30,000 words. Some of the neologisms have been published in the Norwegian Language Council's journal *Språknytt*. The material has been used as a basis for the edition of the second dictionary of neologisms in Norwegian, *Nye ord i norsk 1975–2005* (edited by Tor Guttu & Boye Wangensteen), to appear in 2012. This is a joint project between the University of Oslo and the Norwegian Language Council. Otherwise, of course, anyone who has been editing dictionaries of modern Norwegian has been collecting new words and expressions more or less systematically to make their dictionaries cover most of the contemporary Norwegian vocabulary. However, it is difficult to extract precisely those words in a separate list for the documentation of different new words of a special era. This would require a comparison of the lemma lists of all the dictionaries that were published in that period, which would be very time consuming and likely to get poor results. Unfortunately, several years of documentation of the neologisms in modern Norwegian have been lost.

The largest project for collecting new words in Norwegian Bokmål is *Nyordsprosjektet* 'The Neologism project' at the University of Oslo, led by Dag Gundersen. This project has resulted in a database of more than 300,000 citations collected by volunteers representing different parts of the country. The excerptors were given free subscription of newspapers in order to register and submit words and phrases they found interesting or new. They were not linguists; most of them were retired teachers who after a short tutorial were certified for that work. One of the tasks was to pay particular attention to words and phrases that were hedged by the word *såkalt* 'so called' or citation marks, and to consider them as new word candidates. The excerpts were filed in a database and were PoS tagged and given a standardized form by professional lexicographers. Furthermore, an optional code for type of word formation and semantic development was added to each entry. Since the early 1980s the excerpts were entered directly into an electronic database and that part of the material was then automatically searchable. Through the years, however, the code system was elaborated upon and became quite complicated. When the project was terminated in 2000, there were more than a hundred different optional codes, representing a combination of morphosyntactic, semantic and stylistic features, in addition to those required for PoS tagging. There were many different lexicographers who worked in this project, and due to vague editorial guidelines it has turned out that different persons had used the code system somewhat differently. The material is therefore not consistently coded, which must be taken into account when it is used. In spite of these deficiencies, *Nyordsprosjektet* gives an important documentation of the growth and changes of the vocabulary in Norwegian Bokmål during the last part of the 1900s, with many relevant observations and good coverage of neosemanticisms and neophrasemes. The resulting database consists of 266,314 citations, most of them from between 1968 and 1972, the oldest from 1920, the most recent from 1999. The oldest citations were later also digitized and the material is now freely available to interested linguists. A typical example looks like this in the database[3]:

Grunnord	Ordklasse	Forledd-kode	Tilleggs-kode	Publ. type	Tittel	Nr.	Side/ spalte	År	Forf.
fjernsyn	n	a	Xx	Art	Samtiden	1948/7	430	1948	Halvor Lund
	Det er vår egen verden i **fjernsyn**, renset for slagget fra en mekanisert menneskehet, foredlet ved menneskeåndens seier over menneskenaturen ved en radikal omstilling av verdiene.								

This entry documents the first use registered of the new invention television, called *fjernsyn*. The first use of the loan word television is much later registered:

Grunnord	Ordklasse	Forledd-kode	Tilleggs-kode	Publ. type	Tittel	Nr.	Side/ spalte	År	Forf.
televisjon	c	x	Xx	Art	Naturen	1961/1	24	1961	Gunnar Eriksen
	Med kommunikasjon mener vi her overføring av opplysninger fra et sted til et annet. Opplysningene eller informasjonen kan inneholdes i ord, i form av muntlige meldinger eller telegrammer eller i bilder, som i **televisjon** og billedtelegrafi.								

The first documentation of the abbreviation *tv* is as follows:

Grunnord	Ordklasse	Forledd-kode	Tilleggs-kode	Publ. type	Tittel	Nr.	Side/ spalte	År	Forf.
tv	c	x	Io	Lokal	Programbl	1976/31	4/1,2	1976	
	"Bare velstand" er finkornet komedie, vidd og satire over fenomener som i vår tid eter seg inn i de tusen hjem: tomhet, rotløshet, rastløshet og små forsøk på opprør mot den grå hverdagståke over salongbordet. xx Først og fremst er det Sadie, husmoren i familien som forsøker det. Resolutt klipper hun over ledningen til **tv'en** for å få en gammeldags snakkekveld.								

Wangensteen (1995:417) presents this project and some of its results. After an analysis of 1,000 selected citations, he concludes that 28 per cent of the examined words were useful in lexicographical documentation of the general vocabulary, 21 per cent were candidates for new entries, 6 per cent were neosemanticisms and

3. http://www.dokpro.uio.no/Bokmål/new order/nyord_ramme.html

4 per cent were or might be interesting for orthography standardization because the citations represented frequent deviations from the current spelling norms. For documentation of lexical neologisms the value of the results would of course be much higher. The project was terminated for several reasons. Manual registration of new words and other neologisms was a costly and laborious method. The results were also unreliable since they did not show systematically what was not registered of the vocabulary changes in the newspaper texts. What was recorded more reflected the excerptors varying knowledge of and interest in language change rather than the changes in total. Also the selection of excerpted texts was biased. In spite of these shortcomings, the material is a valuable contribution to Norwegian neography and has been important basis for the two Norwegian dictionaries of neologisms and also in the editing of *Bokmålsordboka* (1986), which is the most comprehensive dictionary of the majority variety of modern Norwegian.

7. Statistical studies of neologisms in modern Norwegian

As we have shown, previous studies and documentation in Norwegian neology suffer from an inadequate methodology. The compilation of neologisms was sporadic and often governed by the excerptor's personal interests and prejudices, for instance the perceived risk that the Norwegian language was about to be destroyed by foreign influence, especially from a wave of English import words. In this project we therefore wanted to generate a new and more objective method of retrieving neologisms from corpus studies.

The research department Uni Computing at the University of Bergen has since 1998 to the present day built a large text corpus by automatic acquisition of Norwegian newspaper texts published on the Internet, called the Norwegian Newspaper Corpus (Andersen & Hofland this volume; cf. also http://avis.uib.no). Since we assume that most neologisms in a language first appear in newspaper texts, we have obtained our material from the NNC. This corpus is a vast resource and of invaluable importance to lexicographers. It is also used as basis for our study, which aims to describe recent changes in the vocabulary of modern Bokmål. Our aim is to investigate the new words that had come into modern Norwegian recently, to document their origin and how loan words have been adapted into the Norwegian language. The results from the NNC-based study derive from two methods, a manual and a statistical evaluation procedure.

7.1 Manual evaluation of the automatically generated new word candidates

In 2009 – at the time of our experiments – the total corpus consisted of more than 700 million running words (2011 over 900 million). Each night corpus texts are collected automatically by a web crawler and stored in a large database. The words collected are checked against previously collected words, which means that words with no hits in the existing corpus are seen as potential new words and presented in a special list. The list makes approximately 200 words each night (cf. Andersen & Hofland this volume).

These lists were initially reviewed manually, as each of the candidates was examined as possible lemmas in the general dictionary *Bokmålsordboka*, or as interesting new words for a dictionary of neologisms (Wangensteen 2002). This work turned out to be too time-consuming to be cost-beneficial. Most candidates were spelling errors, misprints and other noise. Also there are many proper names, both for persons, places, companies and brands which were not relevant for these dictionaries. Many of the new words were typical occasionalisms or guest words with little interest for traditional lexicography. Typical examples were *muskelbil* 'muscle car', *notevenderske* 'notepaper turner', *morderhund* 'killer dog' and *låveleder* 'barn manager'. The real catch of new words for dictionary making from these automatically generated lists were merely 2 per cent, according to Wangensteens (2002) calculation. Moreover this method could not be used to register neophrasemes or neosemanticisms. We therefore needed to find a less time consuming and more accurate method than manually evaluation of the generated lists mentioned above.

7.2 Semiautomatic retrieval of neologisms from the Norwegian Newspaper Corpus

We believe that a sound study of neologisms requires a longitudinal method. Fortunately NNC has been collected continuously since 1998, making longitudinal studies possible, and we can now compare frequencies of the candidates over time. Inspired by previous studies like Renouf (1996), Ooi (1998) and Kilgarriff and Tugwell (2002), where corpus studies were combined with statistical calculations, we developed a less time consuming and more accurate and objective method than manual evaluation of the lists mentioned above. Our goal was to detect all neologisms that would fit into our definition presented in Section 2.4. above.

In the spring of 2009 the NNC contained approximately 2 million unique word forms. Of these, 1.3 million were not previously recorded and were thereby considered potential neologisms. By means of three different statistical filters, the number of candidates was reduced to 3,465 word forms.

Filter 1 removed all proper names, i.e. words not following full stop and starting with a capital letter, except when it was the first word in a period. Filter 2 removed word forms under a certain – arbitrarily set – frequency. This method is also used in previous research projects. The result from filter 2 consisted of 17,277 word forms – still a considerable amount to evaluate manually.

Therefore filter 3 was developed, which, as far as we know, presents new methodology, since it includes the longitudinal aspect of the findings. Filter 3 removed frequent words of constant frequency; words with change in frequency were kept as interesting candidates. Frequency change was identified by linear regression, using a standard statistical technique called the least squares measure. This yields a correlation coefficient; a high coefficient indicates that the word's frequency is increasing. Words with increasing frequency over a period of ten years were seen as potential neologisms. This statistical investigation is presented as a graph in Figure 1 below, which shows the point of intersection and ascension coefficient for the word form *bloggen* 'the blog'.

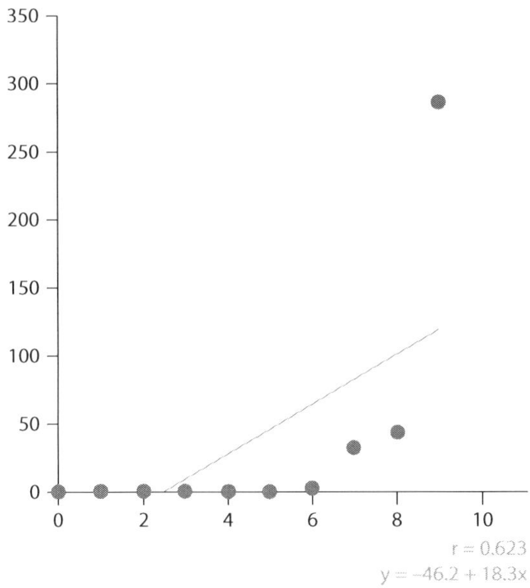

Figure 1. Linear interpolation for the frequency of the word form *bloggen*

The correlation coefficient is 0.63. In the figure, the y axis displays relative frequency; the x axis is the year, and 1998 is year zero.

7.3 Results and discussion

On the basis of the output of the filtering procedure, 1,000 candidates were randomly chosen for manual evaluation by two independent and skilled lexicographers. Only a consensus between both evaluators was counted as a positive result. The main challenge for the method was the possible loss of true neologisms because of the filtering process. The outcome from filter 1 showed that only 1.6 per cent

(16 word forms) of the chosen candidates might be true neologisms. Most of the words filtered out were occasionalisms, mostly three-element compounds such as *arbeidshverdag* 'working week day'. Some of these 16 words were first part in compounds wrongly written as separate words. We therefore concluded that filter 1 functioned to our satisfaction. The results from filter 2 gave approximately 6 per cent candidates of new words, although here also some were separated compounds. Interesting examples from this list were also three-element compounds where one of the elements recently had become productive, like *fastrentetilbud* 'fixed interest offer' and *fastlegereform* 'family doctor reform'. Also *halalkjøtt* 'halal meat' appeared in this list, where only the first element is a true neologism. Thus the results from filter 2 were also regarded as successful.

The words remaining after filter 3 were frequent words that also had increasing frequency. These were examined thoroughly. We found that 300 (30 %) of the 1,000 randomly chosen words were what we call stayer words and real neologisms. Several of these words contained productive first or second word formation elements. Such words are of special interest to map out the development of neologisms in a language, e.g. *barnedrapssak* 'trial for child murder', *barnesoldat* 'child soldier', where the element *child* might be attached to several lexemes as an indication of a perspective that has been given too little attention earlier. Also common slang that has now become accepted in newspaper texts, like *bakfull* 'hung over' was represented. A kind of lacunae was also detected, namely pseudoloans such as *aircondition* 'air conditioning', where the pseudoloan is far more frequent than the correct loan (NNC 249 vs. 26).

The manual revision of the lists showed that the total filter system all in all was a successful method that gave valuable results, even better than expected. The method is time saving and efficient in mapping lexical linguistic change.

The results from the filtering system produced interesting observations and findings about the development of the lexicon in modern Norwegian. The loan word *krash* 'crash' was first registered in Norwegian texts 1955 as a verb, *å krashe* 'to crash'. Still the spelling is not yet naturalised according to the Norwegian spelling system (G. Andersen this volume). Only one year later, in 1956, the dictionary *Nyord i norsk* cites the noun as *krasj,* and slowly this spelling is becoming more common in newspaper texts. In texts from 2009, both *krasj*/*krasje* and *kræsj*/*kræsje* are used, the forms with *æ* documented for the first time in 1972. Through our analysis we are also able to discover a semantic split in the two variant forms, since *krasj* has the literal meaning, cf. *busskrasj* 'bus chrash', *båtkrasj* 'boat chrash', and the more orthophone spelling *kræsj* is used in metaphorical meaning, as in *børskræsj* 'stock exchange crash'.

The manual classification of the 1,000 selected candidates indicates that most of the neologisms in Norwegian newspaper texts from the period of 1998–2009 are compounds of the traditional Norwegian type with common and inherited components, such as *fredagsbønn* 'Friday prayer', *bredbånd/bredband* 'broad band' and *børsfest* 'stock market rally'. New words made out of borrowed material is usually quickly adapted into the Norwegian lexicon, like *blog*, which has the derivations *blogge* 'to blog', *blogging* 'blogging' and even the slang word *bloggings* 'an article in a blog'. In addition there are of course a lot of compounds, such as *bloggemne* 'blog topic', *blogginnlegg* 'blog contribution', *blogginteresse* 'blog interest' and *bloggprinsesse* 'blog princess'.

The results from such a statistical registration will also give more reliable information about the origin of all the neologisms, in contrast with manual excerption where mostly conspicuous words are registered. The general opinion in Norway is that our language is flooded by anglisisms, and protection against English intrusion in the Norwegian language is articulated even among linguists and language researchers. Our results show, however, that only 10 per cent of the neologisms we identified are anglisisms. 2 per cent are Swedicisms, a few are from Italian and French; these are mostly names of dishes and food, such as *scampi* and *baguette*. That means that 88 per cent are compounds of inherited word formation elements, or new word formations. Some of these inherited neologisms have come into general use through slang, like *bakfull* 'hung over' (NNC 83) and *bananas* 'crazy' (NNC 370).

8. Conclusion and further work

A comparison of the manual analysis against the automatically compiled list of possible neologisms showed that our filters worked well. Approximately 30 per cent of the candidates that passed the filters appear to be relevant for the study of neologisms. The words that pass filter 2 but not filter 3 are only rarely interesting neologisms. Thus it seems that our hypothesis of increasing frequency is supported by our study. The quality of the filters is secured through manual and independent evaluation of the results by two experienced lexicographers. Over 30 per cent of the words that passed through all three filters are in some way or other to be seen as relevant neologisms in Norwegian. Our conclusion is that our method is quite time-efficient compared to manual excerption of neologisms, and the quality may possibly be better.

The first direction for further work is the extension of the longitudinal filter to less frequent words. Even though there are relatively fewer interesting words here, there number of words is larger. Reviewing low-frequency words is not feasible without some form of filtering. Since the filter will have less data to work with, one open question is whether the noise level will rise significantly.

The second direction is to include older data, which are slowly becoming available in several corpora, like A-tekst (www.retriever.no), which has electronic texts from the early 1970s. This will allow us to devise a more operational definition of neologisms (e.g. not in use before year X), and will also be more effective in discovering lacunae in dictionaries.

Finally, we plan to develop statistical calculations of neologisms based on context changes. Several neologisms are neophrasemes and will not be found by statistical methods restricted to single words. Statistic lexical analysis from different stages like DeepDict (Bick 2009, Fjeld, Nygaard & Bick 2009) and WordSketch-Engine (Kilgarriff & Tugwell 2002) will probably show more clearly changes in a lexicon than analyses based on single words only.

References

Bick, Eckhard. 2009. DeepDict – A corpus-based dictionary of word relations. In *Proceedings of Nodalida 2009, Odense, Denmark* [NEALT Proceedings Series 4], 268–271.

Brunstad, Endre. 2005. Pingle. Om eit nyord i norsk. In *Nordiske studiar i leksikografi 7. Rapport frå Konferanse om leksikografi i Norden. Volda 20.-24. mai 2003,* Ruth Vatvedt Fjeld & Dagfinn Worren (eds), 78–92.

Elsen, Hilke. 2004. *Neologismen. Formen und Funktionen neuer Wörter in verschiedenen Varietäten des Deutschen.* Tübingen: Gunter Narr.

Fjeld, Ruth Vatvedt. 2008. Talespråksforskningens betydning for leksikografien. In *Språk i Oslo. Ny forskning omkring talespråk,* Janne B. Johannessen & Kristin Hagen (eds), 15–28. Oslo: Novus.

Fjeld, Ruth Vatvedt, Nygaard, Lars & Bick, Eckhardt. 2009. Semi-automatic retrieval of multiword phrases in a corpus of modern Norwegian. In *Computergestützte und korpusbasierte Methoden in der Phraseologie, Phraseografie und der Lexikografie,* Stefaniya Ptashnyk, Erla Hallsteinsdóttir & Noah Bubenhofer (eds).

Graedler, Anne-Line & Johansson, Stig. 1997. *Anglisismeordboka. Engelske lånord i norsk.* Oslo: Universitetsforlaget.

Guttu, Tor & Wangensteen, Boye. Forthcoming. *Nyord i norsk 1975–2005.*

Hargraves, Orin. 2004. *New Words.* Oxford: OUP.

Herberg, Dieter & Steffens, Doris. 2004. *Neuer Wortschatz. Neologismen der 90er Jahre im Deutschen.* Berlin: Mouton de Gruyter.

Jarvad, Pia. 1995. Kryptosammensætninger og skabsafledninger i virkeligheden og i ordbøgerne. In *Nordiske studier i leksikografi 3. Rapport fra Konferanse om leksikografi i Norden. Reykjavík 7.-10. juni 1995,* Ásta Svavarsdóttir, Gudrun Kvaran & Jón Hilmar Jónsson (eds), 221–231. Reykjavík.

Kilgarriff, Adam & Tugwell, David. 2002. Sketching words. In *Lexicography and Natural Language Processing – A Festschrift in Honour of B.T.S. Atkins,* Marie-Hélène Corréard (ed), 125–137. Gothenburg: Euralex.

NLO 1997. *Nordisk leksikografisk ordbok.* Nordisk forening for leksikografi, Universitetsforlaget.

Norsk språkråd. 1982. *Nyord i norsk 1945–1975.* Oslo: Universitetsforlaget.

Ooi, Vincent B.Y. 1998. *Computer Corpus Lexicography.* Edinburgh: Edinburgh University Press.

Renouf, Antoinette. 1996. The ACRONYM Project: Discovering the textual thesaurus. In *Synchronic Corpus Linguistics,* Carol E. Percy, Charles F. Meyer & Ian Lancashire (eds), 171–187. Amsterdam: Rodopi.

Sandøy, Helge. 2000. *Lånte fjører eller bunad? Om importord i norsk.* Oslo: Landslaget for norskundervisning LNU/Cappelen akademisk forlag.

Simensen, Erik. 1995. Påverknaden på mellomnedertysk på norske diplom frå det 14. hundreåret. In *Nordisk og nedertysk. Språkkontakt og språkutvikling i seinmellomalderen,* E.H. Jahr (ed), 55–80. Oslo: Novus.

Sørensen, Knud. 1995. *Engelsk i dansk. Er det et must?* København: Munksgaards sprogserie.

Stene, Aasta. 1945. *English Loan-Words in Modern Norwegian: A Study of Linguistic Borrowing in the Process.* London & Oslo: OUP & Johan Grundt Tanum Forlag.

Thomsen, Johnny. 2002. Præskription og deskription i nyere færøsk leksikografi. *LexicoNordica* 9: 107–119.

Wangensteen, Boye. 1982. *Nyord i norsk 1945–1975.* Oslo: Universitetsforlaget.

Wangensteen, Boye. 1995. Et arkiv over forandringer i moderne norsk ordforråd og dets betydning for norsk leksikografi. In *Nordiske studier i leksikografi 3. Rapport fra Konferanse om leksikografi i Norden. Reykjavík 7.-10. juni 1995,* Ásta Svavarsdóttir, Gudrun Kvaran & Jón Hilmar Jónsson, 411–420.

Wangensteen, Boye. 2002. Nettbasert nyordsinnsamling. *Språknytt* 2: 17–18.

Ash compound frenzy

A case study in the Norwegian Newspaper Corpus

Koenraad De Smedt
University of Bergen, Norway

The creation and use of Norwegian compounds with *aske* 'ash' in the media in the spring of 2010 was remarkable. The Norwegian Newspaper Corpus has provided suitable data for an empirical study concerning neology and 'burstiness' on this topic. The results indicate that the number of new types as well as token frequencies rose markedly and the variety of compounds in use remained elevated for over a month.

1. Introduction

On April 14, 2010, an explosive volcanic eruption at Eyjafjallajökull had broad consequences on Iceland as well as abroad, not in the least because a large ash plume caused air travel disruptions over many parts of Europe, affecting millions of travelers over a period of several weeks. Although earlier volcanic eruptions had been covered in the Norwegian media, the circumstances in the spring of 2010 were of a nature and scale seldom seen and discussed before, so that a new vocabulary was a necessity in the extensive media coverage that followed.

It did not take long before creative Norwegian compounds with the word *aske* 'ash' were observed in the media. Ash had apparently become established quite immediately as the central concept in discourse about the events. Soon, the multitude of compounds was commented on by the general public as well as among linguists. In particular, the word *askefast* 'ash stranded' caught on very well and often produced smiles. In December 2010, the Language Council of Norway chose *askefast* as the word of the year.[1]

So far, however, the linguistic discussion on this topic has been largely anecdotal; no previous quantitative corpus investigations on compounds with *aske*

1. http://sprakradet.no/nb-no/Aktuelt-ord/Ordet-for-aret-Oskefastaskefast/

have come to my attention. The present case study aims at a first, simple quantitative analysis of the occurrence of these compounds in the Norwegian Newspaper Corpus[2] over a specific relevant time span.

The detection of new words has received much attention in the Norwegian Newspaper Corpus project (Andersen 2005). The corpus website maintains an archive of new words for each day, i.e. words not present in the corpus before that date. However, the corpus does not currently provide for automatically tracking the use of words through specified time periods.

Previous studies of neology have typically had spans of several years. A large scale study of neology has resulted in an influential German neologism dictionary (Quasthoff 2007), compiled by automatic frequency analysis. This dictionary lists all new coinages, loan words borrowed from other languages, and existing words that have taken on new meaning since 2000 and through 2006. Many words have a life span of a few years, while some are permanent additions to German vocabulary, and others are observed for only a very short period of time. Many compounds in the current study seem to belong to the latter category, although repeated volcanic ash eruptions could create conditions for the further study of compounds that remain in active use over the course of several years.

The tracking of words in the media yields new knowledge with interesting potential applications. Sets of words can be used to aggregate news events from many different sources, as in the JRC's Newsbrief[3] and Google News.[4] New words or sudden increases in the frequency of existing words may signal events, places, people or topics that have come into the limelight. The Wortschatz portal[5] presents, among other things, an overview of salient words per day, which can be helpful for obtaining an overview of topicality and news interest.

Kleinberg (2002) developed metrics of *burstiness* to find topics that dominate information streams at a particular time by scanning collections of documents for sudden, rapid bursts of words. His example materials include American presidential State of the Union addresses throughout history. The analysis reveals, for instance, that *housing* showed a burst between 1946 and 1950, whereas *women* peaked between 1981 and 1984, which suggests that these topics were central in society at different times. Such methods may be useful for societal trend analysis,

2. For an introduction to this corpus, see Andersen & Hofland (this volume).

3. http://emm.newsbrief.eu/

4. http://news.google.com

5. http://wortschatz.uni-leipzig.de/

while some results may indicate shifts in wording rather than themes, such as the fact that the word *nuclear* has replaced *atomic*.

The present study concentrates on neology coupled with burstiness during a very short time frame. All material was taken from the Norwegian Newspaper Corpus and quantitative methods were used in order to document interesting short term trends. What seems like a sudden broadly witnessed 'frenzy' in the coinage and use of new compounds is hereby possibly documented.

The remainder of this article describes the steps of data collection and subsequent quantitative analysis. In particular, the rate of creation of new compounds within a chosen time span will be discussed, as well as the variety of compounds in use. The article concludes with some notes on the morphosyntax, semantics and collocates of the compounds.

2. Data, method and results

2.1 Selection and preparation of material

For any corpus investigation which is limited to a specific time span, it is essential that language materials are annotated with the time of authorship, or at least of publication. The Norwegian Newspaper Corpus is a monitor corpus which provides such time information. Every night, the web newspapers of the previous day are automatically harvested and the publication date is preserved in the annotation. The Norwegian Newspaper Corpus therefore provides basic data for establishing a chronology of the appearance of words during a specified period.

The first step in the study was an exercise in data collection and filtering in order to obtain suitable material. At the beginning of August 2010, when the data were collected, it was not yet possible to access precompiled lists of new words recorded in this corpus after 2009. Furthermore, the main system for accessing the Norwegian Newspaper Corpus at the time of data collection was based on CWB (Christ 1994; Christ et al. 1999). Although a new corpus management and query system Corpuscle has been in development since the spring of 2010 (Meurer this volume), this new system was not fully functional at the start of the present study and was therefore not used. In the CWB interface to the Norwegian Newspaper Corpus, searches could be limited to a specific year, month or day, but it was not possible to specify start and end dates. Data collection therefore relied on searching in CWB and processing the resulting KWIC concordance with the author's own scripts.

For the present study, the Norwegian Newspaper Corpus was queried with the regular expression *aske.** which covers all words starting with the string *aske*.

On the one hand, this query resulted in the inclusion of some irrelevant words, which needed to be filtered out. On the other hand, some spelling errors, such as *akseskyer*, which was observed in the corpus, did not get included in this list. Also the Nynorsk forms starting with *oske* were not included. The decision not to include these forms was due to the lack of sufficient data. A search in the Nynorsk section of the corpus yielded only five occurrences of relevant compounds with *oske* for the period under consideration.

The keywords matching the query were easily extracted from the KWIC format. Since each line in this concordance was annotated with the news source, consisting of a two-character code for the newspaper and a six-digit code representing the publishing date, it was easy to extract this date as well. A manual inspection of the extracted material revealed that it still contained some noise and errors which had to be removed.

Firstly, a superficial sanity check of the data revealed that items which were recorded in the corpus as being published in the newspaper VG on April 13, 2010, the day before the volcanic eruption, were actually published on April 20. The corpus maintainers could, however, verify that this was an exceptional error while other VG items were coded with the correct date. Obviously it has not been practically possible for the author to exhaustivily verify all dates or other annotations in the whole corpus. The VG materials incorrectly annotated with April 13, amounting to seventeen KWIC lines, were corrected before further processing.

Secondly, all keywords matching the search expression but which were not intended compounds of *aske* had to be excluded. Among these unsuitable strings were *aske* itself and its inflected forms *asken* (definite) and *askens* (definite genitive). Furthermore, all words starting with the string *aske* but unrelated to the lemma, such as the place name *Asker* and its compounds, were excluded. A small number of true compounds with *aske* but referring to different lemmas or different contextual meanings of *aske* were filtered out, such as *askeparkett* 'ash parquet', *askebeger* 'ash tray', etc. The words *askeonsdag* 'Ash Wednesday' and *Askepott* 'Cinderella' were special cases in this respect, since they were occasionally used with a new meaning relevant to the present context. These two words were nevertheless excluded since their original meaning is not related to the domain of the current study and the frequencies of their new meanings remained so low as to be of anecdotal relevance only.

Thirdly, a number of apparent duplicate items were found. These were mainly due to repetitions of whole sentences within the same newspapers, but occasionally two different newspapers would have the same sentence. It was decided to suppress apparent duplicates occurring on the same day.

2.2 Selection of time frame

In order to get a somewhat long term overview, a preliminary inspection was performed on news material from the second quarter of 2010. This revealed that news coverage containing words with *aske* related to the Icelandic volcano events started on April 14 and virtually ceased by the end of May. On May 24, the UK MetOffice announced on its website that "the volcano is no longer emitting any ash". The present study therefore focused mainly on the period from April 14 through May 23, a forty-day span for which all occurrences were extracted and processed with the considerations described above.

The total number of selected compound tokens in the processed KWIC-concordance from April 14 through May 23 was 2,298. A frequency count was computed of tokens per day, presented as a bar plot in Figure 1. These daily token frequencies were not scaled in any way. Although daily accrual statistics are available for the Norwegian Newspaper Corpus, the proportion of daily tokens to a volume of varying newspaper content harvested on that particular day would

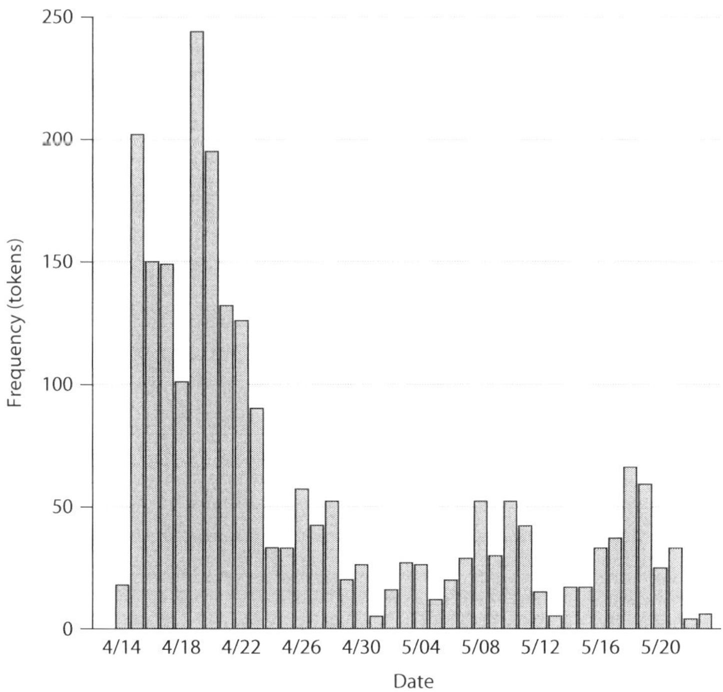

Figure 1. Number of tokens per day

not be very meaningful.[6] A more interesting scaling could be the based on the proportion of daily number of compounds to the daily word count of text dealing with the volcanic eruption, but it would be far from straightforward to separate out that content. Furthermore, the emphasis of the quantitative analysis described below will not be on the token frequencies *per se*, but on the relation between tokens and types, which is independent of the corpus size.

Figure 1 suggests that the news coverage did not have a linear development, but that the first ten days were characterized by blanket coverage, whereas from April 24, the number of tokens remained well below 100 per day, with smaller peaks.

In order to investigate whether compounds were actually new, an additional search was performed for all compounds with *aske* prior to April 14, 2010. It is difficult to verify neologisms with certainty, so approximations are in order. The Norwegian Newspaper Corpus goes as far back as 1998, but it does not seem straightforward to specify searches before a particular date; nor is possible to simply ask for the date of the first occurrence of every string matching a regular expression. After searching for *aske.** in the corpus from 2005 until April 14, 2010, and applying the same filtering of irrelevant items as described above, a relatively small number of low frequency compounds pertinent to volcanic ash eruptions were discovered, which will be discussed below.

2.3 Quantitative analysis

After the list of relevant occurrences in the period between April 14 and May 23, 2010 had been fixed and charted, the second step consisted of a quantitative analysis of the material. A frequency list was constructed of all items in the processed KWIC-concordance. There were 248 distinct word forms. The list of types, exclusive of hapax legomena, which make up half of the list, is included in Appendix 4.1. No attempt has been made to derive lemma frequencies. Still, it is easy to see that by far the most frequent compound lemma is *askesky* 'ash plume', while the second most frequent one is *askefast* 'ash stranded'.

In contrast, the number of types found from 2005 onward but before April 14, 2010 amounted to only 26 forms. Furthermore, their frequencies were considerably lower in that period than in the period after April 14, 2010. The most frequent pre-existing compound, *askesky* 'ash plume' and its inflected forms and compounds, occurred only sixteen times during the four years prior

6. Apart from the fact that daily variations in newspaper *section* sizes are not documented, the daily accrual numbers of the Norwegian Newspaper Corpus refer to the harvesting time and not to the publication date, which further complicates the matter.

to April 14, 2010, as compared to 1,368 times in the following forty days. From the analysis of pre-existing compounds it can be concluded that almost nine out of every ten compounds with *aske* used from April 14 to May 23, 2010 probably appeared as entirely new to the reader, and even the remaining one out of every ten were quite unlikely to have been encountered before and remembered.

A count was made of all new words per day, *new* meaning the first occurrence in the period from April 14, 2010, since the focus now is not on neology *per se* but on the short development of the vocabulary in active use within the studied period. Figure 2 shows a sharp increase in new compounds during the initial ten days with blanket news coverage. However, even after April 23, when coverage had become less extensive, new compounds kept appearing at a rate of about two per day on average, 60 in total for the rest of the period.

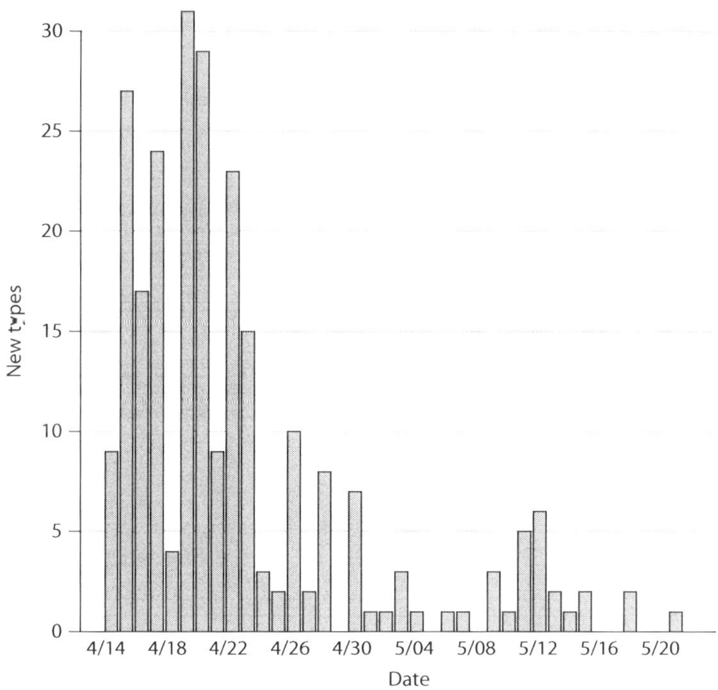

Figure 2. Number of new types per day

Appendix 4.2 presents a list of the words first occurring on April 14 and 15. It is easy to see that the vocabulary used on the first day is quite small and mostly related to physical objects and phenomena related to the volcano eruption, such as the pre-existing *askesky*. On the second day, compounding clearly became more creative. A much wider range of words describing physical phenomena appeared, as well as some terms describing societal consequences. That day saw the appearance of the word *askefast* 'ash stranded', which eventually became the most frequent true neologism of the lot. It appears that this word may have been coined independently by two journalists at two different newspapers. One of the two, journalist Andreas Fosse at the newspaper VG, commented that he did not suspect that this word would become so popular.[7] At the beginning of August 2010, this word yielded about 227,000 results on Google Search.[8]

In order to study the *variety* in the vocabulary in actual use on each date, one has to first consider the number of different types occurring on each day. These counts are plotted[9] in Figure 3. At first sight, it may appear that the general trend of number of types roughly follows that of the tokens.

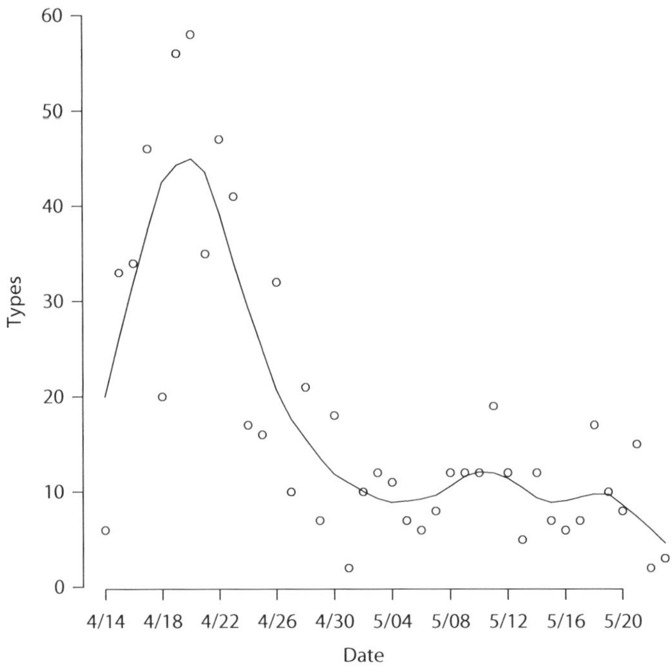

Figure 3. Number of types per day

7. http://www.kampanje.com/medier/article567608.ece

8. http://www.google.com/search?q=askefast+site%3Ano. Later searches showed a decline, apparently due to news items disappearing from the web.

9. A trend line has been drawn with the R function *lowess*, which is a local weighted polynomial regression smoother. A setting of $f = 1/4$ was chosen for this smoother function since this value provides enough detail to show the fast development.

However, in order to visualize the relation between types and tokens on the timeline more clearly, the type counts per day divided by the corresponding token counts are plotted[10] in Figure 4. The numerical data for this analysis are in Appendix 4.3. The trend is an initial increase in the proportion of types to tokens, indicating a growing variety in the active vocabulary. The trend line subsequently levels off, or at least does not show any considerable decrease. However, care must be taken to interpret these results, especially in the second half of the time span, when there is also great variation from day to day, in part due to days with very low frequencies.

3. Discussion

3.1 Remarks on the empirical and quantitative methods

The goal of this contribution was to carry out a case study in which the Norwegian Newspaper Corpus provided empirical data for a simple quantitative analysis of a sudden burst in linguistic creativity and high frequencies of otherwise rare words. The overwhelming news coverage of the events that spurred this investigation made it easy to track the use of compounds with *aske* in time without obtaining too much noise in the data. The emphasis has been on visualization of the quantitative materials. No metrics for burstiness were applied, since the burst was obviously extreme; the vocabulary with *aske* as referring to volcanic ash went from being practically nonexistent to a very substantial volume in terms of tokens and types.

It is not clear whether the trend (cf. Figure 4) can be given one simple explanation. The increase in the variety of compounds may in part be explained by the developments in real world situations referred to in the reporting. Whereas initial reporting dealt with mostly physical phenomena related to the volcanic eruption, the reporting of consequent broad societal effects required a more varied vocabulary. Another possible factor may be the journalists' usual tendency towards a varied, eye-catching vocabulary. The process of creative compounding is likely to have proceeded with a certain timidity at first, before it accelerated with more confidence after common acceptance in the language community. Eventually, the new vocabulary may have provided a certain entertainment value beyond the information value in the news.

The main time span under investigation was limited to 40 specific days in the past. This study is fully replicable even if the corpus is a monitor corpus with

10. Also here, a scatter plot smoother line has been drawn with the R function *lowess*; the setting $f = 1/2$ produced sufficient detail for the main trend.

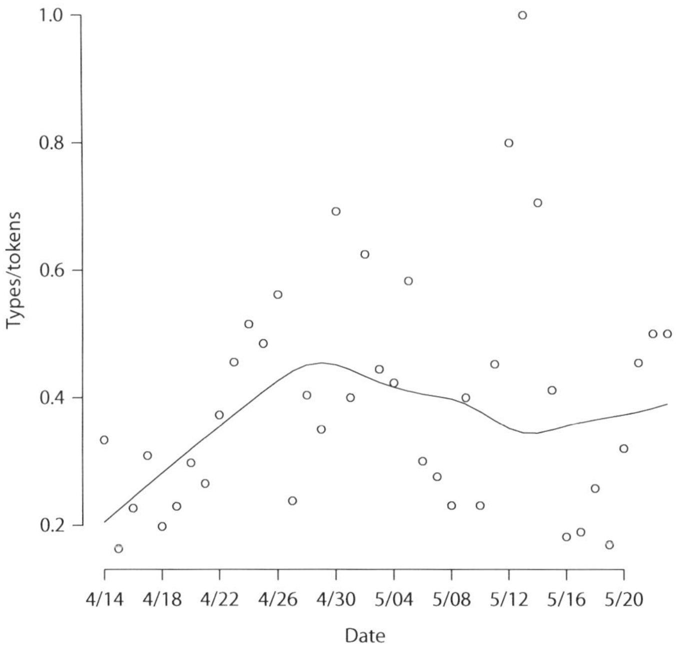

Figure 4. Number of types divided by number of tokens per day

daily changes. It has been an advantage in this respect that search results in the form of KWIC-concordances are coded with the newspaper source and date. Unfortunately, the corpus query interface which was used did not have straightforward provisions for restricting searches to specified time spans. Furthermore, even though the KWIC-concordances were usable for the purpose of this study, it might have been even more practical to download search results in a format such as XML which would be more suitable for further processing. The new Corpuscle query system which is presently (2010–2011) being developed implements improved functionality for restricting searches to arbitrary periods and for downloading materials.

It is furthermore hoped that future corpus query systems will make it easy to obtain token and type counts per day or other time span for arbitrary regular expression queries, to scale frequencies to the relevant volume of material, and to obtain dated lists of the first occurrences of words. In the absence of such facilities, the present case study was made possible through special purpose Unix scripts[11]

11. Inspiration was provided by Ken Church's tutorial *Unix™ for Poets*, available in various editions, e.g. at http://www.stanford.edu/class/cs224n/handouts/kwc-unix-for-poets.pdf

and R scripts[12] written by the author. The present study might also have benefited from full lemmatization and compound analysis of the Norwegian Newspaper Corpus, and even spelling correction. In the present study, such linguistic processing was not applied. Lemmatization and automatic tagging is now gradually being applied to the whole corpus.

A troubling experience was the discovery of a few incorrect date annotations. Without adequate quality assurance of the corpus, the possibility of occasional errors that might go undetected must be taken into account in any corpus study, not just the present one. It is a nearly impossible task to perform a *post hoc* verification of each occurrence in the corpus against the original material.

3.2 Linguistic remarks on specific compounds

Since the main goal has been an overview based on empirical and quantitative methods, an exhaustive linguistic study of each and every compound has not been in order. I will nevertheless conclude with a few remarks on morphological and semantic aspects of some observed compounds.

Besides the expected combinations with nouns, adjectives, and participles used as modifiers, such as *askeavlyst* 'cancelled due to ash', there was one combination with an infinitive, *askesnu* 'turn back due to ash', and one nominalized verb in *på askevent* 'on ash wait'. Remarkable was the caption *aske-o-rama* under a panoramic photograph of the volcano. There were complex compounds such as *askeskyfritt* 'ash plume free' and *askeskykrisen* 'the ash plume crisis'.

Several occurrences of compounds contained unnecessary hyphens, such as *aske-strandet* 'ash stranded'. There does not seem to be a clear trend in this. However, in at least one case, i.e. *aske-onsdag* 'ash Wednesday', the hyphen might have been added to signal its special meaning in the present context, so as to distinguish it from the existing *askeonsdag* 'Ash Wednesday' which was suppressed from the list. However, upon closer inspection, the unhyphenated form seems to have been used also in the new contextualized meaning three times. The use of quotation marks around new compounds was occasionally observed but not investigated. There were obvious typing errors such as *askeksyen* instead of *askeskyen*.

Although the word *aske* itself, being a mass noun, was used somewhat more frequently in the indefinite than the definite form, most countable nominal compounds, such as *askesky*, occurred overwhelmingly in the definite. Apparently the ash plume was continuously referred to as a known phenomenon after it had been introduced to the newspaper readership. The word *askekrise* 'ash crisis' did not

12. http://www.r-project.org/

occur in the singular indefinite at all, but occurred 22 times in the singular definite. Apparently, this term referred to the situation at hand which did not need to be explicitly introduced in the discourse.

From a semantic viewpoint, some compounds were not very transparent due to complex metonymic chains, such as *aske-portefølje* 'ash portfolio', which apparently referred to a portfolio of investments which were assumed to be secure even if the economic situation was disrupted by the ash eruption. As mentioned before, some compounds were ambiguous, perhaps intentionally so. The existing name *Askepott* 'Cinderella' acquired a new meaning as a common noun *askepott* 'ash fund' based on one of the possible meanings of the *pott* element. This coinage was certainly an intended pun. The fact that no automatic disambiguation was available was also a potential problem for *askespredning* 'ash spreading', a pre-existing compound normally used to refer to a funeral procedure. An inspection of this word in context revealed, however, that between April 14 and May 23, 2010, it was used overwhelmingly to refer to the spread of the volcanic ash plume.

As mentioned earlier, a number of relevant words were found to occur in the corpus prior to the main period studied. It is apparent that the majority of these pre-existing compounds refer to physical features of a volcanic eruption, such as *askesky* 'ash plume', *askelag* 'ash layer', *askeregn* 'ash rain', etc. In contrast, *askefast* did not occur at all in the corpus previously, and neither did *askekaos* or any of the imaginative compounds primarily referring to the societal consequences. The only pre-existing evaluative word was *askemareritt* 'ash nightmare', which had occurred previously only once. It was recorded in the corpus in 2008 but was in fact not used at all in the spring of 2010. The word *askespredning* 'ash spreading' seems to have been used exclusively in a funeral context previously.

While a study of deep syntactic relations so far could not be undertaken due to the lack of reliable syntactic annotation in the version of the corpus applied in this study, the superficial collocates of *askefast* were briefly inspected. All words immediately preceeding *askefast* were extracted from the corpus; this search was extended to August 7, 2010 in order to maximize the data and yielded 150 occurrences. The results indicate that 53 of the immediately preceeding tokens were forms of *sitte* 'sit', whereas only seven were forms of *stå* 'stand' and eighteen were forms of *være* 'be'. These three verbs are all compatible with the second part of the compound *fast* 'stuck' or 'stranded' and its other compounds, such as *værfast* 'weather stranded', *snøfast* 'snow stranded' etc., after which the new compound *askefast* appears to have been modeled.

At least one compound, *askesky*, has started appearing in the media as a new metaphor. On August 23, 2010, the newspaper BT wrote *Sjalusi kan vere ei sterk og vond kjensle som ligg som ei svart askesky over mange parforhold* 'Jealousy can be a strong and hurtful feeling which lies like a black ash plume over many a relationship'.[13] Clearly, the use of ash in this metaphor might appear somewhat strange without the background of the volcanic ash eruption episode and its consequences.

Undoubtedly, further interesting analyses could be made about particular words collected in this corpus-based exercise. Furthermore, the volcanic ash eruption of Grimsvötn on May 21, 2011 has opened the possibility of a follow-up study. A number of new compounds, such as *askefastsitter* 'someone stranded due to ash', *askeunntak* 'ash exception' and the verb *askefly* 'fly through ash', have been observed in the days after that eruption, but a detailed study has not been possible yet.

In the present study, the emphasis has been on the selection and processing of materials from the Norwegian Newspaper Corpus and their quantitative analysis in order to discover trends during the small time frame that was the focus of this study. It is hoped that a future research infrastructure for language studies, as that promoted by the CLARIN[14] initiative, will enable such studies in a more direct and practical way and with a more detailed linguistic annotation than is available in the version of the corpus that has been used at present.

The material collected in this case study is available from the author for any further investigations.

References

Andersen, Gisle. 2005. Assessing algorithms for automatic extraction of anglicisms in Norwegian texts. In Corpus Linguistics 2005, Birmingham.

Christ, Oliver. 1994. A modular and flexible architecture for an integrated corpus query system. In COMPLEX'94, Budapest, 22–32.

Christ, Oliver, Schulze, Bruno M., Hofmann, Anja & König, Esther. 1999. The IMS Corpus Workbench: Corpus Query Processor (CQP) User's Manual. Tech. rep., Institut für Maschinelle Sprachverarbeitung.

Kleinberg, Jon. 2002. Bursty and hierarchical structure in streams. In Proceedings of the 8th ACM SIGKDD International Conference on Knowledge Discovery and Data Mining, 91–101.

Quasthoff, Uwe. 2007. *Deutsches Neologismenwörterbuch: Neue Wörter und Wortbedeutungen in der Gegenwartssprache.* Berlin: Walter de Gruyter.

13. http://www.bt.no/forbruker/samliv/Ei-svart-askesky-i-parforholdet-1139377.html

14. http://www.clarin.eu

4. Appendices

4.1 Frequency list exclusive of hapax legomena

929 askeskyen
244 askesky
114 askefast
86 askeskyene
73 askeskyer
63 askefaste
32 askekaoset
30 askepartikler
26 askeproblemene
22 askekrisen
20 askekonsentrasjon
19 askefritt
18 askespredningen
18 askeskyens
17 askesituasjonen
16 asketrøbbel
16 askelaget
15 askeproblemer
15 askepartiklene
15 askefri
14 askelag
11 asketeppet
11 askestøv
10 asketrøbbelet
10 askeskya
9 askestansen
9 askekonsentrasjoner
8 askespredning
8 askenedfall
7 askeutslippet
7 askeprognosene
7 askeproduksjonen
7 askekaos
6 askeutsatte
6 asketap
6 askestøvet
6 askestrålen
6 askestoppen
6 askestans
6 askenedfallet
6 askebølge
6 aske-krisepakke
5 askevarsel
5 askestrømmen
5 askeregnet
5 askerammet
5 askeområdet
5 askegrå
5 askefylt
4 askevarslene
4 askeutslipp
4 askestengte
4 askeregn
4 askeprognose
4 askehumor
4 askehjelp
4 askefaren
4 aske-portefølje
3 askevarselet
3 askeutslippene
3 asketomt
3 askesøylen
3 askesøyle
3 askestrandet
3 askestengt
3 askerammede
3 askenivået
3 askekartet
3 askehelgen
3 askefare
3 aske-strandede
2 askevarsler
2 askevansker
2 askeutbrudd
2 asketåken
2 asketur
2 asketrussel
2 asketetthet
2 asketeppe
2 asketapene
2 askestopp
2 askesonene
2 askesnu
2 askesmell
2 askeskader
2 askesalg
2 askesaken
2 askeregning
2 askeregler
2 askeprøver
2 askeprognosen
2 askeproblemet
2 askeproblematikken
2 askepermitteringer
2 askeperioden
2 askepartiklenes
2 askenivåer
2 askenivåene
2 askemengden
2 askekrisa
2 askekonsentrasjonene
2 askekonsentrasjonen
2 askeintensitet
2 askeholdige
2 askefylte
2 askefrykt
2 askeforekomster
2 askeforekomsten
2 askefnatt
2 askefjerningsteamene
2 askefall
2 askedryss
2 askedekket
2 askedekkede
2 askedal
2 askebølgen
2 askeangst
2 aske-situasjonen
2 aske-problemene
2 aske-krisen
2 aske-kaoset
2 aske-håndtering

4.2 New words on April 14–15

4/14 askepartiklene
4/14 askepartiklenes
4/14 askeproblemene
4/14 askesky
4/14 askeskyen
4/14 askeskyene
4/15 aske-kaoset
4/15 askedryss
4/15 askefast
4/15 askefri
4/15 askefritt
4/15 askekansellering
4/15 askekaos
4/15 askekaoset
4/15 askekrisa
4/15 askeksyen
4/15 askelaget
4/15 askemengder
4/15 askenedfall
4/15 askenedfallet
4/15 askepartikler
4/15 askeperioden
4/15 askeproblemer
4/15 askeskya
4/15 askeskyens
4/15 askeskyer
4/15 askespredning
4/15 askespredningen
4/15 askestansen
4/15 askestøvet
4/15 asketeppet
4/15 asketaken
4/15 askeutslippet

4.3 Type and token frequencies per date

types	tokens	date						
6	18	4/14	21	52	4/28	12	15	5/12
33	202	4/15	7	20	4/29	5	5	5/13
34	150	4/16	18	26	4/30	12	17	5/14
46	149	4/17	2	5	5/01	7	17	5/15
20	101	4/18	10	16	5/02	6	33	5/16
56	244	4/19	12	27	5/03	7	37	5/17
58	195	4/20	11	26	5/04	17	66	5/18
35	132	4/21	7	12	5/05	10	59	5/19
47	126	4/22	6	20	5/06	8	25	5/20
41	90	4/23	8	29	5/07	15	33	5/21
17	33	4/24	12	52	5/08	2	4	5/22
16	33	4/25	12	30	5/09	3	6	5/23
32	57	4/26	12	52	5/10			
10	42	4/27	19	42	5/11			

Financial jargon in a general newspaper corpus

Marita Kristiansen
NHH Norwegian School of Economics

The present paper presents an investigation of financial jargon evident in Norwegian newspapers that can be related to the recent financial crisis. The study is a first step in exploring whether newspapers are useful sources from which to extract Norwegian terminology to be included in for instance termbases. In addition, it will provide a basis for considering whether there may be a need for a planned development of financial terminology in Norway. The paper reports on how financial jargon is used in Norwegian newspapers in relation to the concepts of *financial crisis, credit crunch, subprime* and *hedge fund*. In particular, the analysis focuses on whether Norwegian terminology is formed or English terms are maintained to describe these concepts.

1. Introduction

The recent financial crisis, which is said to have originated in the U.S., has brought with it a number of concepts such as *credit crunch, subprime* and *hedge fund*, which have become as global as the crisis itself. As a result, English is frequently used as the lingua franca when discussing these financial concepts. The global impact from the financial crisis has made it a topical issue also in Norway, not only for the financial specialists, but for society at large. Obviously, the effects of the crisis have affected financial markets in which both institutional investors and private individuals trade. In addition, the severeness of the crisis has also had an impact on Norwegian trade and industry and in turn people in general. Thus newspapers have covered the crisis at length. Since English is the language used to a great extent within the domain also in Norway, the coverage has been done by means of much English-based jargon.

The present paper aims at investigating this financial jargon as it has been used in Norwegian newspapers during the financial crisis, including the years 2007–2010. The overall purpose of the analysis is to see how newspapers may be explored to retrieve terminological data which may be used in terminological resources such as termbases. In particular, the study aims at mapping the use of financial jargon, including anglicisms, evident in *Norsk aviskorpus* ('the Norwegian Newspaper Corpus' henceforth the NNC) which can be related to the global financial crisis of 2007–2010. Thus the aim of the study will be two-fold:

1. to investigate the usefulness of newspapers in extracting terminological data
2. to describe the domain-specific language used in the NNC in relation to the domain of Finance, and in particular the financial crisis

In terminology work, the excerption of data is usually conducted from domain-related texts, such as textbooks on the domain or standard-setting documents like international or national guidelines (cf. Kristiansen 2004, 2011). In order to carry out a corpus-driven terminological analysis, for instance between English and Norwegian, an ideal methodology would be to establish parallel or comparable corpora on the domain. In such corpora extracts of text could be aligned to allow for an easy extraction of terminological units in the two languages (Innselset et al. 2008). This way a large amount of terminology could be efficiently extracted and registered for example in a termbase. However, in the case of Finance, and in particular concepts related to the financial crisis, parallel or comparable texts are difficult to find. The reason is that this is an emergent field in which the actual knowledge items, the concepts, and terms are far from fixed, but highly dynamic (Kristiansen 2011). Thus, existing textbooks in English or Norwegian on the domain will not have the most updated information and will therefore not provide the most valid sources for conceptual descriptions. Also, standard-setting documents which relate to many of the key concepts discussed in connection with the financial crisis have yet to be written. Recent legislation has for instance been passed in the U.S. (e.g. the *Dodd-Frank bill*) which is expected to bring in the "most sweeping changes to America's financial regulatory system since the 1930s" imposing regulations for instance on bank and hedge funds (Economist.com). In such a situation the most current corpus data material is likely to be topical popularised texts, such as newspapers.

Firstly, the analysis will focus on how a set of concepts which have been especially central in connection with the recent financial crisis, are represented in Norwegian news articles. These concepts are *financial crisis, credit crunch, subprime* and *hedge fund* (cf. Section 3.2). To what extent these concepts have been discussed in the NNC prior to 2007 will vary, something which I will comment on below in connection with the discussion of the various concepts. A closer delineation of these concepts will be given in Section 4. Secondly, the study will investigate whether it is possible to extract data in order to establish concept relations and/or fields in popular texts such as newspapers as discussed in Storjohann (2005). Thirdly, the study will map term variants and equivalents which are used in the NNC, something which will give a good basis for terminology development (Quirion 2003). In particular, it will be relevant to investigate whether new Norwegian terminology is formed or whether the English terms or phrases are maintained, with the addition of Norwegian explanatory paraphrases. Finally, the adoption of loan words into a language may involve different degrees of adaptations. The analysis will therefore investigate to what extent the anglicisms used in the NNC have retained their English orthography or whether morphological modifications have taken place, such as normalisation or norwegification (cf. Section 3.2). The analyses relate to the more overall question of whether there is a need for a planned terminology development in Finance.

To distinguish between concepts, terms and equivalents in the text, concepts are indicated by italics, i.e. *financial crisis*, whereas their designations or terms, are indicated by single quotes, i.e. 'finanskrise' and their translations are given in parentheses i.e. (financial crisis), respectively.

2. Background

As stressed in Antia (2000), language planning is important if a society is to be able to communicate specialised knowledge outside the specialist communities. Also, it is important to increase the pace at which languages may adapt to rapidly changing social circumstances. In Norway this perspective has received increasing focus in recent years and measures have been taken to establish national and institutional language policies in higher education to promote the development of Norwegian terminology (cf. e.g. the Norwegian Association of Higher Education Institutions' language policies, UHR.no). However, whereas guidelines have been established, little practical terminology work has been initiated.

In recent years there have been several diachronic studies in LSP on the formation and development of terms as evidenced in texts (cf. Ahmad & Collingham 1996; Temmerman 2000; Humbley 2009), focusing on the initial stages of observation and description. In some of these studies, newspapers have been promoted as a sound source of information, since, as Humbley (2009) argues, term formation is not the prerogative of scientific fields. Relevant examples are studies of economics metaphors in newspaper articles (Salway & Ahmad 1997; Musacchio & Ahmad 2009) and analyses on how information on contextual relational patterns may contribute to additional lexicographic information in dictionaries (Storjohann 2005).

Quirion (2003) promotes corpus analysis as a method to measure the acceptance of terms used in the aftermath of planned terminology development carried out by governmental language agencies. Following Quirion, Karabacak (2009) has studied the implantation success of economics terminology in Turkey. In particular, Karabacak investigates to what extent the economics terminology made official by the Turkish Language Society (TDK) is in fact used in Turkish newspapers. Although there is no planned terminology development in the field of Finance in Norway, the findings from Karabacak's study indicate that Norwegian newspapers may offer much useful information about terminology development. Furthermore, data from Norwegian newspapers may provide a basis for recommending financial terminology which may become accepted among its domain specialists in Norway.

In recent years there have been several studies on foreign words in Norwegian such as Andersen (2005); Graedler (1995, 2004) and Sandøy (1997, 2000). In Andersen (2008), financial terms are studied in particular as used in a general language corpus. The choice to study jargon in the present study and not terms as such has been made because it will not be a focus to discuss whether the expressions analysed qualify as proper terms or not. The concept of *jargon* as applied in the study may be described as "words and expressions that are used in special or technical ways by a particular group of people, often making the language difficult to understand" (Collins COBUILD 2006: 774). Thus, jargon will be domain-specific language, and for the purpose of the present study, language used to describe financial concepts, including unadapted anglicisms used in the NNC, norwegified anglicisms, translation loans and alternative Norwegian terms as used in the years 2007–2010.

In the present study, the concept of *anglicism* will be delineated as an expression borrowed from English into Norwegian, or in other words, any word composed wholly or partially of English lexical material (based on Graedler 2004: 4). Its intension includes English syntax, grammar, meaning, and structure used in Norwegian with varying degrees of adaptation. As discussed in Sandøy (2000) and Andersen (2005), anglicisms may retain their English orthography when used in Norwegian, e.g. 'monolines'. Anglicisms may also be hybrids, for instance as used in compound form, where the anglicism appears either in initial, medial or final position of the term, such as in the compound term 'subprime-lån' (subprime loan; initial position). Finally, loan words may be spelled in a normalised, or norwegified way to resemble more closely Norwegian pronunciation or spelling conventions. The concept of *norwegification* is in the present study used to describe degrees of orthographic adaptation in the anglicisms analysed (Graedler 2004; G. Andersen this volume), such as for example 'kredittskvis' for the English equivalent 'credit squeeze'.

3. Methodology

The present study is corpus-based in that the scope of the study is guided by *a priori* selected jargon which is central in discussions concerning the ongoing financial crisis. The global financial crisis has clearly coloured the language used in the media the last decade. *The Global Language Monitor (GLM)*, an enterprise which tracks language trends globally with special focus on the use of English, lists several expressions among the top words and phrases of the decade 2000–2009 including *bailout, derivative, subprime, financial tsunami* and *Enron*. The GLM analysis is based on their predictive quantities indicator which tracks words and phrases in the media and on the Internet, including blogs and Twitter. Another overview is made by *Time.com*, which has its own top ten financial crisis buzzwords list, including expressions such as *naked shorts, spread, credit default swap (CDS)* and *collateralized debt obligation (CDO)*. The anglicisms investigated in the present study either correspond with or are closely related to the above-mentioned expressions. To check for possible Norwegian equivalents that are used in addition to the anglicisms, an English-Norwegian specialised dictionary on business economic and legal terminology (Hansen & Lind 2008) has been used as reference material.

3.1 Corpus material and selection of financial jargon

The NNC is mainly a general language corpus, including Norwegian newspapers aimed at society at large. Still, the corpus provides a solid representation of relevant financial jargon used in Norwegian in the period of the financial crisis (2007–2010). The NNC includes one daily newspaper, *Dagens Næringsliv (DN)*, which is a financial newspaper likely to have a much higher frequency of financial jargon than the other newspapers (cf. Andersen 2008). Nevertheless, since the purpose of the present study is to retrieve as much terminological data as possible without comparing the findings with a Norwegian reference lexicon as such, no analysis to compare frequencies in DN compared with the other newspapers has been done at this stage.

In order to retrieve data, the KWIC concordance (IMS CWB), based on both an exact pattern matching (untruncated) and truncated pattern matching of Norwegian headwords, has been used. For instance, both 'hedge*' and 'hedge funds' have been used as headwords to retrieve all instances of expressions containing 'hedge' and inflectional forms, all instances of the term 'hedge fund' and also anglicisms used as part of compound terms such as 'hedgefondindeks' (hedge fund index) and 'hedgefondstrategi' (hedge fund strategy). Furthermore, occurrences where the whole concordance consists solely of English, or where the occurrences clearly refer to other concepts than those analysed within the scope of this study, have been excluded from the analysis. Examples of the latter may be 'sikringsfond', 'spread' and 'CFD' (contract of difference) which in addition to denoting financial concepts, are used in discussions of the concepts of the *Norwegian bank's guarantee fund, fashion spreads* and *computational fluid dynamics*, respectively.

Combining a quantitative analysis of the use of English loan words in the NNC with a qualitative analysis of concepts is somewhat difficult since the statistics that can be easily rendered by means of KWIC concordances, giving the number of tokens, do not necessarily indicate something which is relevant for the concept in question. An example may be the term 'financial crisis' (truncated pattern matching) which occurs 18,680 times in the NNC. The frequency does not necessarily mean that the tokens refer to the concept of *financial crisis* which is subject to analysis in the present study, since the newspapers report on both several international financial crises in modern time and also local crises that have hit for instance only a sector or even a local soccer club. In the following the main analytical categories that have been guiding in the analysis will therefore be described, and then next, the analysis will be discussed from the point of view of the concepts subject to analysis.

3.2 Investigating the influence of English loan words

The fact that Finance has become highly internationalised makes it likely to assume a steady increase in the use of English-based jargon. In this connection it is relevant to investigate what kind of terminological information can be found. To investigate this, the analysis will focus on four analytical categories in particular: (i) central concepts and related term candidates; (ii) concept relations and/or concept fields; (iii) terms, variants and equivalents, and (iv) the morphology of the term candidates.

i. Central concepts and related term candidates

Initially, four concepts have been singled out as being especially central when discussing the global economic situation, i.e. the concepts of *financial crisis, credit crunch, subprime* and *hedge fund*. Relevant term candidates (headwords) will be lexical items which denote these concepts, or concepts related to them as discussed in 3.1 above, such as 'finanskrise' (financial crisis), 'kredittskvis' (credit crunch) and 'CDO'.

In addition to these four concepts, a number of other concepts have been analysed as well, as the investigation of concept relations and/or concept fields has progressed. These will be introduced in connection with the discussion of findings in Section 4.

ii. Concept relations and/or concept fields

The second category that has been investigated is concept relations and/or concept fields. This is an important data category in a termbase, indicating which concepts are coordinated or which concept is the superordinate concept of the coordinated concepts. Searching the NNC for information about concept relations or data which could help establish concept fields has therefore been a good test to see how useful such a corpus is. The focus in the study has been to see whether it is possible to find information regarding how a concept is related to other concepts belonging to a particular subdomain, including superordinate concepts, coordinated concepts, subordinated concepts and other relations. Examples of relational information that may be found in the NNC may be utterances such as in examples (1) and (2):

(1) *de mest risikable boliglånene "subprime" og alt-A* (DN080725)
the most risky mortgages, subprime and alt-A

(2) *alt som lukter subprime og andre typer amerikanske boliglånsprodukter* (DN080606)
anything that smells like subprime and other kinds of American mortgage products

In example (1), the representation of the concepts of *subprime* and *alt-A* indicates that we are dealing with two coordinated concepts which have as their superordinate concept *mortgage loan.* In example (2), the concept of *subprime* is grouped as an instance of *American mortgage product.* Together, the two examples give relational information to form an initial concept system of *mortgage product* as the superordinate concept, with two subordinate concepts of *subprime* and *alt-A*. A further discussion of relational information is given in Sections 4.1 and 4.2 in connection with the concepts of *financial crisis* and *subprime,* respectively.

iii. Terms, variants and equivalents
For terminological purposes it is highly relevant to investigate the use of different English and/or Norwegian terms to denote the same concept(s). An example to illustrate this third category which will be investigated may be that of the concept of *hedge fund,* which in the corpus is described as 'hedge fund', 'hedgefond' and 'risikofond', as illustrated in examples (3)–(4), respectively:[1]

(3) *Målet for nordmennene er å finne frem til "hedge funds-forvaltere"* (AP000409)
The aim of the Norwegians is to find hedge fund managers

1. There are also two occurrences of the expression 'risikotakingsfond' (BT100512); however, this expression is excluded from the analysis since it is a term suggested by the current author in that particular newspaper.

(4) *Hedgefond blir ofte betegnet som risikofond.* (DN050316)
Hedge funds are often called risk funds.

iv. The morphology of the term candidates

Three different kinds of morphological processes that have taken place as the anglicisms are adapted into Norwegian will be discussed. Firstly, when borrowed directly, anglicisms may retain their English orthography when used in Norwegian without any modifications, cf. example (5):

(5) *såkalt naked short-selling* (AA100527)
so-called naked short-selling

Secondly, anglicisms are frequently used as part of compound terms, where the English component makes up either the initial, or final position of the term as illustrated in examples (6)–(7), respectively. The study has not returned any compounds with the English component in medial position.

(6) *en kommende finanskrise basert på subprime lån* (DB080704)
a future financial crisis based on subprime loan

(7) *situasjonen for de som er fanget i "norsk subprime"* (DN080626)
the situation for those trapped in a Norwegian subprime

In Norwegian, compounds should be written as one word. Thus the compound in (6) is not according to the spelling norm even if 'subprime' were to be accepted as an import word. In fact, for several of the terms studied, there is much inconsistency in the spelling conventions used. An example may be how compounds are spelled by means of either the use of the hyphen ('subprime-lån'; 59), lack of such ('subprime lån'; 4) or as a fully integrated compound ('subprimelån'; 68), of which the latter spelling is by far the most frequent in connection with 'subprime' (29.9 per cent; cf. Table 3 below). Thirdly, the borrowed words may also be norwegified in that they are orthographically adapted to the spelling norms of Norwegian, as illustrated in example (8):

(8) *stigende råvarepriser og kredittskvis* (DN080415)
increasing commodity prices and credit squeeze

Finally, the NNC shows evidence of new Norwegian terms that are created as well. An example may be the term 'råtne boliglån' to denote the concept of *subprime* in example (9):

(9) *USA, som veltet verden ut i en finanskrise med råtne boliglån* (DA080710)
The U.S. which forced the world into a financial crisis with rotten mortgages

4. Results and discussion

In the following I will present some findings related to the four analytical categories described in Section 3.2 above. These categories have been investigated in relation to the concepts of *financial crisis, credit crunch, subprime* and *hedge fund*. A more detailed analysis of concept relations and term variants will be presented in connection with the concepts of *financial crisis* and *subprime*. Finally, some of the related concepts have been investigated further in terms of the morphology of the term candidates, with focus on two aspects in particular, namely the use of acronyms and inflectional forms.

4.1 The concepts of *financial crisis* and *credit crunch*

Being the overall concept of analysis in the study, the concept of *financial crisis* should be briefly delineated although it is not expressed in form of an anglicism in the NNC. It may be described as "a situation in which the supply of money is outpaced by the demand for money" (BusinessDictionary.com).

The concept of *financial crisis* is a general concept, and the analysis of the use of 'finanskrise' and its synonym 'økonomisk krise' in the NNC in the period of 1998–2010 shows that the terms actually refer to several crises, i.e. the current global crisis (2007–2010), a Russian and an Asian one (1997–98), in addition to financial crises in general ('finanskriser'). Furthermore, there are instances of financial crises which have no relation to the concept in question, as illustrated in example (10):

(10) *investorgruppen som i fjor reddet Rissa-verftet fra økonomisk krise* (AA080717)
the investor group that last year rescued the Rissa yard from a financial crisis

Nevertheless, by retrieving both 'finanskrisen' (the financial crisis) and 'finanskriser' (financial crises) it is possible to gather information about specific crises, including the current one, as well as the general concept. Thus the corpus-based approach provides data that may be used to delineate the concept relevant for the present analysis compared with historical information, as illustrated in examples (11)–(13).

(11) *internasjonale finanskriser får grobunn* (AP990621)
international financial crises gain ground

(12) *slik som krisene i Russland og Brasil som var en følge av den asiatiske finanskrisen i 1998* (DN001130)
such as the crises in Russia and Brazil following the Asian financial crisis in 1998

(13) *Den internasjonale finanskrisen er i ferd med å sette sitt preg på Japan* (DN081226)
The international financial crisis is now beginning to affect Japan

As shown in Table 1, several related concepts are used in addition to *financial crisis* in the NNC, with several term variants, such as 'nasjonal krise', 'norsk krise' and the above-mentioned near synonym 'økonomisk krise'. The latter has a wider intension than *financial crisis*, but the terms are used synonymously in the NNC.

Table 1. Term variants and frequencies of the concept of *financial crisis*[2]

Concept	Terms, variants, and paraphrases in the NNC	Frequency
financial crisis	finanskrise (financial crisis)	17,716
	finansiell krise (financial crisis)	224
	økonomisk krise (economic/financial crisis)	3,130
	nasjonal krise (national crisis)	155
	norsk krise (Norwegian crisis)	37
	global krise (global crisis)	115
	verdensomspennende krise (global crisis)	20
	bankkrise (bank crisis)	590
	gjeldskrise (debt crisis)	747
	boligkrise (housing crisis)	193
	Total	22,927

A fourth variant is 'finansiell krise' (financial crisis), as illustrated also in Figure 1. Figure 1 shows the various terms that are used and how these may be grouped according to whether they refer to the financial crisis on a national or global level. Some expressions are used in both settings or in a general setting without indicating the level of focus (non-specific level).

For instance, although the terms 'nasjonal krise' and 'global krise' refer to concepts which are closely interrelated and share a common core of meaning, they are not true synonyms. The two terms 'global krise' and 'verdensomspennende krise' are, on the other hand, true synonyms. It may be difficult to clearly separate

2. In order maintain a common presentation of the various concepts throughout the article, all tables include both term variants and frequencies. However, in Table 1, the frequencies relate to the expressions only and not to the actual concept of *financial crisis* analysed here since an in-depth analysis of this would go beyond the scope of this article.

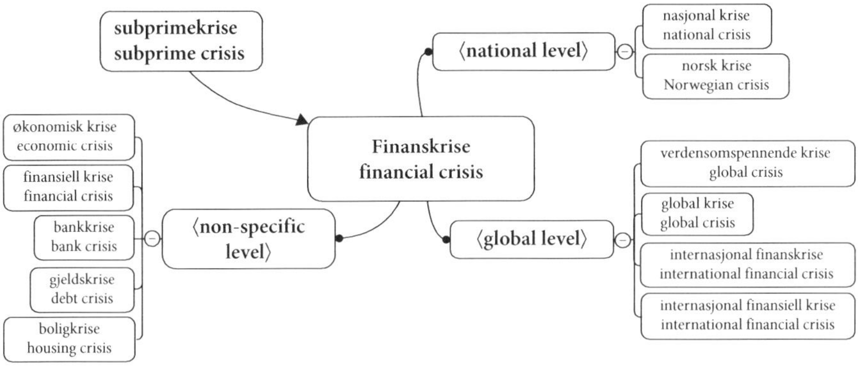

Figure 1. Term variation and near synonyms of *'finanskrise' (financial crisis)*

other terms such as 'bankkrise', 'gjeldskrise' and 'boligkrise', which are all obviously related to the concept of *mortgage*, in connection with this particular domain, both nationally and globally. Some of the terms, i.e. 'finansiell krise', 'økonomisk krise', 'bankkrise', 'gjeldskrise' and 'boligkrise', are all used at both a national, macroeconomic level and at a global one. Thus only the context will disclose to which concept the terms refer.

The well-known crisis in the 1930s, is interestingly enough not described as a financial crisis in the corpus, but only as 'krakket' (the crash) as illustrated in example (14) or 'børskrakk' (stock exchange crash).

(14) *verdensøkonomien står overfor en situasjon tilsvarende krakket i 1929.* (OD981027)
the world economy is facing a similar situation as the crash in 1929.

A *stock market crash* may be described as a "precipitous and rapid decline (that may persist for months or years) in the prices of shares traded on a stock exchange, caused by panic selling" (Businessdictionary.com). It is thus a closely related concept of *financial crisis*. The expression 'krakk', which is used 1,502 times in the NNC, refers to several market crashes in history, i.e. the 1929 crash, the period of 1986–87 where several markets crashed, one in 1992, next the period of 1997–99, then the period of 2001–2002 and finally the current period of 2007–2010. The crashes will naturally correspond closely with the number of financial crises during a given period of time. While the expression is used 772 times in the latter period of analysis, it is still used to refer to all the market crashes referred to here. A more thorough conceptual analysis is therefore required to be able to say to what extent the expression is used as a description of the recent financial crisis. Nevertheless, it shows that the expression, although highly associated with the 1929 crash, is still much used as financial jargon.

Another central concept in the wake of the financial crisis is that of *credit crunch*. The concept may be described as a "Money Market situation in which loans are hard to get. [...] occurs usually when a government tries to control inflation by imposing restrictions on lendings to consumers and small businesses" (Businessdictionary.com). Both Norwegian businesses and private individuals experienced this consequence of the global financial crisis. In the NNC, the anglicism 'credit crunch' appears four times in the analysis period, but only one is relevant for the present analysis; when used as an explanation to the Norwegian 'utlånsstopp' (stop in lending), indicating a cause-effect relationship with 'credit crunch'. As shown in Table 2 below, the Norwegian equivalent (translated) form is 'kredittskvis' which is used frequently and consistently in the NNC. With two exceptions (1998, 2001), the term is only retrieved during the recent financial crisis period. Thus the concept of *credit crunch* is relatively new to Norwegians although we have experience with lending stop during earlier periods as well. As discussed above in Section 3.2, 'kredittskvis' is a translation of the equivalent English term 'credit squeeze', which does not occur in the NNC. It should be noted though, that the English term 'credit squeeze' is less common as English jargon than its synonym 'credit crunch'. The norwegified term is still the one used consistently in the NNC, whereas a possible counterpart to 'credit crunch', 'kredittkrønsj', does not exist in the corpus.

Table 2. Term variants and frequencies of the concept of *credit crunch*

Concept	Terms, variants, and paraphrases in the NNC	Frequency
credit crunch	credit crunch	1
	credit squeeze	1
	kredittskvis (credit squeeze)	60
	Total	62

4.2 The concept of *subprime* and related concepts

The concept of *subprime* was particularly salient in the initial phase of the financial crisis. In fact it was selected as *the* financial expression of the year in Norway in 2007 (E24.no). It can be defined as "a mortgage (which) is granted to borrowers whose credit history is not sufficient to get a conventional mortgage. Often these borrowers have impaired or even no credit history" (About.com).

In contrast to 'credit crunch', 24 terms or explanatory paraphrases have been retrieved which all denote the concept of *subprime*. These expressions are rendered in Table 3 below, including explanatory English equivalents and frequencies.

Table 3. Term variants and frequencies of the concept of *subprime*

Concept	Terms, variants, and paraphrases in the NNC	Frequency
subprime	subprime (subprime mortgage)	70
	subprimes (subprime mortgage)	1
	"subprimes" (subprime mortgage)	1
	"subprime" (subprime mortgage)	10
	("subprime loans") (subprime mortgage)	1
	"subprime" lån (subprime mortgage)	2
	"subprimelån" (subprime mortgage)	6
	"subprime-lån" (subprime mortgage)	7
	subprime lån (subprime mortgage)	4
	subprimelån (subprime mortgage)	68
	subprime-lån (subprime mortgage)	59
	subprime boliglån (subprime mortgage)	14
	subprime-boliglån (subprime mortgage)	7
	subprimegjeld (subprime mortgage)	1
	råtne boliglån (rotten mortgages)	38
	råtne boliglån (subprime) (rotten mortgage (subprime))	1
	"råtne boliglån" (rotten mortgages)	1
	råtne boliglånsprodukt (rotten mortgage products)	1
	råtne boliglånsporteføljer (rotten mortgage portfolios)	1
	høyrisiko-boliglån (såkalte subprime-lån) (high-risk mortgage (so-called subprime mortgage))	1
	høyrisiko-boliglån (high-risk mortgage)	1
	høyrisiko boliglån (subprime) (high-risk mortgage (subprime))	1
	høyrisikolån (high-risk loan)	13
	lavt gradert lån (subprime) (low grade loan (subprime))	1
	Total	227

As is evident from Table 3, many of these terms are simply orthographic variants of 'subprime loan', whereas others refer to near synonyms of the concept, such as 'amerikansk subprimelån' and 'norsk subprime'.

The overview includes the use of expressions which refer to the concept of *subprime* as such and not to related concepts and expressions, such as 'subprime-portefølje', 'subprimekrise', 'subprime-låntagere', something which adds an even longer list of variation in expressions, both in terms of actual concepts, but also orthographic choices. In fact, within the period of analysis, 114 unique expressions are used (cf. Appendix I), including all variants (both conceptually and orthographically). Several of these are orthographic variants only, such as 'subprime-låntaker' vs. '"subprime-låntaker"' vs. '"subprime" låntaker' which all refer to the concept of *subprime borrower* together with the expressions 'subprimekunde' and 'subprime-kunde' (directly translated: subprime customer).

Based on the overview in Table 3 it is evident that 'subprime', 'subprimelån'/ 'subprime-lån' and 'råtne boliglån' are by far the most frequent terms.

Looking at the morphology of the term candidates, the concept of *subprime* is described by means of true anglicisms including inflectional endings (15), compounds with English component in initial position with a norwegified spelling convention (16), new Norwegian terms (17) and new Norwegian terms with explanatory paraphrases (18):

(15) *I dag kalles dette subprimes.* (AP081021)
Today this is called subprimes.

(16) *Banker ble pålagt å gi såkalte subprimelån til låntagere uten egenkapital.* (AP081119)
Banks were forced to offer so-called subprime loans to borrowers with no equity funding

(17) *Råtne boliglån kan skremme flere investorer fra aksjemarkedet* (DN070305)
Rotten mortgages may scare several investors off the stock market

(18) *I året som fulgte, begynte utlånere av høyrisikolån (såkalte "subprimelån") å melde seg konkurs* (DA090106)
In the following year, lenders of high-risk loans (so-called subprime loans) declared themselves bankrupt

Throughout the period covered by the data analysed, the anglicism 'subprime' is maintained also in Norwegian. However, out of the number of expressions used in the NNC in connection with the concept of *subprime* it is evident that many compound expressions have been created with a norwegified spelling (subprime + Norwegian word; see Appendix I). In addition, three new Norwegian terms have been created, i.e. 'høyrisikolån', 'lavt gradert lån' and 'råtne boliglån' of which the latter is the only Norwegian expression used consistently on its own in the NNC without the addition of 'subprime' as an explanatory comment (cf. Table 3).

A reason for the reluctance to use other expressions than 'subprime' may be that what seems to be the preferred Norwegian term, 'råtne boliglån', cannot easily be used as a leftmost compound component in Norwegian to generate compounds such as 'subprimeboble' (subprime bubble), 'subprimemarked' (subprime market) or 'subprimekrise' (subprime crisis). Internationally, subprime lending is also referred to as near-prime or non-prime lending as opposed to prime loans. These synonyms actually offer a possibility of translating "subprime" to "subprima" ('sub' and 'prima' both originating from Latin) or "ikke-prima" (non-prima). In Norwegian 'sekunda' is also established as an antonym to 'prima' and could therefore have been a possible norwegification, e.g. "sekundamarked" for 'subprime market' or "sekundalån" for 'subprime loan'.

Investigating the 558 instances of 'subprime' (truncated pattern matching; see Appendix 1) has provided information about a number of its related concepts, as illustrated in Figure 2.

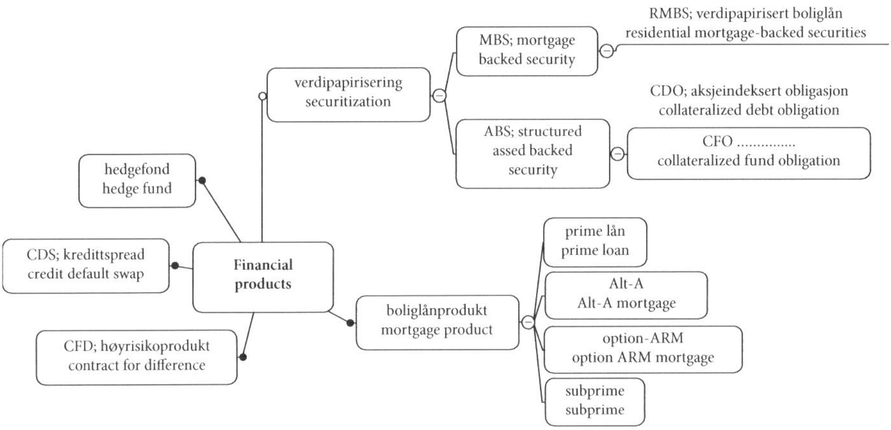

Figure 2. *Subprime* and related concepts based on the NNC

Figure 2 gives an overview of the most frequent concepts that are discussed together with *subprime* in news items in the NNC. Note that the overview should not be read as a concept system in the traditional terminological sense although a certain subclassification has been made to group concepts into different kinds of financial products. The expressions in the various nodes are retrieved from the NNC, with the addition of English translations. There is one exception, though, and that is that the concept of *CFO* or *obligasjon med pant i aktiva*, collateralized fund obligation) which appears in Figure 2 as a coordinated concept of *CDO* but does not occur in the NNC (the acronym is used though to denote the concept of *finansdirektør* (chief finance officer), which is commonly used also in Norwegian companies).

I will in the following comment on some of the concepts in Figure 2, beginning with that of *hedge fund*.

4.3 The concept of *hedge fund*

The situation with rising defaults on subprime mortgages in the U.S. is said to have triggered the global financial crisis. Hedge funds and banks all over the world were suddenly exposed and the financial crisis became a fact. The concept of *hedge fund* may be defined as:

> pooled investment vehicle that accept investors' money and generally invest it on a collective basis. [...] Hedge funds are primarily organized as private partnerships to provide maximum flexibility in constructing a portfolio. Hedge funds can take both long and short positions, make concentrated investments, use leverage, use derivatives, and invest in many markets. (based on Uslegal.com)

In the period of analysis, 'hedge' is used 1,043 times in the NNC (2007–2010), of which 947 refer to the concept of *hedge fund*. In addition, several term variants are also used in the corpus to denote the same concept. Table 4 gives an overview of the various term variants and frequencies.

Table 4. Term variants and frequencies of the concept of *hedge fund*

Concept	Terms, variants, and paraphrases in the NNC	Frequency
hedge fund	hedge fund	9
	hedgefund	7
	hedge fond	7
	hedgefond	886
	sikringskontrakt (hedging contract)	16
	risikofond (risk fund)	22
	Total	947

As can be seen from Table 4, several variants are used to describe the concept of *hedge fund*, including 'hedge fund', 'hedgefund', 'hedge fond' and 'hedgefond'. The already established Norwegian term 'risikofond' (cf. Hansen & Lind 2008) is also used in the NNC. Another term suggested in Hansen and Lind (2008), i.e. 'sikringsfond', is also frequently used in the NNC, however, not in connection with the concept of *hedge fund* (cf. Section 3.1 above). Nevertheless, six synonyms or variants have regularly been used in Norwegian newspapers to describe the concept throughout the analysis period, 'hedgefond' being far the most frequent (93.5 per cent). Thus a compound with the anglicism in initial position and with the norwegified spelling convention for compounds has gained ground.

The semantically related concept of *hedge*, i.e. "an investment position taken in order to protect oneself from the risk of an unfavourable price move in a security" (Investordictionary.com) is described by means of the anglicism 'hedge' in Norwegian as well, as illustrated in example (19).

(19) *preget av ineffektive hedger i* SPP (DN080818)
characterised by inefficient hedges in SSP

Some of these anglicisms are also used as verb forms in specialised collocations, such as 'å hedge' (to hedge), i.e. to manage risk, as well as, 'å hedge i' (to hedge in), 'å hedge seg mot' (to hedge yourself against), cf. (20)–(21).

(20) *flere stater forsikrer seg mot denne usikkerheten gjennom å hedge i* (DB080710)
several countries safeguard themselves against this insecurity by hedging in

(21) *Sentralbanker, pensjonsfond og private investorer kjøper gull for å hedge seg mot mulig depresiering av valuta og inflasjon.* (DN091202)
Central banks, pension funds and private investors buy gold to hedge against a possible currency depreciation or inflation.

This use of the anglicism *hedge* both in noun and verb forms has been frequent since 1998, totalling 1,780 tokens throughout the period and in particular frequent in 2005–06 in addition to the analysis period of 2007–2010.

4.4 A note on the use of acronyms

The analyses of the financial products of *subprime* and *hedge fund* have returned a number of related financial product concepts which are all labelled by means of acronyms (cf. Figure 2). These concepts, i.e. *CDO, CFD, CDS* and *RMBS* (residential mortgage-backed securities), are presented in Table 5. All these four concepts have emerged in the NNC during the years 2007–2010, with the exception of *CDS*, which is used four times also in 2005. Table 5 gives an overview of Norwegian terms and paraphrases which are used to denote these concepts, together with their frequencies in the period of 2007–2010. The overview shows truncated forms only (cf. Table 6 below for an overview of inflectional forms). For each of the four concepts, the bare acronyms are listed, in addition to compounded terms used in the NNC. Acronyms used in compounded expressions are used in initial position only, with the exception of 'syntetisk CDO' (synthetical CDO).

The concepts these terms refer to may in many ways be called true financial crisis concepts, being related to activities which lie at the heart of the reasons behind the fall-out of the global financial markets. The acronyms are consistently based on the English terms and no instances of norwegified acronyms have been retrieved in the NNC in relation to these financial concepts. What is retrieved is a number of variants (e.g. 'aksjeindeksert obligasjon' for 'CDO'), near synonyms (e.g. 'høyrisikoprodukt' for 'CFD') or paraphrases ('obligasjon med pant i lån' for 'CDO') used in Norwegian to denote the various concepts. Note that there is an inconsistency in the frequency in connection with *CFD* due to the fact that the acronym is misspelt in two connections ('CDF' instead of 'CFD').

Table 5. The use of financial acronyms in the NNC, variants and paraphrases

Concept	Terms, variants, and paraphrases in the NNC	Frequency
CDO (collateralized debt obligation)	CDO	67
	collateralized debt obligation	10
	collateralized deposit obligation	1
	collateral debt obligation	2
	aksjeindeksert obligasjon (stock indexed bond)	3
	sammensatt obligasjon (composite bond)	5
	CDO-investering (CDO investment)	4
	syntetisk CDO (synthetical CDO)	1
	CDO-obligasjon (CDO bond)	3
	CDO-marked (CDO market)	2
	CDO-struktur (CDO structure)	2
	CDO-relatert avsetning (CDO related provision)	1
	CDO-relatert investering (CDO related investment)	1
CFD (contract for difference)	CFD	3
	CDF	2
	contract for difference	5
	CFD-navn (CFD name)	1
CDS (credit default swap)	CDS	33
	credit default swap	47
	valutaswap mot mislighold (currency swap against default)	1
	kredittforsikringskontrakt (credit insurance contract)	1
	kredittforsikring (credit insurance)	2
	mislighold i obligasjonslån (default on bond loans)	1
	stasgjeld (sovereign debt)	2
	gresk statsgjeld (Greek sovereign debt)	3
	gresk CDS (Greek CDS)	1
	gresk femårig CDS (Greek 5-year CDS)	1
	spansk og portugisisk gjeld (Spanish and Portuguese debt)	1
	CDS-kontrakt (CDS contract)	3
	CDS-marked (CDS market)	5
	CDS-omsetning (CDS turnover)	1

(*Continued*)

Table 5. (Continued)

Concept	Terms, variants, and paraphrases in the NNC	Frequency
RMBS (residential mortgage-backed securities)	RMBS	6
	verdipapirisert boliglån (mortgage-backed securities)	1
	verdipapirisert huslånsportefølje (mortgage-backed portfolio)	1
	verdipapirisert boliglånsstruktur (mortgage-backed structure)	2
	boliglånsstruktur (mortgage-backed structure)	1
	Total	226

The use of the full English terms in connection with the concepts outlined in Table 5, such as 'collateralized debt obligation', has only been made in relation to their respective acronyms. In connection with the concept of *RMBS*, the Norwegian 'verdipapirisering' (securitisation) is retrieved, which is used consistently in Norwegian. This has resulted in two Norwegian terms, i.e. 'verdipapirisert boliglån' and 'verdipapirisert huslånsportefølje' that are especially descriptive.

In addition to the use of acronyms and other term variants, a number of new compound terms that do not denote the concepts as such, have been produced as well using a norwegified spelling convention of a hyphen to link the two components, such as 'CDO-marked' (CDO market), 'CFD-navn' (CFD name), 'CDS-indeks' (CDS index), and 'CDS-premie' (CDS premium). This underlines the acceptance of the English acronyms in Norwegian.

Finally, a number of more general concepts are used in connection with the acronyms in the NNC (frequencies indicated in parentheses), i.e. 'strukturert kredittprodukt' (structured credit product; 3), 'strukturert kreditt' (structured credit; 12), 'høyrisikoprodukt' (high-risk product; 13), 'finansiell kontrakt' (financial contract; 1), 'komplisert spareprodukt' (complex savings product; 70) and 'kredittderivat' (credit derivative; 23). Although these expressions are used in this context, it would be wrong to call them term variants. These expressions are rather denotations of what may be described as superordinate concepts, since for instance the concept of *CFD*, is in fact a type of *high-risk product*. This is a common naming strategy which is also evident in the use of 'derivat' to denote the concept of *CDS*; 'kredittderivat' to denote the concept of *CDO*, and finally, 'strukturert kredittprodukt' to denote the concept of *RMBS*, respectively. These Norwegian superordinate terms may be used to group several of these financial products.

4.5 Inflectional forms

Based on the retrieved data from the NNC, there is a general tendency to use target language inflectional forms when anglicisms are introduced in Norwegian, as illustrated in example (22):

(22) *opprettholder hedgingstrategien for 2010 på 50 prosent, og har nå hedget 50 prosent* (DN100128)
maintains the hedging strategy for 2010, and has now hedged 50 per cent

This is also the case for the acronyms which are outlined in Table 6. However, as shown in Table 6, several competing plural forms are used with the acronyms, e.g. *-er/er*. This calls for a need to standardise the orthography of the inflected forms in Norwegian in accordance with recommended Norwegian spelling rules, something which would in effect require the form *-er*.

Table 6. The use of inflected form of acronyms in the NNC (2007–2010)

Concept	Inflected form of acronym	Frequency
CDO (collateralized debt obligation)	CDO	10
	CDO-en (the CDO)	5
	CDO-er (CDOs)	23
	CDOer (CDOs)	15
	CDOs (CDOs)	4
	CDO-ene (the CDOs)	12
	CDOene (the CDOs)	1
CFD (contract for difference)	CFD	6
	CFDer (CFDs)	8
	CFD-er (CFDs)	4
	CFDene (the CFDs)	1
CDS (credit default swap)	CDS	29
	CDSen (the CDS)	2
	CDSer (CDS's)	25
	CDS-er (CDS's)	12
	CDSene (the CDS's)	7
RMBS (residential mortgage-backed securities)	RMBS	1
	RMBSer (RMBS's)	2
	RMBS-er (RMBS's)	3

In particular, target language inflectional forms are used to a high degree with the financial acronyms described above, i.e. 'CDO', 'CFD', 'CDS' and 'RMBS'. Graedler (1995: 71f) argues that inflected forms are likely to take on a norwegified orthography, something which is supported by the acronyms retrieved from the NNC.

There is one exception, though, with the concept of *monoline*, i.e. "two companies that insure against the risk of a bond or other security defaulting" (Financial Times.com). In the NNC, 'monoline' does not appear until 2008. However, all 13 occurrences have the inflectional source language form (plural -s) when used as a monoword term, as illustrated in example (23):

(23) *selskapene som driver med forsikring av andres lån i USA, såkalte monolines* (DN080423)
the companies which offer insurance on second-hand loans, so-called monolines

In addition, two occurrences are compounds, where the English component is used in initial position. i.e. 'monoline-motpart' (monoline counterpart) and 'monoline-selskap' (monoline company), respectively.

5. Concluding remarks

Exploring whether newspapers can be used as a source of terminological information for a planned development of Norwegian financial terminology has been a promising and exciting journey. It is evident from the analysis that Norwegian newspapers contain much terminological information which will not necessarily be found in other sources such as for instance textbooks. Thus they offer a solid basis for considering a planned term development.

In the study I have focused on four analytical categories which are especially relevant for gathering terminological information. Firstly, headwords based on international financial word surveys made by The Global Language Monitor (GLM) and Time.com have been singled out to investigate relevant concepts and term candidates. Only a small subset of all the financial anglicisms retrieved has been investigated, including those most closely related to the concepts of *financial crisis, credit crunch, subprime* and *hedge fund*. A more comprehensive study should therefore survey the finiancial jargon evident in the NNC. In the present study, the publication period studied has been limited to 2007–2010. Based on the findings from this analysis, it is evident that the jargon is highly emergent and it is therefore too early to give any definite answers concerning the language development in the domain.

Secondly, data from the NNC has made it possible to outline relations that hold among several of the most topical concepts and to discover new concepts belonging to the concept field of the recent financial crisis. In this connection it will be interesting to expand the study to an in-depth analysis of disambiguation strategies used in the newspaper articles since such information is likely to provide much essential data for the description and definition of concepts. Also, investigating to what extent the metainformation provided at the emergent stage is reduced over time will be relevant in order to see whether expressions have become established unofficially as accepted terms in the domain.

Thirdly, the study has focused on investigating possible Norwegian equivalents or term variants. Based on the findings from this corpus analysis, I will argue that the generally established belief that few Norwegian terms are to be found in the domain is in fact a misperception, since most anglicisms have Norwegian counterparts in the NNC. The many retrieved terms indicate that journalists make a considerable effort to create new Norwegian terminology. Nevertheless, there is much term variation and not all terms are perhaps suitable as Norwegian terms.

Also, both the emergence of new Norwegian terms and the norwegification of anglicisms seem to happen more or less by chance rather than as the result of a planned process. This has been the fourth analytical category accounted for here, including the investigation of the morphology of the term candidates. Based on the findings, there is little indication of a gradual development in which terms take on a more correct Norwegian orthography. On the contrary, the many variant forms, ranging from unadapted anglicisms, via norwegified expressions and translation loans to new Norwegian terms, seem to co-exist over time. Still, the analysis shows that the more norwegified expressions are more frequent than the non-adapted variants, as is the case for 'hedgefond' and 'subprimelån'. A more comprehensive study over a longer time span is, nevertheless, necessary to be able to say more about the development of financial anglicisms and possible trends, in contrast to general language studies of the same development. What is clear from the present study is, however, that acronyms are consistently established by means of English initialisms and that they are commonly used with target language inflectional forms.

To conclude, the findings from the study underline the need for a systematic approach towards monitoring, collecting and discussing domain-specific language challenges, whether they concern finding a good Norwegian term or more popularised expressions that may explain complicated financial matters in a satisfactory and consistent way. This calls for language planning and an infrastructure to collect and disseminate the terminology as it is developed and while the concepts are still of topical interest.

References

About.com ⟨http://useconomy.about.com/⟩ (14 March, 2011).

Ahmad, Kurshid & Collingham, Steven. 1996. Renewable Terminology. In *EURALEX '96: Proc. I–II*, Part II: *Papers submitted to the Seventh EURALEX International Congress on Lexicography* Martin Gellerstam et al. (eds), 759–771. Göteborg: Göteborg University.

Andersen, Gisle. 2005. Assessing algorithms for automatic extraction of anglicisms in Norwegian texts. Paper presented at *Corpus Linguistics 2005*. Birmingham, July 2005.

Andersen. Gisle. 2008. Quantifying domain-specificity: The occurrence of financial terms in a general corpus. In *Synaps 21/2008. Festskrift for Magnar Brekke*, Trine Dahl, Jan Roald & Ingrid Simonnæs (eds), 37–52.

Antia, Bassey E. 2000. *Terminology and Language planning: An Alternative Framework of Practice and Discourse* [Terminology and Lexicography Research and Practice 2]. Amsterdam: John Benjamins.

BusinessDictionary.com ⟨http://www.businessdictionary.com/definition/⟩ (12 July, 2010).

Collins COBUILD advanced learner's English dictionary. 2006. Glasgow: HarperCollins.

E24.no. ⟨http://e24.no/boers-og-finans/article2145134.ece⟩ (2 June, 2010).

Economist.com ⟨http://news.economist.com/cgi-bin1/DM/y/eCJh10cLfAj0Mo0Gg4w0Ek⟩ (1 July, 2010).

Financial Times.com ⟨http://lexicon.ft.com/term.asp?t=monolines⟩ (7 July, 2010).

Global Language Monitor ⟨http://www.languagemonitor.com⟩ (20 June, 2010).

Graedler, Anne-Line. 2004. Modern loanwords in the Nordic countries. Presentation of a project. *Nordic Journal of English Studies* 3(2): 5–22.

Graedler, Anne-Line. 1995. *Morphological, Semantic and Functional Aspects of English Lexical Borrowings in Norwegian*. Dr.art. dissertation, University of Oslo.

Hansen, Einar & Lind, Åge. 2008. *Engelsk norsk økonomisk-juridisk ordbok*. Bergen: Cappelen Akademisk forlag.

Humbley, John. 2009. Accounting for term formation. *Terminology science and research* 20: 1–15.

Innselset, Kai, Kristiansen, Marita & Øvsthus, Kari. 2008. Looking back to move forward. Challenges related to deceitful parallel texts and slippery terms. In *Synaps 21. Festskrift for Magnar Brekke,* Trine Dahl, Jan Roald & Ingrid Simonnæs (eds), 73–89.

Investordictionary.com ⟨http://www.investordictionary.com/definition/hedge⟩ (14 March, 2011).

Karabacak, Erkan. 2009. Acceptance of terminology sanctioned by the Turkish Language Society. *Terminology* 15(2): 145–178.

Kristiansen, Marita 2011. Domain dynamics in scholarly areas. How external pressure may cause concept and term changes. Special issue of *Terminology* 17(1): 30–48. *The Dynamics of Terms in Specialized Communication. An Interdisciplinary Perspective,* edited by Rita Temmerman & Marc Van Campenhoudt.

Kristiansen, Marita. 2004. *The Multi-Disciplinary Nature of the Social Sciences. Investigating Disciplinary Autonomy in Organisational Behaviour by means of Terminological Analysis.* Dr.art. dissertation, University of Bergen.

Musacchio, Maria Teresa & Ahmad, Kurshid. 2009. Variation and variability of economics metaphors in an English-Italian corpus of reports, newspaper and magazine articles. *Corpus-Based Approaches to Figurative Language. A Corpus Linguistics 2009. Colloquium,* 20 July, Liverpool, UK.

Norsk aviskorpus ⟨http://avis.uib.no/⟩ (10 March, 2011).
Quirion, Jean. 2003. Methodology for the design of a standard research protocol for measuring terminology usage. *Terminology* 9(1): 29–49.
Salway, Andrew & Ahmad, Kurshid. 1997. The role of *Metaphors* in financial texts. ⟨ftp://ftp.ee.surrey.ac.uk/pub/research/AI/A.Salway/finmeta.ps.gz⟩ (10 June, 2010).
Sandøy, Helge. 2000. *Lånte fjører eller bunad? Om importord i norsk.* Oslo: LNU/Cappelen akademisk.
Sandøy, Helge. 1997. *Lånte fjører eller bunad? Om norsk skrivemåte av importord.* Oslo: The Norwegian Language Council.
Storjohann, Petra. 2005. Corpus-driven vs. corpus-based approach to the study of relational patterns. Paper presented at *Corpus Linguistics 2005*. Birmingham, July 2005.
Temmerman, Rita. 2000. *Towards New Ways of Terminology Description. The Sociocognitive Approach* [Terminology and Lexicography Research and Practice 3]. Amsterdam: John Benjamins.
Time.com ⟨http://www.time.com/time/specials/packages/articles/article/0,28804,1847213_1847216,00html⟩ (20 June, 2010).
UHR.no ⟨http://www.uhr.no/ressurser/temasider/sprakpolitisk_plattform⟩ (10 March, 2011).
USLegal.com ⟨http://definitions.uslegal.com/h/hedge-fund/⟩ (14 March, 2011).

Appendix I

The use of 'subprime' in the NNC 2007–2010

Subprime	Tot. Frequency
"norsk subprime"	1
"subprime"	10
"subprime" lån	2
"subprime" lånegalskap	1
"subprime" låntaker	2
"subprime-hovedstad"	1
"subprime-industri"	1
"subprimelån"	6
"subprime-lån"	7
"subprime-låntaker"	2
"subprime-marked"	1
"subprime-problem"	1
"subprimes"	1
amerikansk lånekrise	1
amerikansk subprimelån	1
amerikansk subprime-lån	1

(Continued)

Appendix I. (Continued)

Subprime	Tot. Frequency
amerikansk subprimemarked	1
amerikansk subprime-portefølje	1
høyrisikolån	13
ikke-subprime	1
lavt gradert lån	1
Norges subprime	6
norsk subprime	1
subprime	70
subprime boliglån	14
subprime karakter	1
subprime lån	4
subprime lånevirksomhet	1
subprime- problem	3
subprime segment	1
subprimeaffære	1
subprime-arena	1
subprime-bekymring	1
subprime-bekymring	1
subprimeboble	4
subprime-boble	2
subprime-boliglån	7
subprime-bombe	1
subprime-eiendel	1
subprime-eiendom	1
subprime-ekspert	1
subprimeeksponering	2
subprime-eksponering	1
subprime-frykt	1
subprimegjeld	1
subprime-institusjon	1
subprime-investering	2
subprime-kaos	1
subprime-katastrofe	1
subprime-katastrofens ansikt	1

(*Continued*)

Appendix I. (Continued)

Subprime	**Tot. Frequency**
subprime-kollaps	4
subprimekrise	81
subprime-krise	41
subprimekunde	2
subprime-kunde	4
subprime-kvalitet	1
subprimelån	68
subprime-lån	59
subprime-lånemarked	2
subprimelånstap	1
subprime-låntaker	7
subprimeleilighet	1
subprimelignende trekk	1
subprimemarked	24
subprime-marked	22
subprime-måte	1
subprime-nedskriving	3
subprimepapir	2
subprime-plaget folk	1
subprime-portefølje	2
subprimeposisjon	1
subprimeproblem	7
subprime-problem	10
subprime-relatert eksponering	1
subprimerelatert forbrukerlån	1
subprime-relatert investering	1
subprime-relatert kreditt	1
subprimerelatert nedskrivning	3
subprime-relatert nedskrivning	2
subprime-relatert problem	1
subprimerelatert produkt	1
subprimerelatert tap	2
subprimerelatert verdipapir	2

(*Continued*)

Appendix I. (Continued)

Subprime	**Tot. Frequency**
subprime-relatert verdipapir	2
subprimes	1
subprimesafari	1
subprimesegment	1
subprime-segment	3
subprimesektor	2
subprime-sektor	4
subprimeselskap	1
subprime-selskap	2
subprime-sentrum	1
subprimeskandale	2
subprime-skandale	1
subprimeskygger	1
subprime-smell	1
subprime-søpla	1
subprime-studentlån	1
subprimetap	1
subprime-tap	1
subprimetaper	1
subprime-tendens	1
subprimetime	1
subprime-trio	1
subprime-trussel	1
subprime-type	1
subprime-uro	1
subprime-utlån	1
subprime-utlåner	1
subprime-versting	1
subprime-virksomhet	1
suprime på norsk	1
Total	558

Metonymic extension and vagueness

Schengen and *Kyoto* in Norwegian newspaper language*

Sandra Halverson
University of Bergen

The language sample provided by the Norwegian Newspaper Corpus (NNC) provides an appropriate corpus for the investigation of emerging uses of existent linguistic forms. A case in point is the development of new metonymical uses of place names; such uses often involve reference to events located at specific places, or the participants or results of such events. The same metonymic uses also exhibit signs of vagueness between one or more metonymic readings. In this study vagueness is defined in cognitive terms, using Tuggy's model (1993/2006), and the development of metonymic senses is studied in two place name categories at different stages of development. The findings are discussed in light of Peirsman and Geeraerts (2006a, b) prototype model of metonymic relationships.

1. Introduction

Place names often acquire meanings that extend beyond reference to a geographical location. These developments constitute an interesting case for the investigation of semantic relationships and the fluid nature of semantic change. In some cases, the relationship underlying a change is a metonymic one. For instance, in Norwegian, the place name *Schengen* may be used metonymically to refer to the Schengen Agreement (an international treaty to guarantee free movement of people within

* The bulk of the work on this paper was done during a sabbatical stay with the Interdepartmental Program in Linguistics at Purdue University, West Lafayette, IN. Thanks to the program for their hospitality during the 2009–2010 academic year. Thanks also to Jan Oskar Engene for insightful discussions during analysis of the *Schengen* data, and to the members of the EURLING project group for thoughtful comments on earlier analyses.

a defined European area), as in (1), taken from the Norwegian Newspaper Corpus (NNC) (for description of the corpus see Section 3):

(1) *Vi har brukt Interpol, Schengen, Europol – rett og slett alle muligheter* (VG060113)[1]
We have used Interpol, Schengen, Europol – virtually every possibility

Or, similarly, to the membership, or group of Schengen treaty signatories, as in (2):

(2) *… og flere land som i dag er med i Schengen* (NL060210)
… and several countries who are currently members of/belong to Schengen

Or to the geographical territory defined by the agreement, its area of jurisdiction, as in (3):

(3) *… ikke har lov å komme inn i Schengen, …* (DA060526)
… don't have permission to enter Schengen, …

In what seem to be more fluid cases, there is more than one possible interpretation of an utterance. This is illustrated in (4), which may be taken to refer to either the group of Schengen signatories or the geographical area that the treaty created:

(4) *Norge er bare en buss-, fly- eller fergebillett fra landene i Schengen.* (VG061014)
Norway is only a bus, airline, or ferry ticket away from the countries in Schengen.

In this paper, a cognitive linguistic view of semantic structure and metonymy is adopted and the focus is on uses such as (4). Tuggy's (1993/2006) model of the ambiguity/vagueness cline and Langacker's account of sense categories (1987/1991, 2008) serve as the starting point for the corpus analysis of two place names in Norwegian newspaper language. The investigation of these two place names also builds on the Peirsman and Geeraerts account of metonymy (2006a, 2006b), in which metonymy is described as a prototype category of contiguity relationships. These accounts are brought together in the service of two main objectives:

i. to investigate the nature of the ambiguity/vagueness manifested in the data, more specifically to consider how vagueness is related to domain knowledge and the recruitment of conventionalized metonymic patterns
ii. to consider whether patterns of ambiguity/vagueness might be related to different stages of semantic development.

1. For all examples taken from the newspaper corpus, the reference includes an acronym for the name of the newspaper and the date of the occurrence, given in the standard format with the last two digits of the year first. See Andersen & Hofland this volume for a list of the newspapers and the acronyms.

These objectives constitute the two research questions to be posed in the present study. While the study makes use of quantitative corpus data, it is intended as an exploratory, hypothesis-generating study, not a hypothesis-testing one. In previous studies of place name metonymies, the issue of ambiguity and/or vagueness has rarely been addressed (e.g. Markert & Nissim 2003a, b).

A previous analysis of *Schengen* in the Norwegian Newspaper Corpus (Halverson & Engene 2010), revealed that approximately 10 percent of all of the metonymic occurrences of that place name were what was, in that paper, referred to as 'indeterminate'. This term was used rather pre-theoretically to categorize cases in which more than one interpretation was possible. While the indeterminacy found in that data was discussed in light of the Peirsman and Geeraerts model, the precise nature of the indeterminacy was left unresolved. In this paper, the 'indeterminate' *Schengen* cases will be reconsidered, and a more precise description of this indeterminacy will be given. Furthermore, as an extension of the analysis, all occurrences of another place name with comparable metonymic extensions, i.e. *Kyoto*, will be studied in a comparison of metonymic sense categories at different stages of development.

In Section 2 of the paper, the relevant theoretical framework is presented. Section 3 describes the Norwegian Newspaper Corpus material and the method of analysis. Section 4 comprises results and discussion, and concluding remarks are given in Section 5.

2. Theoretical framework

In the following sections, a very general overview of Langacker's Cognitive Grammar is given, and the relevant discussions of semantic change are referred to. The outline is necessarily very brief, and readers are referred to the full accounts in Langacker (1987/1991, 2008). For the purposes of the current study, the issue of ambiguity/vagueness is key, and as a consequence Tuggy's account (1993/2006) is incorporated in the overview.

2.1 Metonymic categories and the ambiguity/vagueness cline

In Langacker's Cognitive Grammar, a language is a conventionalized inventory of symbolic structures, each of which constitutes a bipolar form-meaning pair (1987:73ff, 2008:5). In linguistic expressions, the form side is described as a phonological pole, which may also be realized as an orthographic or gestural representation (2008:15). The semantic pole is constituted by a conceptualization, which makes use of a conceptual substrate and a construal, or 'one of the countless ways of conceiving and portraying the situation in question' (2008:4).

At a higher level of organization, conceptualizations which have become 'entrenched' in the speaker may be cognitively manipulated to create categories of related conceptualizations paired with the same phonological representation (sense categories). This process of category growth, or semantic change, proceeds by one of two possible processes: extension or instantiation.

In the categorization process by which linguistic structures accrue new and additional meanings, the notion of schema is central. A schema may be understood as 'what two cognitive structures have in common' (Tuggy 1993/2006: 172). In other words, if a conceptualization (and hence its phonological representation) is used in a new way, then the new usage shares some or all meaning with the original meaning associated with that symbol. To cite a metonymic example (in which some meaning is shared), in the extension in (6),[2] *maple* is used about the material created from the tree by the same name, as in (5):

(5) dappled shade cast by mature apple trees and maples (21941).

(6) most of the original furniture was maple and some is still in use today (13296)

If the new meaning makes use of all of the content but is more specific, then it is considered an 'instantiation'. In (7) and (8), a schema such as 'geometric shape with three sides of the same length or three acute angles' can link the uses of *triangle* to refer to a musical instrument with this shape, as in (7) or to the shape formed by connecting three geographical points, as in (8):

(7) a relatively straightforward rendition of the song itself on panpipes and recorders, punctuated by the sound of castanets, triangles and whistles (43650)

(8) the governments of the Czech Republic, Germany and Poland have signed an agreement to clean up 'the Black Triangle' (13650)

The linguistic status of the schema and its instantiations can vary. As Tuggy points out:

> Both schemas and their instantiations can coexist in a language; they exist to the degree that they are established (entrenched) in speakers' minds through repeated usage. Well-entrenched structures, *ceteris paribus*, are more salient than less-entrenched structures, [...]. (1993/2006: 173)

2. Examples (5)–(10) are taken from the BNC, accessed through the Sketch Engine interface (www.sketchengine.co.uk). The citation identifications are the references assigned in Sketch Engine.

'Salience' is to be understood as a form of cognitive prominence, which, in turn, is posited as some sort of correlate to levels of neural activation (Langacker 2008: 31), and presumably linked to ease of access and likelihood of production. In Tuggy's account, the notion of schema (shared conceptual content) and the fact that schemas and instantiations[3] manifest varying degrees of salience are used to describe ambiguity, vagueness and polysemy. More specifically, ambiguity and vagueness constitute the two ends of a cline, (a.) and (e.) respectively, in which schemas and their instantiations demonstrate varying degrees of salience in context. In the middle of this cline are situated cases of polysemy (c.). This is demonstrated in Figure 1:

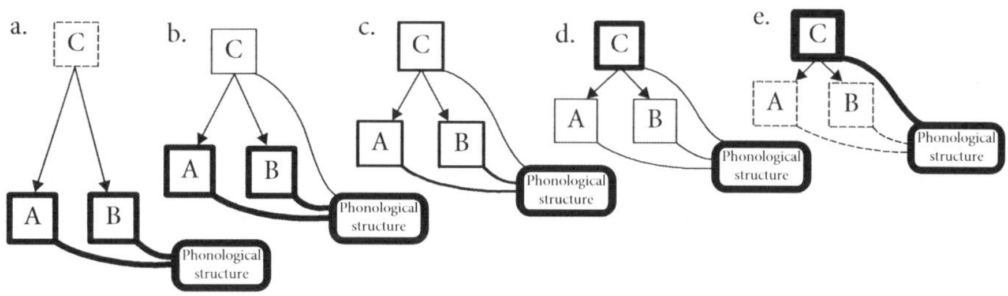

Figure 1. Tuggy's (1993/2006) ambiguity/vagueness cline. Reprinted with permission from Mouton de Gruyter.

In the figure, the schema is represented in the box labeled C, representing what is shared by the instantiations (A and B). The degree of salience of any of these is shown in the figure by the thickness of the box around A, B or C. In addition, the length of arrows linking the schema to its instantiations represents the 'elaborative distance' between schema and instantiation, or the amount of semantic specification required to form the instantiations, or, conversely, the amount of 'despecification' required to form the schema to link two instantiations.

In order to see this more clearly, consider the examples discussed by Tuggy (1993/2006: 176). In his analysis, Tuggy suggests that *aunt* ('parent's sister') is vague between the meanings 'father's sister' and 'mother's sister'. The schema linking these two is claimed to be easily retrievable and better established, i.e. more salient (as depicted in (e.)). The opposite is true, according to Tuggy, of *bank*,

3. As mentioned above, Langacker distinguishes between schemas and instantiations, which share all of the content of the schema but also have more specific content, and schemas and extensions, in which the structures linked by a schema share only part of its content. As this distinction does not impact the issue of ambiguity/vagueness, in what follows the term 'instantiation' will be taken to refer to both types (see Tuggy 1993/2006: 180–181, n7).

which is ambiguous between 'edge of river' and 'financial institution'. It is difficult to find a schema to link these two meanings, which are themselves firmly established (as depicted in (a.)).

What remains is to link this view of semantic structure and semantic relationships to a view of metonymy. Where do metonymic links come into the picture? In Langacker's view, metonymic extensions are often created through conventionalized patterns (2008: 250) that enable category extensions (like for *maple* in (5) and (6)). The types of relationships that are recognized as conceptual metonymies, like OBJECT FOR SUBSTANCE with *maple*, or PLACE FOR INSTITUTION[4] in (9) and (10), are wide-spread in many languages:

(9) Brussels will be able to grant permission to exceed limits in particular areas (12947)

(10) Beijing takes steps to tackle water shortages (11116)

In (9) and (10), the relevant semantic domain within which the metonymic relationship is established is described by Peirsman and Geeraerts (2006a) as 'action/event/process'. Within this domain, conventionalized and highly productive metonymies link agents, patients, locations, time and instruments (2006a 292). According to the authors, some basic domains (e.g. SPACE, TIME, etc.) provide access to a set of conventionalized pathways, or templates, for metonymic semantic change.

Given the Tuggy account, it may be expected that also metonymic semantic change can result in vagueness or ambiguity (1993/2006). Tuggy points out that both instantiation links and domain profiling extensions may give rise to the relationships outlined in the ambiguity-vagueness cline (1993/2006: 180–81, n.7). The question is whether metonymically changing categories will demonstrate ambiguity or vagueness or both. As Tuggy points out, the difference between ambiguity and vagueness lies, among other things, in the relative salience of the instantiations and the schema that links them. In the case of metonymic extensions based on conventionalized patterns, it seems safe to posit that, at least in categories that are undergoing change, the underlying schema must be salient. The reasoning is as follows: in referential metonymies, such as place name metonymies, reference-shifting usages necessitate access to a domain or domains in which the relevant semantic notion, e.g. PLACE, frequently occurs. That is, once a speaker recognizes a referential shift, s/he will look for interpretations based on knowledge of the

4. In the paper, the orthographic conventions of cognitive linguistics are followed. As a consequence, the names of cognitive structures such as domains, conventionalized metonymies, etc., are given in small CAPS.

domain and relevant conventionalized (e.g. metonymic) uses. This implies that the schema (here the metonymic pattern linked to its underlying domain) sanctioning a particular use will be salient, or cognitively prominent, which means that in such cases we might expect uses at the polysemy-vagueness end of the Tuggy cline.

In cases involving metonymic shifts, the schema linking the two meanings must be to some degree salient, or the referential shift will not be interpretable. In place name metonymies, two kinds of knowledge are needed: knowledge of the conventional metonymic patterns associated with PLACE, (schemas linking PLACE to something else, for instance an event), as well as real-world knowledge of, for instance, an institution or an event associated with the place named (i.e. What happened in Schengen and Kyoto?)

2.2 Domains and dimensions in metonymy

In their paper, Peirsman and Geeraerts (2006a) also provide a cognitive linguistic account in which metonymic shifts of meaning are a form of construal (see also Langacker 2008: 69–70). In their view, such shifts come about through the use of patterns of contiguity, many of which are conventionalized and not all of which involve shifts of reference. Moreover, the authors argue that metonymy constitutes a category of contiguity relationships with a prototype structure. Their contribution to the field is the proposed structure for the category, based on the analysis of an inventory of established metonymical relationships taken from the linguistics literature. Well known examples include WHOLE FOR PART as in (11)[5] and PRODUCER FOR PRODUCT in (12):

(11) Spain won the world cup.

(12) Are you sure you want to buy a Toyota?

In deriving the prototype structure of the metonymy category, Peirsman and Geeraerts (2006a) claim that all metonymic relationships can be situated in categorial space defined along two dimensions: strength of contact and boundedness. In keeping with the cognitive linguistic tradition, these dimensions are scalar, and the category is extended from a prototypical core through the process of extension along these two dimensions. For our purposes, the dimension of strength of contact is most relevant. The idea is that moving away from the center of the category represents a 'loosening' of contact, such that the strongest contact (the most prototypical type of contiguity) is 'part-whole' contiguity; a slightly

5. Examples (11)–(16) are constructed to illustrate the Peirsman and Geeraerts types (2006a,b)

weaker level of contact is involved at the level of 'containment', weaker contact yet is associated with 'contact', while the weakest degree of contact is found with contiguity involving 'adjacency'.

These are exemplified in (13)–(16):

(13) That's a purple lilac, not a white one. WHOLE FOR PART

(14) Can you pass the salt please? CONTENT FOR CONTAINER

(15) The West End attracts thousands of tourists each year. LOCATION FOR LOCATED

(16) The twin-set over there just spilled her tea. CLOTHING FOR PERSON

In (13), it is actually the blooms that are either purple or white, not the entire bush (whole – part), and in (14) it is clearly the salt shaker that must be passed (containment). In (15) it is the theaters that attract tourists (contact), and in (16), the twin-set is a person (adjacency).

The examples above demonstrate decreasing degrees of contact in a spatial domain. According to Peirsman and Geeraerts (2006a, 2006b), the same scalar dimensions apply also to metonymic patterns in the temporal domain, in the domain of actions, events and processes and in the domain of assemblies and collections. Thus the same prototypical structure is repeated in the various semantic domains in which metonymic patterns have become established. In this way, the Peirsman and Geeraerts approach incorporates an important role for the two dimensions, as well as the four domains in which they are found to operate. This account provides a sketch of the conventionalized metonymic pathways that are found in four basic domains, and a set of structured relationships between them.

In the previous paper using data from the NNC (Halverson & Engene 2010), the structure outlined for the domain of actions, events, and processes was adopted to describe the metonymic patterns found in the corpus data for *Schengen* and *Maastricht*. The model was able to exhaustively account for all of the occurrences of both of these place names in the data (N=767). In other words, all of the metonymic uses of these two place names represented previously posited relationships within the EVENT domain.

In the paper, it was also argued that knowledge of the EVENT domain was particularly important in the interpretation of compound uses and novel uses of metonymic place names. For instance, in interpreting uses such as *schengenmøter* 'Schengen meetings', *Schengen-visa* 'Schengen visa', or *Schengen-tabbe* 'Schengen mistake', a speaker must rely on knowledge of the conventional metonymies associated with places (e.g. PLACE FOR EVENT, PLACE FOR PARTICIPANT, PLACE FOR PRODUCT) as well as non-metonymic 'real world' knowledge of what actually happened in the place being named.

The Peirsman and Geeraerts approach provided additional leverage with regard to the *Schengen* and *Maastricht* data. In the previous paper, it was suggested that the prototypical structure might provide directionality for semantic development: movement away from the center of the category. On the dimension of strength of contact, this would mean that as a linguistic item acquires new uses, these may involve sequentially co-opting conventional patterns that are increasingly removed from the category center. In other words, it may be that later metonymic extensions utilize patterns in which the degree of contact is gradually decreasing. This was found to be the case in the diachronic development of *Schengen* in Norwegian.[6]

In Figure 2, the scalar dimension of 'strength of contact' is depicted, along with the metonymic extensions of *Schengen* found in the earlier analysis (Halverson & Engene 2010). The metonymic extensions are positioned at the relevant levels along the scalar dimension as they are manifested in the domain of actions, events and processes. The diachronic analysis showed that the frequency of the less prototypical patterns, in this case, TREATY FOR MEMBERS and TREATY FOR GEOGRAPHICAL SPACE CREATED BY TREATY grew over time.

STRENGTH OF CONTACT	METONYMIC PATTERN	EXTENSIONS FOR *SCHENGEN*
Part - whole		
↓		
Containment	PLACE FOR EVENT → EVENT FOR TREATY → TREATY FOR TREATY CONTENTS	
↓		↓
Contact		TREATY FOR TREATY EFFECT (GEOGRAPHICAL SPACE)
↓		↓
Adjacency	PLACE FOR PEOPLE PLACE FOR PRODUCT	TREATY FOR MEMBERS (MEMBERSHIP GROUP)

Figure 2. The Peirsman/Geeraerts 'strength of contact' dimension and metonymic extensions for *Schengen*

6. Halverson & Engene (2010) also included a diachronic analysis which utilized older data from the Atext archive in addition to the newspaper corpus data.

The issue of indeterminacy was also addressed in the study. It was hypothesized that indeterminate cases would involve metonymic patterns that were either at the same distance from the center of the category (at the same 'degree of contact') or that they would involve patterns that were at adjacent levels, for example involving part-whole and containment, or contact and adjacency (see Figure 2). In the analysis, evidence was presented for indeterminacy at the same level, though it was suggested that a more detailed analysis might confirm the uncertain evidence of the latter. This analysis is presented in Section 4.

3. Material and method

This section provides a description of the corpus data and the methods used for the analysis.

The data for this investigation was taken from the Norwegian Newspaper Corpus (http://avis.uib.no). This large, self expanding corpus contains the online versions of a number of major daily newspapers published in Norway. As outlined in Andersen & Hofland (this volume), the corpus includes a range of newspaper types, broadsheet and tabloid, regional and national, general and special business newspapers, and is highly representative of Norwegian newspaper language.

3.1 Material

The Norwegian Newspaper Corpus is divided into several chronologically delineated subcorpora. For this study, the subcorpus collected between 1 April 2005 and 31 December 2006 was selected. The total number of words in this subcorpus is 145,717,669, ranging across ten different online newspapers.

This particular subcorpus was selected on the basis of the time frame it covered, as this relates to political developments linked to the two places in question, i.e. Schengen and Kyoto. With regard to Schengen, the time frame is situated five years subsequent to Norway's implementation of the agreement signed in Schengen, Luxemburg. Norway signed the treaty in 1996, ratified it in 1997, and implemented it in 2001. Thus, in 2005–6, Norway was a decade away from the negotiation process and roughly five years past the initial implementation. With regard to Kyoto, on the other hand, the time span is different. While the Kyoto Protocol to the United Nations Framework Convention on Climate Change was negotiated in 1997 and ratified by Norway in May 2002, it was not implemented until February 2005. Thus the agreement was a brand new political reality for Norway in 2005. In other words, with regard to the Norwegian news coverage in the period from 2005–2006, the Kyoto Protocol was just coming into effect, while the Schengen Agreement had been so for almost five years.

The search strings used were right-truncated matches of *Schengen* and *Kyoto*, respectively. The data include both simplex instances and compounds in which *Schengen* or *Kyoto* is the first element. The reasoning behind identification and classification of the compound instances is discussed in Section 3.2.

In cleaning up the data prior to analysis, instances in which the same text, verbatim, was included in two newspapers on the same date were removed. These double cites are the results of different newspapers taking the same text from a news agency, and are thus considered two instances of the same usage. The total number of hits for each was as shown in Table 1. The Schengen data are taken from Halverson & Engene (2010).

Table 1. Occurrences of *Schengen* and *Kyoto* in subcorpus (row percentages)

Place name	Simplex	%	Compound	%	Total	%
Schengen	176	26	512	74	688	100
Kyoto	192	15	1129	85	1321	100
Total	368		1641		2009	

In the analysis of the *Schengen* material presented in Halverson & Engene (2010), the KWIC concordances used the default setting of 40 characters left and 50 right. As context can be important in disambiguating some of the instances, in this analysis the concordance range was increased to 75 characters left and right. All of the vague occurrences in the *Schengen* data were extracted again from the corpus with the expanded co-text. Of the original 74 vague occurrences, five were disambiguated, and all of them involved the same context (… *hull i Schengen* 'hole in Schengen'). Of the remaining 69, nine were analyzed differently in the new contextual environment, and 7 lost potential readings, while still remaining vague between two readings. One instance was more vague (it gained a potential reading), and one was coded differently. The same procedure was followed with the Kyoto data, though in this case, all metonymic uses were analyzed with a window of 75 characters left and right.

Of course, the question arises of whether the vagueness found in these instances could be eliminated through readings of larger stretches of text, or the entire texts in which the occurrences were found. As expanding the co-text here has had some analytical consequences, this is an important issue. Overall, however, the number of vague cases eliminated was marginal (roughly 4 percent). For the purposes of this investigation, the expanded concordance data will thus be considered adequate. In further work, a more contextualized method would provide a valuable supplement to this analysis.

3.2 Method

As mentioned in Section 2, the Peirsman and Geeraerts approach (2006a, 2006b) to metonymy does not restrict metonymy to cases of involving reference only. In this investigation, however, the metonymies are referential, and as a consequence, substitution tests are used for the purposes of identification and classification. In the first case, a metonymy is identified in cases where the place name does not refer to the city in question, i.e. Schengen, Luxemburg or Kyoto, Japan. For the purposes of classification, the method used in Halverson & Engene (2010), originally adapted from Markert & Nissim (2003a, 2003b), is also adopted here. In short, this method builds on a set of substitution tests using paraphrases. For example, in (17), Kyoto could be replaced by 'the treaty that was signed in Kyoto':

(17) *Mange bedrifter har skiftet holdning og lobbyerer nå for Kyoto.* (DA060907)
Many companies have now changed their view and are lobbying for Kyoto/ the treaty that was signed in Kyoto.

Figure 3 shows the range of metonymic patterns identified in the place name data studied earlier (Markert & Nissim 2003a, 2003b). The metonymies identified in the *Schengen* data in the earlier study are those in category IIB4. The substitution tests for each specific type and an example from the NNC data (in italics) are also given. Not all categories were represented in the data.

One of the analytical categories requires further elaboration at this point: category B4, or PLACE FOR EVENT/TREATY. In the earlier analysis of the *Schengen* data, this category was described as a compression of a metonymic chain involving PLACE FOR EVENT and then EVENT FOR RESULT. It was argued that the final reading, PLACE FOR TREATY, is only accessible through non-metonymic real-world knowledge of what actually happened at the place that is named, i.e. what the specific event was (see also Markert & Nissim 2006: 152). In the *Schengen* data, there were no instances of PLACE FOR EVENT; every metonymic use of *Schengen* included at least this initial compressed metonymy. In analyzing the *Kyoto* data, however, it appears that there are instances that are vague between a PLACE FOR EVENT and the chained PLACE FOR EVENT + EVENT FOR RESULT (i.e. PLACE FOR TREATY). Thus in the *Kyoto* data, it is necessary to allow for this possibility.

Compounds in which the first element was *Schengen*- or *Kyoto*- were classified using the scheme in Figure 3, and the substitution tests were applied in the same manner as with the simplex occurrences. In other words, the compound was the unit that was tested in the substitution test. This is in line with Markert & Nissim (2006: 156), in which coding is determined by the semantics of the head word in phrases. So, for example, in (18), *Kyoto*-årene is classified as an instance

I Literal

A Place line (in newspaper texts), general place reference

for de 500 innbyggerne i Schengen i Luxembourg (BT050709)

for the 500 residents of Schengen in Luxembourg

B Specific place reference (Schengen-avtalen, Schengen-traktaten)

rundt 5 år etter Schengen-avtalen trådte i kraft (AP060203)

about 5 years after the Schengen Agreement went into effect

II Metonymic

A General

A1 Object for name

A2 Object for representation

B Class-specific (location)

B1 Place for product

B2 Place for people

B2a Capital for government

B2b Place for officials (individual or group)

B2c Place for population (majority of)

B2d Place for persons (identifiable subgroup)

B3 Place for organization (originating from or residing in)

B4 Place for event (treaty?)

Test: "event that took place in x"

Test: "treaty that was signed in x"

Under Blair var de uenige om ICC, om Kyoto, om Midtøsten (AP060420)

Under Blair they disagreed about the ICC, about Kyoto, about the Middle East

B4a Place for treaty contents

Test: "provisions/clauses/articles/principles/mechanisms/implications of treaty signed in x"

en kontroll med Schengenregisteret avslørte at han var (AP051230)

checking the Schengen register revealed that he had been

B4b Place for membership, member countries

Test: "membership group or member countries of treaty signed in x"

Britene er nemlig ikke med Schengen-samarbeidet (VG060515)

The British are actually not part of the Schengen group.

B4c Place for geographical area

Test: "geographical area created by treaty signed in x"

er de automatisk nektet visum i Schengen (DB060510)

they are automatically denied a visa in Schengen

C Other

Word play, personification

III Mixed

SIS (Schengens informasjonssystem)

Schengens informasjonssystem skal oversees (AP0600516)

The Schengen information system is to be monitored

IV Other, uninterpretable

Eller forsøke å analysere Schengendyrets vanskelige luner. (DB050805)

Or attempt to analyse the difficult moods of the Schengen animal.

Figure 3. Classification scheme

of PLACE FOR TREATY CONTENTS, as 'the Kyoto years' may be replaced by 'the X (years) implied/specified by the treaty signed in Kyoto'.

(18) *I disse dager arbeider både EU og Norge med kvotesystemet for Kyoto-årene.* (DN061122)
Both the EU and Norway are currently working on a quota system for the Kyoto years.

And in (19), *Schengen-området* is classified as an instance of PLACE FOR GEOGRAPHICAL AREA, as the compound may be replaced by, 'the geographical area created by the treaty signed in Schengen'.

(19) *å bære for innbyggerne i flere av Schengen-områdets naboland i øst.* (DA060425)
to carry for residents of the Schengen area's neighbor countries to the east.

This classification entails that with some of the compounds, the substitution tests actually operate on nouns (e.g. *Kyoto*-årene or *Schengeregisteret* above) which are more specific than the substitution tests can capture. This is tolerated here, as what is actually being classified is the recruitment of the metonymical pattern in the extension process, and not the specific semantic content of the head or the semantics of the relationship between the two elements of the compound.[7]

Compounds in which the second element was *-avtale, -protokoll, -traktat* (agreement, protocol, treaty) were not considered metonymic (Type IB in the classification scheme in Figure 3), as they include specific reference to 'treaty' or 'agreement' and the place name reference does not involve a referential shift. In all other compounds, however, the first element is not a reference to a city, and no reference to 'treaty' is made. These occurrences thus build on at least the PLACE FOR EVENT/TREATY.

The analytical framework developed in Halverson and Engene (2010) was used for the analysis of the *Kyoto* data also. One small clarification is required, however, due to differences in the realities to which the words refer. First, the specific extension of *Schengen* to refer to a geographical area (B4c) is not evidenced with *Kyoto*. We recall that the purpose of the Schengen Agreement was to establish a common external border, which then has consequences for travel and immigration control. The Kyoto Protocol, on the other hand, determines quotas for the emission of greenhouse gases, among other things, and it is not to be expected that the issue of geographical space will be utilized. However, the extension pattern underlying

7. The role of the underlying domain in interpretation of compounds is discussed in Halverson and Engene (2010: 14–15). Clearly the semantic relationships in compounds such as these merits a more detailed investigation in its own right.

this usage TREATY FOR TREATY EFFECT (see Section 2, Figure 2) was also found in the *Kyoto* data; it is just that the treaty effects (in the real world) are different.[8] Thus the classification scheme was still applicable, though the manifestation of the metonymy relationship is slightly different.

As mentioned in the introduction, the earlier study revealed a number of instances in which more than one interpretation was possible. These cases were identified when more than one of the substitution tests resulted in a plausible reading. In the current investigation, these occurrences are the main focus, and the aim is to see exactly how vagueness is manifested in the data, i.e. how vagueness is related to domain knowledge and conventionalized metonymic patterns. To do so, these instances are classified according to the combinations of metonymies the instance allows. Thus a combination of PLACE FOR MEMBERSHIP and PLACE FOR GEOGRAPHICAL AREA, such as (4), would be one type. A combination of PLACE FOR TREATY and TREATY FOR CONTENTS, as in the compound in (20), constitutes another type.

(20) … *i regjeringens egen beskrivelse av Schengen-samarbeidet* (NL 060210)
in the government's own description of the Schengen agreement/program/provisions

A total of eight different combinations were found in the data, and these are given in Table 2, with examples from the NNC. The names of the metonymic patterns are as given in Table 2:

The order of categories is such that the identification number also, very coarsely, represents movement away from the center of the metonymy category. Thus types 1 and 2 involve patterns which are closer to prototypical metonymy than are 7 and 8 along the dimension of 'strength of contact'. The type numbers are not ranks however; thus category 6 is not necessarily 6 increments away from the category center. The ordering is merely intended as a heuristic.

The classification into combination types, or vagueness categories, will allow for the investigation of whether there are certain types that are more predominant than others, for instance whether more or less prototypical metonymies predominate (research question 1), and whether the distribution of types is the same in a sense category that is just beginning to develop as it is in one that has been developing for a number of years (research question 2).

8. It is entirely possible that EFFECT metonymies could become established for *Kyoto* as well, depending on the communicative needs of Norwegian speakers. Such uses would necessarily refer to the effects of the Kyoto Protocol, for instance standards, emission targets etc., rather than the geographical area created by the Schengen Agreement.

Table 2. Multiple readings: combinations found in data

Number	Readings	Examples
1	EVENT/TREATY	*Det er og blir regjeringens ansvar å innfri kravene fra Kyoto.* (AA060122). *It is the government's responsibility to meet the requirements of Kyoto.*
2	TREATY/TREATY CONTENTS	*Kyoto kunne ikke reddet New Orleans fra Katrina.* (DB060906). *Kyoto could not have saved New Orleans from Katrina.*
3	TREATY/TREATY MEMBERS	*Norge knyttet seg til Schengen-samarbeidet* (NL060210). *Norway joined the Schengen agreement/group*
4	TREATY CONTENTS/ TREATY MEMBERS	*De er begge med i Schengen-samarbeidet, EU-landenes politi- og* (AP050805). *They are both part of the Schengen cooperation, the EU police*
5	TREATY/TREATY CONTENTS/TREATY MEMBERS	*SV og SP vil at Norge skal tre ut av Schengen-samarbeidet.* (AP050927). *SV and SP want Norway to withdraw from the Schengen Agreement/ccooperation/group*
6	TREATY/TREATY MEMBERS/ GEOGRAPHICAL AREA	*Et enormt dataregister innenfor Schengen* (BT051028). *An enormous database within Schengen*
7	TREATY CONTENTS/ TREATY MEMBERS/ GEOGRAPHICAL AREA	*Og utvidelsen av Schengen er dårlig nytt* (DA060430). *And the expansion of Schengen is bad news*
8	TREATY MEMBERS/ GEOGRAPHICAL AREA	*Norge er i Schengen.* (DB060505). *Norway is in Schengen.*

4. Results and discussion

This section presents the analysis of the corpus data and a discussion of the results.

4.1 Results

Using the classification scheme given in Figure 3, all instances of *Schengen* and *Kyoto* in the 2005–06 subcorpus were classified. The overall figures are given in Table 3, and the vague uses are counted as instances of each plausible metonymy. Again, the *Schengen* data is from Halverson & Engene (2010).

As is shown in Table 3, *Schengen* is used predominately metonymically, while the reverse is true for *Kyoto* (78% vs. 11%). *Schengen* demonstrates a range of metonymic uses, with three of the main metonymies each accounting for roughly one quarter of the total number of occurrences. All of the metonymies

Table 3. Metonymic uses of *Schengen* and *Kyoto* (column percentages)

	Schengen	%	*Kyoto*	%
Non-metonymic uses	77	11	1,047	78
PLACE FOR EVENT/TREATY	76	11	99	7
PLACE FOR TREATY CONTENTS	181	26	36	3
PLACE FOR MEMBERS	168	24	22	2
PLACE FOR EFFECT OF TREATY	172	25	114	9
Other (also mixed and uninterpretable)	14	2	17	1
TOTAL	688	99	1,335	100

were also found with *Kyoto*, though the frequencies were much lower: from 2–9 percent.

It was mentioned in the introduction that an earlier study found that roughly 10 percent of the *Schengen* occurrences were indeterminate. The later analysis of the *Kyoto* data revealed that 28 instances were indeterminate, of a total of 274, which is also about 10 percent. Thus the two place names demonstrate a similar overall degree of vagueness in this data.

The distribution of the various combinations of multiple readings in the *Schengen* and *Kyoto* data is given in Table 4. The vagueness categories (numbered 1–8) are as outlined in Table 2.

For *Schengen*, there is a relatively even spread across the most prevalent combinations, which are found in second, third and eighth categories PLACE FOR TREATY/TREATY CONTENTS (19%), PLACE FOR TREATY/TREATY MEMBERS (24%)

Table 4. Vagueness categories (column and row percentages)

Vagueness type	*Schengen*	%	*Kyoto*	%	Total	%
1. EVENT/TREATY	0	0	13	46	13	14
2. TREATY/TREATY CONTENTS	13	19	11	39	24	25
3. TREATY/TREATY MEMBERS	16	24	2	7	18	19
4. TREATY CONTENTS/TREATY MEMBERS/	5	7	1	4	6	6
5. TREATY/TREATY CONTENTS/ TREATY MEMBERS	6	9	0	0	6	6
6. TREATY/TREATY MEMBERS/ GEOGRAPHICAL AREA	3	4	0	0	3	3
7. TREATY CONTENTS/TREATY MEMBERS/ GEOGRAPHICAL AREA	1	2	0	0	1	1
8. TREATY MEMBERS/GEOGRAPHICAL AREA	24	36	1	4	25	26
Total	68	100	28	100		

and PLACE FOR TREATY MEMBERS/GEOGRAPHICAL AREA (36%). There are very few instances in each of the other five categories. Each of these three most frequent types allows for only two possible interpretations; all of the less frequent types involved three potential readings.

In the *Kyoto* data, the first two indeterminacy types (PLACE FOR EVENT/TREATY, PLACE FOR TREATY/TREATY CONTENTS) account for 85% of the data. The other six types either do not occur (5, 6, and 7) or occur very rarely (3, 4, and 8). Both of the first two types involve two possible readings only.

The overall picture that emerges here is that the vagueness shown in this dataset seems concentrated in categories 1, 2, 3 and 8. The distribution is very different for the two place names, however. The vagueness associated with *Schengen* involves domain knowledge related to EVENT, PARTICIPANT, and EFFECT, while with *Kyoto* only domain knowledge related to EFFECT is found. In both cases, the non domain-specific conventionalized CONTAINER FOR CONTENT (here TREATY FOR TREATY CONTENTS) metonymy results in vagueness. Thus, in this data, the place name with the broadest range of different metonymical meanings also has the broadest variation in vagueness types among them. The place name which is least metonymical, though it shows evidence of developing metonymical senses, also demonstrates a narrower range of types of vagueness. There is clearly a relationship between the range of meanings (types of metonymies) and the range of vagueness types here.

The patterns straddle different levels in the Peirsman and Geeraerts model of metonymic relationships illustrated in Figure 4. The vagueness in the *Kyoto* data involves metonymic patterns close to category center (the hatched rings numbered 1 and 2), while the vagueness found in the *Schengen* data involves metonymic patterns that are increasingly distant from the center (the rings marked 2, 3 and 8).

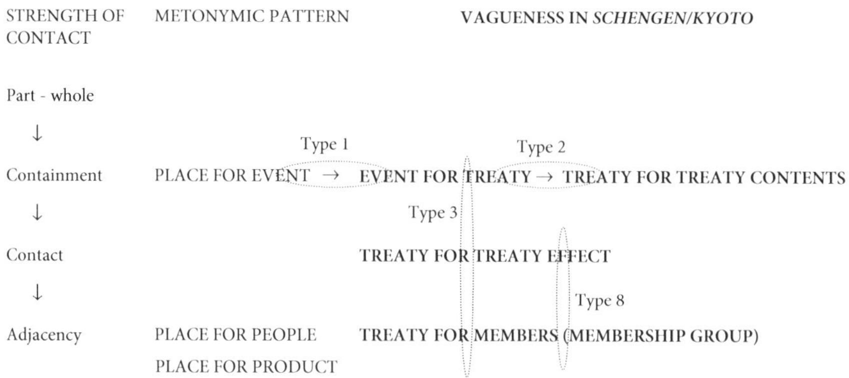

Figure 4. Vagueness types in *Schengen/Kyoto*

Note also that the vagueness in this data involves metonymic patterns at the 'same' level within the category (types 1 and 2) and at different levels (for example types 3 and 8). These patterns will be further discussed in Section 4.2.

4.2 Discussion

In Section 2, it was argued on theoretical grounds that in metonymic extension, the underlying sanctioning schema must be salient enough that indeterminate instances should be considered vague, rather than ambiguous, in Tuggy's (1993/2006) terms. The aim of the present study was to consider two metonymic place names to see whether a more detailed description of corpus evidence might lend further insight into the manifestation of vagueness in developing semantic categories. The analysis of the Norwegian Newspaper Corpus data highlights one interesting feature of semantic development. For the *Schengen* and *Kyoto* data, which involve metonymic extension, the most elaborate category (*Schengen*) is also the one with the most even distribution of types of vagueness. The least developed category (*Kyoto*), on the other hand, is vague in a more limited way. It would seem that in metonymic semantic change, in which underlying domain knowledge is salient and provides a template for extension, accruing new meanings also involves vagueness. If we visualize semantic change in terms of a liquid flow from the center to the periphery of the model in Figure 4, we could say that vagueness, in this data, pools, or collects, where metonymic senses are becoming established.

It may be helpful at this point to recall the political reality that these two place names were being developed to refer to in the 2005–6 period. As mentioned in the introduction, the Schengen Agreement had been in effect for several years, and several of its provisions were in effect and had tangible consequences for travelers in Europe, such as Schengen zones in airports, the physical barriers erected around port facilities, police collaboration on immigration, etc. Specific events involving member countries were frequently reported in the newspapers in the time frame in question. On the other hand, the Kyoto Protocol brought new issues to the attention of the Norwegian public, and the focus was still on the political process through which the treaty was created and the potential effects it might have. It is perhaps not surprising, then, that *Kyoto* was developing new meanings to refer to the negotiation process or its result (the protocol), as in (21) as well as potential treaty effects, as in (22):

(21) … *kan bestrides hvis en tar hensyn til kravene til forurensning etter Kyoto* (DA060301)
…can be contested, considering pollution requirements after Kyoto

(22) … *at Norge skal klare sine Kyoto-mål om å redusere utslippene til bare en prosent over 1990 nivå* (DB051207)
… that Norway shall meet its Kyoto goal of reducing emissions to only one percent over the 1990 level…

While the interplay of semantic extension and vagueness is perhaps not surprising, it is useful to find it demonstrated in corpus data. Moreover, it is interesting to see vagueness associated with domain knowledge and metonymical templates. Further research might be more specifically targeted to test whether certain (more prototypical?) metonymical patterns, CONTAINER/CONTENT, PART-WHOLE are more conducive to vagueness than others, or whether comprehensive use of metonymic extension, such as that found for *Schengen*, is regularly accompanied by vagueness.

More interesting, perhaps, is a comparison of *Schengen* and *Kyoto* as instances of metonymic extension at different stages of development. Due to political developments, *Schengen* had been undergoing semantic development for several years, while *Kyoto* was just emerging. In comparing the two, we have already seen that the overall instance of vagueness in the data is roughly the same at 10 percent. However, we also saw in Figure 4 that the main types of vagueness demonstrated by the two place names were situated at different levels within the Peirsman and Geeraerts model of metonymical relationships. As demonstrated by the numbered ellipses, vagueness types 1 and 2 involve primarily relationships at the level of 'containment'; that is, relationships that are closer to prototypical metonymy. The vagueness types that dominated for Schengen, on the other hand, were also situated at less central levels (3 and 8), and involved metonymic patterns at the same level of contiguity and at adjacent levels. It would appear that the more established category also demonstrated what might be effects of a 'loosening of contact'.

At first blush, it might seem that using a model of metonymy as such to hypothesize about the specifics of semantic development in a lexical category represents a category error. However, it is not the metonymy category that is of primary interest. What is actually being suggested is that the directionality provided by the Peirsman and Geeraerts model (e.g. along the dimension of 'strength of contact') is reflected in diachronic change. It does not seem so far-fetched to suggest that, within any given semantic domain, for instance EVENT; early extensions might involve more prototypical part-whole relationships, while later ones might enlist templates built on more peripheral relationships, such as PLACE FOR PARTICIPANT.

This notion remains speculative at present, particularly given the obvious limitations of this data. Only two lexical items in one language were studied. However, even these limited findings suggest areas for further study. Given this, admittedly limited, evidence that semantic development shows evidence of center-periphery directionality, then it seems reasonable, given the apparent link between semantic development and vagueness mentioned above, to hypothesize that also the manifestation of vagueness will show the same directionality effects. This merits further empirical investigation.

5. Concluding remarks

It is important to remember that in both the *Schengen* and the *Kyoto* data, vagueness was only found in roughly 10 percent of the metonymic cases. Moreover, the figures overall are quite low, with only 28 instances of vagueness for *Kyoto* and 68 for *Schengen*. In the other cases, the metonymic senses were more readily identified, and these occurrences constitute the bulk of the data. Given the limitations of the data and the exploratory aims of the investigation, no statistical analyses were carried out. In future work, more targeted analyses should aim at testing hypotheses such as the following, which emerge from the present analysis:

1. In category extension through metonymy, vagueness occurs in the data where new meanings are being established through the recruitment of conventionalized metonymic patterns and domain knowledge.
2. Category extension through metonymy follows Peirsman and Geeraerts' directionality diachronically. This implies that vagueness will be found at more central levels in new categories, and at more peripheral levels in older ones.

The present study provides corpus-based analyses of vagueness in metonymic change. Even though the full benefits of large-scale corpus analysis are not exploited in this study,[9] the accretion of other studies, in other languages, would further illuminate the types of questions posed here. As it happens, vagueness was not very prevalent in this data. However, its behavior is illuminated in corpus-based studies which can generate hypotheses and provide further insight into current theoretical frameworks. This study involves the investigation of over 2,000 instances of *Schengen* and *Kyoto*, and illustrates that the Peirsman and Geeraerts model (2006a) can exhaustively account for the range of senses that these two place names have developed. The same model can capture interesting characteristics of semantic development over time. These findings are only sufficient to warrant further investigation of these and related questions, however, and are not conclusive. It may be hoped that future work may shed additional light on these issues.

9. For instance, the precise dating of all occurrences in this corpus would enable a micro-level diachronic analysis. This was deemed to be beyond the scope of the present study, whose aims were of a different type.

References

Halverson, Sandra & Engene, Jan Oskar. 2010. Domains and dimensions in metonymy: a corpus-based analysis of *Schengen* and *Maastricht. Metaphor and Symbol* 25(1): 1–18.

Langacker, Ronald. 1987/1991. *Foundations of Cognitive Grammar.* Vols. I & II. Stanford CA: Stanford University Press.

Langacker, Ronald. 2008. *Cognitive Grammar. A Basic Introduction.* Oxford: OUP.

Markert, Katja and Nissim, Malvina. 2003a. Corpus-based metonymy analysis. *Metaphor and Symbol,* 18(3): 175–188.

Markert, Katja & Nissim, Malvina. 2003b. Annotation scheme for metonymies (AS1). ⟨http://www.cogsci.ed.ac.uk/~malvi/mascara/scheme.public.pdf⟩ (October 24, 2007).

Markert, Katja & Nissim, Malvina. 2006. Metonymic proper names. A corpus-based account. In *Corpus-based Approaches to Metaphor and Metonymy,* Anatol Stefanowitsch & Stephan T. Gries (eds), 152–174. Berlin: Mouton de Gruyter.

Peirsman, Yves & Geeraerts, Dirk. 2006a. Metonymy as a prototypical category. *Cognitive Linguistics* 17(3): 269–316.

Peirsman, Yves & Geeraerts, Dirk. 2006b. Don't let metonymy be misunderstood. An answer to Croft. *Cognitive Linguistics* 17(3): 327–335.

Tuggy, David. 2006. Ambiguity, polysemy and vagueness. In *Cognitive Linguistics. Basic Readings,* Dirk Geeraerts (ed), 167–184. Berlin: Mouton de Gruyter. (Originally published in 1993 in Cognitive *linguistics* 4(3): 273–290).

Spatial metaphors in present-day Norwegian newspaper language

Leiv Egil Breivik & Toril Swan
University of Bergen / University of Tromsø

"We map our moods onto a vertical, spatial schema, with the good end 'up' and the bad end 'down.'"[1]

The present investigation is a continuation and extension of our previous work on Norwegian OPP/NED ('up/down') metaphors; cf. Swan & Breivik (2005) and Swan (2010). The investigation will be conducted within the framework of cognitive linguistics. Our primary concern will be with Norwegian OPP/NED metaphors. The use of spatial words such as *høy* 'high', *lav* 'low', *topp* 'top', *bunn* 'bottom', *over* 'over' and *under* 'under' will be shown to support Lakoff (1987; *inter alia*) and Taylor (1995); the concepts *oppe/høyt* 'up/high' on the whole have positive associations, whereas the associations of *nede/lav* 'down/low' are negative. This of course mirrors one of the main tenets of cognitive theory, namely that language reflects experience. We will focus on two issues. Firstly, Norwegian uses the spatial words in question less in their concrete meaning than as metaphors; why should this be the case if the concrete use is basic and anterior? Secondly, the frequency of the *opp*-words seems to be lower than the *ned*-words. Our Norwegian data will be drawn from the Norwegian Newspaper Corpus.

1. Introduction

This article explores some spatial metaphors in Norwegian newspaper language from a cognitive perspective. We thus assume that metaphors are an integrated part of human language and thinking, and that meaning change may happen via extensions from a core or prototypical meaning (cf. Geeraerts 1997; Taylor 1995, 2003; Traugott & Dasher 2000: 6–16). Our purpose is to show that in Norwegian newspaper language, the spatial metaphors studied here are used far more frequently than the corresponding concrete terms. In Section 2, we

1. Daniel Casasanto of the Max Planck Institute for Psycholinguistics, Nijmegen. Quoted from Ananthaswamy 2010: 8.

discuss some of those cognitive tenets and concepts that are relevant for metaphor studies, focusing on image schemas, in particular the UP/DOWN schema. We then proceed to present and discuss data from the Norwegian Newspaper Corpus in Section 3. Finally, Section 4 sums up our most important findings and provides conclusions arising from the findings and discussion of the previous sections.

2. Cognitive views on language

Cognitive linguists generally make the assumption that language is a product of human beings in interaction and, crucially, that language is based on human experience (cf. Gibbs 1996, 2006; Heine 1997; Langacker 1987/1991, 1995; Lakoff 1987; Lakoff 2008; *inter alia*). Thus meaning is identified with mental experience and our conceptions, not with truth values.

The claim that language reflects experience is indeed a matter of importance in cognitive (or conceptual) metaphor theory. The term *conceptual metaphor* refers to patterns of conceptual association (Grady 2007) rather than to individual metaphorical items. In other words, we must distinguish conceptual metaphors (which structure thought) from their linguistic realizations. An example of a conceptual metaphor is UNHAPPY IS DOWN, which has various possible realizations such as *She is far down, He's depressed* and *Don't be downhearted,* etc. Linguistic metaphors, then, represent instantiations of pre-existing conceptual 'mappings' between concept domains, which explains how we manage to process them so simply and quickly as it appears we do. In brief, then, the main claim is that metaphors are an integral part of language, and that thought and language function metaphorically.

While undoubtedly many conceptual metaphors are culturally grounded and determined, there are also metaphors that derive from physical, bodily experiences, and via *image schemas* which may possibly be universal, as shown in many works by Johnson and Lakoff, particularly Johnson (1987); Lakoff (1987); and Lakoff & Johnson (1980; cf. also Feldman 2006; Gibbs 2006; Hampe 2005). Note, however, that although bodies, brains, and bodily experiences are common to all human beings, how we interpret and deal with these bodily experiences is often a matter of culture. Feldman (2006: 200ff) suggests that the metaphor system is grounded in the body in terms of what he calls *primary metaphors* (Grady 1996), for instance AFFECTION IS WARMTH and HAPPY IS UP or HAPPY IS MORE. In the present article, then, it is assumed that there exists a limited set of image schemas which are used to structure experience metaphorically and that it is via the basic image schemas we conceptualize abstract categories and phenomena. According to Gibbs, "Image schemas emerge throughout sensimotor activity as we manipulate objects, orient ourselves spatially and temporally, and direct our perceptual focus" (1996: 316).

Thus the image schemas are so deeply founded in human experience that they must be considered a species of universal, prelinguistic, cognitive structures. As suggested above, most of these schemas derive from our most basic and immediate experiences, i.e. our experience of ourselves as bodies and how these bodies function and fit into the space in which we move, and as such underlie metaphorical language to a great extent. For instance, we live in a world of gravity, and this may be seen as the basis of the highly pervasive UP/DOWN schema which is the concern of the present article. Interestingly, Lakoff's work has in recent years been supported by findings in neurology, psychology, and biology. For an overview of such work, see Ananthaswamy (2010) and Lakoff (2008).

The spatial aspect of language that is our particular concern here, then, is vertical spatiality, i.e. the UP/DOWN image schema. Clearly, one of the most salient experiences of human beings is our experience of being bodies in space with gravity, and thus our experience of space and especially up or down movement would seem to be quite basic. As babies we are by necessity down most of the time, we are lifted up and put down again. Even as adults we perceive and experience gravity and space in numerous ways involving up and down. Not unexpectedly, studies show that "the concepts linked in English with the words *up* and *down* appear very early in children's speech, and are used very frequently [...]. At first, these words apply predominantly to the movements of the child's body [...]" (Wierzbicka 1996: 59).

Recently, work in psychology seems to confirm that there is a connection between this type of physical experience and emotional responses (cf. for instance Meier & Robinson 2004). The question is to what extent this bodily, and apparently very basic, experience is reflected linguistically. In English, there is evidence that metaphorical extensions exist which are orientational (cf. Lakoff & Johnson 1980: 14–21) and correspond to the UP/DOWN image schema, i.e. that good and positive is up and bad and negative is down. We will be concerned with orientational metaphors in the UP/DOWN image schema, which involves perpendicular spatial orientation within a gravitational field. Concepts (and linguistic items) related to this schema include for instance Norwegian *høy/lav* 'high/low', *opp(e)/ned(e)* 'up/down', *over/under* 'over/under' as well as verbs such as *løfte/senke* 'lift/lower'.

According to Taylor (2003: 136–138; cf. also Taylor 1995: 136), there are at least three major conceptual metaphors in English which involve the UP/DOWN schema: the domain of quantity (UP IS MORE/LESS IS DOWN), the domain of evaluation (UP IS GOOD/DOWN IS BAD), and the domain of control (UP IS POWER /DOWN IS POWERLESSNESS). In the present article, we will assume two general conceptual metaphors, viz. that of quantity (UP IS MORE/DOWN IS LESS) and that of evaluation (UP IS POSITIVE EVALUATION/DOWN IS NEGATIVE EVALUATION). Subsumed under these there will be subschemas. For instance, specific cases of UP IS POSITIVE EVALUATION could be UP IS BETTER or UP IS RIGHT, referring to higher status or high morals respectively. Mental states will also be included in the evaluative metaphor (UP IS HAPPY), etc. Examples are given in (1)–(2).

(1) UP IS MORE/DOWN IS LESS
  a. She paid a high price for that house.
  b. Unemployment figures rose in 2001.

(2) UP IS POSITIVE EVALUATION/DOWN IS NEGATIVE EVALUATION
  a. Her low morals appalled everyone.
  b. I am feeling down.
  c. Only his high status prevented his arrest.

So in general, for all domains, it is claimed that the states and perspectives associated with being *up* are positive, while those associated with being *down* are negative. However, in the case of the UP IS MORE metaphor, the quantity aspect is more important than the evaluation *per se*, although it is generally the case that more is also good. Given our experiences (especially in childhood) of being bodies in a space with gravity, this tendency is plausible and not unexpected (cf. Lakoff & Johnson 1980: 14; Lakoff 1987: 275 ff.). There are, of course, methodological problems involved in studies of most orientational metaphors; consider for instance the enormous variety of uses of a word like *up*. However, despite methodological problems, it is important to study metaphorical extensions crosslinguistically, as many linguists have noted (cf. Yu 1998).[2]

To sum up, then, we assume that metaphors are an integral part of language, and that thought and language function metaphorically. We also assume that there exist image schemas which are used to structure experience metaphorically and that it is via the basic image schemas we conceptualize abstract categories and phenomena. Finally, we posit that the original domains of UP, DOWN, LOW, etc. are concrete spatial locations or measures, on the basis of which metaphorical meanings develop. These meanings are not secondary cognitively, but we have access to them via physical experience.

2. Obviously there are also problems with the present metaphor analysis; cf. e.g. Croft & Cruse 2004: 193 ff.; Grady 1997; Jackendoff & Aaron 1991; Taylor 2002: 487 ff. Some of these are well known, for instance the technical problem involved in selecting correct superordinate categories and domains. It has been pointed out that it is easy to end up with a counterintuitive extension of the class of metaphor. Neverthelesss, the cognitive analysis explains many phenomena which otherwise are difficult to explain coherently.

3. The UP/DOWN schema in Norwegian newspaper language

The concept of being (high) up or (low) down may of course be realized in language in a variety of ways. In the present article, we have chosen to explore a small selection of linguistic forms which belong to the UP/DOWN schema, viz. the absolutes *høy/lav* and the comparatives *høyere/lavere* 'high/low/higher/lower' (the superlative *høyest* is not included), as well as four verbs referring to rising or falling, i.e. movement along the vertical dimension: *stige/synke* 'rise/fall' and *løfte/senke* 'lift/lower'. Note that the absolutes *høy* 'high' and *lav* 'low' also include their neuter forms *høyt/lavt* as well as the definite or plural forms *høye/lave*. For each of the above-mentioned words, 300 examples from the Norwegian Newspaper Corpus were randomly selected from the periods 2005–2006 and 2007–2010 (up to 16 June 2010), 50 from each year, constituting a total of 2,400 examples.[3] This sample will be subjected to a closer analysis in the subsequent sections. For the sake of convenience, we will refer to the linguistic metaphors in our data simply as metaphors, although as noted in Section 2, conceptual and linguistic metaphors must be distinguished. Table 1 shows the total number of occurrences of the relevant linguistic forms in the two periods under investigation. The data in Table 1 will provide a background for our analysis.

Table 1. Total number of occurrences of UP/DOWN items in the two parts of the Norwegian Newspaper Corpus examined (2005–2006 and 2007–2010)

Year / Type	2005	2006	2007	2008	2009	2010	Total
Høy	7,995	9,634	8,216	10,780	8,216	4,004	48,845
Høyere	8,077	10,033	8,607	11,660	8,836	4,377	51,590
Lav	2,926	3,638	3,258	4,029	3,373	1,798	19,022
Lavere	5,112	6,116	4,942	8,063	6,355	3,059	33,647
Stige	1,478	1,759	1,587	2,231	1,912	867	9,834
Synke	356	476	540	634	525	209	2,740
Løfte	1,424	1,600	1,610	1,967	1,727	637	8,955
Senke	682	788	808	1,133	865	418	4,694
Total	28,050	34,044	29,568	40,497	31,809	15,369	179,327

3. The verbs *løfte* and *stige* have homonymous nouns, meaning 'promise' and 'ladder' respectively. Such nouns were removed from the initial random samples and replaced by an equal number of verbs.

The examples are analysed in terms of being used metaphorically or non-metaphorically (i.e. concretely/literally), and we also look at idioms used in our newspaper data. However, although we distinguish between metaphorical and non-metaphorical (concrete) instantiations, we do not (following Gibbs 1994 and Grady 2007) consider these categories as in any way clearly delimited. As we will show below, the proportion of what we might call completely concrete and literal usage is very small compared to the metaphorical usage. This is one of the main findings of our study. Another interesting fact is that tokens representing the UP dimension (the positive dimension) by far outnumber tokens representing the DOWN dimension (the negative dimension); this is true even for those items that are not affected by the unmarked/marked dichotomy, cf. the data in Table 1 and see below in Sections 3.2.1, 3.2.3 and 4. In what follows, we will deal with the UP dimension in Section 3.1 and the DOWN dimension in Section 3.2.

3.1 The UP dimension

On our analysis, it is expected that the UP dimension represents the positive, the conceptual metaphors being UP IS MORE and UP IS POSITIVE EVALUATION. The present section will discuss two types of linguistic forms belonging in the UP dimension, viz. the absolute *høy* 'high' and the comparative *høyere* 'higher' as well as the verbs *løfte* 'lift' and *stige* 'rise'. Henceforth, the absolute form *høy* will refer to both *høy* and *høyere* unless otherwise noted.

3.1.1 Høy/høyere

Høy (cognate with English *high*) was borrowed into Middle Norwegian from Old Swedish *høger* (the Old Norse form was *hár, hór*), and it is used non-figuratively with reference to the vertical dimension of objects (extensional high) or an upper position in the vertical dimension (positional high). We assume that this is the original and prototypical meaning. (On the diachrony of *high*, see Bjorvand & Lindemann 2007.)

Norwegian *høy* (like its cognate *high*) refers metaphorically to status and rank and more generally to elevated places in a hierarchy, including various religious uses:

(3) *høybåren* 'of high birth, *høyaktelse* 'reveration', *komme høyt på strå* 'become important socially' (literally 'come high up on the straw'), *ære være gud i det høyeste* 'glory be to God on high', *høyesteprest* 'high priest'

Another frequent use of *høy* is with reference to especial quality or more advanced stage of development, as in (4):

(4) *høyt nivå* 'high quality or level', *høyere utdanning* 'higher education'

Høy corresponds to English *loud* (as in 5) as well as to high pitch when referring to vocal activities:

(5) *høy stemme* 'loud voice', å synge/snakke høyt 'to sing/speak loudly'

Table 2. Distribution of metaphorical and concrete use of *høy* and *høyere*

	høy		*høyere*		Total	
	n	%	n	%	n	%
Metaphorical	273	91	282	94	555	92.5
Concrete	27	9	18	6	45	7.5
Total	300	100	300	100	600	100

As appears from Table 1, *høy* is a highly frequent word in the material utilized for the present study; altogether there are 100,435 occurrences in the periods investigated here (including *høyere*). As Table 2 shows, only 45 examples (7.5%) in our sample involve a completely concrete use of these words, whereas the metaphorical use of *høy* is predominant, involving both schemas described in Section 2 above (including many subschemas). This is in line with various studies of individual collocations such as Deignan (1999) and Hanks (2004); see the discussion below in Section 4.

The concrete use of *høy* includes collocations with words referring to human beings or to structures and buildings, as in (6)–(7):

(6) skapt av Israel fordi de har stengt inne 1,5 millioner palestinere bak en *høy* mur hvor de kontrollerer alle innganger. (AA081231)
'made by Israel because they have locked up 1.5 million Palestinians behind a high wall where they control all entrances'

(7) får ansvaret for flytrafikken i de *høyere* luftlagene over 20.000 fot over Sør-Norge (SA060916)
'becomes responsible for air traffic in the higher atmospheric layers 20.000 feet above South Norway'

A large number of the metaphorical examples belong in the quantity domain; cf. (8)–(10). One group of these involve collocations of *høy* with words denoting something that can be measured in some way, such as *alder* 'age', *pris* 'price', *sex-frekvens* 'sex frequency', *inntekt* 'income', *hastighet* 'speed', *trafikk* 'traffic', *valgdeltagelse* 'election participation'. Thus *høy trafikk* implies many cars, *høy valgdeltagelse* many voters, etc.

(8) Selv om sex-frekvensen i Norge er *høy*, har flere noe å utsette på kvaliteteten. (BT??1011)
'even if sex frequency in Norway is high, the quality has been criticized by many'

(9) Bangladesh har avviklet et fredelig valg med *høy* deltakelse. (VG081229)
'Bangladesh has carried out a peaceful election with a high election turnout'

(10) Han fikk jo også en ny vår i nokså *høy* alder. (BT10??17)
'he got a new spring at a relatively high age'

A related phenomenon is what we might call the scalar use of *høy*. We find this when *høy* co-occurs with words such as *IQ*, where the adjective refers to the upper part of a scale. Indeed, any list or scale will have the same characteristics: one might be high or low on a list or scale.

(11) Foreldre og *høy IQ* viktig for utdannelse. (AA100512)
'parents and high IQ are important for education'

(12) det er oppsiktsvekkende at bandet ikke er *høyere* på radiolista med sin "Ambitions" (DB091229)
'it is astonishing that the band isn't higher on the radio list with their "Ambitions"'

(13) Da starter jobben med å føre AaFK mot tidenes beste eliteseriesesong. Vil *høyere* opp. (AA091231)
'then the job of getting AaFK to the best elite series season. Wants higher up!'

Another example in this group is temperature, where the scale of the thermometer is concrete, and high temperature refers to a point relatively high on that scale; cf. (14). It would seem that *høy* here has a half concrete meaning. Nevertheless, *høy* used about temperature as well as in the collocations described above is metaphorical in the sense that it does not refer to vertical states or objects. If high temperature referring to degrees on a thermometer is 'partially metaphorical', high temperature about emotions (as in *the temperature of the discussion got very high*) is completely metaphorical. We therefore assume that there are degrees of metaphoricity. We will return to this point in Section 3.1.3 below.

(14) såkalte organofosfater, som under *høy* temperatur kan utvikle seg (SA061213)
'so-called organo phosphates, which in high temperature may develop'

A further group of *høy* examples subsumed under the UP IS MORE schema involves collocations with words that are not measurable, but more abstract, and where *høy* essentially means 'much, a lot', such as *kompetanse* 'competence', *forventningsnivå* 'expectation', *effektivitet* 'efficiency', *risiko* 'risk', *prioritet* 'priority', *bevissthet* 'consciousness', *selvtillit* 'self-confidence'. Consider (15)–(17).

(15) Trondheim kommune trenger lærere med *høy* kompetanse (AA051106)
'the municipality of Trondheim needs teachers with high competence'

(16) Skanseguttene har *høy* selvtillit om dagen. (BT10??15)
'the Skanse boys obviously have high self-confidence these days'

(17) har vårt teknologiske samfunn utviklet en svært *høy* sensitivitet overfor solstormer. (DB100616)
'our technological society has developed a high sensitivity to sun storms'

Finally, one might analyse *høy* referring to sounds as a species of UP IS MORE. *Høy musikk, høy stemme,* etc. means more sound, as shown in (18).

(18) Det ble spilt *høy* musikk fra ei leilighet i Storgata (NL 100616)
'loud [lit. high] music was played in a flat in Storgata'

Høy is also used evaluatively in various ways; cf. (19)–(22). In collocations with words such as *standard* 'standard', *kvalitet* 'quality', and *nivå* 'level', the meaning is clearly positive in that *høy* means 'better, much valued'. Some collocations might be described in terms of rank, status, power, etc. (i.e. a subgroup in what Taylor 2003: 138 calls the powerfulness domain). Clearly, the positive here interacts with quantity; *høy kvalitet* refers to better quality, but could also be seen as more quality, and high status is good and much valued, but also involves a quantity of status or power. Here we might also group *trivselsfaktor* 'comfort factor', *klasse* 'class', *stjerne* 'star', the latter being an idiom (cf. below).

(19) kompetanse til å få undervisning på et *høyere* nivå (AA081229)
'qualified to get instruction at a higher level'

(20) Innvendig er det *høy* trivselsfaktor (NL091020)
'inside there is a high comfort factor'

(21) Det gir ikke lenger *høy* sosial status å jobbe for sin far (AP071103)
'working for your father doesn't give a high social status any more'

(22) Vi får vinne den med stil og så be til de *høyere* makter (DB071117)
'we must win it with style and then pray to higher powers'

Høy about happy moods is not used much in the present material, except as *høy stemning* 'happy atmosphere'. However, there are examples of 'dope high'. Since *høy* (most likely a calque from English *high)* denotes happiness and positive feelings, there is an easy extension into *høy* meaning drunk or intoxicated; the material contains examples of these as well as examples such as that in (24) which shows a further development of 'dope high'.

(23) og at de får oppleve entusiasme og *høy* stemning (VG090814)
'that they may experience enthusiasm and high spirits'

(24) Jeg har total realitet i å være *høy* på døden, nå kan jeg prøve å være *høy* på livet. (AP090820)
'I have a total reality in being high on death, now I will try to be high on life'

Høyere utdannnelse 'higher education' is education at a top level, whereas *høy utdannelse* refers more to the quantity of education (i.e. the number of years, although of course it will most likely include higher education).

(25) Begge foreldrene har *høy* utdannelse fra Iran, og har vært viktige (AP051230)
'both parents are highly educated [lit have high education] from Iran and have been important'

(26) Det er fortsatt flere menn enn kvinner med en lang *høyere* utdannelse i Norge. (VG070829)
'in Norway there are still more men with higher education than women'

Finally, it should be mentioned that *høy* is used in many idioms. *Høy sigarføring* 'flamboyant' (literally 'holding the cigar high'), *på høy tid* 'high time', *høy terskel* 'high threshold', and *ha en høy stjerne* 'be popular' (literally 'have a high star') are among those used several times in our data.

(27) Jonas Lie hadde en *høy* stjerne i naziregimet i Berlin. (AP071104)
'Jonas Lie was highly favoured [lit. had a high star] in the Berlin Nazi regime'

(28) De glemmer at folk flest har en *høy* terskel for å ringe politiet. (DA091016)
'they forget that most people have a high threshold for calling the police'

As we have seen, *høy* is used largely metaphorically in our material (this also supports the findings of Swan & Breivik 2005 as well as Swan 2010). We have suggested that there are degrees of metaphoricity, in that in some collocations, *høy* actually can be seen as partly concrete. For instance, this refers to measuring temperatures and, slightly differently, to ranking lists where top and bottom may refer to positions that resemble the vertical dimension, but of course are two-dimensional. And note that, obviously, the top of the list, as in the case of ranking football clubs, is best. In addition, however, there are clearly degrees of lexicalization and conventionalization involved in the differences between collocations with words referring to e.g. price, salary, speed, and traffic on the one hand (where there is no other obvious linguistic means to express the same thing), and on the other hand idioms such as *høy stjerne* and *høy terskel*.

3.1.2 Stige *and* løfte

In the UP dimension we also find verbs such as *heve* 'lift, raise', *stige* 'rise', and *løfte* 'lift', i.e. verbs referring to moving vertically in space. Here, we will discuss *løfte* and *stige*, both of which refer to upward motion. Both verbs existed in earlier forms in Old Norse. The former derives from Old Norse *lypta* 'lift', which itself is derived from *luft* 'air' (cf. Bjorvand & Lindemann 2007). *Stige* derives from Old Norse *stiga* 'walk'. The Proto-Germanic ancestor had developed the meaning of moving upwards. These verbs are not as frequent as *høy*, as can be seen from Table 1. The expectation is that *løfte* and *stige* will behave like *høy*, i.e. occur metaphorically mostly in the quantity domain, and that their meaning will be positive. As noted earlier, both *stige* and *løfte* have homonymous nouns meaning 'ladder' and 'promise' respectively.

As Table 3 shows, *løfte* and *stige*, like *høy/høyere* are largely used metaphorically. It is worth noting that the proportion of concrete usage is noticeably higher in the case of *løfte* than in the case of *high/higher*.

Table 3. Distribution of metaphorical and concrete use of *løfte* and *stige*

	løfte		*stige*		Total	
	n	%	n	%	n	%
Metaphorical	244	81	285	95	529	88.2
Concrete	56	19	15	5	71	11.8
Total	300	100	300	100	600	100

Typically, the concrete use in the material refers to (for *stige*) rising smoke, sea levels, the sun, water, etc, and (for *løfte*) to lifting objects or bodies, weapons, body parts (arms, legs), as for instance in (29)–(30).

(29) 25 000 mennesker så tusener av lys *stige* mot himmelen. (VG051223)
'25,000 people saw thousands of lights rise towards heaven'

(30) Han ville knapt nok klart å *løfte* et sverd av den typen de brukte den gangen. (DB061204)
'he would hardly have managed to lift a sword of the type they used at that time'

Since the concrete meaning of *stige* and *løfte* refers to upward movement, their chief metaphorical use in Norwegian has to do with entities or abstract concepts which are interpreted as being located along a vertical dimension, or rather in movement towards upper locations. In our material, most of the examples with *stige* are, like those with *høy*, from the domain of quantity. Thus *stige* will frequently collocate with similar words as *høy* does, for instance *pris* 'price', *rente* 'interest', *tall* 'number', *omsetning* 'sale, turnover', *temperatur* 'temperature'. These refer to measurable entities, often in the domains of weather or economy, and UP IS MORE; cf. (31)–(32). Compare also collocations with *verdi* 'value', such as (33).

Note, however, terms like *arbeidsløshet* 'unemployment', where the rise does not have a positive meaning, but UP is simply MORE.

(31) Dødstallene fortsetter å *stige* etter tsunamien (VG060718)
'the number of people killed in the tsunami continues to rise'

(32) Arbeidsløsheten er på 17,9 prosent og ventes å *stige* til 18,9 prosent neste år. (DN090927)
'unemployment is 17.9 per cent and is expected to rise to 18.9 per cent next year'

(33) Det er noen eiendommer som kommer til å *stige* betydelig i verdi. (SA080429)
'the value of some properties is going to rise considerably'

Feber 'fever' is used much like temperature as described in the previous section, and the implicit reference is to the thermometer. In (34), of course, the fever is metaphorical at a higher level still, referring to the enthusiasm of people. As already mentioned, temperature, too, is used in this way; cf. (35) and (36).

(34) VM-feberen er i ferd med å *stige* i arrangørlandet. (DB060303)
'world cup fever is about to rise in the host country'

(35) regner de med at temperaturen vil *stige* med mellom 2 og 6,3 grader. (BT060718)
'they expect that the temperature will rise from 2 to 6.3 degrees'

(36) fikk debattemperaturen i fagmiljøene til å *stige* flere grader (AP060516)
'got the academic debate temperature to rise several degrees'

The evaluative domain is less represented in the *stige* than in the *høy* material. Emotions are expressed with *stige* to some extent in various ways. Thus when the rejoicing in (37) rises, it becomes stronger. In (38), however, it is shown that not all increased or rising levels of emotions are good; when collocating with negative words, *stige* leads to even more socially unacceptable states (anger, hate, etc.).

(37) var rask med å introdusere Beckenbauer for å få hjemmejubelen til å *stige*. (DA060610)
'was quick to introduce Beckenbauer in order to make the [home] enthusiasm rise'

(38) Du kjenner aggresjonen *stige* inni deg. (VG060717)
'you feel the aggression rise inside you'

With respect to rank, *stige* may be used about hierarchies in positions, etc.

(39) så øker du sjansene for å *stige* i gradene. (AP060519)
'then you increase your chances to rise in rank'

Løfte means, metaphorically, to make something better, get it to the top, improve, or get out of bad situations, and will occur with words denoting entities which may be improved (lifted), such as *kvalitet* 'quality' and *standard* 'standard'. These too, are typically associated with high (or low).

In the quantity domain, *å løfte realfagskompetansen* 'lifting science competence' leads to more competence, as in (40), while in (41) lifting the math subject means improving the status (more status).

(40) Vi ønsker å *løfte* realfagskompetansen allerede i barnehagen. (DN060607)
'we wish to lift the science competence as early as in kindergarten'

(41) å *løfte* matematikkfagets status. (DN060523)
'to lift the status of maths'

With respect to the evaluative domain, one frequent meaning is to improve the situation for an entity, for instance lifting the entity out of a bad situation to a good one, making it better, or to relieve someone of a burden. This meaning is illustrated by (42)–(44).

(42) landets makthavere burde derfor ha gode muligheter til å løfte millioner ut av fattigdom. (DA070421)
'the rulers of the country should therefore have excellent opportunities to lift millions out of poverty'

(43) men skal vi klare virkelig å *løfte* Festspillene, må vi trekke til oss (BT060609)
'but if we really are to lift the Bergen Festival, we must draw'

(44) å *løfte* en byrde av forventinger fra Liverpool-spillernes skuldre. (DB061209)
'to lift a burden of expectations from the shoulders of the Liverpool players'

With respect to the emotional aspect of *løfte,* we found few examples in our material with the verb on its own. A deverbal adjective, *oppløftet*, may, however, exemplify the UP IS HAPPY aspect of *løfte*.

(45) Jeg er ikke begeistret eller *oppløftet*, snarere litt nedtrykt og tankefull. (AA050420)
'I am not excited or enthusiastic, rather a bit down and thoughtful'

As far as idioms are concerned, *stige* is not represented in our material with an idiom. *Løfte*, however, occurs in a variety of idioms. There are many examples of *løfte rumpa fra stolen* 'get going' (literally 'lift your ass off the chair), *løfte en finger* 'lift a finger'.

(46) Døde kjendiser håver inn uten å *løfte* en finger. (BT081030)
'famous dead people scoop up [money] without lifting a finger'

3.1.3 *Summary*

In Sections 3.1.1 and 3.1.2, we have presented a small set of lexical items which share the property of belonging in the UP dimension, viz. *høy, høyere, løfte, stige.* There are great differences between *høy/høyere* on the one hand and *løfte/stige* on the other with respect to frequency of occurrence in the Norwegian Newspaper Corpus; the former occur more than 5 times as often as the latter. However, these four words have been shown to behave in very similar ways in that they are used mainly metaphorically. As expected, their metaphorical use is largely positive, i.e. UP IS GOOD (subsuming UP IS MORE and UP IS POSITIVE EVALUATION). Furthermore, to some extent both adjectives and verbs co-occur with the same type of words (e.g. *prisen er høy* 'the price is high' and *prisene stiger* 'prices are rising' as well as *høy temperatur* 'high temperature' and *temperaturen hennes steg* 'her temperature rose'). It is worth noting that UP IS HAPPY is generally a very important metaphor (see, for instance, Swan 2010), but our sample of Norwegian newspaper language does not seem to have many instantiations of that type. In other words, examples like (23)–(24) and (45) are not very common.

We have also suggested that there are degrees of metaphoricity which may account for the differences perceived in Norwegian and English between the use of for instance 'high' in collocations such as 'high income', 'high temperature' and 'feeling high'. While all these may be considered conventionalized metaphors (in the sense of Müller 2008: 188) in that 'high' indeed has a literal counterpart, we would like to suggest that they differ with respect to perceived metaphoricity. Thus it is hardly possible to express high temperature, income, speed, etc. except using 'high'; indeed, many speakers will not consider 'high' a metaphor at all in such contexts. The expression 'feeling high', on the other hand, is but one of many ways to express happiness and good feelings (although these may very often be grounded in the HAPPY IS UP metaphor), and probably would be perceived as more metaphorical by most. Degree of metaphoricity is clearly related to degree of conventionalization. According to Semino (2008: 19), "Other things being equal, the more conventional a metaphorical expression, the less likely that it will be consciously used and recognized as a metaphor". It is beyond the scope of the present paper to further discuss degrees of metaphoricity and/or conventionalization, notably the much debated categorization of metaphors as dead, alive, sleeping, etc. See however Deignan 2005: 36 ff. and Müller 2008: 178 ff. for valuable discussions.

3.2 The down dimension

On our analysis, it is assumed that the DOWN dimension generally constitutes a mirror image of the UP dimension, i.e. DOWN IS LESS and DOWN IS NEGATIVE EVALUATION. This is consistent with Taylor's (2003) analysis. The present section will discuss *lav* 'low'/*lavere* 'lower' and the verbs *synke* 'sink'/*senke* 'lower', which are the counterparts of the words discussed in Section 3.1. As was the case in Section 3.1 with *høy/høyere*, the absolute form *lav* will refer to both *lav* and *lavere* unless otherwise noted.

3.2.1 Lav/lavere

Lav derives from Old Norse *lágr* and is cognate with English *low* (the English word was borrowed from Old Norse). Its original meaning is indeed 'lying down'; cf. also Modern Norwegian *liggende* 'lying down' and Old Norse *lægr* 'which can lie down'. (On the history of *lav*, see Bjorvand & Lindemann 2007.) *Lav* is used non-figuratively with reference to the vertical dimension of objects and with reference to positions in the vertical dimension. Generally metaphors involving *lav* have negative connotations, but can also be used more or less neutrally. Like *høy*, *lav* can also refer to position in various hierarchies and scales (less elevated positions), and to stages of quality and development evaluation, status, etc. Consider the examples in (47):

(47) *lav* temperatur 'low temperature', *lav* pris 'low price', *lavere/lavt*stående dyr 'lower, primitive animals', *lav*pannet 'low-browed', *lav* kvalitet 'low quality', *lav*ættet 'of low birth'

In the sections of the newspaper corpus represented in Table 1, *lav* is not as frequent as *høy*. In the sample that is subjected to closer analysis, it is also the case that *lav* is used concretely about a small number of cases, as shown in Table 4.

Table 4. Distribution of metaphorical and concrete use of *lav* and *lavere*

	lav		*lavere*		Total	
	n	%	n	%	n	%
Metaphorical	280	93.3	295	98.3	575	95.8
Concrete	20	6.7	5	1.7	25	4.2
Total	300	100	300	100	600	100

Concretely, the word collocates with words for various objects such as cars, buildings, and constructions, as well as words like *sol* 'sun' (the sun's position on the horizon), and *bane* 'trajectory, orbit'; very occasionally it co-occurs with words denoting persons. Examples are provided in (48)–(49).

(48) Muren rundt tigerburet var for *lav* (AP071228)
'the wall around the tiger cage was too low'

(49) Særlig satelitter i *lav* bane er utsatt (DB100616)
'in particular satellites in low orbit are exposed'

Not unexpectedly, we find differences between *høy* and *lav* with respect to concrete collocations, since the former is used about buildings and persons to a larger extent and is the unmarked member of the antonymic pair *høy-lav*. (Apparently, markedness also plays a role in metaphorical collocations.) *Høy* and *lav* are gradable binary antonyms; they are situated at opposite ends of a continuum. Normally it is the upper or positive part of the continuum or scale which functions as unmarked in measurement terminology; cf. **She is 18 years young* and **She is 5 ft low*.

However, in metaphorical usage, *høy* and *lav* resemble each other with respect to collocations. As with *høy, lav* in the quantity domain is most frequent. Thus *lav* is found with words that refer to entities that can be measured, such as *pris* 'price', *fart* 'speed', *arbeidsløshet* 'unemployment', *vekt* 'weight', *alder* 'age', *temperatur* 'temperature', *bemanning* 'staff, workforce'. These can be measured concretely, and *lav* means little, small or less; for instance, *lav bemanning* refers to few people on the job. Examples are shown in (50)–(51).

(50) og Aschehoug regner med langt *lavere* boksalg enn forventet. (AA060815)
'Aschehoug expects much lower book sales than estimated'

(51) Høyre, Venstre og SV bør håpe på *lav* valgdeltagelse. (AP090914)
'Høyre, Venstre and SV [political parties] should hope for a low election turnout'

Furthermore, the quantity domain comprises collocations with more abstract, less countable words, such as *selvfølelse* 'self-confidence', *risiko* 'risk', *trussel* 'threat', *machofaktor* 'macho factor', *vilje* 'will', and *utdanning* 'education'; cf. (52)–(53). *Lav* means little, small or less in this context. Finally, *lav,* as a reversal of *høy,* can be seen as an example of DOWN IS LESS in the realm of sounds, as in (54).

(52) vestlige lands vilje til å bidra har vært skammelig *lav*. (DA081231)
'in the West, the will to contribute has been shamefully low'

(53) fordommer som at kvinner er selvopptatte og har *lav* selvtillit (BT071227)
'prejudices such as that women are self-centred and have low self-confidence'

(54) frukt blir servert, folk prater med *lave* stemmer. (BT050915)
'fruit is served and people are chatting in a low voice'

In our data selection, the evaluation domain is less represented than the quantity domain with respect to *lav*. In the former domain, *lav* refers (as mentioned above) to the bad or the less developed, for instance morals or culture. Similarly, status and rank which are low are less good. Examples are shown in (55)–(57).

(55) Engelsk presse er besatt av journalister med *lav* moral og høyt selvbilde. (DB090927)
'the English press has been invaded by journalists with low morals and a high self-image'

(56) De fortviler over *lav* kvalitet på en del av gavene. (VG091221)
'they despair over the low quality of the presents'

(57) viser at barn til foreldre med *lav* sosial status har 60 prosent mer fysiske plager (FV050604)
'shows that children whose parents have low status have 60 per cent more physical complaints'

It is worth pointing out that the material we investigated has no instances of *lav* illustrating DOWN IS UNHAPPY, a subset of DOWN IS NEGATIVE EVALUATION.

Finally, *lav* occurs in many idiomatic expressions, although only *lav terskel* is found in the present material; cf. (58). (*Lav terskel* 'low threshold' corresponds directly to *høy terskel* 'high threshold'; cf. Section 3.1.1).

(58) Terskelen for å få barn er *lav* i Norge. (DA081227)
'the threshold for getting children is low in Norway'

In conclusion, then, it has been shown that *lav* behaves much like *høy*, but has fewer uses. Part of the explanation for this is no doubt that *høy* functions as the unmarked member of the pair.

3.2.2 Synke/senke

Finally, we turn to the verbs *synke* 'sink' and *senke* 'lower', which correspond to the UP dimension *løfte* and *stige* discussed in Section 3.1.2. These verbs denote downwards vertical movement in space. The form of the verb *synke* is borrowed from Danish *synke*, but is cognate with the earlier Old Norse *søkkva*. The originally causative form ('make sink') appears as transitive *senke*. On the history of these verbs, see Bjorvand & Lindemann (2007).

Again the expectation is that *synke/senke* will behave like *lav*, i.e. that their metaphorical use will refer to low quantities or negative evaluation.

Table 5. Distribution of metaphorical and concrete use of *synke* and *senke*

	senke		*synke*		Total	
	n	%	n	%	n	%
Metaphorical	263	87.7	189	63	452	75.3
Concrete	37	12.3	111	37	148	24.7
Total	300	100	300	100	600	100

These verbs occur in concrete usage a great deal more than their *løfte/stige* counterparts. In our material, many of the concrete *synke* occurrences refer to people sinking into chairs, bathtubs, and the like, and of course also into water as various objects and even tanks do; cf. (59). Naturally, ships and boats may sink, and we also have examples of sea levels, coastlines, and islands sinking into water; cf. (60). Concrete *senke* (which normally is transitive) overlaps to some extent, e.g. with respect to people sitting or lying down. In addition, body parts may be lowered, notably shoulders (this is normally used as a metaphor, see below), as well as various objects or structural items, etc. (including, dramatically, ships); cf. (61).

(59) puster lettet ut når han endelig kan *synke* ned i baksetet i den varme drosjen. (NL051229)
'a sigh of relief when he finally can sink into the backseat of the warm taxi'

(60) øygruppen Tuvalu forsvant i 1999, og flere står i fare for å *synke* i havet (DB051208)
'the archipelago Tuvalo disappeared in 1999 and more are in danger of sinking into the ocean'

(61) Han deltok selv i arbeidet med å *senke* skipet (BT090922)
'he himself participated in the job sinking the ship'

Most metaphorical examples in the material belong in the quantity domain. *Synke* and *senke* behave much like *løfte* and *stige* in reverse. Thus in metaphorical usage they collocate with many of the same words, viz. words denoting price, interest, temperatures, rates of various types (measurable entities), as in (62)–(63). Abstract, uncountable entities belonging to the DOWN IS LESS metaphor schema is for instance *forventning* 'expectation', *ambisjon* 'ambition', and *risiko* 'risk'; cf. (64). In these latter cases, the conceptual metaphor is DOWN IS LESS. Compare also (65) where the number of decibel corresponds to lower or less sound.

(62) jeg tror ikke prisen vil *synke* noe særlig på en stund. (AP051220)
'I don't think the price will sink for a while'

(63) Temperaturen vil *synke* gradvis de kommende dagene (BT051211)
'the temperature will sink gradually in the next few days'

(64) administrasjonen forsøker å *senke* amerikanske forventninger til Irak (DB061203)
'the administration is attempting to lower American expectations to Iraq'

(65) Foreningen har arbeidet med å *senke* antall desibel for det som kan aksepteres (DB061203)
'the club has worked on lowering the decibel level to an acceptable level'

In the evaluative domain, *synke* and *senke* refer to bad states of affairs, as in (66), or to standards and quality or expectations, as in (67)–(68). The status/hierarchy type is rare in the present material, although one's status certainly might sink as well as rise; cf. (69). This is also true of placement in hierarchies such as football clubs, etc. Indeed, teams and clubs may be *senket* 'sunk' by its rivals; cf. (70). This is a relatively new use of *senke*, and seems to be most typically found in sports language. *Synke lavt* 'sink low' (or *lavere* 'lower') refers to moral decrepitude or social badness, as in (71).

(66) og Gaza langsomt er i ferd med å *synke* ned i kaos (AP060316)
'and Gaza is slowly sinking into chaos'

(67) som frister institutter til å *senke* kvalitetskravene. (AP050523)
'which tempt departments to lower standards of quality'

(68) Undersøkelsen er gjennomført jevnlig siden 1982, og nivået fortsetter å *synke*. (BT060302)
'the survey has been carried out regularly since 1982, and the standard continues to sink'

(69) ikke minst gjør Joel Kinnaman en fremragende innsats i rollen fra å være en av overklassen til å *synke* i dypet da han oppdager (NL100529)
'not least does Joel Kinnaman do a wonderful job as the character who sinks from the upper class into the depths when he discovers'

(70) I kveld ønsker Cristiano Ronaldo (22) å *senke* gamleklubben Sporting Lisboa (AP070919)
'tonight Cristiano Ronaldo (22) wishes to sink his old club Sporting Lisboa'

(71) Hver gang man tror at han ikke kan *synke* lavere, slår han til med en ny bunnrekord (AP060526)
'every time you think he can't sink lower he delivers a new low'

There are several fixed expressions or idioms with *synke* and *senke* that do not correspond to *løfte*. One type is phrasal *synke inn*, meaning 'sink in' about events, feelings, or the like; cf. (72). Another type is reflexive *senke*; peace, silence, and the like may for instance 'lower itself' over a place or person, as in (73). This means that peace, etc. envelops the place or person.

(72) Dommen må *synke* inn litt. (AA100614)
'the sentence must sink in for a while'

(73) Han ønsker også at julefreden skal *senke* seg over Byåsen. (AA061220)
'he also wishes that Christmas peace will descend on Byåsen'

The most frequent metaphor idioms in our material are, however, *senke skuldrene* 'relax' and *senke terskelen* 'lower the threshold', as exemplified in (74)–(75). Cf. also the use of *high threshold* and *low threshold* in Sections 3.1.1 and 3.2.1.

(74) Det blir tid til å *senke* skuldrene, prate og kose oss på hytta (AP061214)
'there will be time for lowering one's shoulders, chatting and enjoying ourselves'

(75) Tipset er å *senke* terskelen. Jeg mener at alle er kreative (BT061207)
'the idea is to lower the threshold. I think everyone is creative'

3.2.3 *Summary*

In Sections 3.2.1 and 3.2.2, we have presented a subset of lexical items which belong in the DOWN dimension, viz. *lav, lavere, senke, synke*. These DOWN items do not occur as frequently as the UP items in our material, and again the verbs are far less common than the adjectives. Like the UP words, the DOWN words occur more frequently as metaphors than in concrete usage. However, it should be noted that in our material, the verbs *synke/senke* are much rarer as metaphors than the corresponding *løfte/stige*. Additionally, we have shown that (as expected) their metaphorical use is largely negative, i.e. DOWN IS BAD (subsuming DOWN IS LESS and DOWN IS NEGATIVE EVALUATION).

In concrete usage, the DOWN words are of course situated at the opposite end of the vertical scale from UP words and have been shown to be used with much the same type of words (for instance both *lav* and *høy* collocate with structures, buildings, people, etc.). In metaphorical usage as well, DOWN words resemble the UP words with respect to possible collocations to a large extent (for instance words denoting price, income, speed, morals, and status).

As far as degrees of metaphoricity are concerned, the DOWN words are like the UP words, but the DOWN adjectives differ from the UP adjectives in that the latter are the unmarked members of the *høy-lav* scale.

4. Conclusion

In the preceding sections, we have investigated a number of UP/DOWN words in Norwegian newspaper language from a cognitive perspective. What we have attempted to show is that words like *høy* and *lav* do not occur as isolated linguistic instances in unrelated contexts, but can be related to each other within the framework of the conceptual metaphors of which they are realizations, and the UP/DOWN image schema on which the conceptual metaphors are based. Specifically, we have shown that the UP words studied (*høy, høyere, løfte, stige*) may be subsumed under the conceptual metaphors UP IS MORE and UP IS POSITIVE EVALUATION, and that the words in question are largely associated with positive meanings and contexts. Contrariwise, the DOWN words (*lav, lavere, senke, synke*) represent a mirror image of the UP words, being subsumed under the conceptual metaphors DOWN IS LESS and DOWN IS NEGATIVE EVALUATION. These words are mainly associated with negative meanings and contexts. We have shown, then, that linguistic expressions such as *høy, lav, stige,* and *synke* are used in a number of contexts where the concrete spatial meaning is transferred to many other domains. Traditional metaphor analyses argue that highly conventionalized metaphors (such as most of those discussed here) are dead metaphors, and therefore not metaphors at all. In a conceptual metaphor framework, such as that adopted in the present article, it is of course assumed that the so-called 'dead' metaphors are highly entrenched and indeed an important means of conceptualization. Thus we hope to have shown that the UP and DOWN words discussed here are able to spread to so many domains precisely because they are grounded in a very basic conceptual metaphor.

We should also note that two general findings emerge from the data. Firstly, a large majority of the UP/DOWN words studied here are used metaphorically, while the assumed prototypical use, the concrete literal use, is very infrequent. Secondly, the number of positive (UP) words by far exceeds the number of negative (DOWN) words.

With respect to the first point, we present here Table 6, which sums up the data in Tables 2–5.

Table 6. Distribution of metaphorical and concrete use of UP and DOWN words in the sample examined

	UP words		DOWN words		Total	
	n	%	n	%	n	%
Metaphorical	1,084	90.3	990	82.5	2,074	86.4
Concrete	116	9.7	210	17.5	326	13.6
Total	1,200	100	1,200	100	2,400	100

While the UP words are less used in concrete contexts than the DOWN words, the majority of all occurrences are metaphorical, altogether 86.4 per cent. Clearly, the present article shows the ubiquity and pervasiveness of metaphor (cf. Gibbs 1994; Taylor 2003), even in newspaper language, which certainly is not normally considered to be a poetic genre. The proliferation of metaphoricity is a result of the words under investigation over time having extended their meanings to many domains in addition to the prototypical concrete usage, thus creating a network of related categories. As mentioned above, the predominance of metaphor in the present material is to some extent paralleled in previous work, such as Deignan (1999) and Hanks (2004). However, these studies are limited in scope as they deal with a restricted set of lexical items and their collocations. Indeed, as Deignan points out: "It does not seem to be possible to predict whether a particular collocation will be more frequent for the metaphorical or literal senses. It may be that for individual combinations of words the ratio of metaphorical to literal instances will shift over time" (1999: 25). By contrast, the present work shows a consistent trend for an extended UP/DOWN system, as do Swan & Breivik (2005) and Swan (2010). Finally, it should be mentioned that Sanford (2008) reports very small proportions of metaphoricity. Such variations may be a function of genre differences as his material consists of spoken data.

The second finding is more puzzling. Why should all the positive words outnumber the negative words to such an extent (cf. Table 1)? This has also been the case in other studies of spatial metaphors in Norwegian, notably Swan & Breivik (2005) and Swan (2010). Literal uses of *høy/høyere* would be expected to be more frequent than *lav/lavere* due to the former being unmarked. There would appear to be no reason *per se* for the unmarkedness effect to automatically carry over into the metaphorical usage. However, as we have shown, the UP metaphors are far more frequent than the DOWN metaphors. It should be noted that the verbs studied here of course are not affected by the unmarked/marked dichotomy, i.e. *løfte/stige* are not unmarked in relation to *senke/synke*. Nevertheless they display the same patterns as *høy* and *lav*. For this particular finding we have at present no explanation, but we will address this question again making use of other genres and corpora. In addition, it might be useful to look more closely at the collocations of the spatial terms investigated here; a more fine-grained analysis might provide valuable insights in this important area.

References

Ananthaswamy, Anil. 2010. Let your body do the thinking. *New Scientist* 27 March: 8–9.

Bjorvand, Einar & Lindemann, Fredrik Otto. 2007. *Våre arveord* (Our Inherited Vocabulary). Oslo: Novus.

Croft, William & Cruse, D. Allan. 2004. *Cognitive Linguistics*. Cambridge: CUP.

Deignan, Alice 1999. Linguistic metaphors and collocation in nonliterary corpus data. *Metaphor and Symbol* 14(1): 19–36.

Deignan, Alice. 2005. *Metaphor and Corpus Linguistics* [Converging Evidence in Language and Communication Research 6]. Amsterdam: John Benjamins.

Feldman, Jerome. 2006. *From Molecule to Metaphor.* Cambridge MA: The MIT press.

Geeraerts, Dirk. 1997. *Diachronic Prototype Semantics: A Contribution to Historical Lexicology*. Oxford: Clarendon Press.

Gibbs, Raymond. 1994. *The Poetics of Mind*. Cambridge: CUP.

Gibbs, Raymond. 1996. Why many concepts are metaphorical. *Cognition* 61: 309–319.

Gibbs, Raymond. 2006. *Embodiment and Cognitive Science*. Cambridge: CUP.

Grady, Joseph. 1996. Foundations of meaning: Primary metaphor and primary scenes. Ph.D. dissertation, University of California, Berkeley.

Grady, Joseph. 1997. THEORIES ARE BUILDINGS revisited. *Cognitive Linguistics* 1: 323–340.

Grady, Joseph. 2007. Metaphor. In *The Oxford Handbook of Cognitive Linguistics*, Dirk Geeraerts & Huberts Cuyckens (eds), 188–213. Oxford: OUP.
Hampe, Beate 2005. When down is not bad, and up not good enough: A usage-based assessment of the plus–minus parameter in image-schema theory. *Cognitive Linguistics* 16: 81–112.
Hanks, Patrick. 2004. The syntagmatics of metaphor. *International Journal of Lexicography* 17(3): 245–274.
Heine, Bernd. 1997. *Cognitive Foundations of Grammar*. Oxford: OUP.
Jackendoff, Ray & Aaron, David. 1991. Review of Lakoff & Turner 1989. *Language* 67: 320–338.
Johnson, Mark. 1987. *The Body in the Mind*. Chicago IL: Chicago University Press.
Lakoff, George. 1987. *Women, Fire, and Dangerous Things*. Chicago IL: Chicago University Press.
Lakoff, George. 2008. The neural theory of metaphor. In *The Cambridge Handbook of Metaphor and Thought*, Raymond Gibbs (ed), 17–38. Cambridge: CUP.
Lakoff, George & Johnson, Mark. 1980. *Metaphors We Live By*. Chicago IL: Chicago University Press.
Lakoff, George & Turner, Mark. 1989. *More than Cold Reason*. Chicago IL: University of Chicago Press.
Langacker, Ronald. 1987[1991]. *Foundations of Cognitive Grammar*. Vols. 1 & 2. Stanford CA: Stanford University Press.
Langacker, Ronald. 1995. The symbolic alternative. In *New Trends in Semantics and Lexicography*, H. Kardela & Gunnar Persson (eds), 89–117. Umeå: Acta Universitatis Umensis.
Meier, Brian & Robinson, Michael. 2004. Why the sunny side up: Associations between affect and vertical position. *Psychological Science* 15(4): 243–247.
Müller, Cornelia. 2008. *Methaphors Dead and Alive, Sleeping and Walking*. Chicago IL: University of Chicago Press.
Sanford, Daniel. 2008. Discourse and metaphor: A corpus-driven inquiry. *Corpus Linguistics and Lingustic Theory* 4(2): 209–234.
Semino, Elena. 2008. *Metaphor in Discourse*. Cambridge: CUP.
Swan, Toril. 2010. Spatial metaphors in the history of English and Norwegian. *Neuphilologische Mitteilungen* CXI: 55–67.
Swan, Toril & Breivik, Leiv Egil. 2005. OPP/NED-metaforer i norsk avisspråk. In *Mot rikare mål å trå*, Gulbrand Alhaug, Endre Mørck & Aud-Kirsti Pedersen (eds), 329–345. Oslo: Novus.
Taylor, John. 1995. *Linguistic Categorization*, 2nd edn. Oxford: Clarendon Press.
Taylor, John. 2002. *Cognitive Grammar*. Oxford: OUP.
Taylor, John. 2003. *Linguistic Categorization*, 3rd edn. Oxford: Clarendon Press.
Traugott, Elizabeth Closs & Dasher, Richard. *2000. Regularity in Semantic Change*. Cambridge: CUP.
Wierzbicka, Anna. 1996. *Semantics: Primes and Universals*. Oxford: OUP.
Yu, Ning. 1998. *The Contemporary Theory of Metaphor: A Perspective from Chinese*. Amsterdam: John Benjamins.

Doing historical linguistics using contemporary data

Øivin Andersen
University of Bergen

Retrieving linguistic data from earlier stages of languages is a notoriously difficult task. Using large electronic corpora combined with data on frequency this task can to some extent be solved. In this article I focus on the use of token frequency as described in functional Grammaticalization Theory. Deverbal nouns are non-prototypical members of the noun class. As they get older they tend to develop into more prototypical nouns. In Grammaticalization Theory this process is called lexicalization. This was tested on some zero suffix nouns in the Norwegian newspaper corpus in 2004 using modern texts only. In this article I test these findings using older texts from the same corpus.

1. Introduction

For many languages throughout the world we have little or no access to historical information. As Grammaticalization and Lexicalization Theories have pointed out, token frequency of lexical units in a language may carry information about their history. Using frequency data from large electronic corpora such as the Norwegian Newspaper Corpus we can catch a glimpse of past developments where historical linguistic data are almost absent.[1]

In this article I will draw on data from the Norwegian Newspaper Corpus to give some support to my hypothesis that deverbal nouns (henceforth DNs) tend to develop into prototypical nouns the older they get. A DN is a noun which is derived from a corresponding verb. The DN *ødeleggelse* 'destruction' is derived from the verb *ødelegge* 'destroy' with the addition of the derivational suffix *-else*. Following basic principles from stage theory in Grammaticalization

1. The relevance of the relationship between the frequency of lexical items and their history is also highlighted outside grammaticalization and lexicalization. Consider, for instance, Zipf's (1949) Principle of Economical Specialisation, whereby the age of a lexical item in the language correlates inversely with its size and directly with its frequency.

Theory, I postulated 6 stages in this development in an earlier article (Andersen 2007a), using data from 2004.

2. Stage theory

The process of nominalization has been described as a process of decategorization (Malchukov 2004: 9). Several researchers have listed various operations involved in the process (Lehmann 1988; Givón 1990; Croft 1991; Dik 1997). Givón, for example, mentions that when verbs acquire a nominal form, verbal agreement, tense, aspect and mode marking are either absent or severely restricted, case marking of the subject and object is modified most commonly to the genitive, and various determiners may be added modifying the deverbal noun, among others. A crucial question is whether there is any ordering of features acquired and lost in nominalization; see the typological literature for some proposals (Comrie & Thompson 1985; Noonan 1985; Lehmann 1988; Mackenzie 1987; Croft 1991; Koptjevskaja-Tamm 1993; Dik 1997).

Some studies (like Comrie & Thompson 1985) involve frequency considerations. In particular, aspect and voice may be retained in nominalization, tense rarely so, and mood and verbal agreement virtually never. Lehmann's Desententialization Scale of decategorization (Lehmann 1988, cited in Malchukov 2004: 11) is quite elaborate (> represents a 'prior to' relation):

(a) Constraints on/loss of illocutionary elements > constraints on/loss of mood/ modal elements > constraints on/loss of tense and aspect > dispensability of complements loss of personal conjugation/conversion of subject into oblique > no polarity > conversion of verbal into nominal government > dispensability of subject/constraints on complements

(b) Combinability with adposition/case affix

Loss of sentential properties on the part of the verb and the increasing nominality endow it with distributional properties of a noun, such as combinability with adpositions or case affixes. As Mackenzie (1987) has pointed out, nominalization involves valency reduction. This is also an important point in the development of the Norwegian deverbal nouns.

These stages were based on purely synchronic data from the corpus. In this investigation I use supplementary data consisting of older newspaper texts collected by Uni Computing and used for comparative reference. Data support for a hypothesis like this would normally require two mutually independent empirical domains: the corpus domain where synchronic data are drawn from the corpus based on token frequency on the one hand, and an authentic diachronic data domain on the other hand. The basis for my postulation of stages was, however, based on the first domain only. In this article I will report on corpus data dating back to 1900 in order to investigate whether these data can give further support to my hypothesis.

3. Deverbal nouns, prototypes and diachronic paths

Recent typological research has shown that DNs in various languages tend to develop diachronically into what Vendler (1967) called perfect nouns. Relevant research on nominalization has been carried out by several researchers like Alexiadou (2001), Anderson (1985), Cowie (2000), Comrie and Thompson (1985), Hansen and Heltoft (1994), Grimshaw (1990) and Koptjevskaja-Tamm (1993). Norwegian relevant studies are Faarlund, Lie and Vennebo (2002), Kinn (1994), Lødrup (1989), Sakshaug (1999) and Vinje (1973).[2] The mechanisms involved in the historical development of grammatical and lexical phenomena have been studied both in a formal generative theoretical framework (van Kemenade & Vincent 1997) and in a cognitive functional framework (Kellerman & Morrissey 1992). The latter type of framework will be adopted here.

In the functional tradition there has been an ongoing discussion on the status and validity of Grammaticalization Theory and the hypothesis of unidirectionality. When lexical elements become grammaticalized they will tend to have a considerable rise in token frequency (Hopper & Traugott 2003: 124ff). This rise seems to signal linguistic changes such as semantic fading, phonological reduction, positional fixing, increased compositionality and reanalysis of word boundaries. Lexicalization, however, tends to result in semantic enrichment and reduction/loss of compositionality (Brinton & Traugott 2005: 32ff).

Prototype theory is one of the most central theories in cognitive functional linguistics. Working with mental lexical structures in cognitive psychology, Rosch (1978) found several lexical features exhibiting prototype structures. For the category of birds a prototype feature is the ability to fly. An exemplar like a robin will have this feature, being a prototypical member of the category of birds, whereas an ostrich, sharing important properties with the robin, like laying eggs, will lack the property of being able to fly. Hence a robin is a more prototypical representative member of the bird category than an ostrich.

2. For more details see Andersen 2007a.

Prototype theory was introduced into linguistics by amongst others Taylor (1989).[3] A central point in prototype theory is the notion that some members of a linguistic category are better and more prototypical representatives (members) of the category than others. Applied to word classes this means that some verbs are more prototypical (i.e. more central members of the class) than others. Likewise, some nouns are more prototypical, i.e. more nounlike than others (Hopper & Thompson 1985). This means that the categories of nouns and verbs can be defined as having characteristic features where some features are absent in the non-prototypical members (lexemes). In Vendler's terms a prototypical noun would be a perfect noun and a non-prototypical noun would be an imperfect noun. An imperfect noun is rather colourfully defined as "a noun with a live and kicking verb inside itself" (Vendler 1967: 131).

Hopper & Thompson (1985) and Taylor (2004) see categoriality as a gradient phenomenon. Here it is important to add that categorical gradience does not imply fuzzy concept borders. As I have demonstrated (Andersen 2007b) the border between nouns and verbs is discrete even though both word classes do have distinct denotational gradience.

My central hypothesis is that DNs follow a diachronic path leading from imperfect noun to perfect noun, i.e. from a non-prototypical member of the noun class in the direction of a more prototypical member of the class. Prototype properties both at the morphosyntactic level and on the semantic level may be cancelled in different contexts of use, as Taylor (2004), Givón (1979) and Ross (2004) have pointed out. In this article I will focus on some basic properties that will be applied as the basis for my postulation of diachronic stages.

When a new DN is coined it inherits event process meaning from the corresponding verb. Coining of new DNs typically occurs in technical and scientific writing.[4] Halliday & Martin (1993) and Banks (2004) have investigated the historical development of DNs in Newton's scientific writings. Events and processes are most typically referred to by DNs. These DNs tend to become scientific terms with a very specific event process meaning. In other words, process event meaning is a prototypical property of the verb and is carried over in deverbal nominalization. This property is non-prototypical for nouns.

Whereas process meaning is typical for verbs, result meaning is typical for nouns. The result of a process is a static state associated with a prototypical noun property like time-stability (Givón 1979, 1984). Givón's Time Stability Hypothesis maintains that different parts of speech show gradience as to the ability to denote

3. Geeraerts (1992) gives a nice survey of diachronic semantics within this framework.

4. For discussion and examples see Andersen 2007c

permanence or stability over time. Verbs like *å skyte* 'to shoot' tend prototypically to be less time stable than nouns like *bygning* 'building'. So verbs tend to be less time stable than nouns, and adjectives tend to take a mid position between verbs and nouns (Givón 1984: 55). Result meaning very often gives rise to time stable entity meaning, which is typical of nouns. As Grimshaw (1990) has pointed out, many DNs have a polysemy which is characteristic for many DNs in several languages containing process and result meaning. A DN like *tegning* 'drawing' may refer to the process of drawing something, or to the result of that process, i.e. a drawing hanging on the wall. Pustejovsky (1998) calls this logical polysemy. Pustejovsky makes a distinction between contrastive ambiguity (usually referred to as homonymy) and complementary polysemy. The latter type is category-preserving. Logical polysemy is defined as a systematic type of complementary polysemy where there is no change in lexical category, and the multiple senses of the word have overlapping, dependent and shared meanings (Pustejovsky 1998: 28). These systematically related meanings tend to include large sets of nouns. A typical example is the figure/ground reversals discussed in Pustejovsky (1998: 31f.).

As Bybee (1985:33ff) has demonstrated, some prototypical grammatical verbal properties are more easily lost in nominalization than others. Her basic principle is that the more relevant the category is to the root meaning of the verb, the more likely it is to be retained, i.e. carried over in nominalization. Aspect is more relevant to the root than tense, so aspect distinctions are retained to a greater extent than tense. In Norwegian there is a closed set of zero suffix DNs referring to sound and movement which have an aspectual distinction of imperfect meaning (for the high frequent DNs ending in *-ing*) and perfect or semelfactive meaning for the corresponding zero suffix DNs. Semelfactive verbs express an instantaneous event. Examples are *sparking* (the phenomenon of kicking) vs. *spark*, (an instance of kicking) (Faarlund, Lie & Vennebo 2002: 124). As Taylor (2004: 306) has pointed out, instantiations are typical of nouns, using for instance determiners like *this* or numerals like *one*. Determiners and numerals are seldom used with *-ing* DNs with imperfect meaning, but occur frequently with zero suffix nouns with perfective meaning.

Another important difference between verbs and nouns is the fact that verbs typically have syntactic argument structure and semantic participant structure associated with it, whereas nouns typically lack this property (Chomsky 1970). Chomsky's own example is the verb *destroy*:

(1) The enemy destroyed the city.

In nominalization the direct object is carried over and the subject may occur in the possessive:

(2) the enemy's destruction of the city

Following Grimshaw (1990) the preposition *of* is the marker of the fact that the direct object has been carried over. She calls it a theta transmitter (Grimshaw 1990:73). In Norwegian the corresponding preposition is *av*. Lehmann (1995 [1982]:2f) calls this a grammatical use of the preposition. Normally, prepositions have lexical (often local and temporal) functions. Examples are prepositions like *on*, *at*, *behind* and *in*. The lexical prepositional phrases function typically as adjuncts, i.e. constituents outside the role frame of the corresponding verb. In DNs with transferred argument structure adjuncts are unchanged in nominalization, as in *servere i restauranten* 'serve in the restaurant' and *servering i restauranten* 'serving in the restaurant'.

Prepositions occurring with DNs in postnominal position inside the role frame of the corresponding verb are realized as two different types of prepositional phrase dependents. On the semantic level, these are known as participants and non-participants. Participants are selected by the meaning of the head DN or the main verb, whereas non-participants are outside the selectional frame of the head DN or the main verb. On the syntactic level these correspond to the distinction between complements and non-complements (Saeed 2003:148ff). Complements are subject to the subcategorization restrictions of the head DN or the main verb, whereas non-complements are not subcategorized by the head noun or the main verb. Some examples from the newspaper corpus may serve to illustrate this:

(3) *Liv Grete presterte å treffe med tre skudd-Ø* ***på første***
Liv Grete managed to hit with three shot-NMLZ on first
skyting, *men ble stoppet*
shooting, but was stopped
Liv Grete managed to hit with three shots on the first shooting, but was stopped (AP0315) [5]

(4) ... *Middlesbrough ikke maktet et eneste skudd-Ø* ***på mål i***
... Middlesbrough not power one single shot-NMLZ on goal
løpet av kampens 90 minutter. (DB40925)
during match's 90 minutes
Middlesbrough did not have a single shot on the goal during the 90 minutes of the match.

In (3) the prepositional phrase *på første skyting* is an adverbial referring to place. It is not related to the lexical meaning of the DN *skudd*. Hence it is a non-participant.

5. The codes after the examples refer to name of newspaper and date of issue, cf. http://avis.uib.no/om-aviskorpuset/innhold. Thus, AP refers to the newspaper Aftenposten, and the date is 15 March. The examples are taken from the tagged 2004 part of the corpus.

In (4) the prepositional phrase *på mål* is related to the lexical meaning of *skudd* and hence a participant in the event denoted by *skudd*.

I also distinguish between two types of complements: arguments and non-arguments. Arguments are those complements which grammatically code (or license) functional elements as direct objects both on sentence level in the case of main verbs, e.g. *Læreren løste* ***problemet*** *i klasserommet* 'The teacher solved the problem in the classroom' and on phrase level in the case of DNs, using the grammatical preposition av 'of', e.g. *Lærerens løsning* ***av problemet*** *tok lang tid* 'The teacher's solving of the problem took a long time'.

Within the DNs there is a further distinction between those which code participants as arguments (i.e. *Lærerens løsning av problemet tok lang tid*), using grammatical coding (the grammatical preposition *av* 'of') and those which code participants as non-arguments (using a lexical preposition), e.g. *Lærerens løsning* ***på problemet*** *lå på bordet* 'The teacher's solution to the problem was on the table'). So the DN *løsning* has both process and result meaning. The DN *løsing* has an unambiguous process meaning. In some restricted pairs of words we have an overt distinction between DNs ending in *-ing* (having process meaning only (as in *bygging* 'the process of building something') and DNs ending in *-ning*, as in *bygning* (the result of the process of building something).

4. Methods and data

4.1 Using a synchronic corpus only

Based on relevant elements of Prototype Theory and Grammaticalization Theory (as outlined in the introduction), I postulated 6 stages for the historical development of DNs in Norwegian. I call these the prototype cline of zero suffix DNs:[6]

1. Establishment of event process meaning and reference
2. Development of result meaning, specific reference, development of logical polysemy by reanalysis and analogical spreading
3. Development of idiosyncratic polysemy and increased semantic distance from the verb
4. Development of idiosyncratic morphophonological alternation and increased form distance from the verb
5. Loss of aspect distinctions by analogical spreading
6. Loss of prepositional dependent and lexical differentiation

6. For a more detailed description of the stages I refer to my article (Andersen 2007a: 66ff).

Malchukov (2004: 9) describes the historical process of nominalization as a process of decategorizaton, i.e. the gradual loss of verbal properties. This process can also be viewed as a movement from the periphery members of the noun class in the direction of the nucleus members of the same class.

But as Grammaticalization Theory points out, these stages are not to be seen as consecutive and well defined thresholds of development, i.e. as mutually exclusive time periods. In a comprehensive process like deverbal nominalization involving several different morphological types (for a survey, see Andersen 2007c), different types may not only represent different stages, but different members of the same morphological type may be on different stages of development, as we shall see. Old forms of lexemes may persist for an unpredictable period of time. These forms may live side by side along with newer forms for a long time. This may lead to what Hopper & Traugott (2003:125ff) call layering, i.e. variability of analogical old and new forms.

In most cases, productivity, frequency and compositionality are closely correlated phenomena. In Grammaticalization Theory it has long been recognized that frequency data are important in showing the unidirectionality of how lexical forms move into grammatical roles. Two basic types of frequency are distinguished: type frequency and token frequency. Type frequency refers to the number of items that are available to a particular class of forms (Hopper & Traugott 2003: 124ff.). For instance, the number of lexical items taking the deverbal nominal suffix *-ing* is very high (comprising most DNs in Norwegian), whereas the number of lexical items taking the deverbal nominal suffix *-t* (as in *drive* 'to manage' vs. *drift* 'management') is much lower.

But, as Hopper & Traugott (2003:125) have pointed out, most attention has been paid to token frequency, i.e. the number of times a particular form occurs in texts or the changes in frequency of forms or constructions over time. These frequency data are very characteristic of the grammaticalization of grammatical forms. Token frequency means the number of times a particular form exemplar occurs in texts, or, the changes of frequency of form exemplars or constructions exemplars over time. A marked increase of token frequency may indicate grammaticalization. Conversely a marked decrease may indicate lexicalization.

Changes such as semantic fading (called *bleaching* in Grammaticalization Theory), phonological reduction, positional fixing, increasing compositionality and erasure of word boundaries, are inseparable from the absolute token frequency of the forms and the frequency with which they occur with other forms. In the opposite process, lexicalization, factors such as semantic enrichment and reduction of compositionality will be assumed to have a close connection to token frequency.

But the type frequency of the different morphological types is also an important indication of the status of the DN. Nouns with high type frequency, such as the *-ing* nominals in Norwegian, tend to retain many of their verbal characteristics (such as process meaning and grammatical argument structure), whereas nouns with low type frequency tend to take on noun characteristics (such as result meaning, loss of grammatically, coded argument structure and development of specific reference and use with determiners). Thus, the development of DNs can be regarded as a process of lexicalization (Brinton & Traugott 2005).

Data on type frequency are very difficult to extract automatically from an electronic corpus. This is especially the case for zero suffix nouns and some low frequency types such as *-t* (as in *drift* 'continuous production'). An investigation on type frequency in technical texts revealed that zero suffix DNs had a much higher type frequency than expected, and seem to enter into alternations with the corresponding highly productive *-ing* DNs (Andersen 2007c: 159). I investigated the type frequency of the different DN suffixes in a technical manual describing the steam generation system of the Gullfaks A oil platform. The manual contained 150 pages. I found 154 DNs in the manual. Of these, 57.14 per cent had the *-(n)ing* suffix, 20.13 per cent had the zero suffix nad 10.39 per cent had the *-sjon* ending. The other suffixes ranged from 3.25 to 0.65 per cent. The high percentage of the zero suffix nouns was surprising. Examples from this manual showed examples like *start av maskiner* 'start-up of engines' alternated with *starting av maskiner* (with the same meaning; cf. Andersen 2007c: 159).

The *-ing* vs. zero suffix alternations did not exhibit the perfect vs. imperfect meaning alternations mentioned above (cf. the example *sparking* 'the phenomenon of kicking' which has imperfective aspect, versus *spark* 'a kick' which has perfective or semelfactive meaning), but both members of the alternations had imperfect process event meaning. In these cases the zero suffix DNs occurred with grammatically coded arguments, using the theta transmitter *av*:

(5)	*standardprosedyre*	*for*	***isoler-ing***	***av***	*reguleringsventiler*
	Standard procedure	for	isolate-NMLZ	of	control valves
	standard procedure for insulation of control valves				

(6)	***Sjekk-Ø***	***av***	*manuelle*	*ventiler*	*må*	*foregå*	*etter*	*kontortid*
	check-NMLZ	of	manual	valves	must	take place	after	office hours.
	The testing of manual valves must take place after office hours.							

As for my data on token frequency, I have used the comprehensive Norwegian Newspaper Corpus (Andersen & Hofland this volume). As of April 2011 the corpus is about 900 million words. At the time of my investigation the number size was 430 million words. The corpus allows automatic extraction of absolute token frequency and relative frequency per 100 million words.

Based solely on these synchronic data I investigated the six zero suffix DNs *skudd* 'shot', *slag* 'beat', *brudd* 'breach, violation', *drap* 'murder', *salg* 'sale' and *kjøp* 'purchase' and concluded that they occupy different positions on the prototype cline. The selection of these six DNs was based on the following assumptions:

1. The zero suffix nouns with perfect aspect meaning, like *skudd* 'shot' and *slag* 'beat' would be expected to be closer to the perfect noun (in terms of Vendler 1967) pole of the cline.
2. DNs closer to the perfect noun pole of the cline would be expected to have elements of idiosyncratic polysemy and increased semantic distance from the verb.
3. DNs closer to the perfect noun pole would be expected to have idiosyncratic morphophonological alternations and thus increased distance from the corresponding verb on the morphosyntactic level.

Based on these assumptions the expected distribution of these DNs would be as follows:

perfect noun		imperfect noun
skudd *slag*	*brudd* *drap*	*salg kjøp*
idiosyncratic		predictable
no argument structure		argument structure
no participant structure		participant structure
low token frequency		high token frequency

Figure 1. Different degrees of nounhood of zero suffix nouns

Token frequency showed that the DNs *kjøp* 'buying' and *salg* 'selling, sale' had a much higher frequency than the others, occurring with process event meaning. The difference between these two DNs and the others was especially salient when occurring with the preposition *av* 'of' in the function of a theta transmitter. *Skudd* 'shot' and *slag* 'beat' did not occur with this preposition at all. The DN *brudd* 'breach, violation, fracture' had a much lower frequency but occurred with the theta transmitter in about 50 per cent of the cases. The DN *drap* 'murder' had a higher frequency than *brudd* and about 75 per cent of its occurrences with the theta transmitter *av* (cf. Andersen 2007a: 72).[7] Occurence with the preposition *på*

7. In the 2004 investigation the DNs *kjøp* with the preposition *av* had a relative frequency of 1,817 and *salg* + *av* had a relative frequency of 3,828 per 100 million words. In contrast the

functioning as a participant, as in *skudd* ***på soldater*** 'shots at soldiers' as opposed to *skudd* ***på slagmarken*** 'shot in the battle field', data showed that *brudd* occurred frequently with the participant preposition *på*. The DN *drap* had a lower frequency, but occurred mostly with the same preposition in the same function. The DNs *slag*, *skudd* and *salg* had only few occurrences with this preposition. However, the 6 occurrences with *salg* and the preposition *på* all showed a different meaning of the DN compared to the corresponding verb. The collocation *salg på* (as opposed to *salg av*) means that the selling takes place at a lower price than the standard price. This added meaning component must have occurred after the coining of the DN. This seems to be a case of semantic enrichment, i.e. a characteristic of lexicalization. Enrichment relates to stage 3 of the cline where the development of idiosyncratic polysemy and semantic distance is focussed on.

Table 1. Argument and participant structure with zero suffix DNs

Infinitive	Deverbal noun	Predictability	Frequency	Argument structure	Participant structure
skyte	*skudd*	idiosyncratic	low	no	no
slå	*slag*	idiosyncratic	low	no	little
bryte	*brudd*	idiosyncratic	low	some	full
drepe	*drap*	idiosyncratic	low	some	almost full
selge	*salg*	idiosyncratic	high	full	little
kjøpe	*kjøp*	predictable	high	full	little

As Grammaticalization Theory has pointed out (Hopper & Traugott 2003), grammaticalization paths seem to be organized onomasiologically, i.e. semantic bleaching must occur before phonological reduction takes place. This is iconically the most plausible sequence. According to this iconic principle an increased distance in meaning between the verb and its corresponding DN will give rise to an increase of idiosyncrasy of the relationship between the verb and the DN. This was focussed on in stage 4. As Table 1 shows, the only fully predictable morphophonological alternation between the infinitive form of the verb and the DN is in *kjøpe* vs. *kjøp*. This DN has the highest token frequency and it occurs most

figures for the others were: *brudd* + *av* 30, *slag* + *av* 30, *skudd* + *av* 153 and *drap* + *av* 186. An investigation of the first 200 occurrences revealed that with *kjøp* and *salg* all the occurrences of the preposition *av* was that of a theta transmitter. The figures for the others were: *brudd* 16, *skudd* 0 and *slag* 0.

regularly with argument structure. The alternations *bryte – brudd*, *skyte – skudd* and *slå – slag* have both vowel alternation and an unpredictable final consonant in the DN. In *drepe – drap* and *selge – salg* there is vowel alternation only.

As regards stage 6, there seems to be a nice correlation between the status of being an imperfect noun on the one hand, and the presence of argument structure on the other hand.

To sum up, these data show that the six investigated DNs occupy different positions along the perfect – imperfect noun continuum.

5. Using older texts from the corpus

The next question is then: If we have access to historical data would these tendencies be further supported? As is well known by Nordic linguists, there is very scant historical evidence from written records at least from the Middle Ages. Systematic relevant data in sufficient quantities are at present unavailable.

But the material associated with the Norwegian Newspaper corpus includes some older texts dating back to 1900.[8] This material includes the following:

1. Texts from around 1900: 217,000 word tokens
2. Texts from around 1925: 355,000 word tokens
3. Texts from around 1950: 355,000 word tokens
4. Texts from 1971: 940,000 word tokens
5. Texts from three newspapers 1981: 810,000 word tokens
6. The newspaper *Bergens Tidende* 1995–1998: 8,621,000 word tokens

Item 6 includes four newspaper issues per month. I studied the six DNs in Figure 1, using KWIC-concordances to see to which extent they occurred with a prepositional dependent in the form of an argument coded by the preposition *av* or in the form of a participant coded by the preposition *på*. Occurrence without the prepositional dependent is taken as an indication of the status of the DN as a perfect noun.

In the process I had to resolve the usual disambiguation of polysemy/homonymy. Thus, the DN *slag* has meanings which are not (at least not obviously)

8. These texts are not a part of what we usually refer to as the Norwegian Newspaper Corpus, but a different set of older newspaper material collected by Uni Computing and used for comparative reference.

derived from a corresponding verb, for instance 'sort, type' as in *bøker av ulike slag* 'books of different types'. A different meaning appeared in the collocation å *være i godt slag* 'to be in a good physical/mental condition'. These were all excluded. Likewise, the DN *kjøp* was excluded when its imperative form 'buy' occurred in advertisements.

Table 2. Older text occurrences of *skudd*

	Tokens	Percentages
1900	0	0,000
1925	9	0,007
1950	27	0,002
1971	42	0,004
1981	12	0,001
1994–1998	298	0,003

As Table 2 shows, the DN *skudd* has a very low overall frequency. The data revealed that it consistently occurs without a prepositional determiner. Moreover, it has a perfective, semelfactive aspectual meaning as opposed to the corresponding process denoting imperfective *-ing* DN *skyting* 'shooting', which freely occurs with argument structure. This fact points in the direction of *skudd* being a perfect noun.

Table 3. Older text occurrences of *slag*

	Tokens	Percentages
1900	17	0,007
1925	29	0,008
1950	31	0,008
1971	53	0,005
1981	38	0,004
1994–1998	335	0,003

The DN *slag* has a slightly higher overall frequency than *skudd*, but occurs consistently without propositional dependent. This also points in the direction of *slag* being a perfect noun. Although percentages are consistently low, they seem to have a falling tendency.

Table 4. Older text occurrences of *brudd*

	Tokens	Participant *på*	Percentages
1900	0	0	0,00
1925	7	1	0,01
1950	14	7	0,03
1971	70	34	0,07
1981	27	12	0,03
1994–1998	452	284	0,05
2. half 94	8	6	
1. half 95	56	31	
2. half 95	55	29	
1. half 96	45	29	
2. half 96	39	25	
1. half 97	54	42	
2. half 97	52	33	
1. half 98	64	36	
2. half 98	79	53	

The concordances revealed most occurrences of result meaning of *brudd*. But here there is a distinct presence of a prepositional dependent. The percentages do not reveal any such tendency. However, no arguments with *av* were detected in these texts. What complicates matters here, however, is the fact that dependents may be suppressed in contexts where they are pragmatically considered as given information or considered as our common knowledge of the world.

Example (7) and (8) may serve to illustrate this:

(7) ...*til legeundersøkelse, men slapp med mindre brudd*
...to medical examination, but escaped with minor fractures
[på x] og slagskader. (950614)
[on x] and blow injuries.

(8) ...*er omfattende. Han pådro seg alvorlige brudd*
...are considerable. He received serious fractures
på kraniet... 950614)
on the scull...

The participant in square brackets in (7) is not explicitly mentioned in the text. The overall frequency is higher than for *skudd* and *slag*, but the frequency data from the oldest texts are uncertain. The percentages are again very low, and show no particular tendency. The presence of participant structure coded with *på* is conspicuously present, but again the suppression of this dependent may be due to information structure distribution in different contexts. The consistent absence of argument structure points in the direction of perfect noun status, as expected.

Table 5. Older text occurrences of *drap*

	Tokens	Argument *av*	Participant *på*	Percentages
1900	1	0	0	0,001
1925	3	0	1	0,001
1950	6	0	6	0,001
1971	66	2	33	0,007
1981	26	0	5	0,003
1994–1998	350	2	57	0,004
2. half 94	3	0	1	
1. half 95	60	0	8	
2. half 95	34	0	9	
1. half 96	38	1	9	
2. half 96	32	0	3	
1. half 97	43	1	5	
2. half 97	54	0	11	
1. half 98	44	0	7	
2. half 98	42	0	4	

The overall frequency for *drap* is in fact lower than for *brudd*. The percentages do not indicate any tendency. On the other hand some occurrences of argument structure may indicate a stronger imperfect noun status for *drap* than for *brudd*.

Table 6. Older text occurrences of *salg*

	Tokens	Argument *av*	Participant *på*	Percentages
1900	7	2	0	0,003
1925	23	14	0	0,006
1950	16	10	0	0,004
1971	57	40	0	0,006
1981	42	23	1	0,005
1994–1998	724	370	5	0,008

(Continued)

Table 6. Older text occurrences of *salg* (Continued)

	Tokens	Argument *av*	Participant *på*	Percentages
2. half 94	13	7	0	
1. half 95	85	32	1	
2. half 95	86	44	0	
1. half 96	66	38	0	
2. half 96	83	44	0	
1. half 97	102	53	3	
2. half 97	113	59	0	
1. half 98	86	41	0	
2. half 98	90	52	1	

As expected, the overall token frequency for *salg* is much higher than for *skudd, slag, brudd* and *drap*. Again the percentages show no tendency. But the presence of argument structure is frequent. However, the special meaning of *salg* in the sense 'sale at a lower price than normal' can be detected from 1981 and onwards. It has increased its frequency since 2000 and onwards. It is an interesting fact that this meaning of *salg* never occurs with the theta transmitter *av*, but only with the participant coding preposition *på*.

Table 7. Older text occurrences of *kjøp*

	Tokens	Argument *av*	Participant *på*	Percentages
1900	0	0	0	0,000
1925	25	16	0	0,011
1950	11	7	0	0,003
1971	27	25	0	0,003
1981	30	15	0	0,003
1994–1998	320	216	3	0,003
2. half 94	5	3	0	
1. half 95	40	22	0	
2. half 95	46	33	0	
1. half 96	43	27	0	
2. half 96	36	24	0	
1. half 97	44	30	3	
2. half 97	32	26	0	
1. half 98	45	28	0	
2. half 98	29	23	0	

The DN *kjøp* is the clearest case of an imperfect noun. It has a high overall frequency, and occurs regularly with argument structure.

6. Concluding remarks

The collection of older texts in the Newspaper corpus is a valuable addition to the corpus and can certainly shed new light on the development of the Norwegian language. But these corpora are too small to give further support to my hypothesis. Tables 2 to 7 indicate that these nouns are at the same stage of development as my original data from 2004 show.

This means that my hypothesis has not altered status: it has not been strengthened and it has not been weakened. As regards token frequency, the oldest data are so small in quantity that very little can be concluded from them.

So, is my hypothesis really an empirical one? Is it possible in Popper's (1980: 32f) terms to conceive a method which will allow me to test this hypothesis?

Considering the fact that older diachronic data are at present unavailable the only possible solution is to make further use of the Norwegian Newspaper Corpus to monitor this development more closely over time. The corpus is continuously being monitored and refined, and it is my hope that this study can be pursued further in the future.

References

Andersen, Øivin. 2007a. Deverbal nouns, lexicalization and syntactic change. *Nordic Journal of Linguistics*. 30(1): 55–86.

Andersen, Øivin. 2007b. Indeterminacy, context, economy and well-formedness in specialist communication. In *Indeterminacy in Terminology and LSP* [Terminology and Lexicography Research in Theory and Practice 2], Bassey Edem Antia (ed), 3–15. Amsterdam: John Benjamins.

Andersen, Øivin 2007c. Deverbal nouns as hybrids: Some textual aspects. *In Evidence-based LSP. Translation, Text and Terminology* [Linguistic Insights Series 47], Khurshid Ahmad & Margaret Rogers (eds), 155–171. Bern: Peter Lang.

Anderson, Steven R. 1985. Typological distinctions in the word formation. In *Language Typology and Syntactic Description*, Vol. 3, Timothy Shopen (ed), 3–56. Cambridge: CUP.

Alexiadou, Artemis. 2001. *Functional Structure in Nominals: Nominalization and Ergativity* [Linguistik Aktuell/Linguistics Today 42]. Amsterdam: John Benjamins.

Banks, David. 2004. On the historical origins of nominalized process in scientific text. *English for Specific Purposes* 24(3): 347–357.

Brinton, Laurel J. & Traugott, Elizabeth Closs. 2005. *Lexicalization and Language Change*. Cambridge: CUP.

Bybee, Joan. 1985. *Morphology: A Study of the Relation Between Meaning and Form* [Typological Studies in Language 9]. Amsterdam: John Benjamins.

Chomsky, Noam. 1970. Remarks on nominalization. In *Readings in English Transformational Grammar*, A. Jacobs & P.S. Rosenbaum (eds). Waltham MA: Ginn and Co.

Comrie, Bernard & Thompson, Sandra A. 1985. Lexical nominalization. In *Language Typology and Syntactic Description*, Vol. 3, Timothy Shopen (ed), 349–398. Cambridge: CUP.

Cowie, Claire. 2000. The discourse motivations for neologizing: Action nominalization in the history of English. In *Lexicology, Semantics and Lexicography*, Julie Coleman (ed), 179–207. Amsterdam: John Benjamins.

Croft, William. 1991. *Syntactic Categories and Grammatical Relations: The Cognitive Organization of Information*. Chicago IL: University of Chicago Press.

Dik, Simon C. 1997. *The Theory of Functional Grammar: Complex and Derived Constructions*. Berlin: Mouton de Gruyter.

Faarlund, Jan Terje, Lie, Svein & Vannebo, Kjell Ivar. 2002. *Norsk referansegrammatikk* (Norwegian Reference Grammar), 3rd ed. Oslo: Universitetsforlaget.

Geeraerts, Dirk. 1992. Prototypicality effect in diachronic semantics: A round-up. In *Diachrony within Synchrony: Language History and Cognition*, Günther Kellermann & Michael D. Morrissey (eds), 183–205. Frankfurt: Peter Lang.

Givón, Talmy. 1979. *On Understanding Grammar*. New York NY: Academic Press.

Givón, Talmy. 1984. *Syntax: A Functional-Typological Introduction*, Vol. 1. Amsterdam: John Benjamins.

Givón, Talmy. 1990. *Syntax: A Functional-Typological Introduction*, Vol. 2. Amsterdam: John Benjamins.

Grimshaw, Jane. 1990. *Argument Structure* [Linguistic Inquiry Monograph 18]. Cambridge MA: The MIT Press.

Halliday, Michael A.K. & Martin, John R. 1993. *Writing Science: Literacy and Discursive Power*. London: The Falmer Press.

Hansen, Erik & Heltoft, Lars. 1994. Kentaurnominaler i dansk (Centaur Nominalizations in Danish). In *NORDLEX-Prosjektet. Sammensatte substantiver i dansk*, Irene Baron (ed), 57–67. Copenhagen: Institut for Datalingvistikk, Handelshøjskolen i København.

Hopper, Paul J. & Thompson, Sandra A. 1985. The iconicity of the universal categories 'noun' and 'verb'. In *Natural Syntax: Iconicity and Erosion*, John Haiman (ed), 151–183. Cambridge: CUP.

Hopper, Paul J. & Traugott, Elizabeth Closs. 2003. *Grammaticalization*. Cambridge: CUP.

Kellermann, Günter & Morrissey, Michael (eds). 1992. *Diachrony within Synchrony: Language History and Cognition*. Frankfurt: Peter Lang.

van Kemenade, Ans & Vincent, Nigel. 1997. *Parameters of Morphosyntactic Change*. Cambridge: CUP.

Kinn, Torodd. 1994. Prepositional phrases in Norwegian: Internal structure and external connections – an LFG analysis. MA thesis, University of Bergen. (Department of Linguistics and Phonetics. Skriftserie nr. 45, Serie B).

Koptjevskaja-Tamm, Maria. 1993. *Nominalizations*. London: Routledge.

Lehmann, Christian. 1988. Towards a typology of clause linkage. In *Clause Combining in Grammar and Discourse* [Typological Studies in Language 18], John Haiman & Sandra A. Thompson, (eds), 181–225. Amsterdam: John Benjamins.

Lehmann, Christian. 1995. [1982]. *Thoughts on Grammaticalization* [Lincom Studies in Theoretical Linguistics 1]. Munich: Lincom.

Lødrup, Helge. 1989. *Norske Hypotagmer. En LFG-beskrivelse av ikke-verbale hypotagmer* (Norwegian hypotactic constructions: A description of non-verbal hypotactic constructions). Oslo: Novus Forlag.
Mackenzie, Lachland. 1987. Nominalization and basic constituent ordering. In *Ins and Outs of Predication*, Johan van der Auwera & Louis Goosens (eds), 94–105, Dordrecht: Foris.
Malchukov, Andrej L. 2004. *Nominalization/verbalization: Constraining a Typology of Transcategorial Operations*. Munich: Lincom.
Noonan, Michael. 1985. Complementation. In *Language Typology and Syntactic Description*, Vol. II: *Complex Constructions*, Timothy Shopen (ed), 42–141. Cambridge: CUP.
Popper, Karl Raymond. 1980. *The Logic of Scientific Discovery*. London: Hutchinson.
Pustejovsky, James. 1998. *The Generative Lexicon*. Cambridge MA: The MIT Press.
Rosch, Eleanor. 1978. Principles of categorization. In *Cognition and Categorization*, Eleanor Rosch & Barbara B. Lloyd (eds). Reprinted in *Fuzzy Grammar. A Reader*, Bas Aarts, David Denison, Evelien Keizer & Gergana Popova (eds), 91–109. Oxford: OUP, 2004.
Ross, John Robert. 2004. Nouniness. In *Fuzzy Grammar. A Reader*, Bas Aarts, David Denison, Evelien Keizer & Gergana Popova (eds), 351–423. Oxford: OUP.
Saeed, John I. 2003. Semantics, 2nd edition. Oxford: Blackwell.
Sakshaug, Laila. 1999. Norwegian compound deverbal nouns: An autolexical analysis in morphology, syntax and semantics. Dr. artium thesis, University of Trondheim.
Taylor, John R. 1989. *Linguistic Categorization: Prototypes in Linguistic Theory*. Oxford: Clarendon Press.
Taylor, John R. 2004. Grammatical categories. In *Fuzzy Grammar. A Reader*, Bas Aarts, David Denison, Evelien Keizer & Gergana Popova (eds), 293–309. Oxford: OUP.
Vendler, Zeno. 1967. *Linguistics in Philosophy*. Itacha NY: Cornell University Press.
Vinje, Finn-Erik. 1973. Verbalsubstantiv avledet med *-else*, *-ing* og nullsuffiks i moderne norsk, især bokmål (Deverbal nouns derived by *-else*, *-ing* and zero suffix in Modern Norwegian, especially Bokmål). Ms, University of Trondheim.
Zipf, George Kingsley. 1949. *Human Behavior and the Principle of Least Effort: An Introduction to Human Ecology*. Cambridge MA: Addison-Wesley Press.

Name index

Subject index